Remembering A.J.

A selection of Reviews by Film and
TV Critic Andrew Johnston

ANDREW JOHNSTON

EDITED BY MARTHA ORTON

REMEMBERING A.J.
A SELECTION OF REVIEWS BY FILM AND TV CRITIC ANDREW JOHNSTON

iUniverse books may be ordered through booksellers or by contacting:

iUniverse
1663 Liberty Drive
Bloomington, IN 47403
www.iuniverse.com
844-349-9409

ISBN: 978-1-6632-3237-3 (sc)
ISBN: 978-1-6632-3236-6 (e)

Library of Congress Control Number: 2021925643

Print information available on the last page.

iUniverse rev. date: 01/20/2022

Contents

Preface and Acknowledgements

This collection of reviews and recaps written by film and TV critic Andrew Johnston has been created in order to preserve some of his writing for the future and also to convey a sense of who Andrew was as a person. The initial idea of publishing a collection of Andrew's film and TV reviews came from his good friend and fellow critic, Matt Zoller Seitz, in the days after Andrew's funeral. I am grateful that the idea which was planted on that occasion has now come to fruition. I would like to express my gratitude to Matt for his encouragement in pursuing this project and also for his permission to include two of his pieces about Andrew, one from *The House Next Door/Slant Magazine* and the second from RogerEbert. com. The first of these was written at the time of Andrew's passing and the second ten years afterwards. I especially would like to express my sincere appreciation to *Time Out New York*, *Time Out London* and *Slant Magazine* (formerly *The House Next Door*), for their permission to include the reviews and recaps which comprise the majority of this book.

In compiling this collection of Andrew's writing, I have been fortunate to have the assistance of two of Andrew's good friends who are also critics, Matt Zoller Seitz and Keith Uhlich. Since Andrew's writings were prolific, their assistance with making the initial selection was crucial to moving forward with this project. My heartfelt appreciation goes to them both. While Matt and Keith should be credited with the quality of their choices, the final selection is mine and any blame for omissions of prominent material should be laid at my door. I am grateful for their help in making the selection of the contents and also for their continued interest in making this book a reality.

In attempting to create a memorial volume which would also be of interest to a larger audience, I have included some of Andrew's early writing from his days at Earlham College and also biographical information which I hope will serve to develop a perspective on Andrew's personality as well as his personal history. Towards that end, the draft book proposal for Andrew's never-published book *Cruising towards Manhood: A Moviegoer's Memoir* is included in the section titled "About the Lad" since it includes biographical details which don't appear elsewhere. Andrew's remarks introducing the film *Slacker* are also included in this section for reasons which I hope will be clear upon reading. Apart from this section of biographical content, the book is divided into sections of reviews that appeared in *Time Out* and recaps that appeared in *Slant/The House Next Door*. Although Andrew wrote for numerous publications., these choices were made based on Andrew's fondness for these particular publications, his longevity of writing for them, and also on permissions received. This book could consist entirely of formal, critical reviews; however, I have chosen to include Andrew's extensive recaps of some of his favorite TV series which appear in *Slant* magazine, at the time called *The House Next Door*. It is in these recaps that Andrew's personality comes through somewhat more vividly than in his reviews. Also, the recaps include some personal perspectives and biographical asides which I have found meaningful and I hope the reader will also.

The general sequence of the material included is chronological, with the exception of dividing the reviews and recaps into sections based on the publication in which they appeared. I found this particularly helpful to compiling the book and I also found this sequence appealing since it reveals Andrew's progress as a writer. In addition, it indicates his dedication to his work up until the end of his life. The title index at the end of the book should be helpful in identifying the contents and searching for specific content.

I would also like to express my gratitude to my husband Robert Orton for his support and patience during the process of developing the text.

Martha Orton
Charlottesville, Virginia
November 17, 2021

Introduction

When Andrew's friends talk with me about him, one thing stands out above the rest—their appreciation for his love, actually his passion, for knowledge. Andrew was an enthusiastic omnivore of information, consuming books, newspapers, films, TV series, music recordings, as if they were the literal stuff of life itself. He was a true lover of life in all its rich and variable artistic expressions, finding his way to seeing the value in virtually all art forms. Such a perspective was consistent with his breadth of vision and also his sense of egalitarianism. Although Andrew had the opportunity to hold an elitist perspective and could be quite discerning in his personal tastes, he had a natural way of finding the good in something when there was good to be found. He also had a keenly developed social conscience, which translated fully into his personal politics and also underlay his generosity to others.

This book includes some autobiographical elements; however summarizing some key points about Andrew's life seems important to do also. Andrew was born in Washington, DC, in 1968, moved to Charlottesville, Virginia in 1970, and to Pondicherry, India in 1975, and returned to the US in 1980. The move to India was difficult for him, especially since the school which he attended there offered classes primarily in French. This was the Sri Aurobindo International Centre of Education, part of the Sri Aurobindo Ashram, to which I (his mother) had moved with Andrew and his younger brother, Stewart. Andrew patiently made the necessary adjustments to this challenging change in his life situation and I will be forever grateful to him for his forbearance and his ability to find positive elements in being deprived of TV and many favorite foods. He credits living in India with his developing an intense interest in books over TV, both because books were available to him while TV was not and also because he found much solace and escape in exploring the virtually infinite possibilities they offered. A film offered every Saturday night in the Ashram playground became another significant aspect of Andrew's life in Pondy. Occasionally he and some friends branched out beyond this and saw a film at the Ratna Cinema, which was a nominally forbidden territory on the far side of the town. In fact, Andrew endured briefly being suspended from school for going there to see the film *Enter the Dragon* with a group of boys from his school. One of them ratted him out, but then a large contingent of older students confessed in his defense that they had also attended the film, and Andrew was readmitted to his classes.

Returning to the US at age twelve presented more cultural challenges and, after settling in at Tandem School, now Tandem Friends School, Andrew found his niche more comfortably. This led to his attending Earlham College, a distinguished college in Richmond, Indiana, also associated with the Society of Friends. Here Andrew's interest in writing intensified and he wrote a weekly column for the *Earlham Word*, the student newspaper. This column primarily reviewed music and became a meaningful endeavor of those years along with Andrew's early morning radio show, "Biscuits and Gravy." During these years at Earlham, Andrew's interests in American and English literature of all genres and American and European history and politics also became rich fields of pursuit.

After college, moving to New York seemed a natural next step for an aspiring writer, especially since there was the opportunity to join a group of friends and share an apartment in the East Village near Tompkins Square Park. This neighborhood was to become Andrew's home for the rest of his life. He loved the East Village, even in its ungentrified iteration in which it first presented itself to him. He loved Tompkins Square Park and having sunny days to sit on a bench under the towering elms or, later, walking his quirky Belgian Malinois, Grover, there and turning him loose in the dog park.

Andrew's first job was at Tower Books, alas no longer in existence, and after this a couple of publishing assistant jobs followed. Seeking a clearer direction for developing his writing, Andrew then applied to the Journalism School at Columbia. He greatly enjoyed this program and happily received his MS in Journalism at the spring commencement ceremony at the Cathedral of St John the Divine in 1996. It was a happy day for Andrew and also for us, his family. We celebrated with a relatively lavish dinner at an elegant Indian restaurant, Andrew's carefully made choice.

Soon after being awarded his journalism degree, Andrew began writing occasional film reviews for *Time Out New York* and subsequently was taken on full time as a film critic. Andrew was truly in his element and, as usual with his enthusiasms, put his whole heart into the work. He loved writing film criticism and was happy working at *Time Out*, enjoying the companionship of colleagues, some of whom ultimately became life-long friends. During these years, Andrew was invited to become a member of the New York Film Critics Circle, a distinction which he appreciated.

The quality of Andrew's writing attracted increasing attention and led to his being invited to be lead film critic at an even more widely circulated magazine. This was in the phase of this publication in which engaging film criticism was more emphasized as a component. When film reviews were reduced in length a couple of years later, that spelled the end of Andrew's tenure there. He went on to do freelance writing and to write for other publications, before returning to *Time Out New York* as editor of their "Time In" section. This section was phased out after Andrew's death. In this role, Andrew wrote and edited TV criticism and also reviews of DVD and game releases, as well as writing an occasional book review or interview.

Writers in the field of criticism are better informed and better able than I am to speak to Andrew's enthusiasms and influence as a critic. But I can relate the enthusiasms which came forth from my own awareness and memory of what he shared with me. Perhaps what stands out most is his love of Peter Jackson's *Lord of the Rings Trilogy*. During Andrew's tenure as Chair of the New York Film Critics Circle, he readily cast his vote for *The Return of the King* as the best film of 2002. In conducting the awards ceremony in January 2003, it was a great pleasure to see Andrew have the enjoyment of announcing this award, along with so many others for films for which he had appreciation. Andrew was very literary in his interests and extraordinarily well read, having enjoyed all of Tolkien years before. His fine appreciation of language no doubt added to his enthusiasm for the *Deadwood* TV series. Although he advocated for *The Sopranos* as the best TV series of all time (so far) in debate with Matt Zoller Seitz and Alan Sepinwall, he was very enthusiastic about *Deadwood*. This enthusiasm led him to share the series with me while he was recovering from his first surgery for cancer in July 2006. Sometimes I wonder how much he was trying to challenge my tolerance for violence and foul language, as well as trying to offer me the chance to enjoy something he greatly appreciated. In any case, watching all of *Deadwood* together in the weeks after the traumatic and frightening experience of his major surgery, became a definite bonding experience.

The cancer diagnosis came somewhat later than it might have, apparently because initially the possibility of colon cancer was ruled out based on Andrew's age. He was treated for gastrointestinal symptoms and weeks passed with no relief for the nausea and abdominal pain which he was experiencing. The timing of the cancer diagnosis probably would have made no difference in the ultimate outcome since the cancer was so advanced. The weekend of Andrew's 38th birthday was exceptionally painful for him. My husband Robert, our son Arthur (Andrew's half-brother) and I had gone to New York to celebrate Andrew's birthday together. The birthday fell on a Monday and we were there for the weekend. Andrew had made a reservation at an Indian restaurant in the East Village which he thought we would all enjoy. All Saturday he was in excruciating pain. I tried to ease this with massaging his back, but this gave little relief. Andrew was only marginally able to cope with the pain by staying curled up in bed. He encouraged the three of us to go to dinner without him. There were two happy results of the weekend, however. One is a pleasant photo of Andrew and me together, Andrew's hair somewhat elevated by the effects of having just gotten out of bed. The other result is that Andrew continued to seek medical diagnosis and the real problem was discovered That fact, however, was about as far from happy as one can get—advanced colon cancer.

What proceeded from the point of diagnosis is an entire story in itself. Quite rightly, no one wants to be defined by disease or medical issues. It is the story of their lives, work, interests, passions, accomplishments, that needs to be told. Suffice it to say that Andrew endured an immense struggle to remain in as good health as possible, that he took a strongly pragmatic approach to every challenge he confronted—every chemotherapy session, every radiation treatment, every surgery. His body took a pounding and his spirit rose up strongly to meet each challenge. Andrew's bravery was immense.

The struggle lasted for two years and four months post-diagnosis. Andrew kept working throughout that time, apart from necessary recuperation periods after surgeries, and even to within a few days of his death. The management at *Time Out New York* was very supportive. Friends were very supportive. But finally the cancer took over.

For those who knew him, Andrew's commitment to universal values of social justice, egalitarianism, environmental causes, and his widely caring nature, will live on in memory, as will his wonderfully quirky sense of humor, his wide-ranging interests and knowledge of the world, particularly literature, history, and almost everything related to film and TV. I hope that this book will give some sense of who Andrew was to those who have not known him personally or who have not read some of his writing. No one volume could capture this completely of course, but perhaps this will at least give a vivid indication.

Martha Orton

About the Lad

Death Proof

The Life in Andrew Johnston
BY MATT ZOLLER SEITZ ON OCTOBER 30, 2008, THE HOUSE
NEXT DOOR/SLANT

So many truths only become clear with hindsight. Here's one of them: Unbeknownst to nearly everybody, even those closest to him, Andrew Johnston was a superhero. His influence was as profound as it was largely unseen. Like the hero of *Miller's Crossing*, Tom Regan, Andrew managed to re-order large parts of his universe without anyone being the wiser.

Andrew—the *Time Out New York* film and TV critic and *House Next Door* contributor who died Oct. 26 at age 40—was, to put it mildly, not a glamorous person. Compared to Andrew, Peter Parker was James Dean. He was vaguely birdlike—darting eyes; bobbing head; question mark posture with arms akimbo, as if his body was remembering wings. It was possible to speak to him for minutes at a time without making eye contact, and when his eyes did meet yours, the connection was often brief, even furtive.

And his way of speaking—well, *House* contributor Sarah Bunting, who interviewed him for the web site she cofounded, *Television Without Pity*, told me that transcribing an interview with Andrew for her "Ask a TV critic" feature was one of the more difficult assignments she could recall. Andrew didn't talk in a straight line. On a good day, he was serpentine. He interrupted himself, qualified himself, questioned himself, reversed course, even argued with himself. He was his own interrogator. There were moments when it seemed as though you were talking to two people— Andrew Johnston and his questioning subconscious. His sentences had clauses and sub-clauses and sub-sub-clauses. In retrospect it seems not at all surprising that one of his favorite shows was *Deadwood*, a series built around monologues that could go on for a minute or longer, and only when you looked at them on the page did you realize that the whole monologue was one long sentence.

Reading Andrew in the pages of *Time Out* or in the weekly series TV recaps that he did for *The House Next Door* was a different proposition. He was an incisive, direct critic who managed to combine baseline assessments of a work's entertainment value with a wide-ranging, free associative view of the work's place within the culture—the forces that inspired it, and the message that it hoped to convey.

Here's one brief passage from Andrew writing about one of his favorite series, *Mad Men*, for *The House Next Door*—reviewing an episode entitled "The Benefactor", he segues from a summary of the episode and its function within the show's ongoing storyline into a discussion of narrative itself.

"After the fairly ground-shaking events of "Flight 1"—Pete's Dad dies! We learn the deal with Peggy's baby! Duck emerges as a full-blown Bad Guy!—I was somewhat surprised to find that "The Benefactor" was basically a standalone with only the tiniest bit of follow-up to the previous episode. But then the more I thought about it, the more I realized something: Almost all of *Mad Men*'s "big" episodes, "Flight 1" included, are basically standalones. This approach is a reversal of the main TV model of the 1990s, and proof of just how much series creator Matthew Weiner learned from working on *The Sopranos*.

"I recently absorbed most of *Maps and Legends*, Michael Chabon's collection of critical essays on genre fiction, in addition to rereading Scott McCloud's *Understanding Comics*, so I hope you'll forgive me for getting a bit academic and pin-headed here. Basically, for most of the history of television, dramas were divided into two varieties: Serials (from *Peyton Place* through *Dallas*, *Dynasty*, etc) and series that were basically collections of short stories about the characters (pretty much every crime/medical/science fiction series you can think of). The main similarity is that in both types of series, the characters never really changed.

"Much of this has to do with the nature of the short story, the form that has arguably influenced episodic TV drama more than any other. I'm sure readers of this column will be able to come up with other examples (right now, all I'm coming up with are Ernest Hemingway and John Updike), but sequential short stories following a single protagonist are far less common in the realm of "serious" fiction than in the genre world—and genre fiction characters, like those on TV, are far less likely to experience real change."

I can't say if, in his multi-year battle with cancer, Andrew experienced real change beyond, obviously, the physical; I tend to think he didn't experience change in the simplistic, formulaic sense—becoming a different person, a better person. If anything, Andrew's stubborn fight against his own mortality amplified the man he was—made his fighting spirit, his generosity, his life force not just more visible, but impossible to ignore.

Andrew was a terrific person when I first met him in 1998, when we were young Turks inducted into the Baby Boomer-dominated New York Film Critics Circle. And he continued to be a great person during the whole time I knew him. He could be spacey and impatient, even hotheaded, and as I alluded to earlier, he was often a hard person to read—opaque at times, even Sphinx-like. But beneath those surface characteristics was a rock-solid sense of values and a deep love for, and appreciation of, other driven people. He believed in talent and originality and singularity of artistic expression, and he dedicated his professional and personal life to seeking out those qualities, nurturing them and doing all he could to help anyone who exemplified them find an audience.

Andrew was an influential critic in his 20s, when he started writing about movies for *Time Out New York*. A lot of men would have been content to enjoy that position and be done with it, but not Andrew. He used whatever sway he had to bring other new voices into the fold. Just in the past week, Mike D'Angelo, film columnist for *Esquire*, credited Andrew with helping establish him as a working film critic by recommending him as his replacement when Andrew left *Time Out* for a brief and unhappy stint at *US Magazine*. So did Bilge Ebiri, who writes for *New York Magazine* and *Nerve.com*; Andrew gave Bilge his first paying job as a critic and continued to send work his way up until the weeks prior to his death, when he asked Bilge to review the new DVD box set of Budd Boetticher westerns for *Time Out*.

Many, many more working critics have their own versions of these anecdotes. They all end the same way: Andrew gave me my start.

As chief film critic for *Time Out*—and later, upon his return to the magazine as the editor and chief critic of the TV and DVD section—Andrew made a point of farming out reviews and feature articles to talented but largely unknown writers whom he met in online forums, at parties, in bars, waiting on line at film screenings. Andrew gave me my first paying job as a magazine editor last year, when he asked me to fill in for him as TV and DVD editor of *Time Out* while he was off having yet another round of surgery and chemotherapy.

At no point did Andrew tell me of the good works he did for other people. It's an aspect of his life that we're all very slowly discovering as we talk about him, about his life and work and what it meant.

Andrew's taste was defiantly his own. He didn't take his cues from anybody—no mean feat for a guy who landed a high-profile job as a New

York Film Critic in the 1990s, when critics of earlier generations dominated the profession and insisted, explicitly or implicitly, that younger critics acknowledge the works they enjoyed during their youth in the '60s and '70s as the be-all and end-all. Andrew's taste in film and TV was eclectic; he loved classic horror films, the signposts of mid-century European art cinema, and yes, the high watermarks of American film that made Pauline Kael's heart go pitter-pat.

But at the same time, he demanded that contemporary work be given a fair hearing, even equal weight, and that we not look down our noses at work created for mediums that were considered disreputable, or from source material that was not from the accepted canon. During his first year in the New York Film Critics' circle, he was part of a group of critics agitating to give Terrence Malick's first film in 20 years, *The Thin Red Line*, as many awards as possible. It ended up getting best cinematography and best director in a year that Steven Spielberg's *Saving Private Ryan* dominated critical discourse.

Five years later, as chairman of the NYFCC, Andrew pushed hard to give Peter Jackson's *Lord of the Rings* movies recognition. The final entry in the trilogy, *Return of the King*, won Best Picture—a stunning upset that made many of his fellow NYFCC members furious. "I can't believe we gave best picture to a movie about hobbits," one complained. Andrew considered the award not just a deserved accolade for a mammoth and unexpectedly well-executed project, but a bouquet tossed to fantasy and science fiction buffs whose enthusiasms were more often mocked by the critical establishment. The NYFCC award paved the way for *Return of the King* to sweep the Oscars that year, and for other critics to proclaim their love of the trilogy openly, without the usual qualifiers.

Andrew gave other people permission to be themselves. He believed comic books, video games and series TV deserved to be evaluated as thoughtfully as feature films at a time when even suggesting such a thing marked one as unserious—as a geek. He encouraged critics his age and younger to stop mindlessly genuflecting to their fathers' and mothers' movies and embrace the new, the now.

Andrew was a booster of great TV, closely following *Mad Men*, *Breaking Bad*, *The Wire*, *The Sopranos*, *Deadwood*, *Buffy the Vampire Slayer*, *Battlestar Galactica*, *Rescue Me*, *The Office*, *The Shield*, *Friday Night Lights* and other series worth watching and arguing about. One of his proudest achievements was his championing of *Donnie Darko*, a film that got lukewarm to baffled reviews when it was released in fall of 2001, soon after the attacks of 9/11. Andrew believed it was a future classic and a present-tense masterpiece, a film whose virtues would eventually be recognized. By writing a rave review for *Time Out*, then mentioning it again in print every chance he got, Andrew did more than any working critic to usher that film into the modern pantheon.

Every time Andrew underwent cancer treatment, at a juncture where doctors warned him he was very likely not going to make it, he'd emerge on the other side and get a tattoo to celebrate the fact that he was still alive. At the time of his death he was edging into Illustrated Man country. His prize tattoo was inspired by the team slogan of *Friday Night Lights* "Clear Eyes, Full Hearts, Can't Lose." The screensaver on his laptop and his work computer was Kurt Russell driving that car with the skull and crossbones on the hood from—yep—*Death Proof.*

Andrew knew deep down that ultimately you can't beat death; sooner or later it always gets you. So he decided to fight as hard as he could and enjoy life while he could. He characterized his cancer as a challenge, almost a dare—a battle he had no choice but to engage. After he had surgery on his spine, he showed me a digital photo of the scar. It looked like the handiwork of Michael Myers from *Halloween*. I was speechless; he grinned at me and said, "Yeah…It's bigger than I thought it would be. It's already healing up, but I want to show people what it looked like right after. It's pretty awesome."

Three weeks ago, when Andrew's legs started to give out and he was having difficulty even crossing a room, he asked me to go see Nick

Cave and the Bad Seeds play Madison Square Garden. It took him 15 minutes to get into the Garden, and he left well before the encore was finished because, as he put it, "I don't want to get trampled by the mob." He'd often follow up an especially difficult surgery by going to Austin and spending a couple of weeks catching live bands and hitting barbecue joints. He celebrated his 40th birthday a few months ago, shortly after finishing a brutal round of chemo, at a Brooklyn beer garden, downing pint after pint of dark beer and eating enough sausage to kill a grizzly.

The last time I saw Andrew, he was in a hospital bed, recovering from all sorts of punishing treatments, including an MRI. He said he wanted to see the season finale of *Mad Men*, so I got him a screener and we watched it on my laptop. His reflexes were slow—sometimes he couldn't shuttle back and forth to re-check lines of dialogue as precisely as he would have liked—but his mind was sharp, catching scenes and images that were callbacks to scenes from earlier in the season, or from last season—details I never would have caught on my best days.

On the way out, I said goodnight to him and told him that one of the great pleasures of this time was seeing how his mother, Martha, doted on him, doing everything she could to make his ordeal as comfortable as possible. "You've got a hell of a mom, Andrew," I said. Andrew blushed a little, then grinned at me. "Yeah," he said. "I know."

Andrew endured the loss of a brother, Stewart, who was killed in 1990 in India. He told me about it on the night of the memorial service for my wife. I had no idea he'd been through such trauma. It clearly was hard for him even to mention it, and in subsequent years, we never discussed it again. He told me that the grieving process is like climbing a mountain, reaching what you think is the top, then realizing you've got another peak to climb, then another, then another. I asked him, "Do you ever reach the top?" And he said, "No. But you learn to like hiking."

Andrew Johnston taught me how to live. I love you, brother.

Missing Andrew: Ten Years Without A Dear Friend
By Matt Zoller Seitz
October 26, 2018/RogerEbert.com

I think about Andrew Johnston any time I write about television, or when I think about terminal illness, and how we can never know how much time we have left.

Andrew, who died of cancer ten years ago today at age 40, was a film and TV critic, mainly for *Time Out New York*. I always liked him, and we communicated regularly through email and saw each other at parties. But I didn't become close friends with him until the final 18 months of his life, after he asked me to fill in for him as editor of *Time Out*'s now-defunct TV and home video section while he was on leave to undergo surgery and chemotherapy (the first of many rounds of treatment).

Andrew originally wrote me in the summer of 2007 to ask if I could recommend anyone who might be able to do the job while he was on leave. He wanted somebody who had experience editing a rotating roster of critics with strong egos (which I had, being the founder and editor of the film blog *The House Next Door*, which is now a part of *Slant*), was available to start immediately, and didn't mind that the job didn't pay much. I was a single parent whose wife had died a year or so earlier. I had recently (foolishly) quit a full time job and was making a meager income freelancing for The New York Times film section and a couple of other places. I asked if it was OK if I submitted myself for the job. It turns out that's what Andrew hoped would happen. He wanted somebody who would run the section more or less as he would have, and wouldn't plot to replace him.

Plus, he added, "You're my best friend."

I later told Andrew's mother, the poet Martha Orton, that I felt a stab of guilt the minute Andrew said this, because I never thought of him as my best friend, even though I liked him a lot. Mostly he was just a guy I had a lot of things in common with.

We ran in the same circles of in New York media in the '90s and early aughts, a time when Generation Xers were eager to acquire positions of influence that were then being held by Baby Boomers and a few critics from the World War II generation. (Things have circled around again since then, as they always do; now millennials and the generation after that are itching to become part of the establishment, if only to get good healthcare.) Andrew and I were elected to the New York Film Critics Circle in the same year, 1998, when we were both 29; that made us the youngest members of the organization at that point. We felt like goofy kids sitting across the table from boldfaced names like Andrew Sarris, Rex Reed and John Simon, who'd been at it for decades. We talked up films like "Repo Man» and "Drugstore Cowboy» that meant a lot to us in high school and college but that hadn't entered the pantheon yet (a favorite pastime of young critics from every generation). We agreed that recent developments in series television (including "Oz" and "The Sopranos") were positioning it as a possible replacement for feature films at the center of cultural conversation—a blasphemous idea among Boomer critics, many of whom thought the younger medium was inherently inferior and always would be.

But none of that necessarily qualified me for "best friend" status. So I did my best to try to earn it, belatedly, during what turned out to be the final stretch of Andrew's life.

I hung out with him, talked on the phone with him, emailed back and forth with him, confided in him when I was going through my own problems as a single parent and single man (we both broke up with our girlfriends on the same day, as a result of discussing dissatisfactions that we were both experiencing). I grew to love and admire Andrew's parents. They became a partial replacement for my own mother and stepfather, from whom I was estranged at the time.

Even as I watched Andrew deteriorate from cancer, I didn't understand the magnitude of his suffering until the very end. It became hard for him to walk without help. His speech and thinking became clouded. He began to smell faintly of lead, as cancer patients nearing the end sometimes do. I re-watched "Breaking Bad" with my daughter a few years after Andrew's death—one of Andrew's favorite shows, though one that, like many others, he never got to see all of— and was overcome with sadness over what Andrew went through. I broke down while sitting on the couch next to my daughter as I watched the show's main character get sick, and lose his hair and stamina. It was so upsetting that I had to turn the show off several times and come back to it the next day. I rarely have that powerful a reaction while watching fiction, and in retrospect I'm sure it's because I was suppressing full knowledge of what Andrew had endured. Even though I had a front row seat, I didn't *get* it until later.

I wrote a little bit about that experience in my obituary for Andrew, which was published at *The House Next Door*, where he recapped a number of TV series for me, including "The Wire," "Mad Men" and

"Friday Night Lights." And I included bits and pieces of his "Mad Men" recaps as footnotes in my book about the show, *Mad Men Carousel*, which also includes original poems by Martha. I try to keep his legacy alive in pieces like this one, and Martha and I and our mutual friend Keith Uhlich are working on a book about him, just in case any publishers out there are reading this and happen to be interested Andrew's life story and work.

Andrew was a brilliant man with a quicksilver mind and a heedless, jumbled manner of speaking, the words practically tumbling out of his mouth, one after the other, as if trying to keep up with the thoughts that raced through his head. I often tried to imagine what it might feel like, or sound like, to be in Andrew's brain as he was writing a piece. I imagined it was like being inside a dryer filled with swirling and colliding ping pong balls, each tattooed with tiny, free-associative sentences. The force of his intellect was staggering. He could pivot from a discussion of J.R.R. Tolkien to an analysis of a 17th century piece of French poetry to a Shakespearean insult to a video game reference, then finish off with a quote from a Joni Mitchell or Leonard Cohen song, and somehow tie it all together in a thesis that only Andrew Johnston could come up with.

I think about him every time I sit down to write about a new movie or TV series that I love. What will I say? Can I make it as amazing as whatever Andrew would have written?

No, but I can try. I owe him that, at least.

Andrew Johnston, 1968–2008

TONY staff remembers a dear, departed colleague.

By Time Out editors

Wed Nov 5 2008

Even though our Time In editor, Andrew, had been living with cancer for years, the end is not easy for us. He died on October 26—a passing that his mother tells us was "peaceful as could be."  That's ironic. Feisty until the end, Andrew was a fighter. I remember his polymath's curiosity, his enthusiasm that often spilled over into rage but also effusive emotion. He had a big heart. I choose to recall him on a summer afternoon in 2006. Andrew was about to enter the hospital for his first operation, but beforehand, he wanted to go see *A Scanner Darkly*. I was happy to oblige. We had lunch. As the lights dimmed in the theater, Andrew leaned over and whispered, "Check it out." He rolled up his sleeve to reveal a new tattoo on his shoulder, the colors still hot and flush. Looking closely, I saw it was a quote from Clint Eastwood's Unforgiven: "Deserve's got nothing to do with it." Squinting his eyes, Andrew had the resolve to go wherever this disease would take him. And in my heart, I feel that he beat it. —*Joshua Rothkopf.*

I've pretty much been a geek my entire life, drifting through a series of fascinations: comic books, pro wrestling, rock & roll, politics. One of the advantages of being a geek in our modern culture is that it keys you in to a sort of collective consciousness, a lingua franca that enables you to connect with a wide variety of people (or at least a wide variety of people geeks like me encounter). Sports does the same thing, but without the conspiratorial feeling of belonging to, if not an aggrieved subclass, a defiant minority.

Andrew was a wholehearted geek, and while we may have had nothing else in common, we shared that, and it was enough. We became work friends, then actual friends. We saw *X-Men 3* together, and *The Descent*, the latter right after his first round of chemotherapy. We went to hipster hamburger restaurants and watched the initial presidential debate (the night after the Sarah Palin pick was announced, Andrew was the first person to tell me that McCain had just blown the election). He tried to teach me to play Xbox games that I was way too video-game illiterate to grasp.

Occasionally, his persona could be opaque, as if he was merely the sum of his digital obsessions, but then the humanity would bust through: He'd share the details of an encouraging second date, or brag about his dog, Grover. Several years ago, five minutes after arriving at my birthday party, he hit it off with a female geek friend of mine, and they spent the next three hours talking on my roof (I was really disappointed it didn't happen with those two). And I was with him last New Year's Eve, as we shared a hope for a better 2008 than 2007. Perhaps most relevant in these pages, he was a fine writer, the kind of cultural critic who compensates for verbal awkwardness by expressing himself with eloquence and authority in print.

I remember leaving an advance screening of *Batman Begins* with him. I liked it, but as a longtime Batman acolyte, I was mildly disappointed, and I nit-picked over the costume, the chase scenes, the characterization of minor villains. Andrew, however, was beaming. He got exactly what he wanted: a big, noisy, thrilling good time, featuring Batman beating the crap out of bad guys. Geeky as he was, he didn't let petty geek bullshit get him down. —*Noah Tarnow*

It goes without saying that Andrew's passion for what he did here was exceedingly strong. I know from experience that it's a characteristic he valued greatly in others as well. I had the honor of serving as co-captain of the *TONY* bowling team with him last year—a title he bestowed on me after I'd circulated a particularly awesome smack-talking e-mail to our fellow team members about the victory drinks we would all have after defeating that week's opponent. He recognized my passion right away and weeks later assigned a story to me: a Q&A with Zane Lamprey, the host of a show called *Three Sheets* in which Lamprey travels the world drinking. On offering the assignment, he wrote me this: "I always like to assign stories to people who are really passionate about the relevant subject...."— *Katharine Rust*

For many years, *TONY* has put together an annual issue we call Essential New York; basically, it's our "best of" issue, and in it we used to write little love letters and observations about the things that make living here special to us. In the 1999 issue, Andrew penned one blurb that, even a decade later, I still think of every time I see my West Village street in a movie. I particularly liked it because he captured that oxymoronic feeling perfectly: We New Yorkers feel coolly superior at the time of the film crew's annoying inconvenience, but then become utterly nerdy and giddy when the result of that annoyance shows up in Spider-Man, or most recently for me, *Nick and Nora's Infinite Playlist*. This is what he wrote." — *Billie Cohen*

Seeing your building or block or office on the big screen *There are few things more aggravating than returning from a long day at work to be told by a pimply-faced production assistant that you can't enter your building because a film shoot's in progress. But in a city that never stops changing, having the place where you live, work or buy your morning joe turn up in a movie can preserve a sliver of your NYC experience in an entirely unique way. Surely it's worth putting up with a little inconvenience so that, years from now, when your grandkids ask about life in the '90s, you can just pop a tape in the VCR and say, "I lived there." [AJ]*

People unfamiliar with Andrew's eccentricities can be excused for thinking him a raving, vending-machine-assaulting, apartment-key-misplacing (I once heard him, from across the lobby, go on for about 20 minutes one night about how they disappeared—they were, of course, under one of the many piles of crap he kept on his desk at all times), Hüsker Dü shirt–wearing maniac. For those of us who go to know him a little better, those suspicions were not alleviated so much as they were totally confirmed. But that was him, and exactly what made him such an interesting person to talk to in a city peopled with so many ambulatory, boorish cliches. Contrary to popular opinion, he did not watch TV 24 hours a day; Andrew was utterly well-read (last I talked to him, he was poring over something about Alexander Hamilton and Federalist ephemera, I think) and attended cool shows pretty frequently (ran into him on several occasions, the last being some Times New Viking show in Brooklyn). He was generous (gave me an old N64 of his when I weirdly got fixated on technology from the mid-'90s), encouraging to me professionally and a bold, talented writer whose hilariously exuberant opinions (he summed his much beloved season one of *Friday Night Lights* thusly: "*FNL* is the best series of its kind since the legendary *My So-Called Life*") I will sorely miss reading. Happy trails, friend.—*Drew Toal*

Andrew was a booster of great TV—he was an early champion of *Mad Men, Deadwood, The Sopranos, The Shield, Friday Night Lights* and pretty much any other show that was worth a damn. Every time he underwent cancer treatment, at a juncture where doctors warned him he was very likely not going to make it, he'd emerge on the other side and get a tattoo to celebrate the fact that he was still alive. At the time of his death he was edging into Illustrated Man country. His prize tattoo was the *Friday Night Lights* motto: "Clear Eyes, Full Heart, Can't Lose." The screen saver on his laptop and his work computer was Kurt Russell driving that car with the skull and crossbones on the hood from—yep—*Death Proof.*

Andrew knew deep down that ultimately you can't beat death; sooner or later it always gets you. So he decided to fight as hard as he could and enjoy life while he could. Three weeks ago, when his legs had started to give out and he was having a great deal of difficulty even crossing a room, he asked me to go with him to see Nick Cave and the Bad Seeds play Madison Square Garden. It took him 15 minutes to get into the Garden, and he left well before the encore was finished because, as he put it, "I don't want to get trampled by the mob." He'd often follow up an especially difficult surgery by going to Austin and spending a couple of weeks catching live bands and hitting barbecue joints. He celebrated his 40th birthday a few months ago, shortly after finishing a brutal round of chemo, at a Brooklyn beer garden, downing pint after pint of dark beer and eating enough sausage to kill a grizzly.

He taught me how to live.—*Matt Zoller Seitz*

About Andrew—In His Own Words

Posted on March 7, 2000.
Self-introduction for a film critics' discussion group

Following in the footsteps of everyone else, here's my introductory post and ballot.

My name's Andrew Johnston, I'm 31 and live in New York City. Education-wise, I have an undergraduate degree in English Lit from Earlham College in picturesque Richmond, Indiana, and a MS in Journalism from Columbia University.

From 1975-80, from the ages of 7 through 12, I lived in India (where my mom moved to join an ashram after my parents split up), an experience that played a big role in my becoming the movie freak that I am. There was only one theater in the town we lived in that got English-language movies, and I didn't get to go there very often. What they got was usually several years old-- DIRTY HARRY and SLEEPER came through as "new" movies in 1977-8--so most of the films I saw over there were Hollywood movies from the '60s that our school booked on their weekly movie night plus lots and lots of Soviet films of the '70s (the cultural office of the USSR's consulate in Madras rented 'em out real cheap). My relative inability to see famous and/or new movies (I didn't see STAR WARS until 1981!) did a lot to whet my appetite for them.

When we came back in 1980, I was fortunate enough to wind up in a town (Charlottesville, Va) with an excellent repertory theater. From '80-'82, I'd ride my bike to the Vinegar Hill Theater at least twice a week after school and catch one of their great double bills, seeing all the classics of the '40s and '50s that my dad had been telling me about for years as well as catching up with good stuff from the '70s I'd missed while overseas. I'd also see an old movie or two every week courtesy of the various campus film societies at UVa., and I read everything by Pauline Kael in the public library by the time I was 14.

In the ninth grade, I was taken under the wing of my English teacher, whose husband was an ex rock critic who had been great pals with Lester Bangs prior to his death. This, coupled with my discovery of UVa.'s great campus station WTJU, my descent into the local punk scene and my growing obsession with the "college" bands of the day (REM, Husker Du, Minutemen, etc.) led me to scale back my cinephilia in favor of music-related fanaticism for the next several years. When I got to college, I wound up scoring a slot as the campus paper's rock critic by the end of the first semester of freshman year and soon got caught up in the world of college radio as well.

When I moved to New York after college, I was bound and determined to make a go of it as a music writer—which I did, in my spare time, for four or five years, writing for magazines most people have never heard of. After getting fed up with the necessary day-job thing, I decided to get serious and went to grad school for journalism. There, I took a class with longtime film critic Judith Crist, who's since become a friend and mentor, and the experience helped reignite my slumbering interest in writing about film. By the time I got out, the local NYC music scene had started to get stale, and there was nothing much going on in the larger music world that really excited me. Through a lucky break, I wound up getting the chance to write some freelance film stuff for Time Out New York, where they like my work so much that they hired me as a film critic in February '97. After three great years there, I recently left to start a new job as the main film critic guy for US Weekly, Rolling Stone honcho Jann Wenner's attempt to beat People Magazine at their own game, the first issue of which will be available all over the United States and Canada on March 17.

I'm doing exactly what I told people I wanted to do when I grew up when I was 13--how many people can say that?

Writing about Cancer, Take One
[August 2008]

There are some kinds of news that (if you have to receive them at all) it's best to receive when you're really fucking high. Finding out that you have cancer is definitely among them.

"There's a significant tumor in your colon," Dr. [1] said in a tone too sincerely sympathetic to have been rehearsed, "and it's spread to your liver, too."

I was sitting on the table/bed in an examination room in Dr. [1]'s office, where I'd just regained consciousness after being given a colonoscopy under the influence of a so-called local anesthetic that had knocked me out for an hour. Drugs like this wore off quickly, I knew from experience, but at this exact moment, if Dr. [1] had told me the test had revealed I was Rosemary's Baby grown up and that he'd found an ingrown tail up my ass, I would have had the same goofy grin on my face and would have taken the news just as calmly.

"I know a really good oncologist on the Upper East Side who can actually see you this morning," he said, handing me a folded print-out of an email containing the address of a Dr. [2]. "I just spoke to him and he can see you at 11:30am."

Still half sedated, I thanked Dr. [1] shook his hand and put on my clothes before heading to the lobby where Bill was waiting for me. Bill— who I'd known since the first day of eighth grade, and who had wound up in New York about six years after me—was the friend I'd drafted (on Dr. [1]'s orders) to make sure I got home OK in case the anesthetic left me acting goofy. A few weeks before, at the pre-Belmont Stakes brunch he hosted every year, Bill had seen me in so much pain that I was unable to stand up straight (later, at the track, the noise made by a crowd of 70,000 had been unable to prevent me from succumbing to bouts of narcolepsy), so he knew I wasn't fucking around when I'd made the appointment with Dr. [1], the second gastroenterologist I'd seen in a month.

"So, what's the story, man?," Bill said as we stepped into the claustrophobic wood-paneled elevator and he pressed the lobby button. "Well," I replied, "I have cancer. At least I finally know what's wrong, so that I can finally fucking do something about it."

It was circa 10am on Wednesday, June 28, 2006, and I was 38 years, one month and six days old.

It was a couple of months earlier, on a Friday night in late April, that things started to get weird.

As was too often the case, I was once again staying in. Being burned out from work had something to do with it; so did the whole all-my-friends-are-married-or-shacked-up-but-I'd-forgotten-to-settle-down thing. There was also the fact that I was now too old to go out in the East Village on a Friday night (not that I'd want to, given the bridge-and-tunnel clusterfuck that enveloped my longtime neighborhood every weekend), but mainly I was just lame. I'd opted to do some work I brought home with me, which isn't as pathetic as it sounds given that the "work" involved watching a stack of *Deadwood* episodes that HBO had sent me in advance. I had just started my third year as the TV critic for a weekly magazine where, many years earlier in the '90s, I'd cut my teeth as a film critic. Hoping to cure my sour mood, I'd turned to one of my favorite substances—glorious grilled fatty meat—up and splurged $16 on ordering Tea-Smoked Duck (Eric Asimov Quote TK) only to wind up on the toilet an hour later, squatting and sweating in vain as I longed for a reprieve from the pain surging through my gut. I could feel the grease coursing through me, which left me sure the duck was to blame. After about half an hour, I chewed my way through three or four chalky tablets, washed them down with a beer and popped a sleeping pill, hoping sleep would provide something resembling relief.

Insert section on the rest of Diagnosis Day—meeting Dr. [2] calling W, telling mom and – – –dad, falling off the weed wagon, seeing Superman Returns, the ironic cancer fundraising at the theater and, finally, telling I. and K.

At the end of the day, even the best job in the world is still a job. George Clooney may get $20 million a movie, but I doubt the money makes him any less bored between camera setups during his ninth consecutive 16-hour day on the set. My TV critic gig was pretty sexy on paper, but the job was a lot less about getting paid to watch TV than about filling three pages of the magazine 51 times a year and frogmarching every last word of it through every step of the editorial process. Having full control of those three pages and being able to write what I pleased was a hard-earned privilege I didn't take for granted—I'd spent the better part of my twenties as a publishing and advertising peon with my nose pushed up against the glass of a media world I longed to be part of—and doing the job right meant working hard all day, then going home and watching at least four hours of TV before passing out at 2am and doing it all over again the next day. On weekends, I typically devoted at least one full day to work, usually stuff I couldn't focus on in our chaotic office—typically, transcribing an interview with a TV actor or writer/producer. I saw my married guy friends about once a month; at the time, most of my social life consisted of beer-propelled sexual encounters with women I'd met through online dating sites. Some of these situations were one-night stands, others were ongoing nebulously-defined relationships that lasted until somebody got bored, met someone else and/ or the whole thing turned. Point being, as the pain in my gut got worse over the next few weeks, I became more and more convinced that it was a stress thing—an incipient ulcer, perhaps, or maybe acid reflux. Around the middle of May, I sought help from my primary care physician, who concurred. She gave me a prescription and, almost as an afterthought, the phone number of a doctor, who I was to call if things got worse. If I had half a brain in my head back then, I would have called him after two days of the medication doing nothing. Instead, in typical Andrew Johnston cowboy fashion I decided to play hurt (so to speak) until the last possible second. That turned out to be two more weeks away, on the weekend before my birthday.

The big 3-8 fell on a Monday, and to my surprise my mother, stepfather and half brother had announced their intention to take a bus up from Virginia for the weekend leading into it. Unsurprisingly,….

[That is where Andrew's writing formally and specifically about cancer ended. His 38th birthday was the last one to be celebrated without the shadow of cancer clouding it.]

DRAFT for a book proposal

Cruising Towards Manhood
A Moviegoer's Memoirs

A Book Proposal
by
Andrew Johnston

"It was very simple really. Where I could not, with syntax, give shape to my fantasies, Gifford could, with his superb timing, his great hands, his uncanny faking, give shape to his. It was something more than this: I cheered for him with such inordinate enthusiasm, my yearning became so involved with his desire to escape life's bleak anonymity, that after a time he became my alter ego, that part of me which had its being in the competitive world of men; I came, as incredible as it seems to me now, to believe that I was, in some magical way, an actual instrument of his success."

—Frederick Exley, *A Fan's Notes*

For Frederick Exley, it was Frank Gifford, the star New York Giants halfback of the 1950s and '60s. For me, it's been Tom Cruise, the biggest movie star of the past two decades. Both are patron saints of great American secular religions who, while symbolizing the homogenous America Exley and I came of age hating, also paradoxically embodied everything we wanted to be. Exley freely admitted that his obsession with Gifford was rooted in lust (for fame), but my interest in Cruise stems from another venal sin—envy. My road from adolescence to adulthood has been a rocky one, but his has been, well, a cruise.

I'm not talking about the *real* Tom Cruise — the three-time Oscar nominee and ex-husband of Mimi Rogers and Nicole Kidman — but the persona he's tailored over the course of a 20-plus-year career in Hollywood. Yes, every Cruise character from Joel Goodson (*Risky Business*) and Pete "Maverick" Mitchell (*Top Gun*) to Ethan Hunt (the *Mission: Impossible*s) and Dr. Bill Harford (*Eyes Wide Shut*) has to work his ass off to overcome serious obstacles, but there's never any doubt that they're going to succeed—because they're all that innately skilled, that intuitively gifted. Because under the skin, they're all Tom Cruise.

If you're a straight, white American male born in the late 1960s, the films of Tom Cruise have been encouraging your fantasies and mocking your failures since 1983. Every stage of the road to adulthood life has been explored in a Cruise film, often a year or two before we experience it ourselves: The loss of virginity *(Risky Business)*. The discovery of the joys

(*Top Gun*) and dark side (*Born on the Fourth of July*) of macho conformity. The difficulty of finding one's way through the professional world (*A Few Good Men, The Firm*). The battle to overcome fear of commitment (*Jerry Maguire*) and the subsequent difficulty of making a meaningful monogamous relationship work (*Eyes Wide Shut*). Even the ultimate passage to manhood, the death of one's own father and the resulting confrontation with the past (*Magnolia*). On one hand, Cruise movies offer flattering, reassuring advice on how to process these experiences. On the other, they're counterproductive: they lull us into believing that we're at fault if our messy lives aren't as neat and organized as things are in the movies.

Directors are generally the ones credited as authors of films, and Cruise has worked with some of the most significant names in American cinema: Stanley Kubrick, Oliver Stone, Martin Scorsese, Cameron Crowe, Steven Spielberg and others. But through the choices he's made, Cruise himself is the author of a larger text: a biography of the archetypal Generation X (for lack of a better term) American male, a narrative that's wormed its way deeply enough into the national consciousness to attain the status of latter-day myth. Like Bible stories or the adventures of Greek heroes, Cruise films are parables that inform our daily lives.

I'm interested in writing a book that doubles as a memoir and a critical text: the story of one guy growing up in the shadow of Tom Cruise, with a study of what his movies say about American manhood woven into it. Exley's great "fictional memoir" *A Fan's Notes* is one of my chief models, but Dave Eggers' *A Heartbreaking Work of Staggering Genius*, Nicholson Baker's *U&I* and Nick Hornby's *Fever Pitch* also number among my influences. In the process of telling my own story, I want to deal with one of the key issues of our media-saturated age: The American tendency to treat Hollywood movies as a guide to life and how — for better *and* for worse — they become substitutes for actual human experience. After all, who wants to learn life lessons through messy interactions with other people when we can just get them from the movies?

"Our fathers were our models for God. If they bailed, what does that tell you about God?"

—Tyler Durden, *Fight Club*

[I know, it's not a Tom Cruise movie, but bear with me for a minute.]

To some extent, all Americans born in the 20th century are children of the movies—me moreso than most. In 1975, when I was seven years old, my parents divorced and my brother and I left a wealthy Virginia neighborhood right out of *The Ice Storm* and relocated to Pondicherry, in the south of India, where my mother signed on as a member of the Sri Aurobindo Ashram. Deprived of television, I became a voracious reader. But most of the books available to me were of British origin: My only connection to American culture was the movies.

The Ashram had a weekly movie night, but Soviet movies were featured far more often than American ones (the rental fees offered by the cultural office of the Soviet consulate in Madras were hard to beat). Seeing semi-recent American movies meant visiting a local fleapit theater where they generally turned up at least five years after their release. As a child of nine, I'd regularly slip off and see such films as *Dirty Harry* and Woody Allen's *Sleeper*—knowing nothing about them beforehand except that they were American—and return home dazzled. The theater was declared off-limits to folks affiliated with the Ashram after a spate of labor riots, and in an act of dutifulness that surprises me 24 years later, I resisted the temptation to sneak away to see *Star Wars* when it came through in 1979 (a "mere" two years late). Despite that remarkable act of self-control, my love of American movies was still the source of my undoing at the Ashram. *Star Wars* was one thing, but Bruce Lee's *Enter The Dragon* was just too appetizing to resist. However, I was spotted going into the forbidden theater by a classmate who then attempted to blackmail me. When I refused to pay up, he ratted me out and the Sri

Aurobindo International Educational Institution promptly washed its hands of Andrew Johnston.

On the day before Ronald Reagan was elected the 40th President of the United States, I returned to this country and entered the seventh grade with little in the way of orientation for American adolescence. Within a couple of years, my mother returned to India (my brother in tow), leaving me with a father who was little prepared for the job. He was so determined to avoid being unlike his own father (a poor guy from the Florida panhandle whose merciless drive earned him a partnership at a top Manhattan law firm and made him both a tyrant and a millionaire) that he became an alcoholic as a teenager and retired at the age of 35 without ever really growing up.

For my models of manhood — my models of God — I turned again to the movies. First came the classic adolescent fantasy figures: James Bond, Superman and Indiana Jones, followed by (thanks to the superb revival house Charlottesville boasted at the time) male icons of previous eras such as Humphrey Bogart, James Stewart and Steve McQueen.

And in the summer of 1983 came *Risky Business* and Tom Cruise.

If you didn't see *Risky Business* when it came out, it may just seem like an above-average coming-of-age movie, a film with a plot that could have served any of the bra-bursting comedies of the era, albeit slightly elevated by first-time director Paul Brickman's strong sense of style. But if you were there at the time — and happened to be the right age — it's something else entirely.

It may seem odd to say that a movie about a high-schooler who only achieves his dream of getting into Princeton after destiny and circumstance turn him into a pimp as inspirational, but if you were boy of 15 in 1983, that's exactly what *Risky Business* was. Not because it served as a sort of beginner's guide to the spirit of capitalism that would define the heady '80s (though the film certainly works at that level) but because of the honesty of its take on the teenage experience. Tom Cruise's Joel Goodson is struggling to find his way as an individual in the face of massive peer pressure and lofty parental expectations, and *Risky Business* is one of the rare films to acknowledge universal truths about teenage life — yes, your friends are full of shit, yes, your parents are out of touch, and yes, sex *is* scary — without patronizing its audience.

But though I thought the movie was throwing me a life preserver, it also warped my adolescent mind. The romantic portrait of Joel's relationship with the beautiful young call-girl Lana (Rebecca De Mornay) led me to spend years pursuing damaged women — smart and charismatic women who also happened to be incest survivors, rape victims and/or former prostitutes— in the misguided belief that if I saved them, they'd save me. And my identification with Joel kicked off a trend that dominated my life for the next ten years, a tendency to transform more-confident peers into surrogate fathers.

Like many of those ertzatz fathers, Cruise quickly betrayed me — by starring in *Top Gun,* a movie that symbolized everything I despised about the might-makes-right, looks-and-guts-trump-intelligence-and-sensitivity America of the 1980s. When Cruise was put in his place by Paul Newman in *The Color of Money,* an alpha male of a previous generation laying the smackdown on the whippersnappers who've come up behind him, I couldn't have been more pleased.

Over the following years, Cruise was an actor I loved to hate: a poster boy for aspiring lawyers, politicians and CEOs, a natural enemy of the sensitive and confused (i.e., people like me). Then things gradually thawed: I grudgingly admired his work in *Rain Man* and *A Few Good Men,* got a kick out of his scenery-chewing in *Interview With the Vampire,* and was finally dragged back into the fold by *Jerry Maguire* — even though it kicked my ass almost as hard as *Risky Business* did.

I saw *Jerry Maguire* alone on a rainy Sunday afternoon, still euphoric from having spent the night at the apartment of a woman I'd known for years, been dating for a few weeks, and had come to believe was The One

For Me. For the first time in my life, or so I thought, I was really in love with someone for whom the feeling was apparently mutual. It's no surprise, then, that Jerry's struggle to get over himself and reach the point where he could share his life with another person seemed to dovetail perfectly with my situation and provide guidance vis-à-vis the steps I needed to take in life. But as much as I treasure the memory of seeing *Jerry Maguire* under those circumstances, the experience came at a steep price.

A couple of weeks later, six weeks into my relationship with the aforementioned woman, I said the words "I love you" to a member of the opposite sex in complete sincerity for the first time in my life. And two days later she dumped me, confessing that she'd gotten drunk and had a one night stand with a stranger while I was at home visiting my family for Christmas. No matter how well we got along with each other, she said, my declaration of love freaked her out and she was just too confused to reciprocate my feelings. Once again I'd fallen into the trap of mistaking my life for a Tom Cruise movie.

But do I love *Jerry Maguire* and *Risky Business* any less because of the bad choices they encouraged me to make? Not at all. I'm no idiot—I know life's not a movie. But sometimes, movies reach you so deeply that you can't help trying to apply what you get from them in the real world. Over time, I've learned that the best way to do this is to treat them as parables rather than literal how-to guides. In that sense, both *Risky Business* and *Jerry Maguire* argue that happiness is obtained by passing up the superficial pleasures of sex, money and success in favor of meaningful human relationships, a ridiculously obvious message that we all need to be reminded of from time to time.

After *Jerry Maguire* proved that Cruise could turn that most uncommercial of things, an intelligent romantic comedy, into a major success (and earned him his second Oscar nomination in the process), he could have lazily cemented his star power with the kind of superficial hits that Mel Gibson phones in several times a year. Instead, he spent two years making *Eyes Wide Shut* with the notoriously demanding Stanley Kubrick, then followed that up with a role in Paul Thomas Anderson's unwieldy ensemble drama *Magnolia*—two challenging and oblique movies that flaunt their status as parables rather than templates. For all their problems, both films are rich with meaning about the biggest problem facing me and all my peers: the difficulty of growing up.

Let's face it — we're living in an age where arrested development is a cultural norm. The vast majority of videogames and comic books — two art forms conventionally held to be children's entertainment — are purchased by men in their 20s and 30s. In the 1950s and 1960s, the ultimate TV dads were Ozzie Nelson and Ward Cleaver, men whose Talmudic quips always held the key to wrapping up Ricky or the Beaver's problem du jour in 30 minutes or less. But in the 1990s, pop culture's chief exemplars of fatherhood were Homer Simpson and *Home Improvement*'s Tim Taylor, men less sophisticated then their own offspring.

Tom Cruise — our biggest movie star — is 41 years old now, and *Risky Business* is 20 years behind him. Yet practically every movie he makes is still a coming-of-age film: No matter the plot or milieu, they're all the story of a guy who has to overcome just one obstacle — be it a withdrawn father, fear of commitment, or the Cruise character's misguided belief in his own prowess — to stand on his own as a man. Of course, becoming a man isn't about overcoming a single obstacle — it's about overcoming every obstacle that Tom Cruise has had to conquer in every one of his movies put together, and then some. And if you didn't have a father capable of teaching you these lessons, you take your guidance where you can find it — in my case, for better or worse, at the multiplex.

I write about movies for a living: I recently wrapped up a long stint as the principal film critic for *US Weekly,* and before that held the same position at *Time Out New York* for three years. Presently, I'm the film critic for the newly launched magazine *Radar* and a freelance writer and critic for publications such as *Time Out New York, Playboy,* and the New

York *Post*. In college, I'd wait with breathless anticipation for the annual announcement of the awards given by the New York Film Critics Circle, a group I've belonged to since 1998 and of which I'm currently the chairman. While a life spent marinating my brain in cinematic fantasies has enabled me to land the career of my dreams (getting paid to go to the movies almost every day and share my thoughts on it), devoting my life to pop culture has also kept me from having the life that I want. How does a guy like me learn to tackle the problems inherent in real-life relationships — with girlfriends, with my peers, with parents, with employers — when I subsist on a diet of four or five happy endings a week?

That's the question I hope to answer with *Cruising Towards Manhood,* a book that I hope will consist less of self-indulgent navel-gazing than of testimony about the difficulty of growing up in the face of the expectations created by Tom Cruise movies. *Risky Business* provided false hope as I grappled with making sense of sex, a process my peers were groomed for in this country while I was in a school halfway around the planet where it was kept under the tightest of wraps. *Top Gun* and *Cocktail* made me despise Alpha Maledom even as I bent over backwards to cultivate the friendship of confident boys whose swagger was increased by the sense of superiority they gained letting me hang out with them. *A Few Good Men, The Firm* and *Mission: Impossible* teased me with the message that skill, intelligence and virtue always equal success as I was getting my ass handed to me trying to get started writing about pop culture. And *Jerry Maguire, Eyes Wide Shut* and *Magnolia*, for all their complexity compared to Cruise's early films, made forging meaningful relationships and coming to terms with my father seem deceptively easy when I decided it was time to do so.

My plan is to write a book that comes in between 250-300 pages, broken down into ten or eleven chapters dealing with various stages of the road I've traveled en route to something approximating adulthood. Each chapter will juxtapose anecdotes on the subject at hand — my discovery of sex, my love/hate relationships with the male peers I've turned into surrogate fathers, etc.— with an analysis of the take that Cruise's films present on the subject. Though there will certainly be some jumping around, the book will present both my metamorphosis from a 15-year-old boy into a 35-year-old semi-man and the evolution of Cruise's screen persona in chronological order, as the two have certainly evolved along parallel lines.

> "Yeah, Mommy wouldn't let me play soccer, and Daddy, ooh, he hit me. So that's who I am? That's why I do what I do? Bullshit."
>
> —Frank T.J. Mackey, *Magnolia*

In some ways, it's the height of egotism to presume that one's life is worthy of turning into a book, especially when you're (a) a child of privilege and (b) still as young as I am. I may sound like just another disaffected crank who wants to write a book to get revenge on my father, or settle scores with women who've done me wrong. Sure, I've had to overcome some pretty intense and exotic obstacles: My ass was dragged to India, then thrust back into the heaving bosom of America just in time for a hellish puberty. I basically raised myself because my father was too self-involved to do the job. I finally came to terms with my long-estranged brother only to endure his abrupt death (a homicide that remains unsolved to this day), then learn that he would have died of AIDS inside of three years if he hadn't been killed. I endured long struggle to launch a career as a magazine writer and saw God knows how many relationships with women go south because of the celluloid fantasies that warped my mind even more effectively than the drugs I consumed to ease my pain. But I know that I'm hardly the first rich white guy to have a rough life. I know that (to quote Tyler Durden again) I'm no beautiful and unique snowflake.

> "The book says, 'We may be through with the past, but the past ain't through with us'."
> —Jimmy Gator (among other characters), *Magnolia*

What I *am* is cocky enough to assume that I can write an interesting, relevant and (it may not be obvious going by this proposal, but trust me) funny memoir about growing up in the '80s and '90s as the child of parents whose minds were scrambled by the '60s (and the foibles of their parents' generation before them). A book about learning to balance independence (that manliest of virtues) with dependence ('cause no man is an island, right?). A book that explores how popular culture helps and hinders us as we navigate our way through the world. A book that can help other men get their lives in perspective and help women understand men. A book that looks at the situation my generation is in without bitching and moaning about why we're being the redheaded stepchildren of history (if we were, our ranks couldn't have yielded a star as iconic as Tom Cruise). A book that's fun to read. And a book that — maybe, just maybe — makes people question their ideas about manhood and helps redefine the subject as we enter the 21st century. A book I hope that you, dear reader, are willing to take a chance on

Text for introducing Slacker at the Museum of the Moving Image

Thanks for coming!

It's my great pleasure to be able to introduce this screening of Richard Linklater's *Slacker*. This is the fourth time I've had the opportunity to select and introduce a film here at AMMI, and the greatest thing about it is being able to give people the chance to see a film on the big screen that they might only otherwise get to see on video—or not at all. If you take a big-picture look at the history of independent film, *Slacker* may not be the landmark that this afternoon's previous attraction was, but it's still a very influential film, even if the movement it helped influence never gathered as much steam as its fans would have liked. *Slacke*r came out in 1991, the same year as Nirvana's *Nevermind*, and at the time, the two events seemed to define a real moment—the first time when people born in the 1960s were able to express themselves honestly in the realm of pop culture, without kowtowing to mainstream standards, and reach a wide audience without having to compromise. I saw the film in 1991, the weekend it opened at the Angelika just after I moved to New York at the age of 23, and felt that for the first time ever I was seeing a world onscreen that I'd really lived in, a world of smart misfits in which being yourself and speaking your mind was the highest possible achievement. The conspiracy theory about the Smurfs being intended to get kids used to seeing blue people so they'd be more likely to embrace Krishna—the references to Brian Eno's "oblique strategies" cards—here, for the first time, was a film that was speaking my language.

Independent film, at the time, felt like an extention of baby boomer culture—and there's nothing wrong with that. But this film told my generation that it could be ours, too. Of course, generational solipsism is one of the great sins of the boomers and one that my generation always loved to mock—and one I don't want to succumb to. *Slacker*'s historical importance lies in how it came at the vanguard of a movement that, like the one spearheaded by Nirvana, flourished before getting assimilated and drowned out by the larger culture. It arrived a year after Whit Stillman's *Metropolitan* and a year before Quentin Tarantino's *Reservoir Dogs*, three films that, together, created a renaissance of movies about conversation, movies which used a glorious cavalcade of words to transcend their low budgets and open a new window on the world. As the musical movement launched by Nirvana gathered steam through the early '90s, so did this cinematic wave. Linklater and Stillman dodged the sophomore slump syndrome and equaled their previous achievements with *Dazed and Confused* and *Barcelona*. Inspired by seeing *Slacker* at the Angelika by chance, Kevin Smith made *Clerks*. Linklater delivered a true masterpiece in the form of *Before Sunrise*. Noah Baumbach chimed in with the brilliant *Kicking and Screaming*. And, of course, Quentin Tarantino won the Palme d'Or, opened the New York Film Festival and made $100 million with *Pulp Fiction*.

And, like all cultural moments with a whiff of the revolutionary to them, it ended all too soon. When Oliver Stone filmed Tarantino's script for *Natural Born Killers* and Linklater adapted Eric Bogosian's *Suburbia*, I—and a lot of likeminded film lovers my age—found ourselves becoming increasingly cynical as it seemed as if the boomers were horning in on something that belonged to us. Tarantino's achievements were diminished by a flood of bad imitators. Kevin Smith fell too much in love with the sound of his own voice and got addicted to the easy laughs he could get with dick and fart jokes. And Noah Baumbach and Whit Stillman seemingly fell off the face of the Earth after Mr. *Jealousy* and *The Last Days of Disco* failed to connect with audiences.

But Linklater is still out there pushing the envelope, taking his vision in new directions, breaking new ground in animation with *Waking Life* and proving himself as a phenomenal actor's director with the little-seen gem *Tape*.

Slacker and *Nevermind* came out close to twelve years ago. It's impossible to listen to the Nirvana album on its own terms now, because the knowledge of Kurt Cobain's suicide inspires deep sadness over what might have been. Fortunately, that's not the case with *Slacker*, a film that, seen today, emits the glorious radiance of a promise fulfilled rather than the sadness of one that was broken.

Thanks again for coming.

Early Reviews and Writing at Earlham College

Musical Miasma, **Earlham Word** [College Newspaper]
September 16, 1988

Singles gone steady
by Andrew Johnston

A few weeks ago, Rolling Stone published a special issue centered around what a survey of their editors and writers had determined to be the hundred best singles of the last twenty-five years. It was pretty much what one would expect from them—a mishmash of the Beatles, the Rolling Stones, Stax/Volt/Motown sixties soul, token nods to punk plus the odd surprise or two. In general, not a bad list, but not without its problems. Probably the best thing about it is the thought it provokes on the exact definition of a single.

In the past, people bought more singles than they did albums, and that determined what got put on the singles. Singles were were released to stand or fall on their own merits. If they sold well, an album might be released as an afterthought. A direct result of this was that a hit song would overshadow the artist that performed it, and several songs were hit singles for more than artist because of this.

In England, a point was made not to include singles on albums at all. This explains why the first Beatles albums were released in drastically different versions in the United States than in the rest of the world.

In many ways, the Rolling Stone list can be taken as a memorial to a medium that is dying if not already dead. Beginning with Bob Dylan's "Like A Rolling Stone," singles began to come off of albums that were complete works in and of themselves instead of being showcases for singles.

Gradually, singles became commercials for albums instead of independent entities, a tendency taken to its extreme by Michael Jackson in the early eighties. By releasing more than half of the songs on his album "Thriller" as singles and having all of them reach the top ten, singles officially began to exist as merely a means towards the end of selling albums. Today, thanks to MTV, they now sell movies and goods. No would-be hit film is complete without a soundtrack single whose video is 70% composed of film clips. Robert Plant's "Tall Cool One" became a Coke commercial less than a month after it was in the top ten.

The Rolling Stone list really is, more than anything, a throwback to a much simpler era—an era when all an artist needed for a shot at fame was one song—three minutes of all the gusto they could muster up to put their foot in the door of stardom. Even if all their other songs were lousy, all it took was one single—a "Louie, Louie" or a "96 Tears" to gain immortality (if not riches).

Today, a single is only a step to what is, in our more complicated time, considered success—videos, commercial endorsements, big tours, and is more often than not a song written with the sole intent of being a commercial song, and the selling point of the album. What it boils down to is fewer artists making more singles that all sound the same. At this rate, I doubt that the editors of Rolling Stone will be able to put together another "Top 100 Singles of the Last 25 Years" in 2013 without a hell of a lot of difficulty.

Friday, Jan. 27,1989
Musical Miasma

Reed's 'New York' cliche

By Andrew Johnston

At first glance, it would appear that Lou Reed couldn't do anything that would be a bigger cliche than to release an album called "New York." Here it is, twenty full years after the break-up of the Velvet Underground and Lou releases an album that features Velvets drummer Maureen Tucker on two songs, one of them being a tribute to Andy Warhol.

Looking only at these surface details, it appears that all that's missing is a tribute song to the late Lester Bangs (the critic who is primarily responsible for Lou's still being taken seriously at this point in time) to make the album into the most obvious and redundant cliche of all time. The album even comes with seif-conscious listening instructions, telling the listener that the album is intended to be consumed in a single 58-minute, 14-song sitting, as if it were a movie. Unfortunately, all of the above will probably intimidate many people away from listening to "New York" by making them think that Lou Reed has become a pretentious middle-aged boob who wants to relive his glory days.

This unfortunate, since "New York" must surely be a classic example of why not to judge an album (or book, or person, for that matter) by its cover. Lou would probably be the first to admit that he's surrounding himself with hoary cliches, but it's done with a purpose.

Lou's sincerity, maturity and stubbornness turns the cliches on their ears, resulting in the emergence of the definitive Lou Reed, artist and opinionated S.O.B. (not necessarily in that order) as future generations will probably remember him.

In many ways, the album comes across as a late-1980s remake of his 1973 album "Berlin". Both albums are loose concept albums consisting of story-songs charting troubled lives set against a common background of a city where all of Reed's characters live. Since the setting is contemporary New York instead of postwar Berlin, the problems are different, even if many of the people aren't. Lou tends to talk his way through all of the songs, making them essentially monologues on whatever the subject at hand is. Some of the subjects are interesting and relevant (family violence, hypocritical politicians and preachers) while some of them are about the last things in the world you'd ever expect to hear Lou singing about (having kids, for instance). He even manages a passable stab at keeping up a rebellious facade by putting his single most offensive lyric (one of the single most offensive lyrics in recent memory, in fact) on the album's first single, "Dirty Blvd.", as well as throwing in the rousingly political call-to-arms "There Is No Time."

Occasionally, he pulls off a real surprise—his AIDS sermon, "Halloween Parade", is a forthright and honest love song and a real celebration of urban gay life, and the Andy Warhol tribute "Dime-Store Mystery" is a subtle and ironic representation of the spirit of Warhol's work instead of a maudlin eulogy. If Lou ever was going to write a song about Lester Bangs, it would hopefully be as well-crafted and appropriate as this one.

The band he's put together is a pretty good one, although most of the time the music they lay down is just window-dressing for Lou's wordy monologues, but they do get to kick ass once in a while. Lou himself plays lead guitar, and doesn't do a bad job of it. In general, the musical portion of the album is solid, timeless arid tasteful rock and roll, music that'll never go out of style. There's nary a single top-40 drumbeat to be found, which is refreshing.

The only real millstone around the album's neck is the fact that it's sure to date badly. His references to Oliver North, crack, and other signs of the times are only the tip of the iceberg—one song, "Dear Mr. Waldheim", doesn't just skewer Kurt Waldheim but Pope John Paul II to boot, as well as containing a mean-spirited (and unjustified) attack on Jesse Jackson. This, alas, is the album's fatal undoing. Lou has obviously worked long and hard to create an album that will fine-tune his image, creating a definitive Lou for the ages, but it's so grounded in today that it can't help but be regarded as a baroque relic once a year (or less) has passed. Which is a shame, but so it goes.

Friday, May 12, 1989
MUSICAL MIASMA
BY ANDREW JOHNSTON

Bob Mould goes it alone

The release of Bob Mould's *Workbook* makes him the second member of Husker Du to begin a solo career out of the ashes of that venerable band. Like his ex-bandmate Grant Hart's *2541*, *Workbook* is a melancholy, personal album filled with sincere emotions. Both records feature an emphasis on the mellow, acoustic sounds Husker Du flirted with before their breakup, but *Workbook* has much more of the fire that propelled the Huskers through the barrier between generic hardcore (which they practically invented) and the bizarre musical dimensions they explored on such classics as *Zen Arcade* and *New Day Rising*. Both records feature songs with metaphors for the breakup of Husker Du, but on *Workbook* those metaphors are enhanced by the subjects that surround them on this rich, 50-minute plus album whereas on *2541,* a short 3-song EP (but a fantastic record nonetheless) leaves one wanting more.

The breakup of Husker Du was sudden and bitter. Last spring, in the middle of recording their third Warner Bros. album, they pulled the plug on themselves amidst a flurry of finger-pointing as to whose fault it was. Mould blamed Grant Hart's heroin addiction for the split, while Hart claimed he quit because Warner Bros. wanted to emphasize Mould, the lead guitarist, as the band's singer and songwriter (since, he said, the label felt uncomfortable about having Hart, the band's drummer, act as a singer/songwriter for Husker Du as well). Hart also said that he couldn't quit heroin until he quit the band—implying that he might have been a junkie in part because of creative friction with Mould. Whoever was at fault, no one hurt more as a result than the band's many loyal fans who had followed them as they moved from the thrash of *Land Speed Record* (without a doubt the loudest, fastest hardest recording in human history) to the diverse and more melodic (but still very raw-both musically and emotionally) sounds of their later albums.

Mould's *Workbook* is a more- or-less "homemade" album. He wrote all the songs and produced the record, as well as playing (through the magic of overdubs) guitar, mandolin and keyboards. Anton Fier, of Golden Palominos semi-fame, plays the drums; while Tony Maimone of Pere Ubu plays the bass and Jane Scarpatoni of Hoboken, N .J.'s Tiny Lights plays the cello. The music alternates from the mellow to the fierce on an emotional roller coaster mirrored by the lyrics, which often recall the manic perspective of David Byrne on the first two or three Talking Heads albums. Mould sings with irony and insight about the joys and sorrows of love on "Wishing Well" and "See A Little Light", and deals, a la Byrne, with the anxieties of life in the modern age in "Compositions for the Young and Old" and "Brasilia Crossed With Trenton." Most off-the-wall of all is the closing song, "Whichever Way The Wind Blows", a cautionary tale with allusions to Uncle Remus and the "why-did-the-chicken-cross-the-road?" joke. Mould's guitar playing is finer than it's ever been, and he also shines on the mandolin. He accompanies himself on both instruments (thanks to those crazy overdubs) to great effect on several songs. Jane Scarpatoni 's cello sounds a tad hokey on some songs, but on many it adds a lush extra layer to the music and rounds out the sound very well. A couple of songs are built around what could be incredibly "pop" riffs, but Mould the producer knows how to bring out the best in those riffs so as to prevent Mould the artist from sounding like Bon Jovi or something, as a more commercially oriented producer might have. Luckily, Virgin Records let Bob do things his way.

Considering the quality and consistency of both *Workbook* and *2541* (as well as the fact that Grant Hart has a new band, the Swallows, with an album out this summer), one can begin to perceive the silver lining to Husker Du's breakup. If Bob Mould and Grant Han keep it up, they could forge brilliant careers and reputations for themselves as well as insuring Husker Du's status for the history books. America may have lost one of her most creative bands, but she's gained two individual and insightful solo artists—which is as close to a happy ending as we're gonna get.

An Afternoon in Early Spring
[For a Poetry Class]

An afternoon in early spring—
He hears random chirps and twitters that
(to her) comprise a chorus of specificity
(Cardinal, Mockingbird, Thrush)
Just a paradigm shift away.

As far, he thought, as poetry:
You can't reach in the toolbox
And find the right trochee for the job
Or amputate a fractured dactyl
And implant a more accurate anapest in its stead
Unless you've made the shift
Thant lets things click.

To some the music of the spheres
Is chaos
And one man's metric cluster
Is another's line of verse.

Andrew Johnston
May 21, 1991

Andrew Johnston: Film and Literary Criticism

Time Out New York, 1996-2008

1996

Scare Tactics
Poe on film, from Corman to Fellini By Andrew Johnston

Every year at Halloween, TV stations blanket the airwaves with the classic Universal horror films of the 1930s, but decades of overexposure have made Dracula, Frankenstein and the Wolfman about as threatening as Papa Smurf. Time has been much kinder to Edgar Allan Poe, whose monsters—men and women driven to murder, madness, addiction and incest by the skeletons in their family closets—seem tailor-made for our dysfunctional age. Poe's track record at the movies has been erratic, but a few films have managed to capture the unique flavor of his work. Any of the following will serve you well.

House of Usher
Dir. Roger Corman. 1960. N/R. 85 mins. Vincent Price, Mark Damon, Myrna Fahey, Harry Ellerbe.

Boston brahman Philip Winthrop (Damon) goes to visit the ancestral home of his fiancee, Madeline Usher (Fahey), and discovers that thanks to a family curse—which her death-obsessed brother Roderick (the bleached-blond Price) describes as a "morbid acuity of the senses"—she's on the fast track to insanity. The first of eight Poe films that Corman made in the '60s, *Usher's* tight screenplay by Richard Matheson does a great job of using the nature vs. nurture debate as a jumping-off point for a Gothic thriller complete with premature burials and a spectacular chandelier crash. Price's monologues about the futility of trying to avoid insanity and addiction when they run in one's family make *Usher* seem remarkably contemporary. Anyone who has ever found themselves regressing during a visit home will find this one especially disturbing.

Creepiest moment: Philip's nightmare, in which he meets the rogues' gallery of Usher ancestors, is a blue-filtered psych-out that anticipates the Corman-produced LSD movies of the late '60s.

The Masque of the Red Death
Dir. Roger Corman. 1964. N/R. 86 rnins. Vincent Price,
Hazel Court, Jane Asher, David Weston, Patrick Magee.

Price turns in another bravura performance as one of Poe's trademark Renaissance madmen. This time he's the devil-worshipping Prince Prospero, who stages a decadent orgy in his palace while trying to wait out the plague that stalks the countryside. Corman fleshes out Poe's story by making Prospero as eager to seduce a pious virgin and force her to embrace Satan as he is to avoid the plague. The virgin was played by Jane Asher— then famous as Paul McCartney's girlfriend, today known as England's answer to Martha Stewart. Elaborate sets and costumes and Nicholas Roeg's lush technicolor photography make this as close as Corman ever came to real greatness. Another Poe story, "Hop-Frog" is grafted on as a subplot, featuring Magee as a scenery-chewing villain not unlike the vengeful writer he would later play in *A Clockwork Orange.*

Creepiest Moment: Prospero's concubine (Court), afraid she's losing him to Asher, tries to win his favor by consecrating herself to Satan in a grotesque "wedding" ceremony.

Spirits of the Dead
Dirs. Roger Vadim, Louis Malle, Federico Fellini 1968.
R.1.17mins. In French with subtitles. Jane Fonda, Peter
Fonda, Alain Delon, Brigitte Bardot, Terence Stamp.

An anthology with three European directors each taking a shot at a different Poe story, the stiffly titled *Spirits of the Dead* is a mixed bag. Roger Vadim's "Metzengerstein" is an unqualified clunker. It's the story of Frederique (Jane Fonda), a hedonistic Hungarian countess who develops an incestuous obsession with her cousin Wilhelm (Peter Fonda), her designated rival in an ancient feud. While it's fun to see *Barbarella-era* Jane staring longingly at her brother (complete with *Easy Rider* sideburns), the adult fairytale atmosphere Vadim strives for never materializes. Too much of the film consists of Jane wandering around listlessly through awkwardly staged tableaux of sexual excess, set to some of the most ponderous narration ever recorded. Decadence shouldn't be this boring. Much better is Louis Malle's "William Wilson," the story of a sadistic bully (Delon) whose evil deeds are thwarted at every turn by the intervention of his benevolent doppelganger. Fellini's "Toby Dammit" is a freewheeling riff on Poe's "Never Bet the Devil Your Head," which stars Terence Stamp as a drugged-out movie star who loses his mind while in Italy to shoot a spaghetti western. Stamp does a great job of satirizing Mick Jagger-esque jaded ennui, and the tripped-out awards-show sequence, in which he has a psychotic meltdown while reciting a speech from *Macbeth*, is as disturbingly accurate a portrayal of a bad trip as you'll ever see on film.

Creepiest Moment: Delon's ritual humiliation of Brigitte Bardot after he beats her in a card game.

Two Evil Eyes
Dirs George Romero, Dario Argento . 1990. R. 115 mins Harvey Keitel, Adrienne Barbeau, Ramy Zada, Madeline Potter, Sally Kirkland.

Two Poe stories are given a contemporary makeover by two cult goremeisters. Romero's staging of "The Facts in the Case of Mr. Valdemar"—the story of a gold digger (Barbeau) and the evil therapist (Zada) with whom she teams up to bilk her dying millionaire husband—could pass for an episode of *Dynasty*. Argento's "The Black Cat" is much more fun: The story of a crime-scene photographer (Keitel) who develops an obsessive hatred of his girlfriend's cat, the segment is loaded with in-jokes for Poe buffs. All the characters are named for people in other Poe stories (Keitel plays Rod Usher) and all the crime scenes Keitel visits feature grisly, Poe-inspired deaths. Argento's tendency toward pretension occasionally gets in the way, but his skill at blending horror and comedy puts "The Black Cat" in a class with Joe Dante's *The Howling* and Peter Jackson's *The Frighteners*.

Creepiest Moment: Keitel's nightmare of his girlfriend leading a pagan rite in which he's ritually impaled as a human sacrifice.

What a Betty!

If the cartoons of Max and Dave Fleischer are better known to film buffs than the general public these days, it's because history is always written by the winners. From the '20s through the early '40s, Fleischer cartoons starring original characters like Ko-Ko the Clown, Bimbo the dog and Betty Boop (not to mention licensed properties such as Popeye and Superman) were among the most popular and innovative around. But sibling rivalries, labor disputes and artistic conflict brought on by the Fleischers' desire to beat Walt Dlsney at his own game forced their pioneering studio to shut its doors before World War II was half over. Thanks to "Out of the Inkwell: The Cartoons of Max and Dave Fleischer," a retrospective at the American Museum of the Moving Image beginning on December 14, the public will get a chance to see more than 80 of the now-rare cartoons that for a few glorious years made the Fleischers' Manhattan studio the envy of Hollywood.

Although AMMl is offering an excellent program of the Fleischers' best-known Popeye cartoons, the true highlights of the retrospective are the brothers' early films. Ko-Ko the Clown, who emerged from an inkwell to do battle with a live-action Max Fleischer in a series of delightful silent cartoons between 1919 and 1929, is the star of three terrific programs. The two-part "Cuckoo for Ko-Ko," will feature live accompaniment by Donald Sosin, and in "Samm Bennett meets Ko-Ko the Clown," the avant-jazz percussionist performs a score he wrote for eight Ko-Ko cartoons, including the brilliant "Ko-Ko's Hypnotism" (1929) and "Ko-Ko's Earth Control" (1928).

Betty Boop Is by far the best known of the Fleischer characters, and she gets her due in "Betty Boop's Rise to Fame," a nine-cartoon program. Highlights include "Silly Scandals" (1930), a vaudeville parody starring Bimbo, Betty's frequent canine love interest; "Betty Boop for President" (1932), in which she morphs her features to spoof then-candidates Woodrow Wilson and Al Smith; and "Betty's Boop's Bamboo Isle" (1932), which features a terrific musical score by the Royal Samoans. Although "Bamboo Isle" isn't the most racially sensitive cartoon ever made, "Betty Boop's Big Boss" (1932) earns bonus points for its vicious send-up of workplace sexual harassment. Also of note is a program devoted to the works of Myron Waldman, one of the few living Fleischer animators, who will be introducing a selection of his work that includes more excellent Betty Boop cartoons, plus the rarely screened Technicolor mini-feature "Raggedy Ann and Andy" (1941) and "The Billion Dollar Limited" (1941), one of the best Superman cartoons.

Many 1930s Fleischer animations were essentially music videos for jazz and pop performers whose hits were incorporated into the adventures of Ko-Ko, Bimbo and Betty. These are being spotlighted in a program that includes 1932's "Minnie the Moocher" (which reveals that Betty Boop is the daughter of German Jews) and "The Old Man of the Mountain" (1933), both with Cab Calloway and his Orchestra; "I'll Be Glad When You're Dead You Rascal You" (1932) with Louis Armstrong; and "Let Me Call You Sweetheart" (1932) with Ethel Merman. A program entitled "Scary Stuff" includes what is perhaps the best Fleischer musical cartoon,

1932's "Snow White," in which Ko-Ko (his movements rotoscoped off a film of Calloway) performs a blistering rendition of "St. James Infirmary."

It was the Fleischers' decision to move their studio to Miami and begin making features that led to the company's eventual collapse. AMMl will screen the two feature films they did complete: the well-known *Gulliver's Travels* (1939) and the rarely seen *Mr. Bugs Goes to Town* (1941), a lavish musical about country insects who move to New York—for which the Fleischers constructed an elaborate revolving 3-D model of Manhattan for use as a background.

Many Fleischer cartoons—especially "Mr. Bugs" and1934's "Ha! Ha Ha!" in which the laughing gas Betty Boop and Ko-Ko unleash from a dentist's office escapes into the live-action streets of Manhattan, causing fits of laughter—have a strong New York flavor, making "Out of the Inkwell" an important part of the visual record of our city. Mickey wouldn't last a day on the streets of Max and Dave's Gotham. *"Out of the Inkwell" runs December 14-January 5 [1997] at the American Museum of the Moving Image.*

The rest is silence
A fascinating compilation celebrates the Shakespeare movies of the silent era.

Today, the notion of filming a Shakespeare play using no dialogue whatsoever would seem as audacious and gimmicky as Baz Lurhrnann's decision to transplant *Romeo and Juliet* to Latin America and load it up with John Woo-style gunplay, but in the early days of cinema, it was the only option filmmakers had. These days, people often think of the Bard's gift for wordplay and character development as his greatest qualities, but the astonishing number of Shakespeare films that were produced in the silent era—at least 90, according to the Internet Movie Database—makes it clear that back in the day, his plots (most of which he borrowed from other writers) were equally prized. Seven of these silent films, covering all of the major genres Shakespeare worked in—history *(King John, Richard III)*, tragedy *(King Lear)*, comedy *(Twelfth Night, The Merchant of Venice)* and fantasy (A *Midsummer Night's Dream, The Tempest)—were* recently restored by the British Film Institute and released on video by Milestone Films as the anthology *Silent Shakespeare.* While none of them does a particularly impressive job of capturing the subtleties of their source material (which is understandable, considering most of them are around ten minutes long), they do offer a fascinating look at the imagination and ingenuity of forgotten filmmakers from the first decade of the medium's existence.

Since the contents of *Silent Shakespeare* are presented in chronological order, the compilation offers the chance to see how dramatically the vocabulary of cinema developed over a short time span. First up is a snippet (all that remains, apparently) of the first-ever Shakespeare movie, *King John* (1899), directed by and starring Sir Herbert Beerbohm Tree. Shot on a bare stage set, the clip consists of nothing more than Tree writhing in agony on a throne for a minute or so while a group of courtiers look on with baffled expressions. The excerpt from *King John* seems to have been included merely for its curiosity value, but the next film, a 1908 take on *The Tempest* from Britain, has legitimate cinematic interest for its use of special effects (there's a great shot where the papiermache wall of Prospero's cave opens up to reveal superimposed footage of crashing waves), location photography and ingenious combinations of the two (in a scene where Ariel confounds Caliban by morphing into a squirrel that scampers back and forth, following his gaze with startling precision).

The Tempest's minimal title cards ("Antonio's party trapped by Ariel," for example) make it clear that it was intended for an audience familiar with the play; as a result, it seems more like a series of tableaux than a proper adaptation (a condition that also bedevils the 1911 *Richard III*).

Other films in the collection, including American versions of *Dream* (1909) and *Twelfth Night* (1910) use lengthy cards to encapsulate their plots—a strategy that's less than successful given the wildly complicated nature of both stories. Indeed, there's so much info to communicate in each of these films that very little of the actual text of the plays ever makes it onto the screen.

Dense plot summaries also weigh down the two Italian films in the compilation, *King Lear* and *The Merchant of* Venice (both from 1910 and directed by Gerolamo Lo Savio) but they're redeemed by their high production values and nuanced performances (Francesca Bertini does particularly well as Cordelia in *Lear*). Both films were meticulously hand-tinted (each character's costume is rendered in a different color), and while *Merchant* was actually shot in Venice, the canals and gondolas that appear are presented matter-of-factly instead of being tarted up as gratuitous eye candy.

Naturally, the films don't have much in common with each other apart from their roots in Shakespeare's work, but they gain a certain unity from the striking strings-and-piano music of Laura Rossi, who provides the score for the compilation. Most new music for silent films slavishly follows the onscreen action, but Rossi is more interested in evoking the thematic feel of each play. Her music is a little too New Agey at times, but when it works, it makes these strange, quaint films seem just as magical as they must have when they were new.

1997

Here's Looking at Him
Bogie is remembered with a major retrospective and a new biography.

Can a weather-beaten actor graduate to leading-man status in his forties and go on to become not just a huge box-office draw and a sex symbol but an American icon? Maybe not today, but in the '40s that's what happened to Humphrey Bogart. "He was the perfect star for a country that had gone through two world wars and a depression," says Eric Lax, coauthor of the newly published *Bogart* (William Morrow, $27.50), the most comprehensive biography of the actor to date. "You could see in his face that he'd lived through it. It really broadened his appeal."

The publication of *Bogart* (a collaboration between Lax, whose 1991 biography of Woody Allen was a best-seller, and the late A.M. Sperber) coincides with a three-week Bogie retrospective at the American Museum of the Moving Image. The actor's signature films are all represented (including his four collaborations with Lauren Bacall, his fourth wife), but the retrospective is most noteworthy for offering the chance to catch the rarely seen *Black Legion* (1937), a hard-hitting indictment of white supremacists. The film stars Bogart as an all-American factory worker who, after seeing the promotion he covets go to a man named Dombrowski, joins a Klan-style vigilante group. It came a year after Bogart's first tough-guy role (in *The Petrified Forest*), and Lax believes it to be a key film in Bogart's development. In the film's most dramatic moment, the robed-and-hooded Bogart succumbs to mob psychology and shoots his best friend during a hate rally. As Bogart is overcome with self-disgust and tears off his robes in shame, Lax says, "You really see him coming together as an actor."

Born on Christmas Day, 1899, Bogart enjoyed a privileged Manhattan childhood as the son of a doctor and an illustrator. It seems an unlikely background for someone best known for playing salt-of-the-earth types, but Lax feels it gave Bogart singular insight. "He really knew the difference between appearance and reality," the author explains. "He grew up in this ostensibly privileged family, but his father was addicted to morphine and his mother was so remote from her children. His characters have this sense of being separate from society, and I think that came from feeling separate from his home life."

After Bogart was kicked out of Andover and did a stint in the Navy, he landed a gig as a stage manager for a touring theater company, a job that required him to understudy several roles. This led to more than a decade on Broadway, where he generally played juvenile playboys in comedies and melodramas. Bogart was 36 when producer Arthur Hopkins cast him against type as escaped convict Duke Mantee in *The Petrified Forest* (a role he'd recreate on film). Mantee, who holds the play's other characters hostage in a desert restaurant, was, according to Lax, the role that created the Bogart persona we know.

"Duke Mantee is a killer who's a rugged individualist living by a code," says Lax. "All the other people are meant to be as petrified and ossified as their surroundings at the Black Mesa Bar-B-Q." *The Petrified Forest* was filmed by Warner Bros., for whom Bogart would go on to make more than 50 films as a contract player. "[Warner's] films were the most grounded in reality," Lax says. "They were the studio of dark streets and hard rain and blood on the pavement. Those films really reflected the turmoil of the Depression-ridden and war-torn society."

The AMMI retrospective tracks Bogart's career from '30s tough guy through his classic leading-man roles in the '40s (*Casablanca* opens the retrospective and is followed by a panel discussion with Lax) on to his more nuanced roles in *In a Lonely* Place (1950) and *The Caine Mutiny* (1954). Missing, alas, are some of Bogart's less characteristic parts: his turn as a

Western gambler in 1939's *The Oklahoma Kid* (memorably parodied by Joe Pesci in GoodFellas), his mad scientist in *The Return of Dr. X* (1939) and his comic role in the bizarre gangsters-versus-Gestapo potboiler *All Through the Night* (1942). "Even In bad movies, he's pretty good," notes Lax.

But why do we celebrate Bogart today, when other stars of his era have faded? Lax thinks it's because of the archetypical Bogart character's uniquely American qualities. "In his most famous roles, he was a man who lived by a code," he says. "If that meant sacrificing his love, he'd do it for the greater good. Americans like that because it's what we'd like to think of ourselves. The times can get tough, but we'll fight through."

A Mongolian Tale
Dir. Xie Fei. 1996. N/R. 103mins. In Mongolian, with subtitles. Tengger, Naranhuar, Dalarsurong.

On Oscar night, we were reminded *ad nauseam* that film is the "universal language." Watching *A Mongolian Tale,* though, one starts to think that perhaps soap opera is more deserving of that tag. The plot of Xie Fei's sudsy melodrama could take place in any nation on Earth. Still, as the global popularity of the Spice Girls and Danielle Steel reminds us, universal appeal is no guarantee of quality.

As the film opens, Beiyinpalica (Tengger), a musician, returns to the Mongolian prairie of his youth, after years in the city, and an extended flashback reveals his childhood. After the death of his mother, the newly orphaned boy is sent to live on the grasslands with Nai Nai (Dalarsurong), an elderly woman. Someyer, a young girl, is also in Nai Nai's care, and the two children enjoy an idyllic childhood steeped in Mongolia's folkways, until Beiyinpalica's father summons him to the city to study for a veterinary degree. On the eve of his departure, Beiyinpalica and Someyer (played as an adult by the radiantly beautiful Naranhuar) swear to marry someday—a pledge that sours when she gets pregnant by one of his drinking buddies.

By the time of Beiyinpalica's prairie homecoming, he's found fame as a folksinger crooning maudlin ballads about Mongolia's natural beauty and the girl who got away. Reunited with Someyer (now a mother of five and married to an alcoholic), he must choose between her love and his stardom.

This *Tale's* greatest assets are panoramic vistas of Mongolia's open spaces, courtesy of cinematographer Fu Jing-sheng. But the pretty pictures can divert you from the film's shortcomings for only so long. Naranhuar infuses Someyer with a noble gravity, but every time Tengger has to get emotional, he starts channeling the spirit of Harvey Keitel at his most overwrought. Tengger is a big pop star in China and Taiwan, so it would seem that the impulse for musicians to embarrass themselves in crossover attempts is yet another phenomenon that crosses all borders.

Chasing Amy
Dir. Kevin Smith. 1997. R. 105mins. Ben Affleck, Joey Lauren Adams, Jason Lee, Dwight Ewell, Jason Mewes.

Chasing Amy, Kevin Smith's third feature, does to romantic comedies what Stan Lee and Steve Ditko's *Spider-Man* did to superhero comics in the '60s: It makes a tired genre newly relevant by giving its characters motivations and problems that seem real. Turning date movie conventions inside out, Smith's new film makes even the insightful *Jerry Maguire* look as shallow as pre-Spidey comics in comparison.

Lifelong pals Holden (Affleck) and Banky (Lee) have found success as comic-book creators, but Holden doesn't realize how empty his life has been until he meets Alyssa (Adams), a fellow cartoonist, at a Manhattan comics convention. He's instantly smitten, even though she happens to be a lesbian. They develop a close friendship that, to his amazement, turns into something more. But it's when Holden's dreams come true that his problems begin.

Amy is every bit as bawdy and irreverent as *Clerks,* but here those qualities are means to an end—Holden's road, though paved with dirty jokes, leads to emotional maturity. Alyssa is a far more complex character than she first appears to be, and Adams's tough charm makes her vividly real, while Lee's short-fused Banky is the comic engine that drives the film. As their straight man (in more ways than one), Affleck complements the two of them perfectly. Smith returns as Silent Bob, who lived up to his name in *Clerks* and *Mallrats* but here delivers a poignant anecdote that gives the film its title. And Ewell, as a gay cartoonist who sells himself as an Afrocentric militant in order to gain street cred, is hilarious in his too-few scenes.

Chasing Amy is obviously a personal film for Smith, a chance to work through his masculinity issues on-screen. But it's the best kind of personal movie, one that makes its concerns universal and ends with a message that, while obvious, is one we'd all be better off for learning.

The Designated Mourner
Dir. David Hare. 1997. R. 95 mins.
Mike Nichols, Miranda Richardson, David de Keyser.

A dazzling meditation on the role of intellectuals and the slow death of high culture, David Hare's film of Wallace Shawn's play is one of the most daring—and successful—stage-to-screen translations of recent years.

Three characters on a bare set address the camera from behind a table: Jack (Nichols), a one-time grad student turned middle-aged never-was; his wife, Judy (Richardson); and her father, Howard, a famous poet (de

Keyser). They live in an unspecified country at an undetermined time. The piece seems to start as a domestic drama, as Jack and Judy discuss their marriage and the influence of Howard on their lives. Gradually, it becomes political as we realize that their country's authoritarian government is changing from a mere dictatorship into a full-blown Orwellian dystopia, where writers like Howard are considered enemies of the state. Judy quickly reconciles herself to the inevitable, while Jack doesn't realize what's happening until it's far too late.

Although it has parallels to *Death and the Maiden* and *Closet Land*, *Mourner* is superior to both because it never lets philosophy eclipse the characters. Nichols, in his screen-acting debut (and one of his few performances since he and Elaine May retired their legendary comedy act in the early '60s), is nothing short of astonishing. As Jack discusses his love/hate relationship with the academic world and reveals his masturbatory and excretory habits, Nichols makes him a vivid Everyman. Richardson is at her best with a graceful portrait of a woman who's never lived outside an ivory tower. De Keyser only addresses the camera a few times, but does so with the required gravitas.

The film's final scene, in which Jack has an epiphany that inverts the one experienced by Winston Smith at the end of *1984*, is sublimely harrowing. Like all great political art, *Mourner* offers no easy answers; instead it used the bond between the audience and the characters to jerk us out of our apathy and remind us that it's always later than we think.

Better living through surgery
Frankenheimer's subversive '60s classic
Seconds comes to video at last.

John Frankenheimer's *The Manchurian Candidate* (1962) has long been justly praised as one of the most original and daring films of the '60s. But an equally brilliant film Frankenheimer made four years later—*Seconds*, a dark morality tale featuring Rock Hudson in perhaps his most intense and revealing performance—has remained a relatively unknown cult item. Mainly, that's because it's never before been released on video—and today, if a movie isn't available on tape, it has, for all intents and purposes, ceased to exist. Now that *Seconds* is here, It can finally receive the recognition It deserves.

Tersely shot In black-and-white by James Wong Howe, *Seconds* begins during a typical rush hour at Grand Central Station. Successful fifty-something banker Arthur Hamilton (John Randolph) Is about to catch the train home to Scarsdale when a stranger hands him a slip of paper bearing an address on Lafayette Street. That night, in the comfort of the mansion he shares with his bored wife, he gets a phone call from an old college friend—who's supposed to be dead—who tells him to go to the address the next day. After a sleepless night, he makes the trip downtown and is led to the office of a mysterious bureaucracy, where he finally discovers what's up.

Arthur's friend, it's revealed, is a client of this mysterious cartel and has recommended Arthur as a potential customer. The group specializes in faking the deaths of wealthy men bored with their jobs and families, shaving 20 years off their age via advanced cosmetic surgery and setting them up with new, carefree lives In California. When Hamilton is less than enthusiastic about signing, up, they threaten to ruin him. He signs on the dotted line.

After a series of operations that alter his face, his voice and even his handwriting, the bandages come off, and suddenly, half an hour into the movie, he's Rock Hudson. After an orientation period with a counselor (Khigh Dhiegh, a memorably oily bad guy in *Candidate*), he's off to Malibu with a new identity: Antiochus "Tony" Wilson, a painter complete with a fake portfolio. As he leaves, his counselor tells him, "You've got what almost every middle-aged man In America wants—freedom."

Seconds is easily one of the most subversive films ever to have come out of Hollywood: Even as It exposes the folly of selfishly abandoning one's commitments, it also makes a passionate case for following one's heart and rejecting conformity. But what's most subversive of all is Hudson's performance. In his struggle to suppress his true identity, he plays out the studio-enforced suppression of his real-life homosexuality for all to see. This Isn't the Hudson who walked through all those comedies with Doris Day—this chilling portrayal of a well-meaning guy stuck in a Kafkaesque nightmare is unlike anything else he did.

Seconds is much bleaker than *The Manchurian Candidate*; there's no humor to speak of, nor a conventional hero for the audience to root for. With its stark photography, jittery hand-held camera and deeply rooted pessimism, it feels like a '70s movie that was somehow made ten years before its time. A remake is in development at Paramount, but in an era when studio films take as few risks as possible, it's extremely unlikely that the remake will even come close to matching the nihilistic beauty of what just might be Frankenheimer's masterpiece.

Chronicle of a Disappearance
Dir. Elia Suleiman. 1996. N/R. 88mins. In Arabic and Hebrew, with subtitles. Elia Suleiman, Ula Tabari, Nazira Suleiman, Fuad Suleiman.

While Suleiman's debut initially seems to take the Seinfeld concept of being "about nothing" to new extremes, the ultramundane vignettes that make up *Chronicle* (voted Best First Feature at the '96 Venice Film Festival) ultimately advance an intriguing thesis, using humor rather than rhetoric to do so.

The "disappearance" in question involves Palestinian identity. Playing himself. Suleiman returns to his hometown of Nazareth after 11 years in the U.S. to discover that his people are becoming irrelevant in their own country. The film's first half, "Nazareth: Personal Diary," sees the director's friends and family going through the motions of life. When they're not napping or smoking endless cigarettes, they gossip, argue, fish and work. Radios and TVs constantly play in the background. bombarding them with tennis matches, news of the Balkan conflict—every possible distraction from their own political situation.

Part two, "Jerusalem: Political Diary," takes Suleiman to the big city. where we see Adan (Tabari), a young Palestinian woman, placing endless phone calls as she searches in vain for an apartment (all of her prospective roommates either hang up because she's an Arab or say how pleased they are to talk to a Russian who speaks good Hebrew). As Suleiman—and later Adan—have a few brushes with the police, they learn that in today's immigrant-packed Israel, Palestinians are invisible even to the law. But mostly, they just sit around.

Chronicle is structurally indebted to Richard Linklater's *Slacker* and the documentaries of Michael Moore and Ross McElwee, but its quirky sense of humor owes more to Samuel Beckett and Charlie Chaplin. The most ironic evidence of the "disappearance" theory comes from a Palestinian priest Suleiman visits. Gesturing towards the Sea of Galilee, upon which Nazareth's most famous native once tread, he says that it's become "a gastronomic sewer" filled with "[the] shit of American and German tourists who eat Chinese food. It forms a crust over the surface ... anyone can walk over water and make miracles now."

The Pillow Book
Dir. Peter Greenaway. 1997. N/R. 126mins. Vivian Wu, Ewan McGregor, Ken Ogata, Yoshi Oida.

When directors like Robert Altman and Sidney Lumet return ad infinitum to the themes and devices that established their reputations, it's easy to suspect that they do so out of laziness. That's never the case with Peter Greenaway. When he revisits ground he's covered before—as he does in

The Pillow Book—you get the sense that he does so because he's obsessed with making that perfect Peter Greenaway film, which, for the moment, exists only inside his head. *The Pillow Book* is his most successful—and accessible—attempt thus far.

As in *A Zed and Two Noughts* and *Prospero's Books,* the director creates a visual catalog that serves as a road map to an inevitable conclusion. Here, the catalog is composed of "pillow books," ancient Japanese court diaries. The film's theme is revenge—not Hollywood-style revenge, but the bloody poetic justice of Jacobean melodrama. Like *Prospero's Books, The Pillow Book* argues that revenge is defensible in the name of art, but here Greenaway throws family honor and sexual identity into the mix and, surprisingly; delivers his most optimistic and life-affirming film.

We first meet the film's heroine. Nagiko (Wu), in the 1970s, when she's a toddler in Kyoto, Japan, Every year, her father ritually paints an ancient blessing on her face as her aunt reads to her from the 10th-century pillow book of Sei Shonagon. As an adult, Nagiko moves to Hong Kong, where her love of calligraphy turns into a fetish she explores through the flesh. Her affair with Jerome (McGregor), a translator, sets Greenaway's characteristically simple but ornate plot machinery into gear.

Most of Greenaway's signature visual devices (elaborate title cards, superimposed images) are employed here; but accompanied by U2 songs and traditional Asian music, instead of a Michael Nyman score, they seem fresher and more dynamic than before. The actors are required to submit completely to Greenaway's mechanics, but there isn't one bad performance. McGregor and Oida (as a venal publisher) are especially fine.

One of the most revealing moments in any Greenaway film occurs when Jerome writes a check dated September 1997. Would anyone else set a film in near-future Hong Kong and make *no reference whatsoever* to the colony's return to Chinese control? Politics mean nothing to Greenaway, and he's proud of it.

What *does* matter to him, then? Well, aesthetics, of course. And tradition, as the final scene makes clear. Set at the dawn of the next

century, it proposes artistic continuity as the cure for millennial angst
It's easy for filmmakers to make us fear the future; convincing us that
everything will be all right takes real skill.

Batman & Robin
Dir. Joel Schumacher. 1997. PG-13. 127mins.
Amold Schwarzenegger, George Clooney,
Chris O'Donnell, Uma Thurman.

Poor Bruce Wayne. When he was a child, his parents were slaughtered
right in front of him. And now his life is the subject of *Batman & Robin,*
a movie that does to comic books what Demi Moore's *Scarlet Letter* did to
19th-century American literature.

This time, Wayne (Clooney) and his partner, Dick Grayson (O'Donnell),
suit up to deal with Mr. Freeze and Poison Ivy (Schwarzenegger and
Thurman), two ex-scientists tearing up Gotham City as part of their
respective evil schemes. Along the way, Bruce and Dick have to work out
their relationship issues, deal with the impending death of their butler,
Alfred (Michael Gough), and figure out what to do with the manservant's
spunky niece (Silverstone). who inevitably discovers their big secret and
gets in on the action.

The plot sounds perfectly workable, but a wretched script and wooden
performances make it impossible to get caught up in. If the recent *Con Air*
proved that good one-liners can make a movie. *B&R* shows that they can
break one—with the characters incessantly mouthing the worst possible
puns at the least appropriate moments.

Clooney is the first movie Batman to fill out the suit instead of getting
swallowed by it (though his bland Wayne could sorely use the edge exhibited
by his ER character, Dr. Ross). Still, his performance barely matters, given
the way the hero is sidelined in his own movie. Silverstone and Thurman

project some winning energy, but they're stuck with all the worst lines (and in this movie, that's really saying something). Schwarzenegger and O'Donnell's performances are criminally lazy.

Schumacher seems to have forgotten everything he knows about narrative technique, instead relying solely on instincts developed when he did window displays for Bendel's, but that doesn't mean dick when you're having your intelligence insulted for two hours.

It's hard to tell whom *B&R* is intended for. Anyone who knows the character from the comics or the superb animated show on Fox will be alienated. And though Schumacher treats the Adam West version as gospel, that show's campy humor is completely incompatible with these production values. As Mr. Freeze would say, it's sure to leave the audience cold.

Killer Instinct
By Jane Hamsher. Broadway Books.

Books that venture behind the scenes of turbulent movie sets are nothing new, but most (like Julia Salamon's *The Devil's Candy*) are written by outsiders observing the process. Insiders, one generally assumes, have too much at stake to risk dishing anything really juicy. Jane Hamsher, however, is brave (or foolhardy) enough to seemingly tell all in *Killer Instinct,* a hilarious memoir of her experiences producing Oliver Stone's *Natural Born Killers.*

There's a lot of great dirt on Stone and Quentin Tarantino here, but the story of how Hamsher and her partner, Don Murphy, established themselves as producers coming out of USC film school is equally fascinating. Murphy met Tarantino through a film-business demimonde of comic-book and science-fiction geeks, and Murphy and Hamsher optioned Tarantino's *NBK* script in 1991, before *Reservoir Dogs* put him on the map. Murphy was working in a comics shop at the time, and

Hamsher was a temp. As Tarantino's ascent began, Hamsher and Murphy started to think they'd never get *NBK* made; they kept getting blocked by legal obstructions from Tarantino, whom Hamsher shows screwing over onetime friends with impunity as soon as he becomes famous.

Enter Oliver Stone, eager to make a film that would give him twentysomething street cred. Stone appears as someone ludicrously removed from pop culture: When Hamsher expresses astonishment that Stone had no idea "Sweet Jane" was originally performed by the Velvet Underground, not the Cowboy Junkies, his assistant informs her that the man who made *The Doors* never paid attention to music in the '60s because "be was too busy in Vietnam." Hamsher's Stone may seem like a world-class freak, a man whose appetite for decadence is exceeded only by his formidable work ethic. But ultimately, he comes across as a guru in spite of himself; he taught Hamsher and Murphy how to be real producers by making their lives as difficult as possible.

The best passages deal with the chaotic shoot, during which Hamsher had to haggle with Stone and his cronies continually to ensure that everyone's visions of the film were in sync—even while no one knew if the film's experimental style would pan out. Harnsher's clear-eyed take on the way business is done in Hollywood and her evocative descriptions of the truly bizarre characters she and Murphy met while struggling to get the film made—place *Killer Instinct* among the best of its genre.

The Full Monty
Dir. Peter Cattaneo. 1997. R. 90mins. Robert Carlyle, Tom Wlikinson, Mark Addy, Lesley Sharp.

Like the recent *Brassed Off, The Full Monty* deals with a bunch of guys in the north of England who feel emasculated after losing their jobs, and then try to reclaim their manhood through a quixotic venture. Instead of playing in a brass band, though, the *Monty* boys opt to become male strippers. It's a slight film, but far more entertaining than *Brassed Off* because it's smart enough not to even try taking itself seriously.

On the ropes since the steel plant he used to work in shut down, the constantly exasperated Gaz (Carlyle) discovers how much money a Chippendales troupe pulled in at a local club and improbably decides that launching a company of male strippers is the best way to raise the cash he needs for child-support payments. Caz and his girthsome pal Dave go on a recruiting drive and wind up with a crew that includes their pompous ex-boss, Gerald (Wilkinson), a security guard who still lives with his mum (Steve Huison), and one guy who can't dance but is so well hung it doesn't matter (Hugo Speer). To distinguish themselves from the Chippendale boys, who stopped at their G-strings, the lads vow to take it all off to give their audience "the full monty."

Monty is much less ribald than it sounds. The funniest moments are frequently the most subtle, like when five of the strippers, standing in the dole line, find themselves unable to resist dancing in place when Donna Summer's "Hot Stuff" comes on the radio. There's surprisingly little raunch, in part because the film can't stop thinking of women as enemies of a sort (at least *Monty* is less offensive than *Brassed Off* in that department). And refreshingly, its definition of male bonding is broad enough to let two of the lads find love in each other's arms.

Carlyle was brilliant as the savage psycho Begbie in *Trainspotting;* here, he proves he can be almost as good when kept on a short leash. We don't learn much about Gaz, but he's the most interesting character in the movie, largely because of Carlyle's down-to-earth warmth. Most of the other characters (especially Dave and Gerald) are stereotypes who seem like they've turned up in every British comedy made in the past 50 years. The somewhat-too-truiumphant ending lets the boys strut all of their flabby middle-aged stuff, but thankfully, it's less grotesque than a typical episode of *Married...with Children.*

She's So Lovely
Dir. Nick Cassavetes.1997. R. 97mins. Sean Penn, Robin Wright Penn, John Travolta.

Watching the films of John Cassavetes now, one is struck by how complex and human his characters are, compared with those in even the most sophisticated of today's independent films. This effect is even more pronounced in *She's So Lovely,* an unproduced Cassavetes script given the '90s treatment and filled with big stars by the late director's son. The final product features some of the year's best perforrnances, even if the plot sometimes gets in the way.

Eddie and Maureen (the Penns) are deeply fucked up, but even more deeply in love. They inhabit a grimy, Bukowskiesque demimonde, a low-rent lifestyle made tolerable by booze and their passion for each other. Eddie has been withdrawn since Maureen discovered her pregnancy, though, and one day he flies off the handle and is committed to a mental hospital. Ten years later, his edge blunted by heavy medication, Eddie is released and resolves to get back together with Maureen—who's now living in suburban luxury with her new husband, Joey (Travolta), and their three daughters.

The first half of the film, which emphasizes character development over plot, is riveting. Sean Penn is brilliant throughout, but he really shines in a series of scenes that show Eddie's gift for talking anyone into anything. His real-life wife is better still, conveying Maureen's desperation—and her boundless love for Eddie—with searing immediacy.

In the film's second half, the plot comes to the forefront, and things get a little more stilted. Travolta's Joey may be acting as almost any man in his situation would, but he comes off like a two dimensional jerk. Still, it's a performance that makes an interesting counterpoint to his family-man scenes in *Face/Off.*

The film is bolstered considerably by Petra Von Oelffen's kinetic editing, a killer soundtrack and dead-on casting of the smaller roles. Harry

Dean Stanton and Debi Mazar are terrific as barfly compadres of Eddie and Maureen's, and Chloe Webb and Gena Rowlands give depth and humanity to their brief turns as social workers. Kelsey Mulrooney, as Eddie and Maureen's nine-year-old daughter, is also great. There's not a character here who doesn't remind you of someone you've met.

The stiffness of the second act (which sometimes flirts with cliche) keeps the film from achieving true brilliance, but there's enough rich humor, keen observation and fantastic acting on display here to make *She's So Lovely* a jewel of a movie, if a slightly flawed one.

The End of Violence
Dir. Wim Wenders. 1997. R. 122mins. Bill Pullman, Andie MacDowell, Gabriel Byrne.

After faltering badly with *Faraway, So Close!* (the misguided *Wings of Desire* sequel) and the pretentious *Lisbon Story,* Wim Wenders returns to form with the impressive *End of Violence.* Pullman stars as Mike Max, a producer of violent genre movies whose sensibilities were shaped by his love of such films as a child. After Max receives a confidential FBI file in his email and survives an attempt on his life, be becomes a fugitive, confiding only in a stuntwoman named Cat (Traci Lind). It's a wildly clichéd setup Wenders plays entirely straight. As Max hides out with a clan of Mexican gardeners (a goofy-sounding plot twist that, again, is presented seriously), he's pursued by Doc (Loren Dean), an introspective police detective. Meanwhile, a parallel plot unfolds concerning Ray (Byrne), a NASA engineer hired by the FBI for an Orwellian surveillance project.

The story sounds like it could have come from one of Max's movies, but by focusing on the characters' ethical responses, it becomes a serious-minded parody of conventional thrillers. After he goes underground. Max renounces his violent films, but instead of pulling a Jerry Maguire, he seems to find true happiness as a blue-collar worker. It's an almost spiritual transition—and a highly unlikely one at that—but Wenders and Pullman make it seem entirely natural. Once Max is in hiding, his New-Agey wife (MacDowell) becomes as ruthless a businessperson as he used to be, further complicating his situation.

As in many of Wenders's films, the action unfolds at a contemplative pace, allowing for plenty of character moments. Pullman, Lind and Dean are all excellent, though Byrne and MacDowell are a bit too stiff and whiny.

Many of Wenders's best films have been road movies, and *Violence* qualifies as one thanks to all the time the characters spend on L.A.'s freeways. Like Robert Altman's *Short Cuts* (which it resembles in a lot of ways), it cleverly exploits its Southern California locale and offers a truly challenging analysis of American life.

Stuck in the '60s
Three documentary videos revisit a decade that's still with us.

Almost 30 years after the decade ended, editorials that blame the '60s for all of American society's woes remain a staple of conservative publications. Perhaps that's because the era and its heroes have generated a persistent pop-culture industry. As long as the decade won't go away, it remains an irresistible target for moral criticism. A lot of good came from the '60s, but it's hard to evaluate the results objectively when some of the period's most interesting figures continue to be enshrined on pedestals instead of being submitted to the kind of deeper scrutiny that could actually teach us something. A look at three new documentary videos on the '60s suggests that hagiography is still par for the course.

A.J. Cataline and O.B. Babbs's film *Timothy Leary's Last Trip* (WinStar) is almost more propaganda than documentary. Its rundown on Leary's career as a psychedelic sage (using some of the same archival footage as

Paul Davids's recent doc *Timothy Leary's Dead)* comes off as a training film for aspiring high-school hippies, thanks to the narration of Babbs (the twentysomethlng son of Ken Babbs, Ken Kesey's right-hand man in the Merry Pranksters). The second half of the film, chronicling a final road trip Leary and Kesey took and an internet conference at which they said their final goodbyes before Leary's death from cancer, is almost painful to watch as the two embarrass themselves over and over trying to relive the past. Even if you're a true believer, *Last Trip* could make you start to think that Pat Buchanan might be onto something.

Leary also turns up in *Growing Up in America* (First Run Features), a 1988 documentary by Morley Markson that is newly available on video. Markson's film consists of interviews with '60s icons who provide commentary on footage Markson shot of them in 1969 and talk about how their lives have changed. The Leary seen here—unconcerned with burnishing his legend before he dies, as in *Last Trip*—comes across as genuinely smart, with a great sense of humor about the '60s (which he calls an era of "windbag gaseousness"). *Growing Up's* most interesting segments focus on '60s figures who remained seekers—Allen Ginsberg, for example, via his devotion to Buddhism, and Black Panther Don Cox, who developed as an intellectual after exiling himself to France. The interviews have real depth, but alas, they're mixed in with softball segments on radicals Jerry Rubin and Abbie Hoffman and attorney William Kuntsler, in which the subjects' actual accomplishments are undercut by their grandstanding. It's kind of sad to see Hoffman basking in the glow of the media for his '80s activism, considering that he took his own life a year after *Growing Up* was made.

Abbie Hoffman's life is a fascinating American story, but *My Name Is Abbie* (Mystic Fire Video), a frustrating missed opportunity of a film, blows a chance to explore one of its most interesting chapters. The film consists of a 1980 interview with Hoffman by Nicola Lanzenberg, done just after he resurfaced following seven years as a fugitive. But instead of concentrating on Hoffman's years on the lam—he went underground after a 1973 coke-peddling bust that he claimed was a setup, and altered his appearance via plastic surgery, even testifying before Congress about environmental issues in his new guise—the film records him rambling on about the Chicago Seven trial as if he had watched it on TV instead of having been a defendant. An interview focusing on Hoffman's then-newly-ended fugitive status—an equally interesting episode that almost seems stranger than fiction—would have done more to buttress the film's view of him as an authentic American revolutionary than having him trot out old war stories.

In the future, maybe someone like Ken Burns will make an encyclopedic '60s documentary that offers real perspective on the impact of figures like Leary and Hoffman. But as long as they continue to be the subjects of rose-tinted nostalgia, they'll remain the scapegoats of choice for those who wished the '60s never happened.

L.A. Confidential
Dir. Curtis Hanson. 1997. R. 137mins. Kevin Spacey, Russell Crowe, Guy Pearce, James Cromwell.

Hollywood has made plenty of *noirs* over the past two decades, but the real innovations in the genre of late have been made on the printed page by James Ellroy, whose sprawling period sagas have won him a huge cult following. *L.A. Confidential* may be his finest book, and while Ellroy devotees may quibble with the telescoping of his epic plot, the film truly captures the author's tone. It's a remarkably satisfying and complex thriller that marks a huge step forward for director Curtis Hanson *(The Hand That Rocks the Cradle)*.

Jack Vincennes (Spacey), Bud White (Crowe) and Ed Exley (Pearce) are three L.A. cops who hate each others' guts from the moment Exley rats out White's partner in a police brutality scandal (which also costs Vincennes his prize gig as the technical advisor to a *Dragnet*-style TV show). The three forge an uneasy alliance when they're assigned by the enigmatic Lt. Dudley

Smith (Cromwell) to investigate a mass murder that may be connected to a string of movie-star look-alike call girls being pimped by an eccentric millionaire (David Strathairn). Matters are complicated by White's affair with Lynn Bracken (Kim Basinger), a Veronica Lake clone, and Vincennes's relationship with a scandal-sheet publisher (Danny DeVito).

The script (by Hanson and Brian Helgeland) is a fascinating case study in literary adaptation: To streamline the book's byzantine plot, many characters are artfully assigned functions served by others in the book, which preserves some of Ellroy's greatest set pieces while simplifying the proceedings. Cromwell and the three leads are white-hot, turning in powerful interpretations of their characters that should more than satisfy Ellroy fans. Unfortunately, the (understandable) decision to collapse the book's seven-year time frame into the space of a few months makes the events seem less significant. Instead of being a secret history a la *Chinatown,* the film turns the novel's operatic plot into a more conventional potboiler. Which doesn't stop it from being deeply enjoyable. Large chunks of Ellroy's brilliant (and often hilarious) dialogue are preserved, and the actors clearly relish the meaty lines. Dante Spinotti's lush cinematography and Jeannine Oppewall's crisp, meticulous production design produce an eye-popping tableau of '50s glamour and sleaze.

It would have taken a six-hour miniseries to do real justice to *L.A. Confidential.* But this terrifically engrossing yarn still takes an early lead among the year's best films.

Springfield confidential
The Simpsons don't get older, but that doesn't mean they haven't changed.

Seven years and 178 episodes after *The Simpsons* premiered in 1990—during my Junior year of college—I'm pushing 30 and have a Master's degree, but Bart Simpson is still ten years old and in the fourth grade. As the show gets ready for its ninth season (beginning September 21 on Fox), *The Simpsons* makes its long-awaited debut on home video this week In the form of *The Best of the Simpsons* Vols. 1-3, three tapes each containing two episodes from the show's first season, which make it clear that Bart and his family have gone through some changes even though they're stuck in time.

At least three of the six episodes—"Life on the Fast Lane," in which Marge almost leaves the family for a suave French bowling· teacher; "The Crepes of Wrath," in which Bart is sent to France as an exchange student while the Simpsons take in an Albanian student; and "Krusty Gets Busted," which introduces recurring villain Sideshow Bob (voiced by Kelsey Grammer)—are about as hilarious and subversive as the show has ever been. Episodes from the first season don't tum up in reruns too often, and while they're every bit as funny as more familiar episodes that have followed, there are differences that make seeing them again as disorienting as meeting up with friends you haven't seen in seven years and realizing how much they've changed.

For starters, the animation (by the Klasky-Csupo studio, which did the first three seasons before the Film Roman studio took over) features thicker lines, and is rougher in general—the characters' mouths don't sync with their dialogue as well as they do in subsequent seasons (though Klasky-Csupo made the animation a little smoother starting in the second season, establishing the look that remains to this day). The show's large supporting cast of Springfield citizens was remarkably well-defined from day one, but crucial changes to some characters make it clear that the writers and cast were still getting a grip on the world of the Simpsons.

"There's No Disgrace Like Home" (in which Homer drags the family to a psychiatrist) and "Moaning Lisa" (in which we meet Lisa's mentor, jazzman Bleeding Gums Murphy) feature a Homer who's generally more angry than stupid. His voice is quite different, too—Dan Castellaneta has said he started out basically doing a Walter Matthau impression before developing the voice we know for Homer while preparing for the second season. Homer's dad, Abe, is significantly less senile than he became over the following years, and while Bart is every bit the little devil we know him as, he shows less confidence and ingenuity.

This is most apparent in "Bart the General," in which Grandpa Simpson and Herman (the one-armed proprietor of Springfield's military antiques store) give Bart a crash course in the art of war to help him take down bully Nelson Muntz. Today's Bart probably wouldn't need their help. Nelson (whose laugh has become one of the show's trademarks) is pretty much the same character we know now, except he has two generic kids as subservient toadies instead of being first among equals with Dolph, Kearney and Jimbo Jones, the tough kids to whom he's been attached at the hip for most of the series. "Moaning Lisa" has two plots, as do most episodes today, but the bulk of the first season featured single stories.

One of the things that hasn't changed is the fundamental dynamics of the Simpson family, which have always produced some of the show's best humor. This is the case even in the crude shorts for *The Tracey Ullman Show* that introduced the Simpsons in 1987, some of which are included between episodes on the Best of the Simpsons tapes. Creator Matt Groening is said to have based *The Simpsons* on his own family (his parents were named Homer and Marge, and he has siblings named Lisa and Maggie), so in that light, it's not surprising that their relationships haven't changed much.

The 200th Simpsons episode airs during the coming season. The producers have hinted in the past that they might call it a day after hitting that landmark, but it now looks as if the show will end in 1999, after its tenth season. It'll be a drag to see it go, of course, but look at it this way—after all those years, Bart will finally get to leave the fourth grade.

ANDREW JOHNSTON

Kicked in the Head
Dir. Matthew Harrison. 1997. R. 87mins. Kevin Corrigan, Linda Fiorentino, Michael Rapaport, James Woods, Lili Taylor.

In spite of its abject mediocrity, *Kicked in the Head* is a film that could provide a valuable public service to New York: It makes the city and its residents seem so completely unappealing that it could well discourage any pretentious young artistes who happen to see it from moving here. A hopelessly self-conscious riff on urban wild-goose chases, like Martin Scorsese's *After Hours* and John Landis's *Into the Night,* it combines all of the worst elements of the indie-film boom in one truly annoying package.

Redmond (Corrigan), a ridiculously dense Lower East Side resident, has just been evicted and is wandering the streets on a "spiritual quest" when his uncle (Woods), a small-time crook, persuades him to deliver a package of coke to an associate in Queens. After Redmond fails to do so, he crashes at the apartment of his pal Stretch (Rapaport, whose shtick has now officially worn out its welcome). Over the next three days, he bounces back and forth between his uncle's dirty dealings and Stretch's turf war with a rival beer distributor. Along the way, he falls for an icy flight attendant (Fiorentino) and tries to shed his clingy ex-girlfriend (Taylor).

The script (by Harrison and Corrigan) substitutes endless pop-culture references and cloying quirks for actual character development, and the fine actors are all astonishingly irritating. Woods is unduly hammy, and Taylor plays her potentially amusing role far too straight. Fiorentino is occasionally charming, but seems to be that way purely by accident. Redmond's naïveté defies credibility, making him the film's most headache-inducing element—and considering the script and the obnoxious soundtrack, that's saying a lot.

Scorsese executive-produced the film, but it's easy to imagine him rolling his eyes at the final product. Watching it offers an uncanny simulation of having a boot forcefully applied to your skull for 87 minutes.

Boogie Nights
Dlr. Paul Thomas Anderson. 1997. R. 2hrs 32mins.
Mark Wahlberg, Julianne Moore, Burt Reynolds.

A sprawling and incredibly entertaining epic about the highs and lows of the adult film industry between 1977 and 1983, *Boogie Nights* puts sophomore writer-director Paul Thomas Anderson (*Hard Eight*) on the map in a big way. If not the best film of the year, it's almost certainly the coolest.

The story begins when 17-year-old Eddie Adams (Wahlberg) is plucked from the kitchen at a San Fernando Valley disco by porn impresario Jack Horner (Reynolds). Under the tutelage of Jack and his wife, adult film superstar Amber Waves (Moore), Eddie reinvents himself as stud-par-excellence Dirk Diggler. Eddie/Dirk's 13-inch endowment and superhuman powers of recuperation quickly bring him the stardom he craves. The affirmation his parents denied him comes from Amber, Jack and other members of the porn extended family, including starlet Rollergirl (Heather Graham) and fellow swordsman Reed Rothschild (John C. Reilly). But after a slightly too-symbolic '79/80 New Year's Eve party, things begin to change—drugs start taking their toll on everybody and the home video boom begins to change the porn biz forever.

Boogie's structure and presentation owe a lot to *GoodFellas*, but in a California context the Scorsese vocabulary seems remarkably fresh. And the portrayal of a community of misfits—the most dedicated being Jack—who build their alternative to Hollywood, echoes Tim Burton's *Ed Wood*.

As grotesquely accurate as the '70s scenes are, Boogie's re-creation of the early '80s is even tackier and more detailed. Along the way, Anderson shows that, along with Scorcese and Cameron Crowe, he's one of the few directors who really knows how to use classic-rock chestnuts to spectacular effect.

The casting is close to flawless: Reynolds and Moore deliver what could well be career performances, and Wahlberg displays more charisma and star power than he's shown before, removing any doubts about his talent that may linger from his days with the Funky Bunch. William H. Macy, Don Cheadle and magician Ricky Jay are terrific in their supporting roles, and Alfred Molina turns in a memorable cameo in the film's most chilling scene.

The porn milieu may scare some folks off, but *Boogie Nights* offers laughs, tenderness, terror and redemption—everything you could ask for in a movie. It's an impressive and satisfying film, one that the Academy really ought to have the balls to recognize.

The Wings of the Dove
Dir. Iain Softley. 1997. R. 101mins. Helena Bonham Carter, Linus Roache, Alison Elliott.

The deliciously suspenseful opening scene, in which Kate Croy (Carter) is followed by a man on the London Underground, makes it immediately apparent that *The Wings of the Dove* is more than just another period costumer. A series of bold gambles by director Softley and screenwriter Hossein Amini make Wings the most modern—and the most involving—such film since *The Age of Innocence*.

The plot of Henry James's 1902 novel is as old-fashioned as they come: Kate, saved from poverty by her rich aunt (Charlotte Rampling), is forced to break off her relationship with Merton (Roache), a working-class journalist. At a dinner party, she meets Millie (Elliott), an American heiress, who we quickly learn is dying from one of those mystery ailments that were always killing beautiful young women in 19th-century novels. When Millie falls for Merton, Kate decides to play matchmaker for the two as they all vacation in Venice.

The wrinkle is that Millie seems poised to leave her fortune to Merton when she kicks off; that's where things get interesting. Kate cares deeply for Millie, but she knows that if she sacrifices her own happiness in the short run, Merton might well become so rich that her aunt could never refuse him. The subsequent financial and sexual wranglings, presented with clinical detachment, give the film a noirish air and an unusual immediacy.

Softley and Amini risk making their film seriously anachronistic by emphasizing the plot's pulpish qualities, but the able cast helps make it work. Bonham Carter, hopelessly mannered in *Howard's End*, is more alive than she's ever been on-screen, and Elliott gives depth to her somewhat underwritten part. Roache, too, is fine, and his performance helps make the ambiguous ending as affecting as it is.

The immaculate production design makes turn-of-the-century London and Venice seem vibrant and real. Wings is a masterful and deeply haunting film; it adds genuine relevance to a genre that typically leans toward the static.

Queen B
The films of Ida Lupino gave pulpy melodramas a woman's touch.

Female directors make a relatively small percentage of today's Hollywood movies, but they still make far more than they did in the '50s, when Ida Lupino was practically the only woman directing studio films. Between 1948 and 1953, Lupino made six fascinating B movies that ran the gamut from issue-oriented dramas to terse noir thrillers; three of them—*Not Wanted* (1948), *The Bigamist* (1953) and *The Hitch-Hiker* (1953)—have been reissued by Kino on Video. Considered together, they reveal that Lupino was a pioneer who opened doors often closed to women and tackled subjects Hollywood commonly avoided at the time.

Lupino began her career as an actress In her native England in the 1930s and came to the U.S. after being signed as a contract player by Paramount Pictures. In the '40s, while she was under contract at Warner Bros., she became famous for playing tough women (she once described herself as a "poor man's Bette Davis"). In the late '40s she started a production company and got her break as a director with *Not Wanted* (which she cowrote and coproduced) when director Elmer Clifton suffered a heart attack on the third day of shooting. She stepped in to finish the job, though she refused a directing credit.

A sort of *Reefer Madness* of unwed motherhood, *Not Wanted* is the cautionary story of Sally Kelton (Sally Forrest), a naive 19-year-old who gets knocked up by a sleazy jazz pianist (Leo Penn, Sean's father). The plot is preachy, but *Not Wanted* features impressive, gritty location photography and a few truly memorable sequences. Sally's feverish labor (seen from her point of view) is hauntingly impressionistic; equally powerful is the shot of Sally's fateful clinch with the pianist, in which the camera pans away from them and follows a cigarette butt discarded by her lover as it falls into a stream and floats away.

The Bigamist is another social drama, but it's morally more complex than *Not Wanted*. Edmond O'Brien plays Harry Graham, a salesman who lives in San Francisco, works in L.A. and keeps wives in both cities. Graham tells his story in a flashback after his secret is discovered by a social worker (Edmund Gwenn, *Miracle on 34th St.*'s Kris Kringle), who runs a background check on him after Graham applies to adopt a baby with Eve (Joan Fontaine), his Bay Area wife. Plagued by loneliness while away from Eve on his long trips to L.A ., he finds himself drawn to Phyllis (Lupino), a cynical waitress. As his business partnership with Eve starts to strain their marriage, he begins spending more time with Phyllis. When she gets pregnant, he decides to do the right thing—even if it's illegal—and marries her, too.

Harry is never shown as a cad; he's a nice guy whose sensitivity leads him into deep trouble. Instead of condemning Harry when he faces the law for his actions, or resolving the plot through a cop-out, Lupino serves up an ambiguous ending that lets the audience judge him for themselves. Intriguingly, *The Bigamist* was written and produced by Collier Young, whom Lupino had recently divorced—and who had just married Fontaine.

The Hitch-Hiker is unquestionably the best of Lupino's films. An unremittingly tense thriller/road movie, its influence on the likes of Steven Spielberg's *Duel* and Jonathan Mostow's *Breakdown* is apparent. Two average Joes (O'Brien and Frank Lovejoy) tell their wives they're going fishing but head down to Mexico for a little hell-raising instead. South of the border, they pick up a hitcher named Emmett Myers (William Talman). He turns out to be a wanted man who has robbed and killed the last several people who've picked him up. As Myers forces them to take him to a port city from which he can escape, he taunts his drivers for being up to their necks in debt and boasts that "nobody gave me anything, so I don't owe nobody." The sadistic Myers is a fascinating study in class resentment, and the film itself is a powerful example of the it-could-happen-to-you thriller subgenre. A title card at the beginning reads "This is the story of a man and a gun and a car"—it perfectly encapsulates the taut narrative economy of all that follows.

As TV began killing off B movies, Lupino jumped to the small screen. She directed many episodes of *Bonanza*, *Gilligan's Island* and *Bewitched* through the '60s and ended her career by returning to acting in guest shots on TV shows such as *Columbo*. She died in 1995. Although she's still best known as an actress, these reissues prove that as a woman director in the '50s she was not a mere curiosity, but a filmmaker worthy of comparison to B auteurs such as Sam Fuller and Robert Aldrich.

1998

Death and taxes
The films of Juzo Itami explore Japanese society with cynicism and affection.

When Juzo Itami killed himself on December 20 at the age 64, the world lost one of its most interesting contemporary filmmakers. In the ten features he directed between 1984 and 1997—only five of which are available on video in the U.S.—Itami critiqued Japanese society with a sharp sense of humor reminiscent of Preston Sturges and Billy Wilder, while maintaining a respect for traditional values and family life that recalled the films of Yasujiro Ozu.

During a period in which Japanese audiences exhibited an increasing preference for American blockbusters over homegrown films, Itami's movies were successful because they boldly lampooned sacred cows that other directors avoided, such as the Buddhist establishment and the yakuza gangs.

Itami and his wife Nobuko Miyamoto, 52 (the star of all his films), were major celebrities in Japan, and it was his fame that led to his suicide: Itami jumped to his death from an office building after learning that a national tabloid was planning to publish an article alleging that he'd been having an affair with a 26-year-old woman. In his suicide note, Itami said that he took his own life to prove his innocence. "I cannot find any other means to prove that there was nothing," he wrote.

After a long career as an actor and TV host, Itami reinvented himself as a writer-director at the age of 50 with 1984's *The Funeral* (Republic Pictures Home Video), a comic look at the ways Buddhist priests and other national institutions milk families for cash when they are burying loved ones. Two years later, *Tampopo* (also available from Republic) followed. This movie was Itami's biggest hit outside of Japan. and it's not hard to see why: The film is his broadest comedy by far, and its principal subjects are those great global constants, food and sex. That, combined with the plot's sly evocation of movie Westerns, made it widely accessible to foreign audiences. *Tampopo* is the story of Garo (Tsutomu Yamazaki), a tough truck driver who plays Henry Higgins to an Eliza Doolittle named Tampopo (Miyamoto). She's a shy widow who runs a decidedly mediocre noodle shop, and Goro's master plan is to turn her into a first-class noodle chef with the help of an eclectic team of culinary experts whom they meet over the course of their adventures. Interspersed through the plot are a series of vignettes analyzing different aspects of the Japanese passion for food, the funniest of which involve a snarky gourmand (Koji Yakusho, the star of *Shall We Dance?*) and his mistress doing things with food that make Mickey Rourke and Kim Basinger's antics in *91/2 Weeks* seem mighty tame by comparison.

A Taxing Woman (Fox Lorber, 1987) looks at tax cheating as a Japanese national pastime, and its portrait in league with the yakuza made it Itami's most pointed commentary to date. Miyamoto stars as Ryoko Itakura, a fiercely devoted tax inspector who embarks on a personal crusade to bring down Gonda (Yamazaki), a businessman hiding huge profits from his chain of hot-sheet motels. Ryoko, a tough-but-tender woman who puts public service over everything else in her life (she's a single mother, but her son is never seen) is the template for the persona that Miyamoto would adopt in most subsequent Itami films—a spunky everywoman with a common-sense approach to problem solving whom the director used as his scalpel to peel back the layers of the issue at hand. While her exquisite chemistry with Yamazaki during their game of cat and mouse is a delight, even bigger laughs come from scenes of Ryoko busting small-time tax offenders who go to hilarious extremes in their vain attempts to conceal their assets. A decidedly inferior sequel,

A Taxing Woman's Return (New Yorker Video), followed in 1988. ltami spends too much time on the boring nouveau-riche bad guys (a couple who run a fake religion to hide their cash). It's the only one of his films to cross the line into outright didacticism, and it's a major disappointment as a result.

ltami had eased up on the preachiness by the time of 1992's *Minbo* (Home Vision), which strikes an almost perfect balance between comedy and soclal commentary. Here, Miyamoto plays a lawyer enlisted by the management of a swank hotel to drive out the yakuza types who hang out in the lobby and scare off legitimate guests. While a fine comedy, it's most interesting for its exposé of the yakuza as bullies who are all bark and no bite. Afraid that the film would permanently damage their reputation, yakuza thugs attacked ltami shortly after *Minbo* opened, slashing his face and neck, leaving him with deep scars. The experience didn't scare him away from controversial topics, though: his last film, finished shortly before his death, reportedly satirized the Aum Shinrikyo cult, which launched a nerve-gas attack on the Tokyo subway In 1995.

Following her husband's suicide, Miyamoto announced her plans to honor him in the spirit of his work. Echoing his criticism of Japanese death rituals in his first film, she decided that in lieu of a conventional funeral, his family would screen all of his films at a memorial service. No director could ask for a more fitting tribute.

Mother and Son
Dir. Alexander Sokurov. 1997. N/R. 73mins. In Russian, with subtitles. Gudrun Geyer, Alexei Ananishnov.

Watching *Mother and Son* is more like attending a photography exhibit than seeing a film: Until Alexei Ananishnov's mouth twitches slightly— you may well assume the movie's lengthy opening shot is a still image. But even if precious little happens in Alexander Sokurov's latest work, it's still a unique and deeply immersive cinematic experience.

Ananishnov plays an unnamed young man caring for his mother (Geyer) as she hovers at the brink of death. While we learn very little about their relationship—the dialogue is kept to a minimum as he takes her for a walk, feeds her and reads her some old letters—the actors' body language and Sokurov's masterfully composed images make their emotions intensely real. The film's events transpire in an isolated rural area, where the occasional whistle of a train in the distance is practically the only evidence of a world that exists beyond the character's perceptions.

Cinematographer Alexei Fyodorov makes incredible use of natural light in presenting the often fog-shrouded locale; his camerawork, combined with the evocative sound effects (wind, sea birds, thunder), vividly conveys the isolation of the characters and helps pull the audience into a film that might otherwise be alienating. The images are given additional prominence by the relative lack of dialogue, a quality that enhances the film's realism: Mother and son waste no time telling each other stuff they already know (a too-common tactic in such pieces). As a result, their relationship is more than believable, and the film's ending extremely moving.

A portentous visual metaphor in the final minutes is the only false note here. The bleak minimalism of *Mother and Son* certainly isn't for everyone, but those who appreciate cinema as more than just a narrative medium will find much here that is impressive.

Men with Guns
Dir. John Sayles. 1998. R. 128mins. In Spanish, with subtitles. Federico Luppi, Damian Delgado, Dan Rivera Gonzalez.

The title of John Sayles's latest film suggests a Tarantinoesque lark, but don't be fooled: There are no wisecracking hit men to be found here.

Instead, *Men with Guns* is a somber rumination on the nature of violence and the sometimes disastrous effects of good intentions. While not as epic as his last film, the masterful *Lone Star*, it's still another bold triumph for one of America's most independent-minded filmmakers.

Humberto Fuentes (Luppi) is a successful doctor in an unnamed Latin American capital. Facing his mortality in the wake of his wife's death, he plans to visit a number of students he trained to practice medicine in remote Indian villages. Fuentes is perhaps a little too proud of his students, whose work he views as his lasting contribution to the world. But a chance encounter with the most gifted of them, who has returned to the city under mysterious circumstances, makes him suspect something is amiss.

As he ventures deep into the jungle, he discovers that his students have been killed, the victims of "men with guns"—in some cases the army; in others, guerrilla insurgents. Appalled that he inadvertently sentenced his protégés to death, Fuentes presses on in the desperate hope of finding at least one of them alive. Along the way, he picks up companions including an abandoned boy (Rivera Gonzalez) and an army deserter (Delgado).

Fuentes's odyssey echoes Marlowe's in *Heart of Darkness*, but here the protagonist's innocence proves almost as horrible as the violent forces he uncovers in the jungle. Luppi conveys the doctor's anguish and desperation with heartbreaking subtlety. Still, the film isn't quite as grim as it sounds—Mandy Patinkin and Kathryn Grody provide comic relief as a pair of hapless tourists.

As usual, Sayles serves as writer, director and editor, giving the film an extraordinary feeling of unity and control. By doing so, he has once again breathed fresh life into auteur cinema and delivered another remarkable movie in the process.

Taste of Cherry
Dir. Abbas Kiarostaml. 1997. N/R. 95mins. In Farsi, with subtltles. Homayoun Ershadl, Abdolhosseln Bagheri, Afshln Bakhtiari, Ali Moradi, Hossein Noori.

It's not easy to make a movie about mortality that doesn't turn into a sappy mess (see, for instance, *Wide Awake*). Kurosawa's *Ikiru*—the story of a man's struggle to give his final days meaning—is one of the few that have really worked. And now there's *Taste of Cherry*, which won the Palme d'or at Cannes last year. Like *Ikiru*, *Cherry* stares down the big questions—Why are we here? What makes life worth living?

The main character, Mr. Badii (Ershadi), is first seen driving through an Iranian marketplace in his beat-up Range Rover. The market is clogged with day laborers begging for work, and Badii sizes them up as if he's cruising for hustlers. But he has something else in mind: He's looking for someone willing to bury him after he commits suicide.

Badii leaves town and drives into the countryside, where he encounters three men—a pimply soldier (Moradi), a student of Islamic theology (Noori) and a plainspoken taxidermist (Bagheri)—each of whom he begs to help him. His conversations with them explore the meaning of suicide from various angles.

Badii, whose most distinctive quality is his thousand-yard stare, never reveals why he wants to kill himself. The film plays like an allegory, but for Americans who don't know much about Iran, the symbolic significance of the characters may be hard to discern. Even if you don't see the importance of the soldier's Kurdish heritage or of the seminarian's past (he's a refugee from the Soviet war in Afghanistan), the resultant image of Iran as a multiethnic society is intriguing.

The conversations that hash out the movie's life-and-death issues are fascinating and nonpreachy, although the somewhat metafictional ending of the film seems like a cop-out. Cherry seduces with its casual frankness, but the existential questions it poses will haunt you long after you leave the theater.

The Rich Man's Table
By Scott Spencer. Knopf.

Scott Spencer's seventh novel takes its title from a passage in Luke's Gospel, which tells of a beggar who lived outside a rich man's house and "longed to eat the scraps that fell from the rich man's table." Like that beggar, Billy Rothschild—the novel's thirtysomething narrator—longs to be accepted by his father, Luke Fairchild, who insists Billy isn't his son. Luke's not your typical deadbeat dad, though: He's a folk-rocker who made a huge impact in the '60s and still enjoys an obsessive following in the '90s—in other words, a thinly veiled Bob Dylan. The story involves Billy's attempt to bring Luke to the bedside of his mother—comatose after a DWI accident. It also uses flashbacks delineating Billy's interviews with Luke's friends and enemies for a book he hopes to write about the singer.

The Rich Man's Table is most enjoyable as a satire of the industry that has sprung up around Dylan—the fanzines, the lit-crit dissections of his lyrics, etc. Apart from the Dylan references, it's also interesting—for a while—as a portrait of Billy's discomfort in being the offspring of a Great Man. Unfortunately, it soon becomes apparent that the novel is heading for a treacly, too familiar father-son reconciliation.

If you're familiar with Dylan, it's fun to trace the parallels between Bob and Luke, but when a character is so blatantly based on a real person, a writer can change things only so much. As a result, the differences between Luke and his model become less inventive and start seeming like mere attempts on Spencer's part to avoid a lawsuit. Spencer also serves up big chunks of Fairchild's lyrics from the '60s through the present, most of which are far too literal to seem genuinely Dylanesque. Some of the scenes in which Billy wrestles with his demons evoke the power of Spencer's best novels (*Endless Love, Waking the Dead*). But a lot of what's here will interest only hardcore Dylanologists even if some of the writer's swipes at them do sting a bit.

City of Angels
Dir. Brad Silberling. 1998. PG-13. 112mins. Nicolas Cage, Meg Ryan, Dennis Franz, Andre Braugher.

A Hollywood remake of Wim Wenders's *Wings of Desire* sounds like a nightmare pitch right out of *The Player*; but surprisingly, *City of Angels* is a complete success. Screenwriter Dana Stevens and director Silberling's sensitive take on the material avoids New Age hokum and Americanizes the story with warmth and intelligence.

Cage plays Seth, an angel (the word itself is never used) who patrols Los Angeles and guides the city's dead to the next plane of existence. One day, he goes to collect the soul of a newly deceased patient of Maggie Rice's, a thoracic surgeon (Ryan) who likes to listen to Jimi Hendrix in the operating room. Maggie's grief over losing her patient fuels Seth's curiosity about the human experience, and before long he succumbs to temptation and allows her to see him. Through Maggie, he meets the Falstaffian Nathaniel Messinger (Franz, in a role corresponding to Peter Falk's in *Wings*), another patient of hers and, it turns out, a former angel who joined the human race 30 years before. Following Messinger's example, Seth rejects immortality, only to learn just how hard life can be.

In the opening scenes, Silberling masterfully re-creates some of *Wings'* most memorable devices—sweeping angel's-eye-view shots, scenes in which Seth and his angelic cohort Cassiel (Braugher) eavesdrop on the thoughts of mortals in a way that makes L.A. seem more interesting and alive than it has in any other recent film. The relaxed pace favors character development over plot, creating great opportunities for the cast. Cage is remarkably subtle in the early scenes, and he wisely resists getting hammy when fate turns Seth's life upside clown. Ryan makes Maggie's angst over her career and love life palpable, and Franz and Braugher take full advantage of their vacation from their TV cop roles with fine, well-shaded performances.

In the final reel, what began as a philosophical study of death and longing becomes a blatant tearjerker, but even then the accumulated momentum sweeps you along. Mainstream films are seldom more lyrical.

Wilde
Dir. Brian Glibert. 1998. R. 116mlns. Stephen Fry, Jude Law, Vanessa Redgrave, Jennifer Ehle.

Wilde begins with a panoramic shot straight out of a John Ford Western, showing Oscar Wilde (Fry) riding into Leadville, Colorado, like the new sheriff in town. He's there not to lay down the law, of course, but to give a lecture on Renaissance art to a group of haggard silver miners. It's an inspired way to start a film about the writer (especially one based on Richard Ellrnan's splendid biography, the source for this episode), but Brian Gilbert's movie soon loses its audacious tone and surrenders to Great Man biopic clichés .

The story proper begins as Wilde returns to England from his 1882 tour of North America. As his career as a playwright gathers steam, he marries Constance Lloyd (Ehle) and fathers two sons. But after he's seduced by handsome Canadian Robbie Ross (Michael Sheen), he develops a strong preference for the company of men.

Robbie remains Oscar's close friend even after the writer embraces the petulant Lord Alfred "Bosie" Douglas (Law) as the love of his life.

This relationship proves to be Wilde's undoing after Oscar allows Bosie to use him as a pawn in a scheme against the young lord's brutal father, the Marquess of Queensbury (*The Full Monty*'s Tom Wilkinson, who's great here). The scheme soon backfires, landing Wilde in prison on charges of sodomy.

The first hour—filled with sharp humor and steamy gay sex—delivers a thoroughly modern portrait of Wilde, and Fry (who, in costume, bears an astonishing resemblance to the writer) plays him with a pitch-perfect combination of smugness and warmth. Law is also riveting as a spoiled brat, something like *Willy Wonka*'s Veruca Salt in the body of a handsome young man. But things are severely hampered by the film's choppy structure (years pass between scenes) and awkward exposition. By the time Oscar's in jail, Debbie Wiseman's score is drowning the film in treacle and Wilde has been hoisted onto a pedestal so high that his sad fate has been rendered strangely unaffecting. The man deserves a film with more wit, irony and life than this one.

Bulworth
Dir. Warren Beatty. 1998. R. 108mins. Warren Beatty, Halle Berry, Don Cheadle, Oliver Platt.

The year's most audacious comedy to date, *Bulworth* is also probably the most radical American movie since *JFK*. But the passionate humanity Warren Beatty brings to his film keeps it out of Oliver Stone territory, with results that are unique and thoroughly invigorating.

It's the weekend before the 1996 California primary, and Senator Jay Bulworth (Beatty), a liberal who's been drifting rightward to please the electorate, is paralyzed by a deep depression. Before returning to L.A. for a major fund-raiser, he decides to throw it all away and takes out a contract on his own life. Since he's about to die anyway, Bulworth figures there's no point in telling the voters what they want to hear anymore, and he begins burning up the campaign trail with a series of increasingly incendiary speeches describing how America's rich preserve their power by screwing the poor. Goading him on is Nina (Berry), a homegirl apparently seduced by his newfound honesty. At an after-hours club in Compton, he rediscovers his will to live and desperately scrambles to cancel the contract without compromising his principles.

The film is almost entirely free of the insider cynicism that characterized *Wag the Dog* and *Primary Colors*. More than anything else, *Bulworth* is descended from Preston Sturgess topical farces of the 1940s, which also juxtaposed a deep belief in the promise of America with irreverent attacks on the hypocrisy of its institutions. At the same time, *Bulworth*'s ending (which is a little too easy to predict) undeniably echoes the downbeat films of the '60s and '70s in which Beatty first proved himself to be more than just a pretty face.

Perhaps more importantly, the jokes are fast, frequent and furious. Beatty isn't afraid to make himself look stupid to get a laugh (the scenes in which he starts rapping and wearing hip-hop fashions are a little uncomfortable but still hilarious), and he's generous enough to let Cheadle, Platt and Berry upstage him. It all adds up to a fascinating, challenging and—yes—inspirational film. Beatty's made some poor decisions in the past decade (*Love Affair*, *Ishtar*), but the brilliant *Bulworth* more than atones for his sins.

Third time around
A newly revised *Close Encounters* may be Steven Spielberg's most sophisticated film.

It's rare enough when a director recuts a film after its release; for someone to do so twice is almost unheard of. Yet this week, *Close Encounters of the*

Third Kind: The Collector's Edition—the third version of Steven Spielberg's 1977 film—will be released on VHS and laserdlsc. It has often been said that *Close Encounters* marked the beginning of Spielberg's transformation from the intense director of *Jaws* and *Duel* into the sentimentalist who made *E.T.*, *The Color Purple* and *Amistad*, but a close viewing of the new *CE3K* reveals it as possibly Spielberg's most personal and complex film, and maybe even his best.

Despite shifts in emphasis, the story remains the same in all three versions: UFOiogist Claude Lacombe (François Truffaut) and his assistant, David Laughlin (Bob Balaban}, become aware that aliens are about to make contact with humanity, and they prepare an *X-Files*-style coverup of the aliens' arrival; meanwhile, Indiana utilities repairman Roy Neary (Richard Dreyfuss), obsessed with the aliens after a brief run-in with them, abandons his family and tries to cut through the conspiracy so he can meet them face-to-face.

Now get out your scorecard, because this is where it gets complicated. The 1977 theatrical version of *Close Encounters* was 135 minutes long. Reportedly unhappy with that version, Spielberg created the "special edition" in 1980, cutting 16 minutes from the film and adding seven minutes of material that had been left on the cutting-room floor the first time around, plus an additional six minutes of new stuff he shot during his breaks from 1941. This gave the 1980 version a 132-mlnute running time. The new "collector's edition," which clocks in at 137 minutes, restores most—but not all—of the material cut from the original version and removes the extended climax of the special edition (which showed the interior of the alien mothership).

Most of the material cut from the 1977 version involved the deterioration of Roy's marriage thanks to his increasing obsession with the alien visitors. This fixation leads him to build a huge replica of Wyoming's Devil's Tower landmark—where the aliens would eventually land—in his basement. The special edition made *CE3K* more action- and effects-oriented by reducing the domestic scenes and including the flashy new climax (which the studio is said to have requested as a condition for giving Spielberg the money to re-edit the film). By restoring the material cut from the original film and keeping a long early scene added to the 1980 version—in which Roy fights a losing battle to convince his kids to go see Disney's *Pinocchio* instead of going to play "Goofy Golf"—the new *Close Encounters* is refocused as Roy's story, making much of the film a surprisingly bleak domestic drama.

Roy's kids are whiny, snot-nosed materialists; his superficial wife (Teri Garr) cares more about what the neighbors think than about what's happening to her husband. In his new book on the Hollywood of the '70s, *Easy Riders, Raging Bulls*, Peter Biskind says that Roy's wide-eyed adoration of the aliens makes him "the first of Spielberg's childlike, regressed adults." That's true but a little misleading; the scenes of Neary's family life are so depressing—sort of like an episode of *Roseanne* directed by Mike Leigh— that his regression is a response to the repressive obnoxiousness of his family. If it weren't for the cutaways to Lacombe and Laughlin that fill the audience in on what's happening with the aliens, the middle third of the film would play as the story of a man going insane because marriage and fatherhood didn't meet his expectations. The *Pinocchio* scene introduces the audience to Roy, and the way that this blue-collar worker is presented as a card-carrying film geek, who gets downright evangelical about the Disney cartoon's virtues, implies that Roy is a stand-in for Spielberg himself.

Siskind suggests that the Spielberg/Roy parallel (and similar thematic elements in *E.T.*) is a metaphor for the alienation the teenage Spielberg felt when his family moved to Arizona, where, as basically the only Jewish kid around, "he must have felt like an 'alien' from planet Israel, plopped down among the earthlings, the Middle-American population of Phoenix." *E.T.* can certainly be read that way, but the bluntness of the family-life scenes in *Close Encounters* seems to suggest that Roy's home life is a nightmare vision of what might have happened to Spielberg himself had he married young, blown off college and never become a filmmaker: The very sensitivity that has helped make him the world's most successful director could have driven him crazy had he settled for the life of an average Joe.

Throughout the film, there are a number of scenes that anticipate themes Spielberg would explore in subsequent projects, but his execution of these ideas here is usually more interesting and subtle. In *Amistad*, for example, he devotes much time to illustrating the language barrier separating the Africans from both their captors and their potential saviors. It's an essential plot point, but it's so belabored that the story gets bogged down. In *CE3K*, the language problem is illustrated concisely by a quick scene in which an interpreter translates Spanish Into English for Laughlin so he can turn around and translate it into French for Lacombe. Since Spielberg doesn't ram the language problem down our throats, the aliens' solution—using music to communicate with humanity—seems even more elegant and natural. If only Spielberg could still trust the intelligence of his audience, instead of talking down to us as if we were as simple-minded as the Neary kids, he might yet make another film this accomplished.

Fear and Loathing in Las Vegas
Dir. Terry Gilliam. 1998. R. 119mins.
Johnny Depp, Benicio Del Toro.

A plotless wonder, *Fear and Loathing* is mad genius Terry Gilliam's most shamelessly self-indulgent movie yet. It's both inspired and frustrating, but what else would you expect from an adaptation of Hunter S. Thompson's supposedly unfilmable book?

It's 1971, and Thompson stand-in Raoul Duke (Depp) and his lawyer/ sidekick Dr. Gonzo (Del Toro) are sent to Las Vegas by *Rolling Stone* to cover a motorcycle race. They hang around, consume mind-boggling quantities of drugs, then regroup to cover a DAs' convention across town.

Along the way, they run into a gaggle of guest stars (Christina Ricci, Lyle Lovett, Flea, Mark Harmon and others) who are used as human grotesques to lampoon the tacky self-importance of American society.

Fear is really a Rorschach test of a movie—some people will see a godawful mess, rendered inaccessible by the stumbling handheld camera and Depp's nearly incomprehensible narration. Others will see a freewheeling comedy, a thinking person's Cheech and Chong film. It all depends on your mood, expectations and state of mind (for the record, I was stone sober and basically enjoyed myself).

The cheeseball Vegas of the '70s provides Gilliam with the opportunity to let his visual sensibility run wild—every scene bulges with detail. But except for some amazingly creative special-effects shots, the visuals never overwhelm the actors. For better or worse, Depp and Del Toro's high energy performances, alternately brilliant and annoying, dominate the film.

Fear and Loathing is at its most successful when it addresses its era: A flashback to 1965 San Francisco and a Depp soliloquy about Timothy Leary's wrong turn are poetic moments that make the '60s seem vital without smacking of boomer nostalgia. Scenes in which news coverage of Vietnam seeps out of Duke's TV into his hotel room are also powerful.

Even the film's most ardent defender will have to admit that the final half hour takes the trip a little too far. But while it's often misguided, the film's uncompromising commitment to its own vision makes it something to behold.

Buffalo '66
Dir. Vincent Gallo. 1998. R. 101mlns. Gallo, Christina Ricci, Anjelica Huston, Ben Gazzara.

The last thing I want to do is further inflate Vincent Gallo's already enormous ego, but I'll be damned if *Buffalo '66* isn't truly brilliant and special. An iconoclastic tale about a closed-off man's struggle to accept the possibility of love, it reveals Gallo to be a prodigiously gifted natural filmmaker.

Billy Brown (Gallo) wound up in jail when he couldn't cover a $10,000 bet he made on the 1991 Super Bowl (Buffalo's famous choke on a last-minute field goal was his undoing). Five years later, he's back on the street with nothing to look forward to. In desperate need of a place to pee, he wanders into a dance studio, where he bumps into Layla (Ricci), a teenager he impulsively kidnaps and forces to pretend to be his wife for the benefit of his parents.

Billy's folks, Jan (Huston) and Jimmy (Gazzara) have been living under the delusion that Billy was working for the government all those years he was in jail, but they really couldn't care less about their son's life. Jimmy is too busy leering at Layla to notice Billy, and Jan has never forgiven him for being born on the day in 1966 when Buffalo won its last championship—making her miss the game. She spends her days obsessively watching tapes of old Bills games and has a photo album filled with Buffalo heroes like Jack Kemp and OJ Simpson—her only picture of her son is buried at the bottom of a closet. The savagely funny family dinner scene more than explains Billy's anal compulsiveness and fear of emotional contact.

Filled with rage, Billy decides to kill the man who missed the field goal, even as Layla improbably falls for him and offers him redemption. Billy's battle against his self-destructive side sets the stage for a heart-stopping climax in a strip club.

Ricci and Huston give poignant depth to characters that could have been cartoons, and Gallo makes Billy both annoying and sympathetic with seeming effortlessness. But the film's most potent ingredient is its visual style. The film's washed-out colors and the flashbacks that explode from Billy's head like comic-book thought balloons make *Buffalo* feel less like a movie than a dream given form.

The X-Files
Dir. Rob Bowman. 1998. PG-13. 121mins. David Duchovny, Gillian Anderson, Martin Landau.

The ongoing mythology of *The X-Files* is notoriously complex, but don't let that scare you away from the movie if you're a newcomer. Rob Bowman and Chris Carter's fine thriller draws heavily on the complex back story of their TV series, yet it's a model of narrative clarity compared to the "who needs a plot when you've got special effects?" paradigm of most recent sci-fi epics.

After a creepy prologue set 37,000 years ago, the film finds FBI agents Mulder and Scully (Duchovny and Anderson) being scapegoated by the bureau for the deaths of five people in the explosion of a Dallas office building. As Mulder is drowning his troubles in booze, he's contacted by the mysterious Dr. Alvin Kurtzweil (Landau), who tells him that four of the victims were dead before the explosion. The secret murders are the work of the Consortium—the cabal represented by the nefarious Cigarette Smoking Man (William B. Davis), which has sold out Earth to aliens who want our planet for themselves.

As Mulder and Scully strive to clear their names, they finally learn the extent of the Consortium's wicked ways and wind up in all sorts of trouble as their investigation leads them to a bang-up finale in Antarctica. Along the way, their famously platonic relationship gets a little more personal, and the groundwork is laid for any number of future story possibilities (hopefully involving the return of Armin Mueller-Stahl, who makes a delicious, and all-too-brief, appearance as an ex-Nazi).

The X-Files has always been the most cinematic show on TV, and Bowman (who's directed many of its best episodes) expands the show's scale and impact on the big screen while keeping its charms intact. Meanwhile, Duchovny is given an extra-large helping of the deadpan one-liners he does so well. A thinking person's action movie, The X-Files offers everything the show's fans could ask for, except a chance to hear Mark Snow's classic theme music in floor-quaking digital stereo. Let's hope Carter & Co. won't make the same mistake when it comes time to make the sequel.

Krzysnof Kieslawski: I'm So-So
Dir. Krzysztof Wierzbicki. 1995. N/R. 56 mins.
In Polish, with subtitles. Documentary.

Tranceformer: A Portrait of Lars von Trier
Dir. Stig Bjorkman. 1997. N/R. 52mins. In Danish
and English, with subtitles. Documentary.

Poland's Krzystof Kieslowski and Denmark's Lars van Trier are two of the most fascinating European directors of recent decades, yet while the documentaries in this double feature offer an interesting look at them, both films are plagued with frustrating omissions. Even so, the insights they do offer make them essential viewing for fans, *I'm So-So* is basically a long interview with Kieslowski, shot in May 1995—shortly after he announced his retirement from filmmaking upon the completion of his *Three Colors* trilogy, and less than a year before his death. The emphasis is mostly on the films Kieslowski made while Poland's communist regime was at its most restrictive, in the '70s and early '80s. These films—*Camera Buff, Blind Chance* and others—are seldom seen in this country; and Kieslowski's more well-known works, *The Double Life of Veronique, The Decalogue* and the *Three Colors* series, are barely discussed. The film's best moment shows Kieslowski and his former crew members reminiscing about the importance of Polish filmmaking during the bad old days of Communism while lounging around a film lab decorated with posters for movies like *Ace Ventura, Pet Detective.*

Tranceformer offers a much more well rounded portrait of its subject than *So-So*, featuring rare interviews with the eccentric, press-shy Von Trier, testimony from his collaborators and a look at the production of

Breaking the Waves. Von Trier is frank about his life and background, yet proclaims at the beginning of the film that "everything I've said and written is a lie." This makes Bjorkman's acceptance of Von Trier's outrageous claim that his films are inspired by nothing more than moods he wants to capture—"Let's do something funny, let's do something sad"—annoying indeed. As a result crucial thematic issues, such as the religious subtext of Von Trier's films, go unaddressed.

In the end, one documentary's weakness is the other's strength. Had Bjorkman pressed Von Trier harder about the meaning of his films—or had Wierzbicki explored Kieslowski's technique as thoroughly as his thematic concerns—we might have had at least one definitive documentary instead of two incomplete ones.

Special Delivery
Kiki's Delivery Service brings the work of Hayao Miyazaki to America—in style.

Most people in this country associate Japanese animation with slick cyberpunk imagery and lurid violence. But the most popular cartoons In Japan are those of Hayao Miyazaki, which are often gentle fantasies that couldn't be more different from the idea most Americans have of anime. An animator since the '60s, Miyazaki founded his company, Studio Ghibli, in 1985 to specialize in animated features at a time when most of Japan's animation houses were abandoning theatrical product in favor of TV shows and straight-to-video releases. The huge success of the ten films Studio Ghibli has released since then has made him a major cultural figure in Japan. Still, Miyazaki's films have only sporadically been available In the U.S., usually in editions of uneven quality. Now that's about to change: In 1996, Disney signed a deal with Ghibli for worldwide distribution rights for nine films, the first of which, *Kiki's Delivery Service* (1989), arrives on video this week. Newly dubbed by an all-star cast of voices (for purists, a subtitled version is coming this winter), Kiki isn't just a beautiful piece of animation but also a remarkable piece of storytelling—the kind of kids' movie people always say just isn't made anymore.

Kiki (voiced by Kirsten Dunst) is a young girl who, like her mother, has been raised to become a witch. Tradition dictates that when she turns 13, she has to leave home for a year and find a city without a resident witch, then settle there and help the locals with her magic. Accompanied by her cynical black cat Jiji (portrayed to perfection by the late Phil Hartman), Kiki settles in the oceanside city of Koriko, where she's befriended by a baker named Osono, who lets her move into a spare room. As Kiki uses her powers of flight to launch a courier service, she has numerous colorful misadventures, while also finding herself bedeviled by the insecurity and loneliness everyone faces in adolescence (not to mention her anxiety over her first crush, on a boy named Tombo). With the help of a grandmotherly customer (Debbie Reynolds) and Ursula (Janeane Garofalo), a young artist who survived her own pubescent turmoil not so long ago, Kiki is eventually able to find happiness in her new home.

The film takes place In a fanciful version of Europe that Miyazaki has described as what he imagined the 1950s would have been like had World War II never happened. The bustling streets of Koriko are filled with bulbous, old-fashioned cars, while huge blimps and passenger biplanes float through the skies above. The city is as much a character In the film as Kiki or Tombo, and the scenes in which she floats high above the rooftops on her broom, then plunges down and zips inches above the cobblestone streets, are truly stunning. The film's quiet moments are just as beautiful as the fancy set pieces, and the accumulated details result in a world. that, like those in the best children's stories, is one you'll probably dearly wish you could visit.

Although the story has a clear moral about learning to develop self-confidence, Kiki is never preachy. The story is given time to unfold at a natural pace (the film is 103 minutes long, while most American animated features these days stay under 90 minutes and consequently seem rushed), which contributes greatly to the sense of depth it conveys. Dunst and Garofalo bring sensitivity and enthusiasm to their performances, but Hartman steals the show. His sarcastic inflection makes some awkwardly translated lines ("There are a lot of buildings, yes!") sound howlingly funny and proves again that he was one of the greatest voice-over artists of all time.

Disney has already scheduled another Miyazaki movie (1986's *Castle in the Sky*) for video release early next year and, through Miramax, will release his latest film, the 1997 medieval epic Princess Mononoke (which was briefly the all-time box-office champ in Japan, before *Titanic* came along) in theaters next March, with a voice cast that includes Gillian Anderson, Claire Danes and Minnie Driver. If Disney's first three Miyazaki releases do well, the other six films in the package (including 1988's *My Neighbor Totaro* and 1992's *Porco Rosso*, both considered classics in Japan) will follow on video at regular intervals. Anyone who really cares about animation has a lot to look forward to.

Happiness
Dir. Todd Solondz. 1998. N/R. 134mins. Jane Adams, Dylan Baker, Lara Flynn Boyle, Cynthia Stevenson.

Happiness is the Bizarro World version of *Hannah and Her Sisters*. Like the Woody Allen film, it follows three siblings and various folks connected to them through the maze of modern life as they search for love and meaning. But Todd Solondz's latest is no urban fairy tale: It's a trip to the suburban heart of darkness that offers an even more chilling vision of America's dark side than *Blue Velvet*. There are no leering Dennis Hopper bogeymen here, just normal people whose lives are subverted by their raging desires. *Happiness* is the boldest American film of the year, and one of the funniest as well.

Tying the film together are Joy Jordan (Adams), a hippiefied lost soul, and her older sisters, Helen (Boyle), a successful writer, and Trish

(Stevenson), a housewife who's convinced that she "has it all." Helen and Trish both take comfort in their superiority to Joy, but both their lives are slowly starting to crack: Helen's angst over the lies her career is built upon is making her increasingly vulnerable: "If only I was raped as a child," she muses. "Then I'd know authenticity." Meanwhile, Trish's husband, Bill (Baker), a therapist, is driven by dark longings that make him the film's most fascinating character. Also in the mix are Allen (Philip Seymour Hoffman), a nerdy neighbor of Helen's who thrives on violent sex fantasies, and the sisters' retired parents (Louise Lasser, Ben Gazzara) who show that even 40 years of marriage can't truly stave off loneliness.

As repulsive as some of the characters are, Solondz makes most of them deeply sympathetic. And every scene works on several levels at once: The film's most hilarious moments all have poignant undercurrents, while the saddest—and most disturbing—are frequently sidesplitting at the same time. The casting is near perfect (Camryn Manheim, Jared Harris and Jon Lovitz have never been better than they are here in bit parts), and the dialogue is razor-sharp and insanely quotable. From the word go, *Happiness* carries the incandescent charge that only a truly seminal film can deliver.

Velvet Goldmine
Dir. Todd Haynes. 1998. R. 117mins. Ewan McGregor, Jonathan Rhys Meyers, Toni Colette, Christian Bale.

Velvet Goldmine is several films in one: a roman à clef about the early careers of David Bowie and Iggy Pop, an argument for the early '70s as a forgotten golden age of gay self-expression and a quasi-remake of *Citizen Kane*. But above all, it's about what it means to be a music fan. Like no movie before, it captures the way rock stars appear (to those under their spell) to be both superheroes and philosopher-kings, and the way the music these iconic figures create is literally capable of transforming people's lives.

As disorganized as it sometimes is, *Goldmine* is still a dazzling triumph and conclusive proof that Todd Haynes is a genuine visionary.

Guiding the audience through the maze Haynes has constructed is Arthur Stuart (Bale), a reporter who's assigned to write a "whatever happened to ... " piece. His subject is Brian Slade (Rhys-Meyers), a flamboyant figure who ruled Britain's pop chart in the early '70s until a publicity stunt backfired and his fans turned against him. Eyewitness accounts of the musician's career are juxtaposed with the reporter's memories of his own youth as a sexually confused kid saved from suburban misery by the glam gospel preached by Slade, Iggy stand-in Curt Wild (McGregor) and others.

Stuart's memories give the film a genuine context. something that's essential considering some of Haynes's more extravagant touches (such as setting the framing device in an Orwellian alternate-universe 1984). *Goldmine* is packed with details that may not be appreciated by those without an intimate knowledge of the glam era, but the film's sheer energy helps make it accessible to the uninitiated. And the soundtrack, which combines classics by Brian Eno and others with covers of songs from the era and new compositions by Shudder to Think, Pulp and Grant Lee Buffalo, is nothing short of tremendous. Bale and Rhys-Meyers are both fantastic, but it's Eddie Izzard as Slade's manager Jerry Divine who, half-way through the movie, gets the last word: "The secret to becoming a star," he says, "is knowing how to behave like one."

The Siege
Dir. Edward Zwick. 1998. R. 109mins. Denzel Washington, Annette Bening, Bruce Willis, Tony Shalhoub.

After the turgid *Fallen* and *He Got Game*, it's a real treat to see Denzel Washington in something decent once again. Crisply mounted by Edward Zwick (who also directed Washington in *Glory* and *Courage Under Fire*), *The*

Siege is—for better and worse—basically a Tom Clancy movie for liberals. High-caliber writing and performances eclipse the film's murky patches and make for a compelling ripped-from-tomorrow's-headlines drama.

After Arab terrorists essentially declare war on New York City, killing hundreds of people in a series of bomb blasts, Congress forces the President to put the city under martial law. In charge is Gen. William Devereaux (Willis), a hardass who brags that "the President knows fuck-all about the Middle East and terrorism that I don't write on his cue cards." The goal of the terrorist campaign is freedom for a firebrand Imam, a man who has been imprisoned by Devereaux without the President's or the CIA's knowledge (a stretch, granted). Acting as voices of reason in this mess are FBI agent Anthony Hubbard (Washington) and his Lebanese-born Muslim partner Frank Haddad (Shalhoub), who team up with CIA Arabist Elise Kraft (Bening) to get to the bottom of things before Devereaux further shreds the Constitution.

The film starts out as a police procedural but turns into a truly disturbing cautionary tale after Devereaux opens an internment camp for Arabs in Brooklyn. Willis (whose haircut and scowl give him an ironic resemblance to Rudolph Giuliani) turns in his best performance since *12 Monkeys*, while Washington is as classy as ever as Hubbard. And the script, loaded with first-rate dialogue, makes its case well without becoming a preachy civics lesson. The motives attributed to certain characters and groups are sure to be controversial, but I'll let the op-ed mafia deal with that stuff. *The Siege* works as a movie, and that's good enough for me.

Rushmore
Dir. Wes Anderson. 1998. R. 93mins. Jason Schwartzman, Bill Murray, Olivia Williams.

A breezy comedy about the grey area between adolescence and adulthood, *Rushmore* makes good on the promise of Wes Anderson's *Bottle Rocket*—and then some. Thanks to stellar performances and the director's original comic vision, it's easily one of the year's finest films.

Max Fischer (Schwartzman) is a sophomore at the ritzy Rushmore Academy, where he's the token poor kid. Max may be a lousy student (because of his participation in a staggering number of extracurricular activities), but his arrogance is unbridled—Oxford and the Sorbonne are his first-choice colleges and Harvard his safety. This geeky chutzpah wins him the friendship of Herman Blume (Murray), a gruff millionaire Max suckers into helping him impress Rosemary Cross (Williams), a first-grade teacher with whom he's infatuated. When the plan goes awry, Max is cast out of his personal paradise and has to deal with the public school experience.

The plot takes several twists from there, but *Rushmore* is above all a character-driven movie. Schwartzman makes Max consistently sympathetic even when he spitefully cuts the brake cable on Herman's car after they have a fight), and Murray gives one of his best-ever performances as Herman, a self-hating, alienated Vietnam vet-turned-industrialist. Williams is exquisitely charming, and the film's strong atmosphere is enhanced by the well-defined characters who populate the background (a delightful Seymour Cassel as Max's dad and Stephen McCole as a Scottish bully, among many others). As in *Bottle Rocket*, much of the action is presented in montages set to well-chosen British pop songs from the '60s that, to Anderson's considerable credit, haven't been used in a thousand other movies.

Rushmore is somewhat indebted to *Harold and Maude* and similar comedies of that era, but the complexity of Max and the audacity of the film's set pieces place it in a league of its own. Unfortunately, its R rating (for a negligible amount of foul language) may keep the film from some of the people who'd enjoy it the most. As fond as I am of *Rushmore*, if I were 15 again, I'd probably think it was one of the greatest movies ever made.

Star Trek: Insurrection
Dir. Jonathan Frakes. 1998. PG. 100 mins. Patrick Stewart, Frakes, Brent Spiner, Levar Burton.

The Next Generation crew's third big-screen *Trek* isn't an epic action movie like 1996's *First Contact* but a modest outing that feels a lot like a typical episode of their 1987-94 TV show. *Insurrection* is nothing fancy, but it's still an exciting, enjoyable movie that debunks the theory that odd-numbered *Trek*s always suck (for those of you keeping score, this is number nine).

Captain Jean-Luc Picard (Stewart) and his crew are going about their usual business when they receive a message that Lt. Commander Data (Spiner), who's on loan to a cultural-survey team exploring a distant planet, has gone nuts and started attacking people. When the Enterprise arrives at the planet—populated by a peaceful race called the Ba'ku—Picard discovers a messy situation indeed. The Ba'ku are virtually immortal, thanks to a radiation field in the rings around their planet, and Federation Admiral Dougherty (Anthony Zerbe) has made an unholy alliance with a bunch of sleazy aliens called the Son'a who want to forcibly relocate the Ba'ku and exploit their virtual fountain of youth. Unable to contact the Federation brass and blow the whistle on Dougherty, Picard and his officers decide to go renegade and save the Ba'ku using guerrilla tactics .

The Enterprise gang are all in top form here, although fans of Burton's Geordi LaForge and Frakes's Will Riker may grouse about the minimal screen time their heroes receive. Picard gets to enjoy a little romance with Anij (Broadway star Donna Murphy), one of the Ba'ku, and Data's cluelessness about human behavior is still good for big laughs after all these years. F. Murray Abraham plays Ru'afo, the chief of the Son'a, and proves himself a more than worthy adversary for Picard.

A lot of *Insurrection*'s character-based humor (and references to TV continuity) will be lost on non-Trekkers—but for those who keep the faith, it offers nearly two hours of quality time with some old friends, which is certainly nothing to sneeze at. It's the moviegoing equivalent of comfort food.

The Thin Red Line
Dir. Terrence Malick. 1998. R. 2hrs 46 mins. Sean Penn, Jim Caviezel, Ben Chaplin, Elias Koteas, Nick Nolte.

Terrence Malick's first film in 20 years is a challenging, oblique adaptation of James Jones's novel about the moral quandaries faced by soldiers on the battle-field in World War II. Its scope and subject matter are sure to invite comparisons to *Saving Private Ryan*, but *Line* offers none of the comforting affirmations that Spielburg's epic provides.

The film follows a company of soldiers through the battle of Guadalcanal, an island that, if held by the Japanese, would provide them with access to Australia and the sea lanes to America. The narrators are Private Witt (Caviezel), who questions the urges that lead to war after he goes AWOL and lives with a peaceful Melanesian tribe, and Private Bell (Chaplin), who takes his mind off of combat by constantly daydreaming about his wife (Miranda Otto). Their viewpoints are balanced by that of the pragmatic Sgt. Welsh (Penn), who believes that "there's no world but this one" and that people should just accept the hand they're dealt.

The other main theme is the familial bond between the soldiers, represented most explicitly by Captain Staros (Koteas), the company's commander, who views his men as sons and is extremely reluctant to sacrifice their lives. This brings him into conflict with Colonel Tall (Nolte), who endured years of abuse from the top brass during his prewar career and has no qualms about sending men to the grave to make himself a hero.

Although the assault on a hill held by the Japanese takes up more than an hour of screen time, these philosophical conflicts make up the real meat of the film. By letting the audience eavesdrop on the thoughts of Tall, Welsh and other characters, Malick makes every position seem at least somewhat justified—although the outcome of events ultimately favors Welsh's fatalistic beliefs.

Like Malick's previous efforts—*Bandlands* (1973) and *Days of Heaven* (1978)—*Line* is a film of incredible beauty. However, the atmosphere created by John Toll's breathtaking cinematography and Hans Zimmer's powerful score is occasionally compromised. The parade of cameos (John Travolta, George Clooney, Woody Harrelson and John Cusack briefly appear) is somewhat distracting, and the fact that Bell and Witt both have Appalachian accents sometimes makes the characters hard to differentiate. Yet even though it's confusing at times (and perhaps a little long), *Line* is still a film of rare substance and power. It may not equal Malick's previous films, but it certainly doesn't betray them.

1999

Psycho [DVD]
Dir. Alfred Hitchcock. 1960. N/R. 109mins. Anthony Perkins, Vera Miles, John Gavin, Janet Leigh.

When I first saw *Psycho* on video as a young lad, I knew better than to invest myself in the fate of Marion Crane (Leigh). Like the revelations that Rosebud is the sled and Darth Vader Luke's father, her early demise is one of those things that have been forever spoiled for those who were born too late. Back then, though, I could barely restrain myself from fast-forwarding through all the talky stuff to get to the shower scene. Seeing Hitchcock's masterpiece again recently, I found myself wishing it weren't going to happen. The story of Marion's pre-mortem detour into embezzlement is surprisingly compelling. People often describe *Psycho* as Hitchcock's most lurid movie because of the graphic murders, but to me, the texture of its opening scenes makes it seem more like his most sophisticated.

It's widely held that it doesn't matter what the MacGuffin is in a Hitchcock movie—that the plutonium in *Notorious* could just as easily have been heroin or diamonds. But that's not the case in *Psycho*. The thing that drives the plot here, the $40,000 that Marion steals from her boss, is inexorably tied into one of the movie's strongest themes: the issue of whether money can "buy off unhappiness." The earliest scenes, in which Marion fools herself into thinking that the cash will solve her problems, have a grittiness found almost nowhere else in Hitchcock's oeuvre, and her long conversation with Norman Bates (Perkins)—whose profound misery makes her acknowledge the folly of her actions—is full of emotions seldom found in Hitchcock's films: longing, regret and loneliness. In Gus Van Sant's remake, the scene's subtleties just fell through the cracks.

There's plenty of stuff in the movie that can cause unintended laughter today, but it also contains my favorite gag in all of Hitchcock: Norman's reaction when, for a second, it seems that Marion's car might not sink in the swamp after all. On top of the film's psychological complexity, the precision that Hitchcock lavishes on such a brief joke makes it clear that *Psycho* isn't just one of his best films, but also his most well-rounded.

The Matrix
Dir. the Wachowski Brothers. 1999. R. 136mins. Keanu Reeves, Laurence Fishburne, Carrie-Anne Moss, Hugo Weaving.

According to Pablo Picasso, "Good artists copy; great artists steal." If that's true, there's a strong case to be made for placing Larry and Andy Wachowski in the latter category. *The Matrix* isn't terribly original as action/sci-fi movies go, but the skill and precision with which the Wacbowskis bolt together off-the-shelf parts makes their follow-up to *Bound* an explosive mind-bender, the kind of action movie that inspires cultural-studies dissertations. Reeves plays Thomas Anderson, a.k.a. Neo, a hacker by night and cubicle drone by day whose services are solicited by a cryptic government representative named Agent Smith (Weaving) and an anarchist cabal led by the shadowy Morpheus (Fishburne). He sides with Morpheus and soon discovers that the world around him isn't quite what he thought it was—and that the stakes in the battle between the anarchists and Smith are higher than he could ever have guessed.

Revealing more about the plot would be criminal, but anyone who saw last year's *Dark City* will quickly notice strong similarities. Instead of going for Goth ambience as *City* director Alex Proyas did, though, the Wachowskis co-opt the aesthetic of Asian genre films and do so more successfully than any other Western directors to date. The film combines John Woo-style gun battles and martial-arts action choreographed by Hong Kong legend Yuen WoPing with wild-assed digital effects, but plot and character development are never neglected.

As usual, Reeves is a little out of his depth here, but the film approaches his inherent doofusness with a welcome sense of humor. Fishburne is as smooth as ever, but it's Weaving (as the Bob Dole-esque villain) who makes the strongest impression. Had the Wachowskis not thought everything through as thoroughly as they did, *The Matrix* could have been a confusing mess. Instead, it's one of the rare megabuck effects pictures that, from the first frame to the last, is palpably a labor of love.

Hideous Kinky
Dir. Gillies MacKinnon. 1998. R. 98mins. Kate Winslet, Said Taghmaoui, Bella Riza, Carrie Mullan.

An adaptation of Esther Freud's autobiographical novel, *Hideous Kinky* gives Kate Winslet her first chance in ages to play a character who seems like a real person instead of a symbol—Julia, a single mother who takes her young daughters Bea (Riza) and Lucy (Mullan) to live in Morocco in the early '70s. Her sensitive, nuanced performance is never overshadowed by the film's sumptuously detailed backdrop—which, alas, is more than can be said of the story.

Julia's a classic lost soul: The former mistress of a famous poet, she's gravitated toward Sufism to fill the void in her life that opened when her lover turned his back on her and their children. But she pursues her religious quest rather listlessly, distracted first by Bilal (Taghmaoui), a handsome laborer, and later by Bea's growing discontent with life in the Arab world. At the beginning of *Kinky*, director MacKinnon adds welcome texture to the narrative by taking the time to document the disorientation faced by Julia and her daughters—most notably their difficulty getting the locals to understand that not all Westerners are rolling in cash. But after the meticulous setup, most of what follows is choppy and episodic. Wooden dialogue and rather banal music choices (did they have to use "White Rabbit" and "Somebody to Love"?) don't help much either.

Still, by rooting the film in the girls' perspective (the title comes from a joke in the private language they share), the film avoids the pitfall of turning into a mere travelogue, and focusing on their friendship with Bilal allows him to come off as more than just an exotic loverboy. As someone who was taken to live in India at the age of seven by a mother who shared much with Julia, I can vouch for the authenticity of the girls' mixed feelings about their life abroad—not to mention the conflict between Julia's needs and those of her children. Maybe it's just me, but this kind of emotional accuracy makes the film's narrative awkwardness that much more disappointing.

Two girls and a guy
Jean Eustache's monumental gabfest *The Mother and the Whore* is as scintillating as ever on video.

One of the great, if all-too-infrequent, pleasures of being a film critic is having your mind blown by a film you didn't expect much from. Such an incident occurred in December 1997, when I was assigned to review Jean Eustache's 1973 film *The Mother and the Whore*, then beginning a revival engagement at Film Forum. Yes, I'd heard that it was a classic of French cinema, but I wasn't exactly thrilled at the prospect of catching an early-morning screening of a three-hour-and-thirty-five-minute black-and-white foreign-language film that reportedly consisted of little more than people sitting around and talking. Frankly, I was a lot more excited about seeing *Scream 2* that evening. Little did I know, as I eased into my seat, that I was in for one of the most memorable cinematic experiences of my life.

The Mother and the Whore has just been released on video for the first time in this country, and having just seen it again in chunks over the course of two days, I can testify that it loses nothing on the small screen. The film offers an encyclopedic catalog of male relationship anxieties embodied by Alexandre (Jean-Pierre Léaud), a Parisian slacker who lives with—and is supported by—Marie (Bernadette Lafont) the owner of a clothing store. Unable to commit to their relationship, he seeks affirmation by throwing himself into melodramatic affairs with women he picks up in cafés. When he hooks up with Veronika (Françoise Lebrun), a promiscuous Polish nurse, he never suspects that he's about to be forced to truly question his identity for the first time.

The first two thirds of the film, in which Alexandre gradually gets over the last woman who dumped him by allowing Veronika's tolerance for his endless ramblings to feed his ego, are both funny and poignant. But as Marie grows increasingly jealous of Veronika, the film grows darker. It culminates in a wrenching final act in which the women team up and brutally deconstruct Alexandre's personality. Veronika then opens her heart to Marie while a perplexed Alexandre looks on.

As engrossing as the film is, it's a hell of a lot to absorb in one sitting, On video, where you can set your own pace, it's easier to appreciate the long build-up to the devastating climax and to absorb the nuances of Léaud's and Lebrun's performances. Screen actors are seldom required to execute scenes as lengthy as those in this film, but these actors' energy never flags. Instead of drowning in the massive speeches Eustache makes them deliver, they connect with the dialogue at a seemingly intuitive level, allowing Alexandre and Veronika to emerge as two of the most complicated and fully developed characters ever committed to celluloid. Marie gets significantly less screen time, although she's given one of the most powerful scenes in the film: a silent emotional meltdown while listening to the Edith Piaf song "Les Amants de Paris."

The Mother was released at the peak of the sexual revolution, but there's nothing dated about its mores—it's not a film about bedhopping, really. It's about how the assumption that love will solve all of one's problems can frequently be a symptom of crippling self-deception. When I first reviewed the film in 1997, I considered the title misleading, because Veronika's rampant promiscuity was never condemned, and Alexandre's relationship with Marie wasn't very oedipal. This time, though, I came to realize that it describes how Alexandre sees the two women during the final confrontation: The only way he can dismiss their hurtful yet accurate comments about him is to reduce the women to archetypes. The suspense generated by the emotional realism of the scene makes it easy to miss this and other messages on a fast viewing.

After making two more films, Eustache took his life in 1981. While it seems a travesty that neither of them has been released in this country, this may, odd as it sounds, be for the best. It would be almost impossible for them not to disappoint when compared to this awesomely substantial masterwork.

Hyperspace

[from *Time Out London*]

The first 'Star Wars' prequel has had US cinemas and magazines scrabbling for a piece of the action, while fans relay their queuing antics on the internet. But whether 'The Phantom Menace' delivers or not, it will have proved there's nothing you can teach George Lucas about hype-management.

Most cultural historians will tell you that, thanks to producer David 0. Selznick's gift for generating hype, 'Gone with the Wind' was the most anticipated movie of all time—'was' now being the key word. Yes, people were drooling at the prospect of seeing Margaret Mitchell's book hit the big screen, but back in 1939 they didn't line up at toy stores to buy talking Rhett Butler dolls or Burning Atlanta playsets weeks before the movie's opening.

Manhattan toy superstore FAO Schwarz was one of hundreds of US shops that opened at 12.01am on May 3, the moment when the embargo on selling merchandise based on 'Star Wars: Episode One - The Phantom Menace' was lifted. Inside the store, the 300-plus fans who had started queuing at 7pm found a dizzying array of 'Star Wars' goodies, from the relatively mundane (action figures and spaceships) to the vaguely perverse (a light-sabre-shaped lollipop indistinguishable from a dildo).

As excessive as some of this merchandise may seem, you can't begrudge George Lucas authorising it. Twenty-three years ago, to placate a studio dubious about the commercial prospects of 'Star Wars', he took a massive pay cut on his director's salary in exchange for sequel and merchandising rights. Twentieth Century Fox agreed to the bargain, a decision now regarded as one of the most short-sighted in Hollywood history. As a result, Lucas was able to use the profits from his merchandise empire to finance 'The Phantom Menace' out of his own pocket, making this $120 million film the most expensive independent production of all time. Fox is merely distributing, in exchange for 10 per cent of the gross; 90 per cent goes back to Lucas.

It's been 16 years since Lucas last offered audiences a look at his galaxy far, far away; 16 years that have seen a huge number of effects-heavy movies influenced by the 'Star Wars' trilogy, but precious few with anything approaching its mythic pull. As the May 19 release of 'The Phantom Menace' draws close, cinema owners and magazine editors across the US, well aware that millions see the film as an opportunity to reconnect with their childhoods, have been bending over backwards to please Lucas, doing whatever it takes to get the movie on their screen or an exclusive story in their publication. Multiplex exhibitors have to agree to a lengthy minimum run (up to 12 weeks) on the largest screen at their facility in order to get the film. Since they require permission from Fox to move the film to a smaller screen if business flags, multiplexes which get 'The Phantom Menace' will be forced to open other major summer movies in their second-tier screening rooms.

Since any magazine with a 'Star Wars' cover is instantly a 'collectible', publications as unlikely as *Elle Decoration* and *Popular Mechanics* are joining such usual suspects as *Entertainment Weekly*, *Premiere* and sci-fi geek publications in covering the film. For some of them, it's paid off already: a late-March issue of *Entertainment Weekly* with Ewan McGregor in full Obi-Wan regalia was the highest-selling in the magazine's history; while *Premiere* had to go back for an unprecedented 150,000-copy second printing of its 'Star Wars' issue. Earlier this year, it was rumoured that Lucas was courting *Time* and *Newsweek* with an eye towards scoring simultaneous cover stories in both magazines, a once-in-a-blue-moon occurrence for pop-culture stories. *Time* wound up featuring McGregor, Liam Neeson and Jake Lloyd (the nine-year-old tyke who plays Anakin Skywalker, the future Darth Vader) on the cover of its April 26 issue, which included a lengthy interview with Lucas on the spiritual meaning of 'Star Wars'. The fact that *Newsweek* reported on rumours of Lloyd's lack of on-screen charisma in January, referring to him as 'Mannequin Skywalker', probably didn't help it in negotiations with Lucas.

The micro-management epitomised by the midnight embargo on merchandise sales shows that Lucas is heeding the words of George Santayana about those who fail to learn the lessons of history being doomed to repeat them. The main lessons here come from last year's 'Godzilla'. Roland Emmerich's mediocre giant-lizard movie opened on a record 7,000 screens last summer. This resulted in the extremely rapid spread of bad word-of-mouth about the film, and poor sales for 'Godzilla' toys. which were forbidden from sale before the film opened. A limited release for 'The

Phantom Menace' (around 2,500 prints are going out) ensures crowded cinemas and lots of press coverage about the length fans have to go to in order to see the film, while putting the toys on sale around the country some two weeks before the film opens ensures more news coverage to fan the flames of anticipation.

No matter what happens, Lucas will make an obscene amount of money off 'The Phantom Menace' —the purchase of $500m in merchandise by the Wal-Mart chain alone will net Lucas's licensing arm $50m profit before the film starts playing. But at least he's making sure worthy causes will benefit from the mania surrounding the film. Instead of the traditional glitzy celebrity premiere in LA, 'The Phantom Menace' will debut at charity galas in 11 American cities on May 16, with the tickets going for $500 a pop.

To discourage touting, Lucas originally intended a ban on advance ticket sales for the film. This backfired when people who have jobs and lives started voicing fears that they wouldn't be able to see the film because they couldn't afford to put everything on hold and queue up for days. Advance tickets are now due to go on sale over the phone and at theatres on May 12. In March, Lucas moved the film's opening from a Friday to a Wednesday hoping that by giving diehards a chance to see the film earlier, it would be easier for families to see it on the first weekend. A consequence of the midweek start, though, is that opening-day absenteeism from work could cost US businesses as much as $300m. And who knows how many schools kids will take the day off.

Advance ticket sales also mean that dozens of fans queuing up in shifts outside Grauman's Chinese Theater in LA and the Ziegfeld in Manhattan (their antics chronicled on the net at www.starwars.countingdown.com) get to spend seven fewer days on the sidewalk. The accounts on the website message board ('I had a blast! Got interviewed by *Daily News*...WICKED, COOL!' posted a fan named Steve Lubot, who had just returned from his first shift in line) are so heady, it's almost possible to forget that this is just one of hundreds of movies being released this year, destined, like all of them, to wind up as just another tape among thousands at your video shop. Almost.

'Phantom Menace' - exclusive review!
[from *Time Out London*]

Let' s face it: no film could ever match the expectations some have for· 'Episode I - The Phantom Menace'. Which isn't to say it's a disappointment: on the contrary, it's awesomely entertaining, provided you accept it on its own terms. 'Menace' is not, as some hoped, a dark, operatic melodrama like 'The Empire Strikes Back'. But neither is it a tidy, cartoonish effort à la 'Return of the Jedi'. Like the original film, it's a Boy's Own adventure yarn with a corny but irresistible spiritual subtext. The effects and production design are stunning, but they always serve the story, not the other way around.

The basic plot is simple enough —Jedi Knight Qui-Gon Jinn (Liam Neeson) and his apprentice Obi-Wan Kenobi (Ewan McGregor) undertake a quest to liberate the planet Naboo from the clutches of the sinister Trade Federation—though diehard fans will relish the hints dropped about factors that will lead to the fall of the Republic and the rise of the Empire by the time of 'A New Hope' (which takes place 32 years after 'Menace'). The film doesn't exclude the uninitiated, though: the story of nine-year-old Anakin Skywalker (Jake Lloyd) provides a layer of accessible human drama, and while the film's first act may be rushed and its midsection talky, big set-pieces like the Pod Race (imagine the chariot duel from Ben Hur but with jet engines drawing the vehicles) and the tense climax have all the magic and intensity of classic 'Star Wars'· moments like the Death Star trench run. 'The Phantom Menace' won't bring peace to Kosovo, but it's a hell of a lot of fun.

Force majeure
Menacing advance word and a tidal wave of anticipation can't dampen the irresistible *Episode I*.
Dir. George Lucas. 1999. PG. 131 mins. Liam Neeson, Ewan McGregor, Natalie Portman, Jake Lloyd.

Star Wars: Episode I—The Phantom Menace is neither the glorious epiphany that fan boys were praying for, nor the woeful disappointment that some critics are calling it. But it is far more complex, interesting and subtle than your average summer movie. It's a terrific piece of entertainment, one of the greatest visual spectacles in screen history and a much better film than 1983's sloppy, cartoonish *Return of the Jedi*, the last entry in the series. The catch is that *Episode I* requires you to accept it on its own terms—both as a cornball adventure that proudly flaunts its spiritual trappings and as the first chapter of a larger story.

Like the films in the original *Star Wars* trilogy, *Menace* wastes no time getting down to business. Within minutes of Jedi knight Qui-Gon Jinn (Neeson) and his apprentice, Obi-Wan Kenobi (MacGregor), arrive at the planet Naboo, hoping to head off an imminent invasion by the Trade Federation, they find themselves fighting a legion of Battle Droids, saving the life of spastic alien Jar Jar Binks (more about him later), visiting an underwater city and dodging giant sea monsters as they race through the planet's core in a submarine. It's just as rushed as it sounds, and it's not the most encouraging way to start things off.

The film finally reveals some genuine texture after Qui-Gon convinces Naboo's ruler, Queen Amidala (Portman), to let him and Obi-Wan escort her to Coruscant, the capital of the Galactic republic, where she can appeal to the Senate for help. Mechanical problems force a pit stop on Tatooine, the backwater desert world that figured prominently in the original *Star Wars* (a.k.a. *Episode IV*). There, Qui-Gon meets nine-year-old Anakin Skywalker (Lloyd), a slave boy in whom he senses something peculiar, and *Episode I*'s purpose starts to become clear.

As everyone knows by now, Anakin is destined to become Darth Vader, the great villain of the original tripod. While it's unquestionably sad that a sweet, innocent lad like "Ani" (as everyone calls him) would suffer such a fate, Qui-Gon's optimistic belief in the boy's potential for good seems more tragic still. In the original trilogy, we never got a good look at the Jedi Knights—Yoda and the older Obi-Wan were professors emeritus, and Luke was (let's face it) a bumbling neophyte who mostly got by on luck. Qui-Gon is the first Jedi we've seen in his prime, and he's a remarkable character, a type of hero Hollywood almost never presents: a warrior, yes, but a deeply religious one, a man whose every move is guided by his devout faith in the Force. But he's not a stuffed shirt, either—one is reminded of mythological trickster-heroes like Odysseus when Qui-Gon wins Anakin's freedom through an elaborate series of bets. Lucas has often seemed to be blowing smoke when talking about the influence of Joseph Campbell and classic archetypes on Star Wars, but Qui-Gon lends credence to Lucas's claims, and Neeson deserves a lot of credit for being able to sell the character while sharing so much of his screen time with the ever-distracting Jar Jar.

Jar Jar (a computer-animated creature whose voice, provided by actor Ahmed Best, sounds like that of a Jamaican Bugs Bunny) is a source of broad comic relief throughout the film, and he's already been pilloried as an example of *Menace* being overly skewed toward children. Jar Jar's antics are pretty juvenile, but they don't make *Menace* a kids' movie—instead, it's a movie that happens to welcome children into its audience. By using Jar Jar and Anakin as hooks for the 9-to-12 crowd, Lucas reaches out to a group that most summer movies take for granted. Jar Jar is undeniably annoying, but he doesn't sink the movie the way *Jedi*'s Ewoks did, and the film never completely abandons the adult audience. (If this was purely a kids' film, it probably wouldn't have a major plot point revolving around parliamentary procedure.)

Menace is Lucas's first film in 22 years, and it shows, but in a good way. Its style is almost entirely consistent with that of *Episode IV*—right down to the use of wipes for most transitions—and it has a raw creativity missing from the installments that were directed by others. The originality of creatures like Sebulba (a sinister cross between a camel and a chimp who is Anakin's main rival in the stunning pod race sequence) and places like Coruscant (a planet that's one giant Art Deco city) sets *Menace* apart from most Hollywood blockbusters and underscores the sameness of those films' visual effects. Lucas footed *Episode I*'s entire $120-million budget himself, making it not only the most expensive independent film ever but the most extravagantly uncompromised presentation of a single filmmaker's vision to date. While admirable, this also poses some accessibility problems for those who don't know their *Star Wars* chapter and verse. It's never made sufficiently clear, for instance, that the invasion of Naboo is really a gambit designed to elevate Palpatine (Ian McDiarmid), the planet's senator, to Supreme Chancellor of the Senate (a position from which he promotes himself to Emperor by the time of *Episode IV*). McDiarmid also plays shadowy bad guy Darth Sidious—the "phantom menace" of the title— and it's left open as to whether or not both men are one and the same. Stuff like this gives fans something to debate until *Episode II* comes out, but it's also likely to leave casual viewers baffled.

All of this results in a mighty talky midsection, that, like the minimal screen time accorded to McGregor and to Sidious's attack-dog apprentice, Darth Maul (Ray Park), may disappoint some. But it also gives Lucas the chance to flesh out his remarkable universe and to lay a lot of promising groundwork for *Episode I*. The audience's patience is rewarded by the pod race (an awesomely kinetic celebration of sheer speed) and the climax (which features the most breathtaking lightsaber action in the entire series), sequences with all the magic and intensity of the original trilogy at its best. If you're one of those people who thinks *Star Wars* destroyed American cinema, *Menace* won't change your mind. But at a time when mainstream films are dumber than ever, it seems like a genuine triumph of the imagination.

Trekkies
Dir. Roger Nygard. 1998. PG. 86mins. Documentary.

If ever there was a subculture ripe for documentary treatment, it's Star Trek fandom, a strange and fascinating world that gets a disappointing once-over in *Trekkies*. Roger Nygard's film is packed with sorta-amusing examples of the endearing (and sometimes disturbing) eccentricities of its subjects—who generally prefer to be called Trekkers—but never really gets at the heart of what drives them.

Hosted by former *Next Generation* cast member Denise Crosby (who seems admirably nonspooked by fan art showing her character, Tasha Yar, in compromising positions with Lieutenant Commander Data), the film indiscriminately mulches together interviews with cast members from all four *Trek* series with reportage from conventions and segments on the daily lives of exceptionally devoted fans. One of them—Little Rock copy-shop worker Barbara Adams—wound up in the national spotlight a few years ago, when she was a Whitewater juror and wore her Starfleet uniform to court every day. She seems positively benign compared with Gabriel Köerner, a California 14-year-old who's been attending conventions since since he was six and behaves like an angrier version of *Rushmore*'s Max Fischer. Far more interesting is Dr. Denis Bourguignon, a seemingly normal Florida dentist with a beautiful wife and charming kids; he turned his practice into a *Trek* shrine and coaxed his employees into wearing uniforms (although you've got to wonder about his marriage when his wife talks about how, at home, she occasionally dresses up as *Deep Space Nine*'s Ferengi bartender Quark!).

Somewhat surprisingly (considering that the film is released by Paramount, which owns the *Trek* franchise), *Trekkies* does acknowledge, albeit briefly, the world of "slash" zines, which contain gay porn stories (written primarily by straight women) featuring hot Kirk-on-Spock action. But while Trekkies is encyclopedic, it's also badly organized, jumping from one subject to another and then back to one covered half an hour earlier. Notwithstanding its occasional touching moments (it's surprisingly hard not to be moved when James "Scotty" Doohan starts crying while describing how he once talked a fan out of suicide), *Trekkies* has all the substance of a feature-length *Access Hollywood* segment.

Regret to Inform
Dir. Barbara Sonneborn. 1998. N/R. 72mins. Documentary.

The Oscar-nominated *Regret to Inform* arrives in theaters just two weeks after *Return with Honor*, another Vietnam War documentary with a similar-sounding title. Under no circumstances. however, should the two films be confused. Instead of celebrating the valor of those who served in Vietnam, *Regret*—which takes its title from the words of the form letter received by families of soldiers who died in the war—chronicles the continuing struggle of women on both sides of the conflict to put the wartime deaths of their husbands in perspective. *Regret* may not have much of a thesis beyond the time-honored maxim that war is hell, but it delivers its message effectively, without resorting to cheap sentiment.

On her 24th birthday, director Barbara Sonneborn learned that her husband Jeffrey—they'd been sweethearts since she was 14—had died in combat. Twenty years after his death, she became possessed with an urge to visit Vietnam, and in the film, she uses her trip as a framing device for interviews with other widows of the war.

While the interviews with American widows are often touching, the interviews with Vietnamese women are more affecting still. One—Sonneborn's friend and translator, Xuan Ngoc Evans—talks of resorting to prostitution in order to support her family; another, who spied on American troops by posing as a maid, describes the hideous torture she suffered at the hands of the South Vietnamese after the Americans captured her and turned her over to them.

Regret's evenhandedness may strike some as a concession to political correctness, but if it didn't tell both sides of the story, it wouldn't be such an effective antiwar statement. More than once in recent years, America has seemed disturbingly eager for a new war, but the stories told here powerfully illustrate how just how lucky we are to have escaped a prolonged conflict for more than a generation.

I'm Losing You
Dir. Bruce Wagner. 1998. N/R. 102mins. Rosanna Arquette, Frank Langella, Andrew McCarthy.

Ideally, film critics should bring as little baggage as possible to each movie they review. But after suffering through Norman Mailer's mind-bogglingly dreadful film *Tough Guys Don't Dance* a decade ago, it's been impossible for me to approach the work of novelists who direct adaptations of their own work with anything resembling an open mind. Bruce Wagner's *I'm Losing You* melted my skepticism: Although the film's serious tone is punctuated by moments of unintentional silliness, its thoughtful take on the spiritual vacuum of Los Angeles is undeniably affecting.

Perry Krohn (Langella) is the creator of a hugely successful *Star Trek*-like TV show who discovers, on his 60th birthday, that he's suffering from inoperable lung cancer. Perry's imminent passing kick-starts a series of crises for Bertie (McCarthy), his son, and Rachel (Arquette), the niece Perry adopted after his brother's death. Bertie—a failed actor who supports himself by selling the insurance benefits of dying AIDS patients—seeks refuge in a doomed relationship with an HIV-positive woman (Elizabeth Perkins), while Rachel, who freaks after discovering the truth about her parents' deaths, immerses herself in Jewish mysticism.

If you think this makes *I'm Losing You* sound like an epic downer, you haven't heard the half of it. Except for Perry's cancer, none of these catastrophes are random—they're all the result of people's casual cruelty toward their loved ones, a theme that, while pervasive here, is never explored directly enough. But the point of the story isn't how the characters respond to crises (a good thing, since almost every scene where someone gets emotional is painfully overwrought) but on how they go on living afterward. Wagner's dialogue is too glib at times, but his cast compensates with heartfelt performances that ground the film in reality and keep its melodramatic aspects in check. Wagner's novel was apparently more of a satire in the vein of Michael Tolkin's satirical attacks on L.A. (in *The Player* and *The New Age*), and while the resulting film may not be as probing as Tolkin's efforts, it's definitely more emotionally rewarding.

Iced tease
While it might be too chilly to truly love, Stanley Kubrick's final film is a tantalizing farewell.

Eyes Wide Shut begins with a shot of Nicole Kidman's bare ass—an image as blunt and disarming as the one of a young recruit getting his head shaved with which Stanley Kubrick began Full Metal Jacket. By getting the naked movie-star thing out of the way up front, the great director's final film—a peculiar, powerful and thoroughly engrossing adaptation of Arthur Schnitzler's *Traumnovelle*—is quickly freed to concentrate on storytelling. The portentous opening of *2001: A Space Odyssey* aside, Kubrick has usually been one to cut to the chase, and after years of hype, rumor and anticipation, the simplicity of *Eyes*'s initial scenes is downright comforting.

The kinky trappings of its midsection aside, *Eyes* is a film about the elusive nature of real intimacy. Dr. William Harford (Cruise) and his wife Alice (Kidrnan) have been married for nine years, but it's apparent, as they dress for an opulent Christmas party thrown by a patient of Bill's named Victor Ziegler (Pollack), that a certain anomie has infected their relationship. At the party, Bill chats up a couple of models while Alice is propositioned by a Eurotrash smoothie (Sky Dumont). Neither of them strays, but their flirtations result in a fierce argument the following evening (when they're both stoned) during which Alice reveals her sexual fantasies about a navy officer they encountered on vacation the previous summer. It's a scene that's funny yet unnervingly raw, and easily the best in the film. Their conversation is interrupted by a phone call informing Bill that one of his patients has died, and he ventures into the night haunted by visions of Alice in bed with the officer.

While wandering the streets after consoling his patient's daughter (Marie Richardson), Bill swings by a jazz club where Nick Nightingale (Todd Field), an old friend who dropped out of med school to become a musician, is performing with his band. Nick mentions that he's on his way to another gig—a decadent party where he's been contracted to perform blindfolded for a crowd of masked hedonists. Bill impulsively decides to crash the party, secures the requisite disguise and gets a taxi to take him out to the Long Island mansion where the party is taking place. There, he finds himself in the middle of a bizarre orgy, 65 seconds of which is obscured by digital manipulation that, while indefensible, is not really that distracting: A fateful encounter at these dark revels launches Bill on a journey toward self-discovery that takes up the rest of the film.

As the title of both the film and its source material suggest— *Traumnovelle* translates as "dream story"—the influence of dreams upon reality and the difference between the two states of consciousness are among the main themes here. And indeed, the dreamlike nature of the film helps make its excesses and peculiarities acceptable in context. *Eyes* is set in contemporary Manhattan, but it was filmed entirely in London. Establishing shots show actual downtown locations, yet Bill prowls streets that don't exist in real life—a creative decision that may ring false to some New Yorkers. But the layer of abstraction it provides makes it easier to swallow situations that are unlikely to transpire in the city we know— Bill's run-in with a uncommonly comely streetwalker (Vinessa Shaw), for example, and a detour into *Blue Velvet* territory involving a leering costumer (Rade Sherbedgia) and his randy teenage daughter (Leelee Sobieski). The film's saturated colors and eerie lighting compound the hallucinatory effect of these scenes.

At the screening I attended, the orgy provoked a lot of unintentional laughter, and not without good reason. It's a strange, stiff sequence that feels like an Andrew Blake porn film crossed with one of Roger Corman's Edgar Allan Poe movies. However, in the film's only real departure from Schnitzler's story, there's a powerful scene late in the film that forces one to reconsider those events, which suddenly seem a lot less cheesy in retrospect,

Cruise is in virtually every scene of the film, but he spends much of it not acting so much as reacting. Except for his jealousy, Bill isn't given that much to define him—but if he lacks the determination that's the main quality of Cruise's signature roles, he certainly possesses the naïveté that is its flip side. While it's a little frustrating that Kubrick uses the audience's natural sympathy for Cruise as a crutch, by making Bill a blank slate, the director uses Cruise to draw out phenomenal performances from others in the cast. Kidman's work as the inscrutable (yet outspoken) Alice is unquestionably the best of her career, and her absence from the middle of the film is a real disappointment. It may sound like damnation with faint praise to say that for a director Pollack is an amazing actor, but it's true—he does a remarkable job of making Victor seem simultaneously jovial and sinister. His off-the-cuff casualness makes a crucial scene toward the end a lot more believable than it might have been had the far more mannered Harvey Keitel (who was originally cast in the role) not parted ways with Kubrick.

Like many of Kubrick's films, *Eyes* is a little too chilly to really love (after a single viewing, anyway) but very easy to admire. Even so, it also has emotional moments that are much warmer than anything in his previous work, most notably the scene where Richardson's character puts Bill in a tough spot by unexpectedly declaring her love for him. The film also has the closest thing to an unambiguously happy ending Kubrick has ever crafted, an ironic final note for a director whose films have often been construed as misanthropic.

Despite these tonal variations from his previous work, *Eyes* is full of trademark Kubrick devices: masterful tracking shots, well-deployed (if somewhat overused musical leitmotivs and humor so dry it may elude some people entirely. The resulting film, like a dream, is both straightforward and open to endless interpretation. Unlike dreams, though, films can be revisited at will, and this is one I fully expect to return to time and again.

Frank sentiments
In describing the history of *Joe the King,* actor-turned-writer-director Frank Whaley pulls no punches.

If you attend film festivals with any regularity, it's hard not to be skeptical about actors-turned-directors—every year, the Sundance lineup contains two or thee mediocrities directed by a performer who persuaded a few big-name friends to take bit parts in order to dazzle starstruck investors and selection-committee types. Every now and then, however, one of these films turns out to be genuinely striking—as is the case with Frank Whaley's *Joe the King,* the bleak story of an impoverished 14-year-old boy (Noah Fleiss) in upstate New York in the 1970s. *Joe,* which earned Whaley the Sundance festival's Waldo Salt Screenwritlng Award (in a tie with Guinevere writer-director Audrey Wells) is the rare film to place more emphasis on the actual experience of adolescence than on period nostalgia. "Sherwood Anderson said that no one knows the chair of loneliness more than a child," said Whaley over a cup of coffee. "That's what I remember most about my childhood—being alone all the time, being sad and lonely."

Whaley, whose baby-faced looks belie his 36 years, grew up poor in Syracuse and freely acknowledges that Joe's story contains elements taken from his experiences as well as those of his brother Robert, who composed the film's score. "There's some fact in there mixed in with a lot of fiction," he said, with a wry smile. After making his screen debut as Jack Nicholson's younger self in 1987's *Ironweed*, Whaley had an impressive run with supporting roles In Oliver Stone's *Born on the Fourth of July*, *The Doors* and *J.F.K.*, but he's probably best known as the college student gunned down by Samuel L. Jackson at the beginning of *Pulp Fiction* and for his starring role as studio executive Kevin Spacey's long-suffering underling in the Hollywood satire *Swimming With Sharks*. His decision to get personal by writing and directing *Joe* came about because, he said, "for the past three or four years, I've been feeling really discouraged about the parts I've been getting. [These days] there are basically three kinds of movies—animated films for children, teen soap-opera movies and Tom Hanks movies I could play the third or fourth part in, [and) I find that boring. It started getting to be that or straight-to-video B movies with James Belushi. That all led to the decision to write and direct. It was that simple."

But when *Joe*'s script was complete, Whaley quickly discovered that a period movie with pubescent leads wasn't exactly the world's easiest sell. "[Everybody] wanted to make Joe 18, and to tum it Into a coming-of-age story with Reese Witherspoon as the love interest. They didn't want to make my movie." Eventually, Whaley found support from producer Scott Macaulay (*Gummo*), and the film was shot on Staten Island over 28 days in the summer of '98. To raise some of the budget, Whaley made a strategic decision to accept a role as Dennis Farina's sidekick on the short-lived CBS series *Buddy Faro*. "I was counting on the idea that we'd be cancelled after 12 episodes, and ideally, it was."

To help raise the film's profile, Whaley recruited a number of his friends and former costars, including Val Kilmer (who plays Joe's alcoholic father) and Ethan Hawke (as a guidance counselor) for the adult roles. Without any prodding from Whaley, Kilmer acquired an impressive beer gut for a role that took him just three days to film. "I gave him the script two or three months [before the shoot] and he didn't have the gut. Then I saw him on the set, and be had no shirt on and his belly was out to here, huge." Hawke, a good friend who cofounded the Malaparte Theater Company with Whaley, is also packing a few extra pounds in *Joe*, but as Whaley explained affectionately, "Ethan was just plain fat. His wife [Uma Thurman) was pregnant, and they were just sitting around eating Oreos."

Whaley hasn't completely turned his back on acting—he's in next month's CBS miniseries *Shake, Rattle and Roll*—but he's well aware that, in today's indie-glutted marketplace, his future in his new career will hinge almost entirely on *Joe*'s reviews. "From my acting experience, I've had films come out where I thought, They're gonna say that I'm the best actor in the world, and [the reviews] come out and say 'Mr. Whaley was mildly entertaining,' so I'm not letting my hopes get too high…[but) I have a couple of other scripts that I wrote, a play and an original screenplay, and I'm in the first stages of [adapting] *Winesburg, Ohio*, by Sherwood Anderson. I want to just keep writing."

The Straight Story
Dir. David Lynch. 1999. G. 111mins.
Richard Farnsworth, Sissy Spacek.

Its G rating and Disney imprimatur may at first glance make *The Straight Story* seem like a dramatic departure for David Lynch, but in fact, this genuinely inspirational true story continues themes from his previous works and shines new light on them. Lynch's celebration of "family values" in *Blue Velvet* and *Twin Peaks* certainly felt ironic at the time, but his remarkable new film makes it clear that the man hailed as one of pop culture's most radical visionaries really is a mom-and-apple-pie man in his heart of hearts. The clear-eyed passion he brings to this stranger-than-fiction tale results in what just might be his masterpiece.

Alvin Straight (Farnsworth) is a worn-out, 73-year-old retiree who lives in Laurens, Iowa, with his daughter, Rose (Spacek), in a shabby house where he fully expects to spend his remaining days. One night, Alvin gets a phone call informing him that his older brother, Lyle—whom he hasn't spoken to in a decade—has been felled by a stroke, so Alvin resolves to visit him using the only means of transportation available to a man whose poor eyesight has robbed him of a driver's license: a riding mower.

The trip—it takes him six weeks to travel several hundred miles—is "a hard swallow of my pride" for the stubborn Alvin, but he gives it his all and then some. Along the way, he encounters numerous characters whose problems he solves via homespun advice that will seem wildly hackneyed to some, but Farnsworth makes it clear that a big part of why Alvin repeats these homilies is to convince himself that they're true. As the real stakes in Alvin's quest for redemption emerge along with the details of his troubled past, this folksy tale effortlessly crosses the gulf between the merely quaint and the profoundly moving.

Much will be written about Farnsworth's performance, which is amazing, but cinematographer Freddie Francis and composer Angelo Badalamenti, both previous Lynch collaborators, are just as essential to the film's success. Their knowledge of Lynch's methods (and vice versa) allows for an organic unity between images and music that adds resonance to the film's message without drowning the audience in schmaltz. *The Straight Story* is a simple movie, but it's got a heart as big as all outdoors.

Being John Malkovich
**Dir. Spike Jonze. 1999. R. 112mins. John Cusack,
Cameron Diaz, Catherine Keener, John Malkovlch.**

From *The Wizard of Oz* to *Willy Wonka and the Chocolate Factory*, visionary movie fantasies have often been underrated in their own time, only receiving the recognition they deserve years down the road. With luck, the hilarious and strangely moving *Malkovich* won't have to wait so long to become an acknowledged classic. Music-video directors are frequently slammed as a pox on the face of American movies, but Spike Jonze's first film instantly establishes him as a major filmmaker

Frustrated by the lack of opportunities Manhattan offers for those in his field, puppeteer Craig Schwartz (Cusack) swallows his pride and uses his manual dexterity to score a position as a file clerk with LesterCorp, a business located on floor 71/2 of an otherwise ordinary office building. Craig's been married for years to Lotte (Diaz, dressing down and then some), a pet-store clerk, but that doesn't stop him from becoming deeply infatuated with the icy Maxine (Keener), who works down the hall. One day, Craig discovers a mysterious doorway behind some file cabinets that transports those who crawl through it into the mind of John Malkovich, allowing them to see the world through the famous actor's eyes. Maxine sees this portal as a business opportunity, but after Lotte beams into Malkovich and starts to question her sexual identity, the actor's consciousness becomes a battlefield upon which the unhappy couple slug it out for Maxine's affections.

Malkovich is quite possibly the funniest film I've seen this year, but Charlie Kaufman's script never lets opportunities for humor eclipse the real heart of the story—the deep spiritual longings of the characters, especially Craig. The cast (which also includes Orson Bean and Mary Kay Place in amusing supporting roles) is uniformly terrific, but Keener—who's given the chance to refine and perfect the acerbic bitch-goddess persona she developed in *Your Friends & Neighbors* and *Out of Sight*—is the real standout.

No matter how surreal things get, Jonze keeps the film grounded in the drab world we know, navigating the contrast with a skill worthy, but never derivative, of great screen fantasists such as Tim Burton and Terry Gilliam. There have been a lot of tremendous first films this year, but when it comes to sheer intoxicating originality, *Malkovich* outshines them all.

Mansfield Park
Dir. Patricia Rozema. 1999. PG-13. 105mins. Frances O'Connor, Jonny Lee Miller, Embeth Davidtz, Alessandro Nlvola, Harold Pinter.

Miramax-produced costume dramas are frequently as bland and predictable as McDonald's hamburgers, but every so often, the company lets some filet mignon slip through—Iain Softley's stunning *The Wings of the Dove* two years ago, for example, and now Patricia Rozema's deeply moving *Mansfield Park*. Grafting incidents gleaned from Jane Austen's journals and letters onto the story of the author's third novel, Rozema captures the writer's combination of prickly wit and hopeless romanticism as few filmmakers have.

Fanny Price (played by Hannah Taylor Gordon as a child, and the luminous O'Connor as an adult) is a poor girl who's given the chance to live with her mother's sisters—Mom married for love, but her siblings did so for money—at Mansfield Park, a stately country home presided over by swaggering imperialist Sir Thomas Bertram (Pinter). It doesn't take long for Fanny to forge a deep bond with Sir Thomas's son Edmund (Miller), but as she reaches marrying age, she finds herself pushed in the direction of wealthy rake Henry Crawford (Nivola), whose sister Mary (Davidtz) has her sights trained firmly on Edmund.

Sir Thomas wants Fanny and Edmund to hook up with the Crawfords, because the Bertram fortune is in jeopardy—the family gets its money from a slave plantation in the West Indies, and England is on the verge of abolishing slavery in its colonies. The slave trade is a background issue in Austen's novel, and the only time the film feels forced is when Rozema brings the topic to the forefront. The majority of the time, the focus is on Fanny's internal life and her angst over following her heart versus helping her family—a situation given powerful intimacy and immediacy by O'Connor's amazingly sensitive performance. The rest of the cast is terrific, as well: Miller lends Edmund a quietly impressive nobility, Davidtz makes Mary rapacious without turning her into a cartoonish harpy, and Pinter laces Thomas with just enough humanity to make him complex and sad instead of merely loathsome. You may be able to see *Mansfield Park*'s ending coming from a mile away, but it's so beautifully constructed and dramatically satisfying when it arrives that you probably won't mind at all.

Sweet and Lowdown
Dir. Woody Allen. 1999. PG-13. 95mins. Sean Penn, Samantha Morton, Uma Thurman.

With an exception or two (such as his cokehead-lawyer bit in *Carlito's Way*), Sean Penn has spent the '90s playing brooding types, but Woody Allen's latest gives Penn the chance to deliver his most developed comic performance since his immortal turn as Jeff Spicoli in *Fast Times at Ridgemont High*. Here, he's Emmet Ray, a 1930s jazz guitarist with a squeaky voice and Ronald Reagan hair who spends his off hours (to the perpetual dismay of his female companions) watching trains and shooting rats at garbage dumps. It's a shame, then, that the movie isn't half as interesting as Penn is in it.

Emmet didn't really exist, but the film acts as if he did—*Lowdown* is a mockumentary of sorts, framed by Allen and other notable jazz lovers (including radio personality Ben Duncan, filmmaker Douglas McGrath and writer Nat Hentoff) telling anecdotes about the guitarist that are brought to life by Penn and the cast. A prodigiously gifted player whose fame was hampered by his eccentricity, Emmet is shown romancing Hattie (Morton), a sunny mute girl he eventually dumps for a socialite (Thurman), before his self-destructive urges buy him a ticket to obscurity. The specter of the only man who can outplay him, Gypsy guitarist Django Reinhardt, haunts him all the while.

Emmet's peculiar combination of naïveté and egomania ensures that the film has its share of hilarious moments, and the warm cinematography of Zhao Fei sets the perfect visual tone for the material, making it simultaneously nostalgic and gritty. But Emmet's misadventures keep driving home the same point—that devoted artists can't help pushing away the ones who care about them—and the repetition quickly grows tiresome. The message is obviously important to Allen, but one can assume only that he's still coming to terms with it—otherwise, he'd know that self-absorption is just as alienating to audiences as it is to lovers.

The Green Mile
Dir. Frank Darabont. 1999. R. 3hrs 7mins. Tom Hanks, David Morse, Michael Clarke Duncan.

On paper, *The Green Mile* seems like a movie deliberately designed to make cynical critics gag and wail: It's a three-hour Tom Hanks vehicle containing heavy religious symbolism, a hokey framing device and a subplot built around a cute li'l acrobatic mouse. Yet despite all that, it's also a powerfully effective piece of storytelling, which is beautifully acted by a tremendous ensemble cast. Based on a 1996 serial novel by Stephen King, the film revisits a lot of ground that writer-director Darabont covered in *The Shawshank Redemption* (also adapted from a King story), but the way *Mile* weaves together multiple plot threads and puts a fresh spin on familiar themes makes it a much better film in almost every regard.

Hanks plays Paul Edgecomb, the head guard on death row (its faded lime linoleum provides the film with its title) at the Louisiana state pen during the height of the Great Depression. Edgecomb has his hands full dealing with the antics of cruel rookie guard Percy Wetmore (Doug Hutchison) and a bunch of prisoners both remorseful (a Cajun eccentric played by Michael Jeter) and unrepentant (Sam Rockwell as a hillbilly psycho), but no one on the *Mile* consumes his attention like John Coffey (Duncan). Coffey is a gigantic black man convicted of brutally murdering two young white girls, but his size soon proves to be the least of his distinguishing qualities. In addition to his childlike innocence, Coffey also appears to have been blessed with a healing touch, and the more Edgecomb learns about him, the more he dreads the inevitability of putting this unlikely prisoner to death.

Edgecomb's deep decency makes him a classic Hanks character, but the actor wisely sublimates his star power for the needs of the story, allowing his costars to score most of the film's big moments. Morse is terrific as the ironically named "Brutal" Howell, Paul's trusted lieutenant, and James Cromwell is predictably fine as the prison warden, but the hulking Duncan leaves the deepest impression. The "Yessuh, boss" dialogue he's stuck with seems occasionally demeaning, but he delivers it with a charisma and nobility that's the stuff Oscar nominations are made of, and his warm presence makes some of the strained parallels between Coffey and a certain religious figure with the same initials a little easier to swallow. *Mile* may have its share of cloying (and even butt numbing) moments, but its refusal to sugarcoat the more disturbing elements of King's novel makes it clear that this is definitely one from the heart.

ANDREW JOHNSTON

Any Given Sunday
Dir. Oliver Stone. 1999. R. 2hrs 40mins. Al Pacino, Cameron Diaz, Dennis Quaid, Jamie Foxx.

It's often been said of films about sports that smaller balls equal better movies. Any Given *Sunday* explodes at theory, and not just because of the credible intensity of its gridiron aeon. Oliver Stone's best movie in many years—and one of his finest ever—looks at the world of professional football from almost every conceivable angle, but it never tries to be the definitive statement on the subject. A surprisingly balanced film that merges Stone's hyperkinetic style with a character-centric narrative approach reminiscent of John Sayles and Robert Altman at their best, Sunday proves that powerful human drama and MTV visual pyrotechnics actually can coexist after all.

Sunday is the story of the Miami Sharks, a floundering franchise in the fictional AFFL that, in an opening sequence that's the sports equivalent of the Normandy landing in *Saving Private Ryan*, loses two quarterbacks—including its longtime mainstay, Jack "Cap" Rooney (Quaid)—to serious injuries in a single quarter. Third-stringer Willie Beamen (Foxx) takes over and begins a meteoric rise that poses problems galore for stubborn coach Tony D'Amato (Pacino) and feisty owner Christina Pagniacci (Diaz), not to mention his teammates (including LL Cool J as a running back and New York Giants legend Lawrence Taylor in a very effective performance as the Sharks' defensive captain).

Stone is perhaps the most consistently pretentious of all American filmmakers, but he brings an unexpected off-the-cuffness to *Sunday* that's typified by his cameo as an announcer prone to chugging whiskey in the booth. Even when the old Stone emerges—during a stormy confrontation between D' Amato and Beamen that's intercut with the chariot race from *Ben-Hur*, for example—the actors keep the film from running off the rails. Pacino's hysterics work in his favor for a change, allowing him to deliver a complex portrait of a man terrified that all his sacrifices have been for nothing. Foxx is awesomely magnetic in a role that could well transform him into a superstar, and Diaz works overtime—with impressive results—to ensure that her character is more than just a bitch on wheels. Instead of treating football as a metaphor for society, the film regards the game as a machine that chews people up and spits them out, and focuses on what it takes to survive under those circumstances. Yes, it all ends with the big game, but *Sunday*'s great success is that it leaves you feeling that the victories its characters achieve off the field are more important still.

2000

The Edge of the World [DVD]
Dir. Michael Powell.1937. N/R. 81mins. Niall MacGinnis, Belle Chrystall, Eric Berry.

The reference books may say that *The Edge of the World* is English director Michael Powell's 25th movie (in a career that began just seven years prior to this 1937 release), but one could argue that it's his first as a real filmmaker—the film that vaulted him out of the realm of so-called "quota quickies" and set him on the path toward the greatness he achieved with his collaborator Emeric Pressburger on such films as *I Know Where I'm Going!* and *The Life and Death of Colonel Blimp*. Rarely seen in this country in recent years, *World* is a slight but undeniably moving film that offers early evidence of Powell's two greatest gifts: a remarkable visual sensibility and a knack for creating complex and believable characters from simple material.

 World's story unfolds on Hirta, a remote island off the coast of Scotland in an area the Romans believed to be the literal edge of the earth. Upon returning from six months on the mainland, 24-year-old Robbie Manson (Berry) tells his sister, Ruth (Chrystall), and best friend, Andrew Gray (MacGinnis), that he's engaged but that he won't be bringing his wife back to Hirta: Due to a confluence of economic and environmental factors, he's become convinced that the island can no longer support its inhabitants. Robbie's announcement drives a wedge between himself and Andrew, and starts the ball rolling on a series of events that changes the community forever and lends a tragic air to Ruth's romance with Andrew.

 In *I Know Where I'm Going!*, which also takes place on a Scottish island, Powell helped to invent the quirky-isolated-town minigenre (which remains popular today—see *Waking Ned Devine*, for example), but there's little of that sort of cuteseness here. The location photography is stunning, but not gratuitously gorgeous—Hirta looks as unforgiving as it does beautiful—and many of the most affecting scenes are dialogue-free and rely on silent-era storytelling techniques (a move that helps cover for the stiffness of some of the actors). The theme of traditional cultures faced with extinction by "progress" has been tackled in a zillion movies over the years, but hardly any of them possess the resonance of this striking—and resolutely unsentimental—film.

Full moon fever [DVD]
The documentary *For All Mankind* takes an intimate look at the Apollo program.

Most people who were alive at the time of NASA's 1969–1972 moon landings remember only fuzzy TV pictures of American astronauts bouncing around on the moon, while many who were born later acquired all their knowledge of the Apollo missions from movies (*Apollo 13*) or TV projects (HBO's *From the Earth to the Moon*) that were so long on flag waving and/or technical trivia that the deeper meaning of lunar travel was left largely unexplored.

Director Al Reinert's 1989 Apollo documentary *For All Mankind*—now available in a terrific new DVD edition from the Criterion Collection—begins with the famous soundbite in which President Kennedy guaranteed that an American would walk on the moon before the '60s were over, but that's the only time it indulges in patriotic rhetoric. Comprised of excerpts from the six-million feet of 16mm film that the Apollo astronauts shot on their missions (and featuring narration culled from 80 hours of interviews Reinert conducted with Alan Bean, Jim Lovell, Gene Cernan and other Apollo vets), *Mankind* focuses exclusively on the experience of space travel.

The film has its share of obvious and even hokey moments, but the beauty and quality of the footage make it an absolutely seminal document.

Although *Mankind* features film shot on 11 different Apollo flights, the documentary cuts it all together to provide a sense of a "typical" mission, from blastoff to Earth orbit (which provides the opportunity for some incredible spacewalk footage from the early Apollo flights), and on through the long trip to the moon and the landing process. Some of the astronauts' observations on their experiences sound pretty flaky ("You realize you're not there because you deserve to be there you were just lucky," says Apollo 9's Russell L. Schweickart of his spacewalk. "You're a representative of mankind at that point in history, having that experience, in a sense, for the rest of mankind."). But their awe is totally understandable—the sights they captured on film are stunning enough to turn even the most eloquent poet into a babbling idiot.

Footage actually shot on the moon doesn't appear until after the halfway point of this 80-minute film; before that, in addition to the spacewalk sequence, there's a lot of film of the astronauts horsing around (and trying to feed themselves) in zero gravity. At first, a little of that stuff seems to go a long way. But it also reinforces the humanity of the astronauts—they're doing exactly what you or I would do in such a position, like in a touching scene where Ed Mitchell listens to a tape of performances by Buck Owens and Merle Haggard recorded especially for the astronauts. The zero-g shenanigans serve as a reminder that these are ordinary, middle-class American guys who wound up in the most extraordinary of situations, a fact often glossed over by treatments of the story that highlight the astronauts' heroism.

Mankind's images of the lunar lander en route from the moon's surface to its rendezvous with the orbiting command module are more purely breathtaking than any of the footage from the moon itself, but the images captured on the surface are still quite stunning. The moon's curvature and short horizons provide a genuine sense of otherness missing from fictional portrayals of lunar landings, a feeling enhanced by Brian Eno's superb music. In the liner notes for his album *Apollo* (which contains all the music he was commissioned to write for *Mankind*), Eno writes that when he saw the moon landings on TV, it seemed as if "the fear of boring the general public had led the editors and commentators to present the transmissions from space in an uptempo, 'newsy' manner ... obscuring the grandeur and strangeness of the event with a patina of down-to-earth chatter." The way *Mankind* is edited robs a couple of Eno's compositions of their power, but when Reinert gets generous with the long takes—during the spacewalks and the scenes of actual lunar exploration—the music proves to be the key element in helping the film to achieve its goal: removing politics from the equation in an attempt to capture, as Eno writes, "a set of moods, a unique set of feelings that quite possibly no human had ever experienced before."

Snow business
Quality mercifully triumphs over hype in the feverish climate of Sundance 2000.

If, following the customary anal probe, an alien abductee had been dropped off in the middle of Main Street in Park City, Utah, last week, he could have easily been forgiven for not realizing there was a film festival going on. Yes, flyers for independent films may have covered almost every empty wall in this resort town, but self-congratulatory ads for dot-coms looking to boost their stock price were more ubiquitous still. After evolving from a sleepy event into America's premier film marketplace, the Sundance Film Festival has become increasingly besieged by coattail-riding events—Slamdance, Lapdance, Digidance and others—resulting in a bizarre multimedia carnival where movies that filmmakers had done everything but sell a kidney to finance are forced to compete for attention with concerts by has-beens like Sammy Hagar.

I've long enjoyed mocking what I call the Sundance Effect, a high-altitude fever that leads film buyers to spend millions on features that open to empty houses and drives otherwise-rational souls to spend hours lining up in the cold for movies that go straight to video. But this year, something funny happened: The attention—and the major awards—went to films that actually deserved them. Karyn Kusama's *Girlfight* and Kenneth Lonergan's *You Can Count On Me* split the jury prize in the dramatic competition, with the audience award going to Raymond DeFelitta's *Two Family House*, and I'll be amazed if I see three more purely affecting films this year. *Count On Me*, the tale of the uneasy relationship between two adult siblings (Laura Linney and Mark Ruffalo) who were orphaned as children, and *House*, which stars Michael Rispoli as a restless dreamer in 1950s Staten Island who finds himself trapped by his friends and family, are beautifully written films equipped with complex characters who are allowed to really breathe and grow. But *Girlfight* is all of that and more. The visceral account of an alienated Latina teen from Red Hook (played with searing intensity—and just a hint of vulnerability—by first-time actor Michelle Rodriguez) and her quest for validation through amateur boxing is as tight and confident a first feature as any I've encountered. Kusama deservedly picked up the jury's directing prize, while *Count On Me* bagged the Waldo Salt Screenwriting Award for Lonergan.

A case could be made for each of those films as conventional crowd-pleasers, but the important thing is that they're crowd-pleasers that work. Indeed, the stultifying mediocrity of the festival's trendiest films provided convincing evidence that the Sundance Effect was as prevalent as ever. Case in point the baffling popularity of Miguel Arteta's *Chuck & Buck*. It's a comedy with a premise that the Farrelly Brothers could have worked wonders with—a sexually confused mama's boy forces his way into the life of his now-successful childhood best friend but it just lies there, and Arteta's decision to shoot on digital video only succeeds in making his film look like crap. Another hipster fave, Greg Harrison's hey-kids-let's-put-on-a-rave movie *Groove* (which was purchased by Sony Pictures Classics) is also shallow, but at least it's fun and energetic. Although *Chuck* sold to Artisan Entertainment (the distributors of *The Blair Witch Project*) for a reported $1 million, the jury's decision to give special awards to Donal Logue for his performance as a portly, philosophical Lothario in *The Tao of Steve* and to the ensemble cast of *Songcatcher* (which stars Janet McTeer as a musicologist cataloging Appalachian folk songs in 1907) struck a welcome blow for substance over style.

As the festival's profile has escalated, Sundance's Premieres division has become the launching pad of choice for the spring collections of minimajors such as Miramax, USA Films and Lions Gate. In the early days of this year's festival, nothing was more anticipated than the debut of Mary Harron's *American Psycho* (scalpers' tickets fetched up to $100 each outside Park City's Eccles Center). Christian Bale's superbly hammy performance aside, *Psycho* proved to be much ado about very little. If the MPAA has its way, the movie that reaches theaters in April will be slighter still: *Psycho* has been slapped with an NC-17 for an innocuous three-way sex scene that's actually the funniest and most revealing moment in the film. Much more satisfying among the premieres were Stanley Tucci's *Joe Gould's Secret*—a nostalgic valentine to the Greenwich Village of the '40s starring Tucci as legendary New Yorker scribe Joseph Mitchell and Ian Holm as a hypereducated bum—and Michael Almereyda's *Hamlet*, which overcomes gimmicky casting (Ethan Hawke as the melancholy Dane, Bill Murray as the obsequious Polonius) to emerge as a tough, powerful film that updates its source material with a combination of artistic panache and unerring practicality. For those seeking nothing more than pure entertainment, the cultish "Park City at Midnight" series—in which *Blair Witch* premiered last year—delivered in spades courtesy of *Psycho Beach Party*, a spirited romp based on drag legend Charles Busch's play, and *But I'm a Cheerleader,* a spoof of the gay-rehab movement that plays like a John Waters movie with heart.

At Sundance, the hype surrounding the rollouts and discoveries often drowns out the buzz on documentaries, a phenomenon I freely admit having succumbed to as I strove to see as many of the 156 (or so) films in the festival as I could. As much as I enjoyed *The Filth and the Fury,* Julien Temple's revisionist take on the history of the Sex Pistols, the most impressive of the docs I squeezed in had to be Marc Singer's *Dark Days.* The winner of the audience award for best doc (as well as the cinematography and Freedom of Expression awards), it follows the residents of an Amtrak tunnel beneath Penn Station, allowing them to tell their own stories without telling the audience what to think, the fatal flaw of many a Sundance documentary fave. It's hard not to be cynical about any festival that claims the Mercedes Benz SUV as its official vehicle, but when Sundance bestows recognition on movies as intelligent, human and diverse as *Dark Days, Girlfight, House* and *Count On Me,* it's harder still to deny its value to the culture of film.

2005

Flights of fancy
Three gems from the Studio Ghibli vaults arrive on DVD.

Although Hayao Miyazaki's *Spirited Away* won the Academy Award for Best Animated Feature two years ago, the soft competition (including *Lilo & Stitch* and *Treasure Planet*) reduced the magnitude of the achievement. But the reverent tone of a lengthy profile in *The New Yorker* last month made it official: Miyazaki's standing as a cultural figure in the West has finally begun to approach that which he enjoys in his native Japan.

Ironically, the Miyazaki titles that have received the widest distribution in the U.S.—*Spirited Away* and *Princess Mononoke* (1997)—are probably the ones least accessible to Western viewers. Disney's distribution deal with Miyazaki's company, Studio Ghibli, has resulted in the gradual stateside release of his back catalog, and the latest batch includes films perfectly suited for those who were left wondering what all the hype was about after sampling his more recent efforts.

A delightful blend of swashbuckling adventure, bittersweet romance and whimsical fantasy, 1992's *Porco Rosso* (Italian for "crimson pig") is the only film Miyazaki made specifically with adult viewers in mind, though it's still entirely appropriate for children. Set in Italy and Croatia in the 1920s, the movie deals with a World War I air ace whose cynicism and misanthropy caused him to literally transform into a pig. Instead of wallowing in self-pity (or mud), our hero rolls with the punches and uses his flying skills to take on air pirates, a showy American interloper and the growing power of Mussolini's Fascist regime.

First commissioned by Japan Air Lines as a brief in-flight movie (they asked for something that would help middle-aged businessmen keep their minds off work on transpacific flights), the project grew into a full-blown feature as Miyazaki became intoxicated with the story's visual potential. Although the DVD includes the original Japanese dialogue with English subtitles, Disney spared little expense on a superb English-language dub that is also included, featuring a deadpan, gravel-voiced performance by Michael Keaton as the porcine aviator (the French track includes Jean Reno, whose portrayal of the character is reportedly Miyazaki's favorite).

Also newly released is *Nausicaä of the Valley of the Wind* (1984), Miyazaki's second feature and the first he made after forming his own studio. Since the only previous domestic version was a butchered 84-minute cut released in 1986, the arrival of the new disc is a boon to fans who have had to buy bootlegs or expensive imported videos in order to see the 116-minute original. *Nausicaä* is the Miyazaki film that most closely corresponds to American stereotypes about Japanese animation, insofar as the action takes place in a dystopian sci-fi future. But its strongest visual influence is the work of the French cartoonist Moebius, and the story line has undeniable echoes of Tolkien.

The title character is a plucky girl who discovers that the toxic flora and fauna surrounding her village evolved as a means of repairing environmental damage from several millennia ago. As she embarks on a quest to prevent two rival factions from repeating the mistakes that screwed up the planet in the first place, many signature Miyazaki motifs appear fully formed: The breathtaking flying sequences, strong environmental message and fiercely determined female protagonist presage later triumphs such as *Kiki's Delivery Service* (1989), *Princess Mononoke* and *Spirited Away* (*Nausicaä* is also the film that launched Miyazaki's long-running collaboration with composer Joe Hisaishi). Alison Lohman does an adequate job as Nausicaa on the newly recorded English dialogue track, which is more notable for strong work by Uma Thurman (as the heroine's steely rival, Kushana) and Patrick Stewart (as the Gandalfesque Lord Yupa). All of the new

Ghibli DVDs include background material and Japanese trailers and TV spots, but the *Nausicaä* disc contains a particularly enjoyable bonus: a freewheeling documentary about the studio's origins, featuring oddly quaint, staged reenactments of key events.

Technical issues resulted in the indefinite postponement of *My Neighbor Totaro* (1988), which many consider Miyazaki's finest work. As a replacement, Disney has released *The Cat Returns* (2002), a sharp contemporary fairy tale directed by Ghibli's Hiroyuki Morita that gets the same extravagant treatment as the Miyazaki features. *Totoro* will come in time; until then, *The Cat Returns* bodes favorably for Disney releases of other Ghibli films (Isao Takahata's 1999 *My Neighbors the Yamadas*, an ingenious experiment in 2-D computer animation, would be especially welcome) by directors whose works have yet to make a dent in the United States.

Poetic justice
Martin Scorsese does right by Bob Dylan's artistry in *No Direction Home*. [DVD]

Martin Scorsese's passion for rock music would seem to make him an ideal choice to direct a documentary about Bob Dylan's early career, but there was slight cause for concern when *No Direction Home* was announced. Would Scorsese's reverence for his subject—made obvious by *The Last Waltz*, his 1978 film about Dylan's former sidemen the Band—lead to toothless fawning? At three and a half hours, would the documentary meander? Thankfully, the final product renders any reservations baseless. Available now on DVD and airing in two parts Monday 26 and Tuesday 27 on the PBS series *American Masters*, *No Direction Home* exceeds all expectations. Both scholarly and fleet-footed, the film brilliantly re-creates the cultural moment that produced Dylan, while using his story to explore how tension between an artist and his audience often leads lo the greatest of triumphs.

An extensive interview with Dylan gives *No Direction Horne* its backbone, but the film gets its power from the interpolation of equally revealing anecdotes from others and a wealth of stunning archival footage, including much heretofore-unseen material shot on Dylan's famous 1966 UK tour with an early incarnation of the Band. Despite the heavy use of talking heads, the film is hardly an upscale episode of *Behind the Music*—there's no narration, and no *Rolling Stone* writers chime in to provide context for newbies. Instead, the film features interviews with the singer's peers, many of whom have a complicated relationship with Dylan (friendly rivals Dave Van Ronk and John Cohen, ex-girlfriend Joan Baez). Some have axes to grind, but there are none better qualified to discuss the 1960s folk world and how Dylan transformed it.

The Dylan interview is used to greatest effect in part one, which focuses on Dylan's cultural gestation in Minnesota and his meteoric rise after migrating to New York in 1961. Woody Guthrie is often cited as Dylan's chief influence, but others were equally important—country singers Johnnie Ray and Webb Pierce, primal folkies John Jacob Niles and Odetta—and scratchy clips of their 1950s TV appearances clarify what the young Robert Zimmerman was aiming to do when he reinvented himself.

The placid confidence in the early photos of Dylan, some dating back to high school, supports the repeated claims in his 2004 rnemoir that he never doubted he was destined for greatness. That faith in himself—a paradoxical response to his feeling that he was "maybe not even born to the right parents"—is the key to the inscrutability that allowed so many myths to develop around him. Liam Clancy says the singer changed his name in tribute to Dylan Thomas, and Tony Glover calls the act a response to anti-Semitism in Minnesota, but Dylan says the new moniker "just popped into my head one day."

Dylan's determination to live and create without having to explain himself forms the conflict that drives the second half of the film. Dylan began singing topical material in emulation of Guthrie, and though he obviously had a sincere belief in social justice (evidenced by his moving recollections of Dr. Martin Luther King Jr.'s march on Washington), he soon felt boxed in by political assumptions and expectations. Many fans and peers considered his transition from protest music to rock & roll a sellout, but the sonic fury and lyrical density of his electric music made it a huge commercial gamble.

No Direction Home ends with a title card explaining that Dylan took an eight-year break from touring after a 1966 motorcycle accident, and while the singer never went off the deep end like Howard Hughes, the cycle of persecution, vindication and withdrawal parallels the last hour of Scorsese's *The Aviator*. On the '66 tour, we see Dylan getting bombarded with unbelievably inane questions from European reporters and being heckled by fans too stubborn to realize that he was perfecting his greatest and most influential music before their eyes. Everything builds to the film's greatest discovery: never-before-seen footage of the famously thunderous Manchester performance of "Like a Rolling Stone" that was Dylan's response to a shout of "Judas!" from the crowd. It's a storied moment, made all the more exhilarating when seen in the context of one fearless artist's masterful tribute to another.

2006

Fairy tale of New York (Metropolitan) [DVD]
UHBs rejoice: *Metropolitan* is finally enshrined on DVD.

Whit Stillman's martini-dry comedy Metropolitan takes place "not so long ago," as an opening title card puts it, but the film now seems more like a period piece than it did when released in 1990. "I was trying to make it seem as far back as possible, but we couldn't change things too much," says the director of the low-budget chronicle of high society, speaking from his home in Paris. "But we got a lot of things that soon after vanished—there's no longer a bookstore where the old Scribner's was, and B. Altman is gone."

Metropolitan's evocation of the past extends beyond physical landmarks: Set during the holidays in an unspecified year (Stillman says 1971 "isn't a bad guess"), the film follows a group of young Upper East Side blue bloods as they navigate a gauntlet of pre-Christmas society dances at the Plaza Hotel. Most of the action unfolds in late-night afterparties where the protagonists have endless liquor-fueled, navel-gazing debates that showcase Stillman's remarkable ear for dialogue. Previously available only in a low-quality VHS edition, the film is now available in a blue-chip DVD from the Criterion Collection that treats this understated gem with the respect it richly deserves.

"It's a film about what could be the least sympathetic group in the United States and makes them incredibly sympathetic," says Chris Eigeman, who played the tart-tongued Nick Smith, the most memorable of the film's UHBs ("Urban Haute Bourgeoisie," an acronym one character coins as a more sociologically accurate alternative to preppie). Eigeman went on to star in Stillman's *Barcelona* (1994) and *The Last Days of Disco* (1998), but as the new DVD reveals, he was nearly passed over for *Metropolitan*. The disc includes a scene in which Nick is played by the 6'5" Will Kempe, who was shifted over to the role of the nominal villain, sneering aristocrat Rick Von Slonecker, in part because of how he towered over the other principals, "I thought Chris was a really impressive guy and a great actor, but I didn't think he could do comedy," Stillman recalls. "It shows how misguided and misled you can be."

Although *Metropolitan* received a warm reception at Sundance in 1990, it didn't acquire a distributor until its New York debut at MoMA's New Directors/New Films festival a few months later. The film struggled at the box office until *New York Times* critic Vincent Canby put it on his yearend top-ten list, which attracted enough attention for the film to set a new house record at the Angelika Film Center. "There's a barrier that's hard to break through if you don't play the populist card," Stillman says when asked if contempt for the upper classes posed obstacles. "The film wasn't an unambiguous attack on snobbishness, and I think that makes people uncomfortable. Worse than uncomfortable—it makes them angry."

Somewhat ironically for a film with such a rarefied backdrop, *Metropolitan* was shot for a pittance in borrowed apartments and locations that were used on the sly. "I recommend that the first time someone acts in movies, they do it for a movie made for about a dollar fifty on the streets of New York City, because you learn really fast," Eigeman says. "We'd be shooting scenes on Park Avenue or in front of the Plaza, and people would come up and try to sell us watches, and we'd be like, 'We can't; we're actually in a movie right now.'"

For the original VHS release, Stillman reluctantly reconvened the cast to shoot a deceptively racy box cover designed to attract more attention on video shelves. It was really trashy," Stillman says, "But my friends in the industry congratulated me on opening it up for the market." To his great relief, the new DVD's jacket features an illustration by veteran *New Yorker* cover artist Pierre Le Tan that is far more representative, suggesting that the passage of time has finally made *Metropolitan* 's sophistication a selling point rather than a liability.

2007

A confederacy of dunces (Idiocracy) [DVD]
Mike Judge's *Idiocracy* embodies brilliant stupidity. [DVD]

This week's DVD release of Mike Judge's *Idiocracy* makes it official: When the film opened in Atlanta, Dallas, Houston, Austin and Los Angeles on September 1, New Yorkers were jobbed out of seeing one of the best movies of 2006. Speculation has run rife as to why the film—completed in 2005 and held for a year—was buried with no critics' screenings and zero marketing budget, classic signs of a film released purely out of contractual obligation. Twentieth Century Fox isn't talking, and except for an interview with *Esquire* in June (I've never experienced anything like this," he said), Judge—the director of *Office Space* and creator of *Beavis and Butt-head*—has also remained mum. There are any number of things in *Idiocracy* that could have offended the News Corporation suits, from its depiction of Fox News in 2505 (anchored by a shirtless bodybuilder and a bikini babe) to a tacit pro-eugenics bias. Most intriguing of all, however, is the possibility that Judge's tart spoof was let out the back door because of its subversive (and howlingly funny) approach to class issues that are seldom if ever addressed so frankly in studio films.

Like the most effective social satires, *Idiocracy*'s plot is just a flimsy framework on which to hang the gags and potshots, something that Judge basically acknowledges via the goofiness of the circumstances (which it would be criminal to spoil) that result in Army private Joe Bauers (Luke Wilson) and flinty streetwalker Rita (Maya Rudolph) being cryogenically frozen for 500 years instead of 365 days. Joe and Rita wake up in a world pretty much populated by adult kindergartners, the result of heavy reproduction by dim bulbs while educated folks sat on the sidelines wringing their hands instead of making babies (a prologue mocking childless yuppies makes the eugenics charges moot by proving Judge doesn't think a world dominated by the offspring of NPR listeners would be a better place).

The title is misleading insofar as pure stupidity isn't the main problem with the citizens of the United States of Uhmerica in 2505—rather, the issue is that they collectively embody every negative stereotype about poor, tacky whites, Latinos and African Americans. In the future, everyone smokes oversize cigarettes and reads word-free lad mags, and as Joe soon learns, the slightest sign of individuality or imagination makes one destined to go through life being mocked for "talking like a fag." The ubiquity of the slur (which, as Judge reminds us, has a catchall nature that makes it the moron's insult of first resort) helps Judge develop his case against the film's other main target: the kind of macho aggression that Judge's targets often cite as an American virtue.

The film is loaded with background gags that drive home Judge's point (a cigarette billboard bears the health warning THE SURGEON GENERAL HAS ONE LUNG AND A VOICEBOX AND HE COULD STILL KICK YOUR SORRY ASS). Indeed, the Easter eggs are so numerous that one could argue that NewYorkers (and Judge fans in other cities bypassed by Fox) actually win out by getting the movie on DVD first since many of the best jokes would be nigh-imperceptible in a theater. Right on the surface, however, are gags about Starbucks and H&R Block devolving into "adult" businesses, which hint that the ascendency of idiot machismo has turned all women into sex objects (the female attorney general is universally referred to as "fun bags").

Judge's future world is technically still a democracy, but the citizens obviously choose their leaders on the basis of virility: President Duane Camacho (Terry Crews) is a former porn star and onetime Ultimate Smackdown champ, This, arguably, forms the most controversial argument in the film—that America has consistently failed to live up to its potential because we keep choosing leaders for swagger and confidence rather than smarts and ability. But Judge isn't urging viewers to take to the streets and vote the dumbasses out. Like *Office Space*'s Peter Gibbons, Joe is a decidedly average guy who, despite his problems with society, basically accepts things as they are and wants to be left alone. It's widely believed that Fox left millions on the table by botching the 1999 release of *Office Space*, and the studio's handling of *Idiocracy* brings to mind a familiar maxim: Insanity means doing the same thing repeatedly while expecting different results.

Two Lane Blacktop [DVD]

Any movie in which the leads are credited as the Driver (James Taylor), the Mechanic (Dennis Wilson) and the Girl (Laurie Bird) is obviously going to be about as minimalist as they come. Equipped with a script so full of car jargon that the dialogue often sounds like midperiod Springsteen lyrics, Monte Hellman's existential 1971 drive-in special is rightly hailed as one of the best American road movies. *Two-Lane Blacktop* subverts expectations even more today than it did 36 years ago by featuring superwuss Taylor as a virile and calculating street racer whose rival is an ascot-wearing dandy played by *The Wild Bunch*'s Warren Oates. Taylor and Wilson (the Beach Boys drummer who drowned in 1983) emit a rough, confident charisma that makes it a wonder neither landed more screen roles; at the very least, both would have their pick of modeling offers were they starting their careers today. The film has been available on DVD before (in editions that quickly became out-of-print collector's items), but Criterion's eagerly awaited two-disc package—including screen-test outtakes, loads of publicity materials, and a commentary by cowriter Rudolph Wurlitzer and critic David Meyer, as well as a paperback of the script by Wurlitzer and Will Corry—leaves the previous versions eating dust.

2008

Cape fear (Justice League: The New Frontier) [DVD]
Darwyn Cooke takes a fresh look at Cold War superheroics in Justice League: The New Frontier. [DVD]

The 1992 debut of *Batman: The Animated Series* launched a wave of TV cartoons starring DC Comics superheroes—including *Superman* (1996) and *Justice League* (2001)—that were as well written as prime-time dramas and had as much to offer general viewers as they did devoted comics fans. While these series were more faithful to the original comics than any that had preceded them, the length of a typical episode—scarcely 20 minutes—made it hard to directly adapt stories that originated on the page, especially those from the increasingly serialized comics of today. Multipart crossovers spanning various titles are now all the rage, with self-contained stories increasingly taking place outside the main DC continuity, often in "Elseworlds" stories set in alternate universes or different time periods. The prospect of selling this conceit to the general public might intimidate some people, but not cartoonist Darwyn Cooke.

"The very notion of it being a problem, or ascribing a term like *Elseworlds* to it, is very much a part of direct-market comics thinking," says Cooke, cowriter of *Justice League: The New Frontier,* a straight-to-DVD) animated film set in the 1950s. "When people go to the movies, they just call it a period film. I think a mass-market audience that puts it on will fall right into it, even if they don't have anything to line it up with other than the big archetypes they know."

First published in book form in 2004, Cooke's graphic novel *DC: The New Frontier,* a retelling of how the Justice League of America came together, has now been adapted into a film that re-creates both Cooke's distinctive art style and his grim but ultimately optimistic take on the years between WW II and the Kennedy administration. Here, Wonder Woman (voiced by Lucy Lawless) makes like a feminist-separatist Colonel Kurtz in Southeast Asia, while Batman (Jeremy Sisto) fights satanic cultists and Superman (Kyle MacLachlan) is a government lackey; most other heroes have been driven underground by the Red Scare. The air of cynicism is punctured when a common threat unites them—along with new heroes Green Lantern (David Boreanaz) and Martian Manhunter (Miguel Ferrer) and an army of lesser known DC characters—creating a spirit of cooperation that redefines superheroism just as America enters a new era.

Having worked on the *Batman, Superman* and *Men in Black* animated series before devoting himself full-time to comics, Cooke was well aware of the challenges that come with turning a 420-page graphic novel into a movie running just 75 minutes (a duration dictated by Warner Home Video). "It's very daunting from a budget and scheduling standpoint," he says. "Everybody involved would have loved to have had more screen time to devote to some of the other aspects of the story, but you have to work with what you have. One of the great things about 2-D animation is that you can't make it much cheaper than it gets made right now. It's really a question of applying your imagination to it. With CGI, it's a different story because of the amount of money you need, and the time."

This flexibility allowed Cooke to add characters and situations from the graphic novel to the storyboards long after the script stage. "It's pretty seamless, but Adam Strange, Green Arrow, Jimmy Olsen, the Blackhawks—none of them were in the final script. [The producers] said, 'It's too many characters, it's too much voice talent, you have to be realistic here,'" he recalls. "What we did was, at the storyboard stage, I took care of the designs, and the director and the board guys worked all those characters into the story without dialogue, so they're all there." These and other last-minute additions—including a trove of microfilm evidence pored over by Batman—allowed for more of the backstory to get filled in, giving the film an increased sense of fealty to Cooke's graphic novel.

If *The New Frontier* sells well, it's expected to be the first of several DVDs adapting popular DC graphic novels and story arcs. In addition to the massive popularity of *The New Frontier* imprint, Cooke's animation background helped qualify his work as a test case. "This was a unique opportunity—because I'd worked in the Warners studio before, I sort of had a foot in both camps," he says. "There's more motivation to have the creators involved because they're trying to capture the essence of the original stories [with these movies],and I had enough experience to be useful as opposed to just watching it happen on the sidelines."

Death Proof [DVD]

In its theatrical version, presented as the back half of *Grindhouse,* Quentin Tarantino's *Death Proof* felt like a potentially decent comedy sketch ruined by being needlessly dragged out. But with a half hour of footage reinserted (most of it is the "missing reel" from the middle of the film), it now plays like an actual Tarantino movie and not an overly wordy parody of his work. True, some of this has to do with his talky contribution no longer being preceded by Robert Rodriguez's action-packed *Planet Terror,* but the reinstated material gives us a little more insight into the psychosis of vehicular serial killer Stuntman Mike (Kurt Russell). It also makes it easier to appreciate how *Death Proof* is itself two movies in one: Halfway through the film, when the action jumps forward 14 months, the faded colors and fake scratches are dispensed with. The dramatic change in picture quality accompanies the arrival of Rosario Dawson, who proves herself more naturally suited to the rhythm of Tarantino's dialogue than any actor since Samuel L. Jackson. She and Russell clearly had as much fun making *Death Proof* as the director did, and in this context their enthusiasm feels well warranted.

Time Out New York TV & SLANT Magazine

TONY TV
2005

Beat happenings
**A pair of BBC dramas reflect the transatlantic
evolution of cop shows.**

In recent years, American cop shows have experienced a schism: Broadcast
series such as *Law & Order* focus most of their attention on the case du jour
and scarcely bother with character development, while on cable, the inner
workings of *The Wire's* Jimmy McNulty and *The Shield's* Vic Mackey are
explored at length and long-running story arcs prevail. Each approach has
its merits, a steady diet of either can leave viewers longing for a show that
explores the middle ground.

Two police dramas beginning a six-week run on BBC America on
Monday 31—new arrival *Night Detective,* starring Don Gilet, and the
returning *Murphy's Law,* with James Nesbitt—strike a balance between
plot and characterization that feels like a throwback to the '70s heyday
of *Kojak* and *Columbo,* when shows emphasized their heroes' quirky
personalities as much as their problem-solving skills. The tradition was
sustained and enriched in the '90s by Britain's *Prime Suspect* and *Cracker,*
the complexity of which had a strong influence on NBC's *Homicide: Life
on the Street,* the progenitor of today's cable crime dramas. But while both
these imports have plenty of grit, the lack of loose ends suggests that the
British popularity of current U.S. broadcast shows may be having a tickle-
down effect.

Of the two, *Night Detective,* broadcast in the U.K. as *55 Degrees
North* (the latitude of Newcastle, where the action takes place), is the more

conventional. Gilet plays Nicky Cole, a London detective who blows the whistle on a corrupt superior and is "rewarded" with a transfer up north, While Cole is used to solving sexier crimes than the mundane cases he gets on the night shift in Newcastle, his problems as a city slicker in the sticks are trivial compared with the issues he faces as a black cop in an overwhelmingly white city.

On an American show, Cole would probably experience racism only from uptight bosses and low-life perps; here, sympathetic supporting characters commit casual acts of bigotry that add depth to an otherwise boilerplate premise. In the first episode, Cole gets pulled over while driving his Mercedes and is given the third degree by two officers who realize that Cole is one of their own only when he's called to a crime scene hours later. When the detective is asked why he didn't identify himself as a cop, our hero replies that he didn't want special treatment. And why didn't he report them? "You're a brother officer, aren't you?" he replies. The two constables become valuable allies for Cole, but he never hesitates to call them out for observations of the "you guys like spicy chicken, don't you?," variety, or to dress down his presumptive love interest, prosecutor Claire Maxwell (Dervla Kirwan), when she says "nobody likes it when the new boy does good" without thinking about the double meaning.

All in the Family featured similar exchanges 35 years ago, of course, but honest racial discourse is rarely seen on broadcast television in the U.S. today. Also refreshing is the everyday nature of the featured crimes, which are more likely to involve protection rackets and abusive pimps than serial killers. *Murphy's Law* features more exotic cases, with plenty of angst ladled on top. In the 2001 pilot that introduced him, Belfast-born undercover cop Tommy Murphy (Nesbitt) moved to London seeking a fresh start after his daughter's death in an IRA bombing. And mere minutes into the new season, Murphy's partner from the show's 2003 run, Detective Annie Guthrie (Claudia Harrison), is stabbed to death.

Nesbitt *(Bloody Sunday)* can brood with the best of them, and his skill at delivering cynical wisecracks while convincingly wallowing in self-pity keeps the series from being unbearably glum (as does Murphy's penchant for making the same rnistakes over and over, which could inspire a drinking game—take a shot every time he foolishly trusts a woman who's far less innocent than she seems). The nature of Murphy's undercover investigations—which lead him, among other things, to live at a homeless shelter and join an elite-but-crooked narcotics squad—gives more screen time to guest stars than to the regular supporting cast, but creator Colin Bateman and his fellow writers often provide one-shot characters with complex motivations that make the hour-long episodes feel like miniature films noir. *Murphy's Law* may not have the scope and heft of a series as ambitious as *The Wire,* but the obvious influence of such blue-chip crime writers as Lawrence Block and George Pelecanos makes for a show that will leave genre fans hankering for more once its brief season is done.

Patriot games
The *Family Guy* team gets topical on *American Dad.*

Fans of the animated series *Family Guy* were thrilled last year when its enormous DVD sales and strong performance in cable reruns led Fox, which canceled the show in 2002, to commission 35 new episodes. But for the men behind the cartoon, vindication was undercut by stress: Creator Seth Macfarlane and his collaborators Mike Barker and Matt Weitzman were at work on the pilot for a new show, *American Dad,* and had to face the daunting, time-intensive prospect of cranking out two ongoing cartoons at once.

"I've evolved to a point at which I can walk a pretty steady line between delegation and creative control—unless, of course, I've been drinking," deadpans Macfarlane, who chose to focus on *Family Guy* and let Barker and Weitzman run *American Dad* after the new series received an order for 19 episodes. Fox scheduled the show for a May debut but requested that the first episode be finished in time to run after the Super Bowl on Sunday 6. "We had eight months to get it ready when normally the tightest schedule you want to be on is nine months," Barker says. "It killed a lot of us, but we made it happen."

Fortunately, nothing seems rushed about the first *American Dad,* which offers a well-balanced combination of political satire, traditional family-sitcom shenanigans and goofy surrealism. Macfarlane voices Stan Smith, an ultraconservative CIA desk jockey who lives in northern Virginia with his demure wife, Francine (Wendy Schaal), their left-leaning daughter, Hayley (Rachael Macfarlane, the co-creator's sister), and nerdy son, Steve (Scott Grimes). Rounding out the household are Klaus (Dee Bradley Baker),a goldfish with the transplanted brain of an East German Olympian, and Roger (Seth MacFarlane again),a tart-tongued extraterrestrial with an insatiable appetite for junk food. In the debut, Stan uses the Agency's considerable resources to help his son become student-body president ("Rigging elections is my bread and butter," Stan boasts to Roger) so Steve can impress girls.

Stan's actions—and a wicked joke about President Bush's belief that God supports him make it fairly obvious which side of the red-blue divide the creators fall on. "Mike and Matt and I are among those who are not too thrilled with the way things have been going," Macfarlane says. But because of the lead time involved in animation, most of the scripts for the first season were in the can before the 2004 election. "It was a concern of ours that the man we voted for would not win, which is what happened for most of the writers," Barker says. "Stan would have been a much more frustrated soldier if Kerry had won, but he'd still be taking on the fight," Weitzman says. With Bush staying in the White House, he continues, "Stan can gloat a little bit. He's kind of a happy clam."

Some may find it surprising that such a show, like the puckishly political *Arrested Development,* would air on a corporate sibling of the fire-breathing Fox News and *New York Post,* but according to Macfarlane, "the news division and the entertainment division seem to be separate companies. We've experienced none of that attitude." And Barker and Weitzman hope to avoid alienating conservative viewers by borrowing a page from *All in the Family.* "The left saw Archie Bunker as ridiculous, but the right sympathized with him and his point of view," Weitzman says. "We hope people on both sides of the fence will like Stan for their own reasons." Over Thanksgiving, Barker showed the pilot to his in-laws, one of whom is a die-hard conservative. "Afterwards, I expected him to say, 'Oh, yeah, stick it to the Republicans, really cool,'" Barker recalls. "Instead, he said, 'I get it, The father wants his son to be less of a geek.' That's what he took away with him. If we can poke fun without driving people away, that'd be a pretty nice balance."

High-school confidential

Veronica Mars creator Rob Thomas tells all about making teen TV for adults.

I get a lot of fan e-mail through my website and I swear, every third message has a line in it to the effect of 'I know that as a '37-year-old I'm not in your target audience, however· ...,'" says writer-producer Rob Thomas, whose teen-detective series *Veronica Mars* attracted intense devotion among older viewers the instant it premiered on UPN in the fall of 2004. "I just turned 40 and I'm trying to write a show that I would want to watch. We never sit around the writers' room and go, 'What would teenagers find interesting here?'"

Last year, the titular sarcastic sleuth (Kristen Bell) spent the year searching for her best friend's killer and seeking redemption for her father, Keith (Enrico Colantoni), who lost his job as the local sheriff when he refused to accept that the man who confessed to the murder was the actual perp. Along the way, she solved problems for her classmates at a tony SoCal high school, in stories that usually owed more to David Lynch and James Ellroy than *The O.C.* And although Veronica's pluck made her invaluable to her father in his new gig as a private investigator and bounty hunter, she often left him in the dark as a matter of necessity. "If Keith knew everything that was going on in her life, they would have moved a longtime ago," Colantoni says. "No father in his right mind would have stayed—he'd have packed her up in the middle of the night, shoved her in the car, and they would have gone to Idaho or someplace!"

By the time Thomas finished writing last year's finale, which tied up all of the loose ends, the series's fate was still up in the air. Since the writing staff still had a few weeks on their contracts, Thomas and his team had the time to lay out a new yearlong plot, which considerably ratchets up class tensions at Neptune High, where the student body is split between the children of the ultrarich and their servants' offspring. Although the first-season scripts never deliberately strove for youth appeal, occasional concessions were made in the casting department—Paris Hilton and Jonathan Taylor Thomas appeared as guest stars—and the series's ardent online fan base had a collective conniption early in the summer when a rumor spread that Tara Reid would join the cast. "A lot of people panicked based on stories that came out which were largely untrue," Thomas says. "The network made requests, but they weren't ones we disagreed with. There's no part of me that feels any less proud of what we're doing in season two because of network interference."

The main request—the addition of more characters in their twenties— was in the interest of retaining viewers from *Veronica Mars*'s new lead-in, *America's Next Top Model.* The new time slot puts Veronica Mars opposite *Lost,* with which it shares many fans, but Thomas feels the advantages of following UPN's highest-rated show makes up for the drawbacks. "If I could wish away *Lost,* I would, but I wouldn't trade our slot for any other on UPN.»

The last series Thomas created, *Cupid,* starring Jeremy Piven, was cancelled by ABC after less than a season in 1998. Several years of failed pilots followed, an experience that has made him all the more appreciative of his current series's fan base. He's been known to visit discussion forums at the website Television Without Pity and takes the time, when possible, to correspond with fans via his own site, robthomasproductions.com. The response of his peers has been equally gratifying. "I got the nicest note a few weeks ago from [*Buffy the Vampire Slayer* creator] Joss Whedon, in which he said he was such a fan of *Veronica Mars* that he now better understood the fervor of *Buffy* fans," Thomas says. "He grasps it now that he's on the other end. It's a heady feeling."

The best and worst in TV 2005

THE PEAKS

1. Nlp/Tuck
FX's high-gloss drama about a Miami cosmetic-surgery clinic was already a terrific show, but the third season's fearless exploration of male sexuality elevated the series to another plane entirely. Between Christian Troy's (Julian McMahon) complex response to being raped and teenager Matt McNamara (John Hensley) feeling out his attraction to transsexuals, nothing on the tube came close to breaking as much new ground.

2. Six Feet Under
Great shows that tarnish their rep by sticking around too long are sadly commonplace; those that know when to quit and do so with style are rare indeed. *Six Feet Under's* beautifully paced wind-down yielded one of the most devastating epiodes in TV history (Nate Fisher's funeral) and provided a textbook example of how to craft a finale that pleases fans without pandering to them.

3. Lost

When a show relies on mysterious questions to justify its existence, striking the right balance between providing answers and deriving fresh stories from the premise is brutally difficult. This year's Emmy winner for Outstanding Dramatic Series pulled it off with aplomb, while simultaneously telling rich, character-driven stories in the tradition of Rod Serling and 0. Henry.

4.Deadwood

If history is written by the victors, *Deadwood* is all about giving the losers their due. In the first season, magnificent bastard Al Swearingen (Ian McShayne) came off as a villain; this year, his inevitably doomed campaign to save the lawless town from annexation by the United States and exploitation by robber barons served as a brilliant allegory for the evolution of American capitalism.

5. *Veronica Mars*

One of the best shows of the 2004-05 season got even better this year as the characters gained new depth, refining creator Rob Thomas's inspired blend of *Nancy Drew, Twin Peaks* and *Degrassi High*. Harry Hamlin gets special props for his transformation into TV's most hateful villain, while Kristen Bell and Enrico Colantoni effortlessly eclipsed *Alias's* Jennifer Garner and Victor Garber as the small screen's most believable and affecting daughter-father team.

6. *The Office*

There are a thousand ways this remake of the BBC gem could have failed, but executive producer Greg Daniels avoided all of them. By giving his cast the improvisational breathing room to make his American reinterpretation a legitimately great show in its own right.

7. *House*

TV is a medium typically driven more by premise than by character, but without its acerbic, pill-popping protagonist, *House* would be just another medical show. Hugh Laurie's portrayal of the phlegmatic physician made each episode a master class in the art of screen acting, while the scripts revealed more about the guesswork involved in the actual practice of medicine than *ER* has in a decade-plus on the air.

8.*Weeds*

Suburban angst is one of the most played-out subjects there is, but creator Jenji Kohan's terrific comedy-drama went places other shows didn't, avoiding pat resolutions and rendering the highs and lows of everyday life with a masterful degree of emotional realism. And *damn* was it nice to see Mary-Louise Parker in a role worthy of her gifts.

9. *The Shield*

This year's pair of inspired casting decisions—Glenn Close as an intensely driven veteran cop and comic Anthony Anderson as a canny drug dealer—revitalized the gritty police drama and set the stage for a fifth season (starting January 10) that promises to be every bit as gripping.

10. *Battlestar Galactica*

It was sometimes hard to tell what the war-on-terror parallels meant, but no series did a better job of blending adrenalized action, knot-in-your-stomach suspense and multifaceted characterization.

Honorable Mentions:

Gilmore Girls, Rome, Medium, Rescue Me, My Name is Earl, Project Runway, The Daily Show with Jon Stewart, Alias, Scrubs and *Grey's Anatomy*.

THE PITS

1.*Freddie*

Cynically trading on his Puerto Rican heritage, Freddie Prinze Jr, stormed the small screen with a braying sitcom. Chronicling the misadventures of bachelor whose ethnic stereotype-laden family moves in with him, *Freddie* embodied the genre at its tackiest.

2. *Out of Practice*
Few things are more depressing than seeing a killer cast—including Stockard Channing and Henry Winkler—trapped in a leaden comedy. Unfortunately for them, the momentum of CBS's Monday schedule has kept this clunker around despite costar Paula Marshall's famous series-killing jinx.

3. *The War* at *Home*
Revisionist nostalgia aside, *Married ... with Children* sucked the first time around. Michael Rappaport's smug fourth wall-breaking narration makes this retread even worse.

4. *Sex, Love & Secrets*
Never heard of it? No surprise: Though UPN traditionally tolerates low ratings, this tragically hip L.A. soap starring Denise Richards was pulled after four weeks, and with good reason.

5. *Rock Star: INXS*
How low can reality TV go? The betrayal of the late Michael Hutchence by his bandmates was sad even by the bottom-feeding standards of the reunion-tour circuit.

Not quite as bad (but close):
Starved, Related, Head Cases, The Apprentice, Martha Stewart and So You Think You Can Dance.

2006

The Wire
The gritty Baltimore drama cements its status as TV's ultimate class act.

This week, you'll probably read a lot of reviews of *The Wire's* new season that laud creator David Simon's stunning street drama for its narrative complexity and social conscience. But while those are among the series's many virtues, critics who emphasize them risk making Simon's exhilarating urban panorama sound like a dreary homework assignment. Here's what you really need to know: Never before has there been a series at once as bawdy, chilling, vibrant, disturbing, melancholy, sidesplitting and honestly uplifting as this chronicle of the battle fought daily by cops, drug dealers and politicians for the soul of Baltimore.

As the new season begins, the protagonists are widely scattered: Bad-boy detective Jimmy McNulty (Dominic West) has sobered up and put a uniform back on; Major Cedric Daniels (Lance Reddick) has assumed command of the western district; Thomas "Herc" Hauk (Domenick Lombardozzi) has become a bodyguard for flashy Mayor Clarence Royce (Glynn Turman); and the disgraced Roland "Prez" Pryzbylewski (Jim True-Frost) has left the force to teach eighth-grade math. The latter development is the jumping-off point for an exploration of the sorry state of public education in American cities, a topic that has yielded some of the most mawkish and didactic movies and TV shows ever made. This, it should go without saying, is not one of them.

The genius of *The Wire* has always been its skillful presentation of stories about social problems in purely character-based terms, Simon obviously relishes his freedom from the objectivity that he needed as a reporter for "the Baltimore *Sun,*" but viewers are never cudgeled with his opinion on the subject of the day—season three's story addressing drug legalization was as much about the desire of Major "Bunny" Colvin (Robert Wisdom) to retire with a meaningful legacy as it was about the social upside of a sanctioned, regulated narcotics trade. Here Prez steps into the classroom looking for redemption but quickly has his do-gooder fantasies shattered by a self-serving bureaucracy that makes it nearly impossible for even the most promising kids to avoid the vortex of drugs and violence.

The stories of four such boys (played by the remarkable Maestro Harrell, Jermaine Crawford, Tristan Wilds and Julito McCullum) form a nexus for a number of engrossing plot threads involving characters from years past: Baby-faced city councilman Tommy Carcetti (Aidan Gillen) stages a quixotic campaign to become Baltimore's first white mayor in a generation; the ruthless Marlo Stanfield (Jamie Hector) consolidates his grip on the drug trade now that the rival Barksdale gang is history; and detective Lester Freamon (Clarke Peters) tries to figure out how Stanfield expands his empire without leaving the streets full of bodies.

In interviews, Simon and his creative partner, Ed Burns (a retired Baltimore police officer), have made it clear that many plots and characters are composites of real-life people and events. *The Wire's* air of authenticity can be harrowing, yet it's inspiring. The series's most compelling characters are men and women who know how fucked-up the system is yet refuse to surrender to cynicism, even if that means enraging and alienating their spouses and children. As in life, the good guys often lose, and the victories that come are frequently small. But over time, the little wins add up and coalesce into the kind of leading by example that can eventually change the world. It's a theme found in the muckraking detective fiction of Richard Price and George Pelecanos, whose contributions to the series (along with those of *Mystic River* author Dennis Lehane) have helped make each season richer than the last. The passion that the writers and actors bring to every episode ensures that *The Wire* never feels like a lecture, but it has a lot to teach us nonetheless.

Friday Night Lights

Fancy lighting and camera angles are making TV dramas look more and more like big-screen movies every week, but it's still startling to encounter a series as thoroughly cinematic as *Friday Night Lights*. Actor-director Peter Berg's 2004 adaptation of H.G. Bissinger's nonfiction best-seller about Texas high-school football defied sports-movie conventions, drawing heavily on Steven Soderbergh for inspiration, and the Berg-produced TV spin-off's use of similar techniques—moody handheld shots accompanied by ambient piano music and dialogue from scenes taking place elsewhere—is just as contrarian and refreshing.

The series replaces the real-life team from Bissinger's book with a fictional analog: the Dillon Panthers, a small-town West Texas squad burdened with ulcer-inducing championship expectations of success by the community as it begins its first year with Eric Taylor (Kyle Chandler) as head coach. Taylor can't turn around without 50 people offering him unwanted advice, and the early episodes focus on him shoring up relationships—with his wife (Connie Britton) and with 160-pound second-string quarterback Matt Saracen (Zach Gilford)—that let the coach tune out the hectoring. It's soon clear that the principals are all hiding behind facades that conceal their fears, and the tension is conveyed through telling images and the actors' body language rather than expository dialogue. The technique demands a lot of the cast, but it allows familiar story lines to take on an unexpected emotional subtlety that, while rewarding, may alienate viewers craving the melodramatic raunch of *Varsity Blues*. Bone-crunching tackles aside, nothing else on the fall schedule is as intimate or introspective.

For love of the game
Friday Night Lights' Zach Gilford helps give jocks a good name.

Long on brutal hits and crunching rock music, the early promos for NBC's *Friday Night Lights* offered little hint of the poetic vision and emotional honesty that quickly endeared the series about small-town Texas high-school football to viewers who don't know a safety from a two-point conversion. A key part of the appeal has been the performance of 24-year-old Zach Gilford as Matt Saracen, an introverted Bob Dylan-loving tenth-grader who becomes the quarterback for the Dillon Panthers after an injury turns his golden-boy predecessor into a paraplegic.

Matt's story line may sound like a cliché, but the cinematic vocabulary established by executive producer Peter Berg (who wrote and and directed the 2004 big-screen adaptation of the nonfiction best-seller by his cousin H. G. Bissinger) and the emphasis on the effects of football rather than the game itself have turned *FNL* into the most unique drama on broadcast TV this fall. "The way we shoot this is just so different. I'm dreading having to do something else, because we have so much freedom to improvise and make up whatever we want as we go along," says Gilford, hunkering down with a tuna melt at a Chelsea diner during a recent visit to New York for an appearance on *Today*. "I think that's partially why each of us is so invested in it, because we feel as if we're really contributing. We're not just showing up, saying something someone else wrote and going home. We're actually creating something."

Gilford moved to New York after graduating from Northwestern University in 2004, and lived in Harlem while working at the Patagonia store in Soho and an after-school program in Queens. In his spare time, he slogged away at auditions that brought him little aside from an episode of *Law & Order:SVU* before he was cast as Matt and moved to Austin to shoot the series. Gilford's own high-school football career (as a defensive corner) was ended by a broken leg, but not before he learned enough about the game to appreciate Matt's situation. "'He's a kid who's not a star quarterback but has to be," Gilford explains. "Even when it's scripted and fake, it's still a hard position. I can't imagine being in a game and having to see through all the players to get the ball in the right place."

NBC's original marketing efforts were predicated on a belief that the series would have little interest to women, but that quickly proved false — a devoted fan who describes Matt as "the boy every woman I know wishes she knew in high school, but totally didn't" reflects the views of hundreds of online supporters, and Connie Britton's work as the outspoken wife of hard-pressed coach Eric Taylor (Kyle Chandler) has produced many of the series's most compelling moments. "That's kind of why Pete wanted to make the TV show after the movie — with the movie he could only follow the team and tell the story of what they did," Guilford says. "With the TV show, he can get into the characters and their lives, and that's what's interesting about the book."

Like many TV dramas that defy categorization, *FNL* hasn't had an easy time of it in the ratings (all through the autumn, ABC's *Dancing with the Stars* has dominated the 8pm Tuesday time slot, which Fox's *American Idol* will reclaim in January). Still, its numbers have remained steady, and NBC has asserted a firm belief in the show, recently giving it a full-season pickup. On the other hand, network president Jeff Zucker has talked about devoting all of NBC's 8pm berths to reality TV and game shows, reducing the number of alternative slots. "It definitely adds a little stress to your day," Guilford says of the ratings agita. "It's in the back of your head, and you know there's nothing you can do about it, but when you love your job as much as I do, you want to keep it." That said, Guilford acknowledges that if the show succeeds over the long haul its very nature will bring his gig to an end. "There's not gonna be 'the college years,'" he says. "Some of the characters might stick around and not go anywhere or do anything, but Matt's gonna go to college. I like that commitment to realism and not selling out."

2007

Friday Night Lights: The First Season

Actor-filmmaker Peter Berg's 2004 movie about Texas high-school football and the pilot episode for the TV version (which he wrote and directed) were both technical triumphs, but neither really hinted at the emotional depth the series would attain as its first season progressed. Taylor Kitsch (as a brooding running back), Adrianne Palicki (his sometime girlfriend with a bad reputation) and Scott Porter (a wheelchair-bound ex-QB) are all pretty enough for *One Tree Hill*, but it's immediately clear they were cast for their talent as much as their looks. As coach Eric Taylor and his wife, Tami, Kyle Chandler and Connie Britton deliver rich, lived-in performances that result in the most complicated and believable TV marriage this side of Tony and Carmela Soprano; meanwhile, the travails of introspective bookworm quarterback Matt Saracen (Zach Gilford), who's in over his head on every front, provide bittersweet comic relief. In story line after story line, *Friday Night Lights* illustrates the true meaning of the Dillon Panthers· inspirational slogan ("Clear Eyes, Full Hearts, Can't Lose") instead of merely paying lip service to the motto. *FNL* is the best series of its kind since the legendary *My So-Called Life* (where head writer Jason Katims cut his teeth). Unlike its storied predecessor, this remarkable (but similarly ratings-challenged) series is thankfully coming back for a second season. October 5 can't get here soon enough.

Mad Men

Inspired by cynical Eisenhower-era comedies of manners *(Sweet Smell Of Success, The Apartment)* and the stories of John Cheever, frequent *Sopranos* writer Matthew Weiner's *Mad Men* is a scathing chronicle of the ad industry's boozy midcentury heyday, and one of the freshest series to hit basic cable in years. Set in 1960 at Sterling Cooper, a Madison Avenue agency populated by "more failed artists and intellectuals than the Third Reich," as creative director Don Draper (Jon Hamm) puts it, the series rivals Ang Lee's *The Ice Storm* in skillfully reconstructing the past on its own terms.

Draper's coworkers—including a baby-faced upper-crust schemer (Vincent Kartheiser) and a naive, husband-hungry secretary *(The West Wing's* Elisabeth Moss) initially seem like simple devices to let the series explore class, gender and sexuality, but they soon take on a depth that speaks more to the constancy of human nature. In the early episodes, Draper himself is largely a cipher, defined mostly by Hamm's machete-sharp cheekbones, though hints of wartime trauma and a complicated childhood gradually suggest he's a white-collar Tony Soprano whose emotions are held prisoner by the era's preference for cocktails over therapy.

Weiner can't resist a few pokes at now-primitive technology, and some historical facts are bent for dramatic effect (Draper coins a slogan for Lucky Strikes that actually dates to 1917), yet the series generally protects itself from the ironic laughter that greeted Todd Haynes's equally sincere *Far from Heaven* by appealing to viewers' heads as much as their hearts. Draper's print campaigns may seem quaint, but they push the same buttons as the ads that consume more of our public space every week. Behind the billowing smoke, narrow lapels and beehive 'dos of *Mad Men* lies the most relevant new drama of *2007.*

It's Always Sunny in Philadelphia

The first two seasons of FX's proudly misanthropic sitcom ran in midsummer, when the lack of competition can make it easier for an iconoclastic series to develop a fan base. This year, its return coincides with both the new network lineups and the reappearance of *Curb Your Enthusiasm,* the series that inspired *Sunny* more than any other. And by now, creator-costar Rob McElhenney and his pals have honed their sensibility to the point that Sunny can more than hold its own against the competition.

Amazingly, the series's formula has yet to grow repetitive: Mac (McElhenney), Charlie (Charlie Day), Dennis (Glenn Howerton) and Dee (Kaitlin Olson), the four friends who run Paddy's Irish Pub, encounter a serious situation—in this year's premiere, they find a baby in a Dumpster—which divides them against each other, leading to arguments and scheming that quickly result in chaos. Danny DeVito's season-two addition to the tight ensemble cast as Frank, the supposed father of Dennis and Dee, expanded the comic possibilities. Anne Archer also guest-starred as their mom, a seemingly good idea that largely fell flat. She isn't around this time, and her absence—combined with the revelation that Frank isn't really the siblings' dad; he's Charlie's—has helped the series become more streamlined than ever. The second of the two episodes airing on Thursday 13, a parody of the Mark Wahlberg football movie *Invincible,* is a bit of a clunker, illustrating the pitfalls of depending too much on shticky recurring characters (the incestuous McPoyle clan, used to much better effect next week), but the pair of episodes which follow on September 20—one featuring returning guest Stephen Collins, cheerfully spoofing his 7th *Heaven* persona—are refreshingly rude examples of a sitcom in its prime.

Back in the game
Kyle Chandler and Connie Britton return as TV's most believable couple on Friday Night Lights. [The full version of this interview, which appeared in shortened/edited form in print and in complete form on the TONY website.]

The television academy may have snubbed Kyle Chandler and Connie Britton's consistently terrific work as small-town Texas football coach Eric

Taylor and his wife, Tami, on NBC's *Friday Night Lights* (which kicks off its second season Friday 5), but TONY readers were more discerning: The actors were both decisive winners in our first annual Shadow Emmys. During an August visit to Austin, we had the pleasure of spending an hour with Chandler and Britton in Chandler's trailer while the season's fourth episode was being shot on location at a Lutheran church. Here's the complete transcript of the conversation, which appears in abbreviated form in *TONY* #627.

I wanted to start by saying I'm appalled that you were screwed out of an Emmy nomination.

Kyle Chandler: I didn't see it as getting screwed out of anything. It all went good.

Well, just being on the air is more important than getting any awards.

Chandler: That's the way I look at it

Were you sweating the renewal after last season?

Chandler: I put forward to everyone that there was no doubt we were gonna get picked up again. If we didn't get picked up, I wasn't gonna see anyone for a long time anyway, so it wasn't going to come back at me. I was pretty sure that we would, knowing personally that it's a good show. There's a lot to be found there. The only thing we need to do now is to get people watching.

Tom Carson of *GQ* described your work on the show as being "as perfect as series acting gets." Does something like that put extra pressure on you to deliver?

Chandler: No, it doesn't.... This sounds hokey, I guess, but I really don't pay much attention to those things other than the fact that I like to hear the good things and dismiss the bad things. I've been doing it long enough to where it's just like, you're hot in Hollywood one day... for me, I turn into a bigger fish and get happier swimming around, but then once the show I'm doing is gone, you're starting out at square one, so I don't put much credence into the whole... My ego's not big enough really, I don't think, to let me get involved. My self-confidence isn't great enough to let me take it too seriously when I get those accolades. Certainly my wife and kids don't let me believe too much of it. But it's a great compliment and I thank him for it. This is a perfect job, and the show for me came at just a perfect time, because I've been married now for 12 years and I haven't ever played a father or someone that's married in this way, and I've been able to use so much of the tools that have accumulated in that box on this show. It's new. You know as well, the way the show is presented, the way it's shot and the way the attitude is around this place as to being creative and working with material and exploring things. There is no "wrong" in art. Pretty much you can hang that on a shingle in front of our door. It all just comes together. A lot of people speak about the relationship Connie and I have together and you'll find out from talking with her, she's not a bullshitter, she's straight-up. She's a really good actress. We both love comedy and we have similar comedic timing, I think. We find similar things funny. We both love acting and love actors. We protect each other onscreen as actors. One thing we've found out too is we both enjoy making fools of ourselves, and that makes for a great relationship on just about every level. [*Jokingly*] Here comes the bitch now. Hey, Connie, come on in, she'll have something to say about everything.

[*Connie Britton enters the trailer.*]

Kyle was just talking about...

Connie Britton: Himself?

...well, about how it's not really a funny show but there is a lot of humor that comes through via the marital conflicts and stuff like that, which helps it feel natural and believable. I don't think there's any other show on TV at the moment that feels more like watching normal people living their lives, in a lot of ways. It just blows me away week after week that way. In terms of now that you have a full order for the second season and don't really have to worry about that

for awhile, is the show going to get a little bit deeper, is there a sense of "we don't have to worry, so now we can take it in more interesting directions"?

Britton: I hate to say it, because it was a great vote of confidence that they picked up 22 episodes, but the truth of the matter is they can cancel it anytime they want to. My feeling is, let's just get as many shot as we can before we start to air, and if the ratings don't go up before they get a chance to cancel us.

Chandler: Also too, and I think the cast willingly knows this, even if they said, "We're gonna pick you up for a full season, guaranteed," for us as actors and for us as workers, it's better for us to plant the seed in our heads whether we know it's true or not that we could be canceled at any time, so when we come to work, put forth your best. There's a chance at all moments.

Britton: We're certainly not resting on our laurels this year, that's for sure. I mean, last year going into it, there were a lot of unknowns and a lot of reservations, and so we went into it feeling, "Let's make this the best show we can, and we don't know what's gonna come out of it." And now, even though we had a great first season, surprisingly—well, not surprisingly, we have the same feeling this season. We gotta make this the best show it can be.

Chandler: I think the writers, the producers, I think everyone pretty much feels that way. Everyone who works on this show, though I haven't met them all, obviously, has a passion for the show. I think they really believe in what they're doing.

Britton: People are so passionate about it.

With good reason, and it really shows in every episode. I think it must be kind of different from anything you've done before, if you're here and the writers and producers are out there in Los Angeles.

Britton: It is a most unusual thing, and I would never have imagined that it would work. But it somehow works so beautifully…

Chandler: I'll tell you why it does, too, because I've done it when it didn't work quite so smoothly. And the reason it works so smoothly here, and I've said this before in interviews, and it just sort of sums it up, is because everyone here is asked to do what they do best. No one is told what to do. And everyone that does their best is most creative when they're doing their own thing, and they've got a bunch of talented people who are doing their own thing. I think that comes out and gives everyone that individual sense of, I own a piece of this show. I think that comes down from the editors, the writers, those people are back in L.A., and we're here but there's such a creative effort to share in what we're doing. It goes straight to Pete Berg [director of the pilot and the 2004 screen adaptation of H.G. Bissinger's nonfiction book] and the way he set the tone from the beginning. And he couldn't have found better people than [executive producer and frequent writer] Jason Katims, [producer–director] Jeffrey Reiner and these other folks that are running the show. Their spirits... There are no kings on this show; we're all princes.

Britton: It's all a collaboration, and when you have people feeling, I think it's exactly what Kyle said, but also when you have people doing their best and being trusted to do their best, it instills confidence in them. And then the collaboration works so much better because everyone is feeling not only passionate about doing their best but also they've been empowered to do that. Each person on the show knows they're an important cog in this machine and they're just as important as anybody else. The camera crew know how important they are and the editors know how important their role is to the show and all of that, and [*Her tone gets cheeky as Chandler's eyes suggest he's eager to butt in.*]... Oh, sweetie, do you have something else to say? I can't wait to hear it, I bet it's going to be so interesting.

Chandler: I wanted to say just real quick is that one of the biggest lessons I've learned, it might be one you've learned too, is that creative part and how to deal with other artists in a way, because I've never had that experience, and it's the most freeing experience. It goes down to, this is a silly story, but a fellow this summer who was putting a little gate and a little wall up in my yard, my wife had him come over and he said, "Mr. Chandler," and I came over there and he goes, "How do you want me to do this?" He gave me a few different ways he could do it, and I swear Jeff Reiner, our producer and director here, channeled right through me and all the lessons I've learned here, and I said, "Look, man, you know what? The fact of the matter is, if you build this gate the way you think it's gonna look best, just use your imagination here and I'm sure I'm gonna love it." And I'll tell you what, it's a little simple gate, but you can sure as hell tell that it's tight, it fits, it's creative, it's a *nice gate*. I think it comes from giving people the opportunity to do what they do best. That's not to say there aren't arguments—we get in knock-down drag-outs, but they're *creative* arguments. We're not pulling out guns and shooting at each other

Britton: But that's the best part of the collaboration. That goes to our relationship on the show, too. If you have a true collaboration and an element of trust, and a foundation of trust underneath, then you can argue about anything, because the arguments are all toward the better good. That's true in the relationship between our two characters, and that's something that's been really important in that relationship, and it's also true in the collaboration on this show.

Chandler: Our relationship between Austin and L.A., our relationship between NBC and the show. I've never been part of anything that has been so comfortable and yet so difficult in the sense of there's so much personal responsibility. No one's told how to push a button, you got to figure out how to push it yourself and make it work. You didn't expect all that, did you? [*Chuckles*]

It's great to hear, because this is stuff I'm really fascinated by, 'cause the show has really meant a lot to me.

Britton: It's meant a lot to us, too. We've had a lot of people ask why, why, and we try to figure that out, too. As actors, Kyle and I, unlike these young actors who in a way don't know how great they have it, because for a lot of them this is their first time out.

Chandler: This is the beginning of their technique.

Britton: Yeah, but for us, you know, we're kind of like wow, we hit the jackpot, and we're constantly trying to figure it out. It's the beauty of what we have here.

I interviewed Zach Gilford [who plays quarterback Matt Saracen] in New York last year pretty early in the season, and he could already tell he'd lucked into something really special for his first show. It was not gonna be like this in future jobs.

Britton: We just had a guest director on the show, yesterday was his last day, and I was talking to him about it and he goes— he's going straight to direct another episode of a big hour-long show— and he's like, "I've been here for however long, three weeks, and I'm dreading it. Now that I've done this, getting back into that standardized procedure is gonna be rough going," and I think it is true....

Chandler: It's the difference between a Rockwell and a Pollock.

Britton: We need to patent this. [*Beat, perplexed emphasis*] A *Pollock*?

Chandler: Yeah. [*Mimes squeezing paint tube, makes squoosh sound effect, then mimes even strokes*] Freedom!

[*Britton inquires about Andrew's tattoos; a few minutes of extraneous small talk follows.*]

Britton: Part of what people like about the show so much is that there's a real fullness of heart in the small town and the relationships and the community. I think we experience that on the show off camera as well in terms of our... We really take care of each other here and on the show. I think that's something we've tried to capture in the world of small-town America; in a world like that, it's all about the relationships and people holding each other up and supporting each other. I think that we have so strayed from that in a lot of what we have on television now. It's like that kind of straightforward, heartfelt relationship is not really represented that much anymore, nor in film that much either. So that's part of what our fan base is responding to, and it's a very real thing for us personally as well.

Have you guys started to put down roots here a bit? Are your families here, or are you commuting to see them? I know Taylor Kitsch [who plays running back Tim Riggins] bought a condo in Austin recently.

Britton: We still go back to L.A.; Kyle's got a whole family there.

Chandler: As far as putting roots down here, Austin's the biggest character on the show already, I love this town. When I came back here this year, I was so excited to get back here. I'll cry as much for the show when it's over as I will for leaving this town and not having this place to come back to.

I don't want you to drop any spoilers, but it's going to be really interesting to see where y'all's relationship is going to go on the show, because you had such a believable and interesting conflict at the end of the season over taking the college coaching job. There was a lot of closure at the end of the season, but a lot of danglers, too. It's going to be really interesting to see how it plays out.

Chandler: They opened as many doors as they closed, that's for sure. As far as where our characters go, I don't ask, to tell you the truth. I've expressly said that I don't want to know what's going to happen. I've told them I liked to be surprised by the script. With actors, if you find out what's supposed to happen down the line and it doesn't happen, you might be disappointed, and then you have a problem and start going, "Why didn't we do this, why didn't we do that?" I don't like knowing what's gonna happen. I like finding out what's gonna happen [when the script is delivered] and then discuss that. If it's gonna be in the script, good. If it's not... These writers are very open. You call up and give a suggestion, which they ask for—we're supposed to do that as actors—it doesn't fall on deaf ears by any means. Ninety percent of the suggestions that Connie and I send in are not only put into the script but get a thank-you at the end.

Britton: It's not adversarial at all.

Chandler: This Jason Katims guy, he's a kick-ass SOB.

Britton: They all are.

I was a big fan of his work on *My So-Called Life* and *Roswell*.

Chandler: He's a good person, too.

It seems like that's the case because of how natural the characters feel, as if you're putting a lot of yourself into the characters. It's great they give you the opportunity to do that.

Britton: Again, it's all about the naturalness and the realism that we're entrusted with. It's like what you [Chandler] were saying about not wanting to know what's in [future] scripts. We're living in this world so fully that to know in advance what's gonna happen is like knowing what in your life is gonna happen. To have the spontaneity of having just one script in front of you…even on that day, we don't rehearse it. We may switch the lines around and we may fool around with it when we're doing it in the space for the first time, so there's a real sense of it living instead of being thought out or premeditated. As an actor, it's a gift to be able to do that.

Chandler: I can give you an example too—today in the car, there's a scene with the girl who plays my daughter, Amiee Teegarden. We're driving along, and it's written that a certain thing happens with the car, and they're pulling us in the car with the cameras in the truck and so on, and I asked Jonas Pate [the director] how we're gonna do this, and he says, "What I want you do to is go with the dialogue up to this point and then just use the real world." That's pretty much our show. Take this stuff and put it in the real world. We use the world around us within the material, we don't have a world around us we're trying to fit it into. It brings a reality to it.

Given how fast you're presumably working, cranking them out doing 22 a season, I figured you probably did a lot of rehearsing on camera and going with your gut.

Chandler: That's exactly right. Your faith in the director is when they tell you which direction to take it, and that's when it gets fun. Because you start having those conversations and you start taking it places that even the writers might not know, they might not have seen where it could have gone. Even though the dialogue may be the same or it may change or whatever. And hence the show sort of changes. And within shooting it, you can shoot something five, six, seven times, and if you're still working on it, you've got different scenes with different takes and different emotions and different directions. When the editors get it, they don't know what the fuck they've got, and all of a sudden they're piecing it together and you've got a whole different scene that could change the whole show and go somewhere else. So when we watch the shows for the first time, quite often there are scenes that make us go, "That's where they went with it, 'cause I didn't know, since we did it this way and that way, so what's going to happen in the next script…" It's exciting for us, too, it's a living organism.

Unlike most dramas, it seems like you always have a couple different cameras going at once. They've eased up on the Soderbergh-type editing after the first few episodes last year, but there's still some of that there.

Chandler: It's usually three cameras there when we start up.

Britton: Three or four. And the thing is, even though they slowed up the cameras a bit, the great thing about it… I mean, I was as little worried at first, I thought, Oh no, don't mess with it, but the thing the visual style really accomplishes is we have such a pure sense of intimacy. Even if the cameras aren't moving fast, it doesn't matter. It took me about until maybe episode four last year where I realized, Oh, I don't have to do that much as an actor because the cameras are telling the story. We just go in and start walking around the room and saying our lines and figuring it out and changing it up, whatever, and the cameras are finding it all and the editors are putting it together, so I was like, Oh, we really don't have to do that much!" [*Laughs*]

Chandler: We got some damn good cameramen.

Britton: We have a great camera crew, and they're as passionate about it and as interested in finding the story and the truth of it and telling that story as we are.

Chandler: I truly believe they know the scripts just as well as we do. They keep very in tune with it so they know exactly what's going on.

Connie, I think you're being astonishingly modest when you're saying it's the camerapeople who are really doing some of the storytelling and you don't have to work that hard.

Chandler: [*In a perfect deadpan*] No, she's not.

The scene with your big speech at the roast last year, that was just an incredible piece of acting, it was so moving.

Chandler: [*Tongue still in cheek*] That was me. Okay, you were good too.

Britton: Again, that was one of those moments where, we live so much in these characters, getting up and doing that sort of knowing the conflict that was happening with us, and then getting up and having to say that speech and being nervous about it, that's how you would be. It was tricky for me because they'd written all these football jokes in there and I really don't know anything about football. But I was like, Tami would have it all written down, so I had it all written down.

Even if you don't know anything about it, you can't help absorbing a little bit doing the show, I'm sure. It's sort of funny, because I really don't know jack shit about football...

Britton: So you're the perfect person to be writing this article!

I'm in my thirties and only now through watching the show did I get motivated to really understand the rules.

Britton: That should be the title of the article "I don't know jack shit about football, but..."

Before you came in, Kyle was talking about how the series let him take his life experiences as a husband and father and apply them to his craft. Has that been the case with you as well?

Britton: I've played a mother before, and a wife, but I'm neither. For me it's interesting in a different way, because we are kind of creating this interesting, multifaceted marriage and parental relationship, and I'm neither married nor a mother. So it's interesting in different ways for me.

Well, your relationship with Aimee certainly seems believable.

Britton: I know, it's odd.

Chandler: Well, it's because she's a good actress!

Britton: It's for a lot of reasons, but I just feel really fortunate about it. What I do come from, and what I take a lot from, is that I grew up in the South and was very influenced by the Southern women around me, including my mother, who wasn't from the South originally but became a full-fledged Southern woman, so there's a lot of dedication to those women in the role for me.

Kyle, one of the things I find so fascinating about your character is how he's a really good guy, but he's stubborn and wrong and a jerk sometimes, but his heart's in the right place. There are levels of ambiguity you might be more accustomed to getting on a cable show rather than a network series. Whenever Coach Taylor is being pigheaded with his daughter or whatever, you still like the guy even when he's being a jerk.

Chandler: One thing I like about all the characters I've played up to date since I've been working, is I love the humor. I like playing comedy, and I like making a fool of myself as well. This is a perfect show for me to be... He's a coach and a father [*Seamlessly shifts gears into Coach Taylor mode*], so you know, dammit, things are going to be my way. I'm the father of a family, this is my family, I am in charge of this family... Where is everybody? [*Becomes Kyle Chandler again*] You know what I mean? I don't know if it's my love of, like, W.C. Fields, those kind of characters that are just... Archie

Bunker—how could you not love that SOB racist pig? He was the greatest guy on TV.

Britton: I think the greatest misconception is that as an actor, the only reason your character is going to be likable is if they're somehow perfect. I think the reason characters are likable is if you give them imperfections that everyone can relate to. And if they're redeemable. I think that's true of all the characters on our show—none of them are perfect, but none of them cannot be redeemed one way or another. And I think that's where the sense of humor comes in. I think as long as you can deal with that with a sense of humor, you can go a long way.

Chandler: It's not the sinner, it's the sin. [*Aware that he changed the tone of the conversation*]. Well, I'm just saying...

Well, that sort of speaks to...

Chandler: It's kind of my metaphor for working today. [*Britton shoots him a glance that says, "Come up with another metaphor."*] Hey, the Pollock one was good!

Well, it comes back around to the team slogan—"Clear Eyes, Full Hearts, Can't Lose"—doesn't it? The truth of the motto has always been illustrated through the story lines. It wasn't something you just paid lip service to, which is part of why I've always found the show so incredibly moving. And something else I was curious about, in terms of getting the opportunity to impart some of your experience to these young actors who are just starting out, it must be a cool thing to be able to do.

Chandler: The most interesting thing about the young actors is, when I was starting out, it took me awhile—I started acting really when I was 23 and got out to [L.A.], I mean I had a SAG card and all, but when I got into acting class and started working and started really figuring out exactly what it was and who I am, blah blah blah, well, these young actors, that's where you learn your technique as an actor. These young actors, their technique is being formed on a show like this that for me... For me, it I feel like it started with *King Kong* and then with this show, both of those, because Peter Jackson worked similarly, he gave you the ability to do your thing and come up with ideas. He really wanted you to bring something to it. I can't explain it, but I was ready for this show after doing that. These kids here are starting at that point. I feel like I'm at the top of my game right now, and it's a lot because of what we've been doing. So these kids, I just don't know where they're going to go from here, but they can only go up.

My So-Called Life: The Complete Series [DVD]

Brian Eno once said that while the *Velvet Underground* sold only a couple of thousand albums in the 1960s, everybody who bought one started a band. The same isn't literally true where *My So-Called Life* and TV drama are concerned—even the lowest-rated programs score a few million viewers, and many fans of Winnie Holzman's 1994-95 teen drama are just now old enough to break into the business—but it's hard to understate the influence of the show, which launched the careers of Claire Danes, and Jared Leto, as well as a number of behind-the-camera luminaries (including *Friday Night Lights* producer Jason Katims).

In a feat reminiscent of the letter-writing campaign that spared *Star Trek* from cancellation in 1968, fans of *MSCL* organized a subscription drive that yielded a limited-edition DVD set in 2002, which instantly sold out and until recently, regularly went for several hundred dollars on eBay. The patience of those who skipped the 2002 collection is well rewarded by the extras on this affordable reissue, which include a 1995 cast Q&A and a book with essays by Janeane Garofalo and Joss Whedon. However, most fans would agree that the most important thing is how a new generation of viewers can experience 18 amazing episodes (the penultimate one is universally considered a dud) chronicling the awkward adolescence of Angela Chase (Danes), her lovelorn neighbor Brian Krakow (Devon Gummersall), gay classmate Rickie Vasquez (Wilson Cruz) and cryptic brooder Jordan Catalano (Leto), all of whom rank among the most vivid and believable characters in the history of the medium.

Black Christmas
Johnny Cash and friends celebrate the holiday the old-fashioned way in a fantastic pair of vintage specials.

For Americans born between World War II and the mid-1980s, it's impossible to imagine the holiday season without TV Christmas specials, if only because of the consistency they provide—for someone whose family might have lived in Boise, Idaho, one December and Fort Lauderdale the next, the continuity provided by CBS's annual broadcast of *Frosty the Snowman* is nothing to sneer at. But the animated standbys that get dusted off every year represent only one aspect of the holiday-special tradition. Musical variety shows such as the remarkable Johnny Cash Christmas specials from 1976 and 1977, just released on DVD by Shout! Factory, are an equally significant form of holiday programming, albeit one that has become far less commonplace over the years. Certainly, the Cash shows, unseen since their initial broadcast, have moments that play like high camp now. But the combination of the terrific performances and the deep sincerity of the Man in Black allows them to capture the spirit of the holiday in a way that makes most other Christmas specials seem like mere acts of lip service.

In the 1976 special, Cash and his guest Roy Clark remark that people are always surprised when they say they grew up on the same music as the rest of America, by which they mean the work of singers such as Frank Sinatra and Tony Bennett. Their comments introduce a fantastic segment in which the two perform a duet of Bing Crosby's "Far

Away Places," followed by Cash doing "That Lucky Old Sun" (a 1940s Frankie Lane hit later covered by Louis Armstrong and Ray Charles) and Clark's superb rendition of Nat King Cole's "The Christmas Song." Their introductory comments point at the reason such specials have died off: With the explosion of cable TV in the 1980s, TV programming began to be targeted at increasingly specific audiences, causing shows that appeal across demographic lines to become increasingly scarce. Contemporary holiday specials on the country-themed CMT network, such as this year's *A Toby Keith Classic Christmas* and *Larry the Cable Guy's Christmas Spectacular,* practice a certain brand of outreach by featuring guests such as Jewel and Flavor Flav. But the net effect is a kind of eclecticism for its own sake, which feels mighty hollow next to Cash and Clark's palpable affection for popular standards (a tendency represented in the 1977 special by a smoking cover of Rosemary Clooney's "This Ole House" by Cash and the Statler Brothers).

Notwithstanding Cash and Clark's salute to pop vocalists (and the hokey performance of "Tie a Yellow Ribbon Round the Ole Oak Tree" by Tony Orlando, June Carter Cash and the Man in Black), the special doesn't dilute its country components for a mainstream audience—from a purely musical perspective, the highlight is a virtuoso steel-guitar jam by Barbara Mandrell of all people, displaying a proficiency that was seldom visible on her early-'80s variety show. The special ends with a visit by Billy Graham, who, instead of turning to Scripture, uses a story by the 19th century writer Bret Harte to address the meaning of Christmas, and seeing the famous evangelist in a more or less secular context reveals just how effective a speaker he can be.

While the 1976 special was filmed at Cash's farm with no audience, the one that followed a year later was shot at a theater in Nashville, and while the musical agenda is basically the same, the intensity level is much higher. The presence of an audience has something to do with it, but the spark is as much a function of the guests. In addition to the returning

Clark (with whom Cash performs a medley of Gene Autry Christmas songs, including "Rudolph the Red-Nosed Reindeer"), Cash welcomes three of his Sun Records colleagues from the 1950s: Carl Perkins, Roy Orbison and Jerry Lee Lewis, who are all in peak form. Each contributes a fiery version of one of his signature hits (Lewis additionally does an ace "White Christmas") before all four team up to perform the traditional "This Train Is Bound for Glory," which Cash dedicates to the recently deceased Elvis Presley. The special ends with the all-star quartet (plus June Carter Cash) taking on the Christmas carols "Hark! The Herald Angels Sing" and "Children Go Where I Send Thee." Everything adds up to a juxtaposition of country and rock—and of the religious and the secular—that makes the special a microcosm of Cash's storied career.

The best (and worst) of 2007

THE BEST

1 *The Sopranos* (HBO)
Even before the final episode aired, the last half-season of David Chase's Garden State gangland saga embodied everything that was great about *The Sopranos*. Then came the Chase-directed "Made in America," which miraculously restored Journey's street cred and created the kind of zeitgeist moment that wasn't supposed to be possible anymore in a fragmented, 600-channel cable universe. Lots of TV dramas are compared to novels these days, but few others (maybe only *The Wire*) have achieved the scope and substance of literary fiction while painting between the lines of small-screen convention.

2 *Mad Men* (AMC)
Mere weeks after *The Sopranos* ended its run, David Chase protege Matthew Weiner offered up the next great TV drama. Drawing on the

stories of John Cheever and the films of Billy Wilder for inspiration, Weiner's chronicle of the advertising world in the early 1960s instantly established itself as one of the medium's greatest studies of class in American society. As Don Draper, creative director of the Sterling-Cooper agency, Jon Hamm displayed a George Clooney-caliber charisma that should earn him movie roles galore once the series has run its course (which hopefully won't be for awhile).

3 *Friday Night Lights* (NBC)

The second season, which began in October, has left some fans frustrated, but the 11 episodes that aired between January and April were close to perfect. Kyle Chandler and Connie Britton are never less than eerily believable as a married couple. and Britton and Aimee Teegarden have begun to edge out *Gilmore Girls'* Lauren Graham and Alexi Bledel as the mother-daughter pairing of the decade. On the field and off. it's the most cinematic program on network TV by a mile.

4 30 Rock (NBC)

With each successive episode, Tina Fey's inspired sitcom went further into glorious absurdity—and strayed further from the realm of backstage satire. The bittersweet romantic travails of Fey's Liz Lemon gave the series a strong, realistic female voice unlike anything else on the tube, while the supporting ensemble (led by Alec Baldwin) proved themselves the comedy equivalent of the '27 Yankees.

5 *South Park* (Comedy Central)

After ten years and 167 episodes, Trey Parker and Matt Stone's no-holds-barred cartoon continues to display stunning creativity. This year's "Imaginationland" three-parter, featuring literally hundreds of cameos by characters from fantasy fiction and children's books, was one of the series' finest moments.

6 *The Shield* (FX)

The penultimate season of FX's merciless police drama featured some of the best (and most overlooked) TV acting of the year courtesy of Michael Chiklis, Walton Goggins, CCH Pounder and guest star Franka Potente (Forest Whitaker, in a brief reprise of his searing role from last year, wasn't too bad either).

7 *Curb Your Enthusiasm* (HBO)

Larry David's real-life divorce got his creative juices flowing like the Mississippi. After limping over the finish line of its fifth season in 2005, *Curb* was on fire this year, in no small part thanks to the inspired addition of J.B. Smoove to David's gallery of sidekicks.

8 *Battlestar Galactica* (Sci Fi)

BSG's hard left run into the realm of Cylon mysticism could have been a disaster, but it quickly built to the series' most gobsmacking cliffhanger yet (no small feat for a program where each season has improbably ended on a more shocking note than the last).

THE WORST

1 *Big Shots* (ABC)

For fans of *The West Wing, Alias* and *The Practice* who were psyched to see Joshua Malina, Michael Vartan and Dylan McDermot return to TV, this deadly dull dramedy about rich assholes was a painful reminder about why we should be careful what we ask for.

2 *The Tudors* (Showtime)

Casting Jonathan Rhys-Myers as a rock-star version of Henry VIII was an inspired move (the much-married king didn't blimp out until late in life), but there's really no excuse for decadence being this dull.

3 *Private Practice* (ABC)

The *Grey's Anatomy* spinoff magnifies its big sister's flaws by a factor of ten—and then adds insult to injury by wasting a cast loaded with talented TV veterans.

Final grade: The general mediocrity of the networks' fall lineups was frustrating to say the least—for the first time in years, the fall brought a measly two new shows worth getting excited about (*Chuck* and *Reaper*), which also happened to be eerily similar to each other. Between the slim pickings and the uncertainty created by the writers' strike, 2007 would qualify as an off year for television…if not, that is, for the summer arrival of *Mad Men* and the revitalization of *Lost* and *Curb Your Enthusiasm*, both of which had been starting to go in circles. After starting strong in 2006, *30 Rock* and *Friday Night Lights* really came into their own during the winter and spring, establishing themselves as modern classics in the making. Cable's FX shored up its status as a source of quality trash with *Dirt* and *Damages*, while David Milch's beyond-gonzo *John From Cincinnati* and the explicit relationship drama *Tell Me You Love Me* revealed that HBO is unafraid to take chances and avoid the formulaic in its pursuit of a successor to *The Sopranos*.

2008

The Wire
The brilliant chronicle of urban life begins its knockout final season.

The lavish praise heaped on season four of *The Wire* was the sort that can go to some artists' heads, and that causes others to crumble under the pressure of audience expectations. But it's always been obvious that the devastating drama created by former Baltimore *Sun* reporter David Simon is the work of a supremely confident team. As such, the first seven episodes of the final season, which begins Sunday 6 on HBO, feel as if they were created in a vacuum: They seem entirely unaffected by previous responses to the series, and all exemplify *The Wire* at its best. In other words, they're seven of the best hours of television that have ever been produced.

The aforementioned vacuum only encompasses the reactions of critics and fans, of course, since what makes *The Wire* brilliant is its honest reflection of city life and Simon's willingness to take a stand on what he thinks is wrong with society. Though the urban plague of guns and drugs has been among the chief topics every season, Simon has also used the series as a platform for muckraking exposés of municipal politics, public education and the disappearance of middle-class jobs from American cities. In the final season, he addresses the role of the media, using a fictionalized version of the *Sun* to explore how buyouts and budget cuts have had a devastating effect on journalists to comfort the afflicted and afflict the comfortable (as the industry maxim goes) at a local level.

The action at the *Sun* centers on a trio of new characters, most notably the paper's burnt-out city editor, Augustus Thompson (*Homocide: Life on the Street*'s Clark Johnson, who also directed *The Wire's* 2002 series premiere), and Scott Templeton (Tom McCarthy), a reporter who is beloved by the bosses yet might be a preppy Jayson Blair. Their addition to a roster of characters that has grown every season may worry fans hoping to see plenty of their favorites before the series leaves the air, and it's true that a few mainstays are nowhere to be found. Some fans, however, may prefer this season to the previous one thanks to the large role played by Jimmy McNulty (Dominic West), the bad-boy police detective whose drunken misbehavior has long provided the grim series with welcome comic relief but who largely vanished into the background during season four.

When *The Wire* left off, McNulty—who had decided he could do the most good by wearing a uniform and walking a beat—opted to go plainclothes again to help investigate the deaths of nearly two dozen men whose corpses were boarded up in abandoned row houses by Snoop (Felicia Pearson) and Chris (Gbenga Akinnagbe), the chief lieutenants of rising drug boss Marlo Stanfield (Jamie Hector). As the story resumes, the Baltimore PD, like the *Sun,* is undergoing drastic budget cuts that are reducing its ability to fulfill its primary mission. McNulty, apoplectic that the brass would end an investigation into 22 murders, soon starts doctoring evidence so that the deaths of homeless men appear to be the work of the sort of serial killer that makes the press wet its collective pants.

With prodigious dexterity, Simon and his collaborators (including former Baltimore cop Ed Burns and novelists Richard Price, George Pelecanos and Dennis Lehane) connect the story of McNulty's big lie to plots from previous seasons, including the constant horse-trading of mayor Tommy Carcetti (Aidan Gillen) and a couple of threads that some fans may be surprised to see more of. The connections that are drawn both lend a sense of unity to the entire series and increase the depth and believability of Simon's Baltimore, which can now hold its own against the most detailed fictional worlds in any medium. Three of the four youngsters whose stories drove the previous season appear in the early episodes, and their status (as well as that of Bubbles, the genial snitch played by Andre Royo) provides no small amount of pathos. The main emotion that the new season elicits, however, is righteous indignation: It's impossible to repress a sense of outrage that institutions such as the police and the *Sun* could fall into such disrepair. It remains to be seen whether *The Wire* will inspire anyone to change the world, but there's no doubt that it has changed the face of television and will prompt others to expand the horizons of the medium for decades to come.

The Gates

Credited to four directors (including the *Grey Gardens* team of Albert Maysles and the late David Maysles), this chronicle of Christo and Jeanne-Claude's Central Park magnum opus—which used 3/4 as much steel as the Eiffel Tower—is fascinating and frustrating by turns. The best part comes a few minutes into the film, which marks the third anniversary of the project, when attorney Theodore W. Kheel's account of meeting the artists in 1979 suddenly transforms into a flashback. Believing that "creation is as much a part of the final product as the work of art" (in Kheel's words), Christo and Jeanne-Claude arranged for the Maysles brothers to document their original pitch to then-Parks Commissioner Gordon Davis when New York was just starting to emerge from the long funk that held sway over the city in the 1970s.

Despite Christo's belief in recording every stage of his process, the '70s sequence is the only time *The Gates* goes deep behind the scenes: Most of the film consists of semicandid footage of New Yorkers taking in the finished project during the two weeks it was in place in February 2005. While the archival material is thoroughly fascinating (it's wild to see Koch-era politicians reacting suspiciously to Christo's plan to self-finance the project), brief glimpses of massive bolts of fabric in a Queens warehouse, and of Mayor Bloomberg palling around with the artists offer hints at how much richer the film could have been with a greater focus on the run-up to the installation. Albert Maysles and the other directors obviously hoped to capture the impact of Christo and Jeanne Claude'a project for those who couldn't be there, but the effect is like trying to do justice to the *Mona Lisa* with a postage stamp.

John Adams
Paul Giamatti dazzles as the prickliest of the founding fathers.

No matter how many times you see the credits sequence for *John Adams,* it's almost impossible to avoid getting goose bumps from the montage of Revolutionary War-era flags that introduces HBO's superb miniseries based on David McCullough's 2001 biography of the second President. The credits quickly establish a vivid you-are-there sense of immediacy that is one of this epic's two great strengths. The other is the magnificent performance by Paul Giamatti, who fully embodies the passion, intellect and chutzpah for which Adams is famous, and who makes it clear that those qualities—which Adams himself admitted rendered him obnoxious and unpopular—always served the cause of American independence rather than the politician's own ego.

Screenwriter Kirk Ellis has skillfully isolated the most cinematic moments in McCullough's sprawling book: More than one of the seven episodes is built around events that McCullough described in just a page or two. The first installment (one of two episodes broadcast on Sunday 16) is an electrifying piece of courtroom drama, while the second could well be the finest dramatization ever produced of the events that culminated in the Declaration of Independence. We meet Adams in 1770, when he's a 35-year-old lawyer who, hoping to vault beyond his humble origins, has recently moved from the boonies to Boston with his wife, Abigail (Laura Linney), and their young children. Both to build his reputation and because no one else will take the case, he agrees to defend the British soldiers charged with murder in the Boston Massacre. He thereby earns a rep for impartiality that leads his cousin Samuel Adams (Danny Huston) to persuade the attorney to begin a political career that takes him first to Philadelphia and then to the global stage.

Adams clearly supports the American cause from the beginning ("Massachusetts is my country," he responds when offered a plum job in the British Admiralty court), but no one can blame him for initially harboring doubts about the movement: Many Boston patriots come off as uncouth louts, and the wealthy John Hancock (Justin Theroux) appalls Adams by cheerfully goading a mob into giving a tax collector the tar-and-feathers treatment (which director Tom Hooper presents with the same graphic, almost loving detail that he showed a man being drawn and quartered in 2005's, *Elizabeth I*). After Adams devotes himself fully to independence and becomes a delegate to the Continental Congress, he's frustrated by bureaucracy until Benjamin Franklin (Tom Wilkinson) persuades him that Virginia's Thomas Jefferson (Stephen Dillane) and GeorgeWashington (David Morse), unlike the other Southern delegates, share his intellectual temperament. As engrossing as the first episode may be, it's at Independence Hall that *John Adams* really becomes something special. Wilkinson and Morse masterfully humanize characters who are as iconic as Moses and Jesus, while Dillane shrewdly plays Jefferson—later Adams's great rival—as both modest and inscrutable,

It's also in Philadelphia that Giamatti's performance comes together and Adams emerges as a crusty New Englander with a very un-Yankee lack of reserve. His legendary irascibility appears as he locks horns with stubborn South Carolina delegate Edward Rutledge (Clancy O'Connor)

and Pennsylvania's John Dickinson, a Quaker who favored appeasement (and who, thanks to a brilliant turn by Zeljko Ivanek, emerges as a tragic but dignified figure). Adams's stint in Philadelphia is intercut with scenes in which his wife endures a smallpox epidemic and British assaults on Massachusetts, and it's soon apparent that Linney' s best scenes are those without Giamatti: Abigail's perspective on daily life during the Revolutionary War is invaluable (ditto her take on Europe in the fourth episode), but when John and Abigail are together, their dialogue quickly grows too expository (and while their children prove that the Adamses did, in fact, have sex, the perpetual formality of their relationship makes it seem uncharacteristic when we see them do the deed in their fifties).

With the third episode, the miniseries focuses on aspects of Adams's life that get short shrift in U.S. history classes, most notably his long diplomatic service in Europe. Although a sea battle worthy of a Patrick O'Brian novel vividly communicates the hazards of 18th-century travel, the depiction of Adams's European years doesn't convey the full magnitude of the risks he took on behalf of his country. Nonetheless, there are few dramatic productions in any medium that have done a better job of illustrating the challenges America faced as a young nation—or of bringing life to men and women who often seem too distant and exalted for anyone to identify with.

The Night James Brown Saved Boston

Airing on the 40th anniversary of the events it chronicles, this special VH1 Rock Doc tells the story of how the Godfather of Soul cast a ray of light during one of America's darkest moments. On April 4, 1968, Dr. Martin Luther King Jr. was assassinated in Memphis; as the news spread, riots quickly swept through Baltimore, D.C., Newark and dozens of other cities. Boston started to burn as well, before a hastily arranged broadcast on the local PBS station of Brown's long-scheduled Boston Garden concert on April 5 brought peace to the city.

Although *Night* follows the classic talking-head format, it's easy to discern the outlines of a feature film waiting to be made—the protagonist would be Tom Atkins, a young African-American Harvard Law student and city councilman who came up with the idea and pitched it to newly elected mayor Kevin White. White and Atkins are both candid and engaging as they recount the surreal process of arranging the broadcast, which was planned without Brown's knowledge. The performance footage is as fascinating for the presentation as it is for Brown's legendary moves: The TV announcer introduces "Negro singer Jimmy Brown and his group," while audience members rushing the stage throughout the show keep the police nervous and force Brown to mediate between the cops and the crowd.

Over the past four decades, Dr. King has become so iconic that it's hard to imagine the impact of his death if you didn't experience the aftermath yourself. In the film, Princeton's Dr. Cornel West offers a metaphor that beautifully encapsulates King's significance and the tribute Brown offered from the stage: April 4, 1968, says West, is the day America lost its best friend.

Elvis Mitchell: Under the Influence

By pure coincidence, the first two episodes of public-radio correspondent and former *New York Times* film critic Elvis Mitchell's new one-guest talk show are both major scoops: The premiere features director-actor Sydney Pollack, who died in May, and the second episode offers a rare extended talk with Bill Murray, who has been the subject of much gossip since his wife's recent no-holds-barred divorce petition.

The credit sequence suggests that Mitchell's ego will be a bigger factor than is actually the case—he's clearly a little uncomfortable on camera, so the guests do most of the talking. Pollack and Murray basically speak uninterrupted for 30 minutes each, and the insight provided into their personalities and work is fairly stunning. Pollack, a multiple Oscar winner, surprisingly adopts a defensive stance against "intelligentsia" who say he wasted his career directing nothing but star vehicles. It's obvious his true passion was for acting, and while many won't need his lecture on the history of the Method, the chance to watch someone like Pollack ramble on is a big part of what makes *Under the Influence* so enjoyable.

The Murray interview stresses the *influence* element of the title, as the comic discusses his favorite actors at length (including the Marx Brothers, Barbara Stanwyck and William Holden), with a heavy focus on their physical technique. When talking about collaborators, he offers sincere but iconoclastic tributes to their skill and professionalism (had Murray entered the business at the same time as *Tootsie* ghostwriter Elaine May, "I would have chained her to a typewriter and made love to her every four hours just to keep her going"), instead of puffy platitudes. Future installments will feature Laurence Fishburne and Quentin Tarantino, and watching them be themselves with Mitchell promises to be every bit as absorbing.

Mad Men—Season One [DVD]

Although the regular DVD edition of *Mad Men's* superb first season looks predictably terrific, it nonetheless pales next to the Blu-ray version, which offers countless vivid examples of how ultra-high-resolution imagery is adding fresh creative depth to dramatic journalism. It's not just that we can now read all the copy in the 1960 *Playboy* VW ad that vexes Don Draper (Jon Hamm), creative director at the Sterling Cooper agency, on his train from Ossining. Now, every nuance of Hamm's expressions can be seen, even in long and medium shots in which he's the farthest actor from the camera. TV is often said to be a writer's medium above all, and such scenes reveal how the extra picture depth can allow them to call more thoroughly on the full range of an actor's talent, making it easier for the scribe to follow the "show, don't tell" dictum.

Naturally, the high-res discs are also very kind to the series's amazing production design: The colors have a sumptuous pop to them that increases the show's resemblance to the 1950s and '60s films that inspired creator Matthew Weiner. The audio mix, too, reveals fresh subtleties that were often imperceptible on television. The eternal conflict between Cablevision and Time Warner Cable essentially made *Mad Men* broadcasts unavailable in HD within the five boroughs, and the visual lushness, which makes Weiner's world seem all the more complete, will leave even the devoted feeling like they're watching the series for the first time.

The Shield
The grittiest cop show on cable gets ready to call it a day.

Apart from *WWE Raw*, there's nothing else on TV with story lines as byzantine as those on *The Shield*. When we last saw corrupt but well-intentioned LAPD officer Vic Mackey (Michael Chiklis), he'd just formed an awkward alliance with longtime foe Councilman David Aceveda (Benito Martinez) to thwart an evil politician's partnership with a Mexican drug cartel—and to take down Mackey's rogue protege Shane Vendrell (Walton Goggins) while they're at it.

This season, Vendrell stirs up trouble with a host of bad guys from the series's early days (when Vic was more explicitly corrupt), setting up a fake—or is it?—street war between Mexican and Armenian gangs. Dominating the new season's early episodes, this setup seems likely to pave the way for the series's ultimate resolution. Still, *The Shield* is always at its best when it favors character over plot, and the complicated scheming in the premiere ensures that even the most devoted fans will scratch their heads a few times.

Over the years, the series has established itself as a destination for filmmakers eager to sharpen their skills by working on a tight schedule (David Mamet, Frank Darabont), and for actors seeking meaty, image-changing roles (Glenn Close, Forest Whitaker and, most memorably, comedian Anthony Anderson). The final season takes it easy on the big names and lets the core cast members take an extended final bow doing what their characters do best. On the plus side, this means we get ace comic relief from David Marciano as Detective Steve Billings, a skirt-chasing dullard always on the lookout for ways to scam the city, who is again partnered with "Dutch" Wagenbach (Jay Karnes), another wanna-be player who can turn even the most mundane shooting incident into a serial-killer investigation.

In addition to giving women writers and directors a lot more opportunities than many TV dramas do, *The Shield* has always been notable for its strong female characters, and Catherine Dent (as officer Danielle Sofer, the mother of Vic's illegitimate kid) and CCH Pounder (as Captain Claudette Wyms, the station commander, who continues to suffer from lupus) are wisely being worked into the approaching climax. Unfortunately, creator Shawn Ryan 's desire to let the regulars strut their stuff while addressing as much unfinished business as possible backfires by highlighting the series's unfortunate nepotistic tendencies. Ryan's wife, Cathy Cahlin Ryan, plays Vic's wife. Corrine, and Chiklis's real-life daughter, Autumn, portrays Vic's adolescent daughter, Cassidy. Neither is a particularly strong actor (though Ryan has her moments), and a subplot about the increasingly rebellious Cassidy investigating her dad's secrets and starting to dabble in alcohol feels like a waste of time.

Much of this probably makes *The Shield'* s final season sound like a disappointment, but it's not. Rather, it's an extremely representative season, featuring as much of the good as the bad. The series has always had one of TV's best ensemble casts, and the brinkmanship among Vic, Shane and their cohort Ronnie (David Rees Snell) continues to yield a remarkably subtle and insightful study in alpha-male pack behavior. *The Shield* has never avoided social consciousness, but, as in the work of L.A. crime novelist James Ellroy, it's generally deployed as a plot device rather than to stir moral indignation, as on *The Wire.* At a time when so much television is aiming for the heights and succeeding—it might be easy to underrate *The Shield* for aspiring merely to the level of first-rank crime fiction. But that's a mark plenty of popular shows (such as the entire *CSI* franchise) consistently fail to hit. One sincerely hopes that Chiklis's first-season Emmy doesn't turn out to be his highest achievement; if he spends the rest of his career hollering, "It's clobberin' time!," that'd be a crying shame.

Gimme shelter
Sanctuary creates a familiar world unlike anything you've seen.

The first episode of the new Sci Fi Channel drama, *Sanctuary,* begins with what appears to be an aerial tracking shot of Manhattan at night, in which the camera pulls back over the East River and into Williamsburg, coming to a rest in a street of drab buildings inhabited by Polish immigrants. But as soon as a police car pulls into view, the logos and uniforms suggest the city may not be New York after all.

In movies, such shots are typically created via green screens and computer animation, but on *Sanctuary* the technique extends to mundane sets such as bedrooms, subway tunnels and police stations (like an urban *300).* Set in a crumbling, nameless metropolis that evokes director Christopher Nolan's take on Gotham City, *Sanctuary* unfolds from the POV of Dr. Will Zimmerman (Robin Dunne), a forensic shrink recruited by the enigmatic Dr. Helen Magnus (Amanda Tapping of *Stargate: SG-1* and *Stargate Atlantis)* as her assistant on a mind-bending project. Magnus runs the Sanctuary, a facility for mythological creatures and assorted monsters that live among us in secret, which serves as part shelter, part prison and part mental hospital. Other cast members include Emilie Ullerup as Magnus's daughter Ashley, who hunts monsters in the field for her mother, and Christopher Heyerdahl as John Druitt, a homicidal ex-lover of Magnus with a secret that is one of the series' loopiest elements.

"Every planet that we went to in the *Stargate* universe looked like British Columbia," says creator Damian Kindler, who worked with Tapping on both *Stargate* shows. "With camera systems and visual effects being what they are now, we can go further. If this show had been made five years ago, it would not be as cool."

In the mid-'90s, the syndicated *Babylon 5* used a few virtual sets, but *B5*'s deep-space setting constantly reminded the audience that the backdrops were projected. By using green-screen effects to create ordinary sets as well as elaborate fantasy tableaux, suspension of disbelief is a whole lot easier.

"Having done hard-core sci-fi alien spaceship shows—which are really fun, mind you—I realize that you're cutting off part of your nose to spite your face because there's a whole section of people who will never give a damn about a spaceship show," says Kindler. "Shows that transcend cult status and become a bit more mainstream tend to have a foot in reality, a foot in the here and now, and then a license to go further."

Sanctuary originated in 2007 as a series of three short online films that served as a de facto pilot and were reshot and expanded to make the first episode. After developing a warm working relationship with Tapping on the *Stargate* shows, Kindler persuaded the actor to abandon her series-regular slot on *Atlantis* in favor of periodic guest appearances (she also agreed to be an executive producer of *Sanctuary*).

"I was asked to do season five of *Atlantis,* and I didn't know at that point if *Sanctuary* would be picked up for television," Tapping said, speaking from a studio lot in Vancouver. "I took a massive leap of faith. I thought, if I sign on for *Atlantis,* basically I'm killing *Sanctuary,* and I just have to take the chance. Now that *Atlantis* has been canceled, I know I made the right decision." (Now airing Fridays at 10pm on SciFi, *Atlantis* will broadcast its final episode in January.)

"Nobody can make science gobbledygook sound more entertaining than Amanda," says Kindler. "At the same time, we wanted to make sure she didn't sound like her character on *Stargate*. There was a pressure to take her into places where she hadn't been before, and we did. She gets to show a sexiness and freedom and mystery and power that she never had as Carter on *Stargate*. It was a challenge to do justice to how far she wanted to take things." The net result is a series that takes TV's genre boundaries and impressively renders them fluid. "A lot of people watch TV so they can escape to a version of the world they want to see, not a version they know doesn't exist," says Kindler. "We hope *Sanctuary* plays with those preconceptions. It's not so cut-and-dried; it's not saying this is real and this definitely isn't. It's saying, this is kind of fun. It's somewhere in between."

Slant Magazine/The House Next Door

Wrong Is Right: The Political Jiu-Jitsu of Battlestar Galactica
BY ANDREW JOHNSTON ON DECEMBER 15, 2006

The first episodes of *Battlestar Galactica*'s third season revised the text displayed during the opening credits, thereby distilling the series's premise down to its absolute basics: "The Human Race—Far from Home—Fighting for Survival." In other words, these folks live thousands of lightyears away yet inexplicably worship the Greco-Roman pantheon and are at war with a genocidally-inclined artificial species of their own creation...but *they're us*.

Of course, in saying that, executive producers Ronald D. Moore and David Eick and their creative team are equating the human species in general with the United States, the better to traffic in allegories about post-9/11 America, BSG's stock-in-trade ever since the 2003 pilot miniseries. From both a creative and commercial standpoint, that's a dicey proposition. Given how polarized the U.S. and the world have become since 9/11, any series that tackles the detention and torture of enemy combatants or the suppression of civil rights in a time of national crisis is going to either alienate half its audience or else cling to a milquetoast middleground and come off as either wishy-washy or opportunistic. But Moore and Eick devised an ingenious third option: on *BSG*, they've mastered a form of political jiu-jitsu, coming up with plots that, within the context of the story, at least—put liberal viewers in a position where they're forced to agree with the Fox News crowd and, alternately, make Dittoheads see things through the eyes of Daily Kos readers.

Full disclosure: My personal politics are half Socialist and half Libertarian; by default, given the either/or nature of the American system, I'm what most people would call an extremely liberal Democrat. As such, I can only guess how effective *BSG* is at making right-wingers see the world through liberal eyes. I'm in awe of how Moore and Eick persuaded me to agree, for example, that there are circumstances under which abortion should be banned (via "The Captain's Hand"), but the episodes that seem constructed to make conservatives understand an opposing viewpoint strike me as politically facile (from my perspective, they're preaching to the converted). For that reason, I wonder if episodes like "Hand" seem as thuddingly obvious to those on the right.

With that caveat in mind, let's go back in time to the first appearance of Moore and Eick's jiu-jitsu: the series's third episode, "Bastille Day," which introduced Tom Zarek (Richard Hatch), the radical Saggitron native who has become the show's most useful political figure—his radical politics allow the writers to use him as a hero or villan depending on plot requirements, in addition to articulating arguments that don't quite fit in the mouths of any of the principal characters. In his first appearance, Zarek—then locked up on the same prison ship upon which was being transported when the Cylons first attacked—was presented as a combination of Simón Bólivar, Nelson Mandela and Timothy McVeigh. We learned that the ever-rebellious Apollo (Jamie Bamber) was a big Zarek fan back in his college days. The revelation that Zarek's book was flat-out censored by the authorities provided a intriguing hint that humankind's governing document, the Articles of Colonization, might not resemble the U.S. Constitution as closely as we thought.

Zarek's not in prison for his words, however, but for his actions: though we don't learn the details, it's suggested that Zarek killed an unspecified number of people in an Oklahoma City-type attack. Throughout the episode, Apollo acts like a conservative stereotype of simpering liberals who would rather protect abstract notions of fairness than defend peaceful citizens against terrorists. He travels to Zarek's galley hoping to recruit him and other convicts for a work gang—but his offer to reduce sentences in exchange for hard labor is rebuffed, a mass uprising ensues, and he ends up being imprisoned himself. Zarek holds Lee and other *Galactica* crewmembers as hostages, saying he'll only release them after the resignation of Laura Roslin, who he sees as an illegitimate leader (even though she was elevated to the presidency according to rules laid out in the Articles). Secretly, though, Zarek wants to use the standoff to engineer a bloody showdown between prisoners and the Galactica's marines in the hope of bringing down Roslin and getting publicity that will help him reestablish a power base; so what if a few dozen innocents die in the process? Conservative viewers are given a classic opportunity to say "I told you so!", while liberals are faced with the implication that the Dick Cheney/Alberto Gonzalez wiretapping, rendition-approving, it's-abuse-not-torture crowd might have a point.

But the situation reverses itself again when Apollo quashes Zarek's rebellion by offering to use his clout with Commander Adama (Edward James Olmos) and President Roslin (Mary McDonnell) to force them to stick to a constitutionally-mandated election timetable and succession procedure. For a liberal idealist, this seems a happy ending in which diplomacy and respect for the letter of the Constitution carries the day. For those on the other side, the ending probably just seemed like a setup for the return of a really juicy villain. This could be construed as an argument in favor of negotiating with terrorists, but the desperate situation—the prisoners were needed to help harvest ice needed to replenish the fleet's rapidly-dwindling water supply—allows the writers to avoid taking a firm stance on either side of the issue.

If Zarek is often *BSG*'s ultimate conservative bogeyman, his flipside would have to be Saul Tigh (Michael Hogan), who has come to symbolize authoritarian force. This aspect of the character was most prominent at the start of season two, in the story arc where Adama was sidelined after an assassination and Tigh took command of the fleet and declared martial law. Notwithstanding his raging alcoholism, Tigh has always been *BSG*'s poster boy for law-and-order conservatism. His initial response to the attempt on Adama's life—a dramatic increase in military discipline—may seem logical, but his tenure as fleet commander soon turns into a fiasco thanks to his impulsiveness and drinking. After he officially declares martial law, a poorly-trained solder kills several civilians while trying to suppress a riot; when Adama awakes from his coma, the fleet is on the verge of chaos. To those who agree with Tigh's iron-fisted approach to crisis management, his failure may have played as a legitimate tragedy. But to those who think Tigh's methodology has had toxic effects on American life when applied by the Cheney gang, the sense of sadness comes not from Tigh's personal collapse, but from the inevitability of chaos ensuing from his crackdown on liberty (it's tempting for those on the left to gloat when such tactics backfire, but the body count makes it difficult).

Fixing the political position of any arc, episode or individual character is not easy, because on *BSG,* no element is ever static. By the start of Season Three, for example, Zarek—who had become Vice President of the Twelve Colonies—had morphed into somebody conservatives could admire as an exemplar of principled patriotism, for his unilateral refusal to collaborate with the Cylons. Tigh, on the other hand, seemed to skew leftward as season two progressed, perhaps in response to the Galactica's first encounter with the Battlestar Pegasus (in "Pegasus" and "Resurrection Ship Part 1 & 2"), commanded by the ultra-authoritarian Admiral Caine (Michelle Forbes), who dehumanized her troops.

Liberals and conservatives alike root for the human fleet, and in so doing, root for America's best interests, whatever they consider those to be. But the series goes out of its way to complicate one's sympathies. For instance, in the season two finale when Tigh attempted to steal the presidential election to ensure the re-election of Laura Roslin over her rival Baltar (James Callis), a secret Cylon mole and collaborator, he was unknowingly acting on behalf of humankind's best interests. The inarguable rightness of Tigh's Chicago-style electioneering put liberal viewers in an awkward position. The Supreme Court-decided outcome of the 2000 U.S. Presidential election recommitted Democrats to the sanctity of the one-man, one-vote paradigm, and reinforced their perception of the Republican Party as unrepentant dirty tricksters who would go the extra mile to suppress or disqualify ballots in the name of victory. Yet in identifying with the humans—who in some sense represent American citizens—liberal viewers found themselves cheering for Baltar to get screwed in much the same way they believe Al Gore got screwed by Team Bush. At the same time, G.O.P. voters who believed the 2000 election was a case of the end justifying the means might have found themselves thinking that this episode did a better job of justifying their side through allegory than Team Bush ever did in news reports.

The theft of the election was shot down by Adama and Felix Gaeta (Alessandro Juliani), two of the series's most sympathetic characters, who briefly became "bad guys" for putting an end to the scheme and unknowingly signing the death warrants of thousands of colonists who would perish at Cylon hands on New Caprica a year later (rough cuts of "Collaborators" sent to the press listed the number of survivors after the evacuation of New Caprica as 36,592, which was bumped up to 41,435 when the episode aired). On New Caprica, Tigh became the leader of the resistance against the Cylon occupiers and their human proxies; this led him to embrace tactics favored by groups like the PLO and Hamas and Iraqi insurgents in our world—including suicide bombing. Tigh's innate appeal to conservatives forced them to view events through the eyes of political movements they're inclined to demonize. (That said, this particular trope was irksome from a common sense standpoint: when your race has less than 20,000 women of child-bearing age left alive, suicide bombing, like abortion, is not a good idea.)

Of the humans who made it off New Caprica alive, no one suffered more than Tigh, who lost an eye (unlike Odin, he hasn't received wisdom in exchange—not yet, anyway) and killed his own wife as punishment for her collaboration with the Cylons. But he soon lost the sympathy of liberal viewers by leading a "star chamber" court that tried perceived collaborators on the basis of flimsy evidence and gave the accused little opportunity to defend themselves. The parallels to the Bush administration's limits on the ability of accused terrorists to have their day in court were clear—perhaps transparent. It seems clear that the writers wanted to show conservative viewers the folly of a democratic society restricting legal rights of those held and charged as enemies of the state. If any were led to reconsider their opinions of the Abu Ghraib scandal and the conditions at Guantanamo Bay, I can hardly complain. As an opponent of the Bush administration's interpretation of the Constitution, though, the episode seemed groaningly obvious—especially since it was revealed that the nearly-executed Gaeta, formerly Baltar's aide, was the mole who saved humanity by leaking the Cylon plans. (The script treated this as a big surprise, but there were no other logical candidates, and the preceding episodes were loaded with broad hints.) This time, it was liberals who were left smacking their foreheads at the obviousness of the message, although the progressives and radicals among the characters were hardly let off the hook—the executions and trials (some as brief as Admiral Caine's famous two-second courts-martial) were ordered by Zarek, who briefly succeeded Baltar as president, and Everyman deck chief Galen Tyrol (whose activist bona fides were proven when Moore and Eick had him deliver a speech cribbed from 1960s UC Berkeley campus activist Mario Savio in the season-two finale) sat alongside Tigh on the bench at the kangaroo court.

In season three, *BSG*'s focus has shifted more to religion and philosophy, but political allegory remains a core component of of the series's DNA. Production leadtimes and Sci Fi's scheduling policies prevent the series from literally ripping stories from the headlines as the *Law & Order* shows do, but that's undoubtedly for the best; if the goal is to make people rethink their fundamental assumptions, broad hypothetical scenarios are better than specific questions. Besides, neither a diminished Cylon threat (courtesy of the virus that's floating around out there) or even the discovery of Earth is going to get all of the colonists to agree on the right way to solve any given problem, because they're us.

Andrew Johnston is the television critic for Time Out New York.

Dusty Springfield: The Simpsons Movie
BY ANDREW JOHNSTON ON JULY 27, 2007

Has there ever been a more what-you-see-is-what-you-get title than *The Simpsons Movie*? It's the last word that's the key: The brain trust behind the series (11 of its writers are credited with the screenplay) have emphasized theatrical presentation above all, even building a curtain-raising short (starring Itchy and Scratchy, natch) into the feature. The opening gimmick allows for a change in aspect ratio (from 1.85:1) to the Cinemascope range (2.35:1) that's probably the most effective use of such a trick since *Galaxy Quest*. From there on, there's seldom a scene that fails to make use of the wide canvas the creators have allowed themselves. The visual upgrade (among other things, the linework is cleaner and more fluid than it's ever been on the series) is one of the main reasons I'd strongly encourage anyone inclined to see the film to do so on its opening weekend with the largest crowd possible.

The film's most unique quality is how it offers, pretty much for the first time ever, the chance to see how the series's brand of humor goes over with a big audience. The first 15 minutes are basically a series of vignettes, and for anyone who's spent the better part of their life watching the series, the communal response to the film's first gags involving Milhous, Abe Simpson, Ned Flanders, Monty Burns, et al. is pretty close to exhilarating (ditto reaction to a couple of priceless moments that could never pass Fox Standards & Practices, which I wouldn't dream of spoiling). Seeing the movie at home could never come remotely close to matching the experience.

The biggest problem is that the film peaks before the plot really kicks in. The story itself is awfully similar to that of a great many episodes, and it makes the deadly mistake of separating the Simpson clan from their fellow Springfieldians for the bulk of the running time. And the familiar nature of the plot only serves to underscore a myriad of baffling creative decisions: Lisa and Marge get virtually nothing to do, there are no musical numbers to speak of, and loads of mainstay characters barely appear, with major fan favorites such as Patty and Selma, Principal Skinner, Ralph Wiggum and Krusty the Klown among the near-absentees. Also peculiar is the lack of pop culture references (the series has never been afraid to date itself) and the decision to begin the movie with an ultratopical gag and then avoid such humor thereafter.

If a *Simpsons* movie absolutely had to be made, it should have happened prior to 1998—in other words, before the death of Phil Hartman, whose Lionel Hutz and Troy McClure, two characters with enormous potential to help drive a plot that could remain interesting for seventy-some-odd minutes (the running time minus credits). And if the writers were going to take another trip to a creative well they've visited time and again over the years, they'd have been much better off serving up an epic Bart vs. Sideshow Bob confrontation than a predictable Homer-centric plot. The end credits inevitably include a sequel tease (the manner in which it's done is one of the film's few real eye-rollers, unfortunately), and the producers may well rectify some of their omissions if the charcters make another trip to the big screen. Will they get the chance? *The Simpsons Movie* isn't bad, but neither is it good enough, I suspect, to convince a lot of people to buy the proverbial cow after seventeen and a half years of getting the milk for free.

David vs. David vs. David
or *Which Is the Greatest TV Drama Ever, Simon's The Wire, Milch's Deadwood, or Chase's The Sopranos?*
BY ANDREW JOHNSTON, ALAN SEPINWALL AND MATT ZOLLER SEITZ ON MARCH 5, 2008

Editor's Note: *The views expressed in this podcast are those of the commenters, and do not necessarily reflect the official policies, positions, or opinions of The House Next Door.*

Below is a transcript of a roundtable audio discussion featuring *House* contributors Andrew Johnston (*Time Out New York*), Alan Sepinwall (*The Star-Ledger, What's Alan Watching*), and Matt Zoller Seitz (*The New York Times*).

Throwing Down

MZS: This is Matt Seitz. We're here at Joe Jr.'s restaurant at Sixth Avenue and 12th St. with Alan Sepinwall of *The Star-Ledger* of Newark and Andrew Johnston of *Time Out New York*. Andrew and Alan and I have decided to get together and talk about the greatest drama show on television, because at one point or another, all of us have declared a particular drama show to be the greatest dramatic series in the history of American television. I'll just start with my pick, which is *Deadwood*, and I think we'll go around the table.

AS: This is Alan, and my pick would be *The Wire*.

AJ: This is Andrew, and I'm arguing on behalf of *The Sopranos*.

MZS: OK, Alan, since *The Wire* is freshest in everybody's minds—and we're right next to a dish deposit bin, so watch out, folks, if you're wearing headphones—

AS: And be prepared, food will be served at some point—

MZS: —and it might turn into a Sergio Leone movie, with the loud eating. But anyway, Alan, you want to dive in?

AS: Sure. I like *The Wire* the best of the three. They're all amazing shows, but [*The Wire*] is the most consistent from beginning to end, and there's much less fluctuation in quality than I found in the other two. And I feel like it has more to offer in terms of comedy and action and drama and high culture and low culture. It can be all things to all viewers at different times.

MZS: I'm gonna throw down with *Deadwood*, because although it certainly doesn't pass the consistency-of-quality-over-time test—the highs were unbelievable and the lows were pretty low from scene to scene and episode to episode—but I thought for degree of difficulty, it wins in a walk. It works as a portrait of the West, as a look at America, as kind of a parable about how society is created. And also, just on every level—the acting; the complexity of the characterizations, even the small ones; the filmmaking; the atmosphere and everything else—it's doing more things and doing them better than any of these shows.

AJ: I'm going to start off by saying, really quickly, I guess, that I have an enormous amount of love for all three shows, and they're separated by about—I'm holding my fingers about less than a millimeter apart here—

MZS: Exactly.

AS: Yeah.

AJ: For me, *The Sopranos* is a tough choice, because the three shows deal with America in different ways. *Deadwood* is the past and the origin. *The Wire* is urban problems and just really big issues facing the country as a whole. And *The Sopranos* is really the more individual show, a personal show, the one that's really about the family in the modern era and in the society that's come about. It's easier to identify with in some ways, because you have mostly a single-viewpoint character, Tony, but of course, [series creator] David Chase doesn't really want you to identify with him, because you're always reminded ever so often that Tony's a really scummy gangster. One of the things that really distinguishes it from *The Wire*, Alan, is that sometimes it's definitely not an all-things-to-all-people kind of a show. It's a show where Chase, I think, critiques his audience. It's interesting that you were saying that being all things to all people is kind of a good thing about *The Wire*, because I find sometimes that, as much as I love *The Wire*, sometimes I find that—and I was talking about this with a friend of mine the other day—it really caters to viewer expectations much more than the other shows do. That's not necessarily a bad thing, but I find that of the three, it's the one that's most inclined to give the fans what they want.

MZS: I would amend that only to say that it pays much more attention to plot and delivering setups and payoffs, whereas *The Sopranos* and *Deadwood* were more willing to wander into an alley and hang out for awhile. And I thought that was a good thing, because I think atmospherically, *Deadwood* is the best of the three shows. Watching it, I feel that I am in another mental space, I'm in another time, another place. I get that with *The Sopranos* and *The Wire* some of the time, but not as often as I did with *Deadwood*, even when it wasn't firing on all cylinders.

AS: And I think that if [*Wire* creator] David Simon really wanted to give the fans what they wanted, then Omar would still be alive right now. I think what you're seeing, Andrew is—as Matt says—[*The Wire*] is more focused on plot. It's a slightly easier show to predict because it teaches you how to watch it—

MZS: That's true.

AS: —and by now, at the end of the fifth season, we understand where things are going and people on Matt's blog and on my blog, too, kind of thought Omar was gonna go, and was gonna be killed by somebody *like* Kenard.

MZS: True. Once they're conditioned to know the rhythms of the show, they're conditioned to expect the *right* outcome—

AS: Yeah.

MZS:—not necessarily the one that's gonna make them personally happy, but you know, the dramatically correct outcome.

AS: Yeah.

MZS: And I will say that all three of the shows were actually pretty good about that—

AS: —yeah—

MZS: —and whether or not they really surprised you, or whether they gave you what you expected or something unexpected, or if they did the David Chase double-fakeout, they all were definitely attuned to that, [and] after a while, you got a sense of what the world view of the show was, and if the show was not true to that, then you were disappointed.

AS: Yeah.

AJ: Yeah.

A Whole Organism

MZS: Talking about degree of difficulty, about the variety of things that a show does, one of the things that I appreciated so much about *Deadwood* was that, whereas *The Wire* is great at putting you in the moment, and *The Sopranos* did that, I think, as well, except when it was getting into Tony's dreams, what I loved about *Deadwood* was that you got the sense of an entire community *simultaneously*. You get a sense of the entire community with *The Wire*, certainly, and sometimes with *The Sopranos*. But [with *Deadwood*] you got the sense of [elements of] an entire organism functioning, sometimes at cross-purposes with each other, and also, sometimes, [of] people doing or saying things for a particular reason and not knowing why they did it, and having an effect other than the one that they intended. That happened constantly and consistently on that show in a way that felt very true to life for me.

AS: I would say it happens pretty consistently on *The Wire* as well, where you see how a decision that's made in city hall winds up affecting a kid in the eighth grade; how Herc the cop does something, doesn't even know what he's doing [and] destroys some other kid's life; things along that line. If it seems more like a whole organism on *Deadwood*, it's just because the show took place over about three square blocks, so it's very easy for Swearengen to stand on his balcony and see everything that's going on at the high and low ends of the town, whereas Carcetti has no idea what Bubbles' life is.

MZS: That's true, and maybe the caveat we should have thrown in at the beginning is, we know that we're comparing apples and oranges and pears here.

AS: Yes, yes.

AJ: Exactly, yes. On *The Sopranos*, I think the community is, in many ways, something that exists in the past. You're really aware of all of these connections that came from when [the characters] were all—when everybody's family was in the Italian neighborhoods of Newark before the riots of the '60s. And then it just fragmented, [with] people going to different suburban neighborhoods in New Jersey. You're aware of these things that happened in the past, like Tony having had the fling with Charmaine Bucco in high school, and that having an impact on all these relationships years later with Tony and Artie [Bucco] and the restaurant and all this stuff. There are all these references to this shared past that the characters have. It's far more fragmented in the present, which maybe keeps you from realizing that that element of community is there on the show. I was fortunate to have the experience of watching the entire run of *The Sopranos* from the beginning going into the final episode. When you watch the entire show over the course of about a month, these things really just, like, pop together.

MZS: And you did watch the entire show over the course of a month? All six seasons?

AJ: Yeah, yeah, yeah, yeah.

MZS: Wow.

AS: I'd imagine that put you in a very dark frame of mind by the end of it.

AJ: Kind of, yeah, kind of.

MZS: What you're reminding me of there is that *Deadwood* had that aspect as well, although it was not just happening in real time as you watched it. You saw a character's personality changing, sometimes in ways they weren't aware of. That's something that almost every character, even the small ones, had in common on *Deadwood*, whereas not so much on *The Sopranos*, and only in certain cases on *The Wire*.

AS: Well, I mean, the motto of *The Sopranos* is, "People don't change."

MZS: Exactly.

AJ: Yeah, yeah.

AS: That's one of its firm beliefs. So [*The Sopranos* and *Deadwood*] are working at cross-purposes. On *The Wire* you see that *some* people can change, but they have to work very hard to do so, within the strictures of the institutions they work and live in.

MZS: But one of the many things that all three of them have in common—and I'm discovering more similarities as we talk about them—is [that] they're sort of meditating on the idea of identity. Who are we, and how responsible are we for who we are? And to what degree can we change it? And under what circumstances? I think that's a big part of it.

AJ: Fundamentally—and I suppose we're supposed to be defending our own shows here—one of the things that appeals to me most about *The Wire* is its belief that under the right circumstances, people can change. In the penultimate episode, Bubbles' big scene at the AA meeting was probably one of the most moving things I've ever seen on television.

MZS: It was.

AS: Andre Royo is an amazing actor.

MZS: He is terrific. And of course, it probably goes without saying that one of the reasons [that scene] was so effective was because you had a five season build-up to that.

AS: Yes. They earned that, entirely.

MZS: They did. But you know, Andrew, I would have to say the same thing about *Deadwood*, only to an even more pronounced extreme. The thing that appeals to me personally—and ultimately I think we're talking about personal preference here, because they are shows that stand head and shoulders above almost everything else that's been done—what I appreciate most about *Deadwood* is two things. First, the sense of almost symphonic complexity—of all of these interlocking pieces working together dramatically, and all of the different, multiple levels that it's operating on. It could be structurally interesting, in the way that a season builds over 12 episodes; and then from scene to scene, it can be interesting, just the arcs that the characters undergo within a particular scene; and then on top of all that, there's the language. The language itself is as complicated as a lot of individual shows are.

AS: Yeah.

AJ: Yeah.

MZS: There's more going on, not just in Swearengen's monologues, which I think everybody who's seen the show appreciates, but throughout. I was actually pulling some quotes from *Deadwood* before I came over here, just trying to remind myself of some of the highlights. Some of the things that popped out of Francis Wolcott's mouth were extraordinary, and they sounded very different from what Swearengen said. But over and above everything else, *Deadwood* appeals to my sense of life, in that it is aware of how dark and how cruel people can be, and yet I feel like [series creator David Milch] has something in common with Robert Altman, in that he appreciates the complexity of human beings, all of them. *All* of them. Even a character like Steve the Drunk, who you would think would be just one-note, reveals new shadings each time you see him. Every single character on that show, right on down the line. There are many characters on *The Sopranos* and *The Wire* that are basically a plot function. You know they're there to be a foil to other characters, and so forth, and I don't get a sense of an infinite potential lying within every human being in the way that I did with *Deadwood*.

AJ: I'm inclined to agree there. Definitely there are characters on *The Sopranos* that have felt that way. It seemed like, toward the end of the show—I can't decide if they became more than plot devices, or if they became a different *kind* of plot device. Paulie Walnuts was always a pretty consistent comic relief character throughout the run of the show, and then there's the episode where he and Tony go on the road trip, and then Tony starts thinking about him as just, really, this potential liability in his organization—

MZS: Where they get on the boat?

AJ:—yeah, and the nature of their relationship, a lot of things. Also, Janice had become sort of a one-note shrew, [but by the end of Season Six] you see that she's gonna be raising Bobby's kids as a single mother. You really see that she's becoming Livia, to a full extent that you hadn't seen before. It's hard to say if it's real complexity that's coming out or if [the characters are] becoming just a different kind of plot device; it's hard to say.

MZS: It's also a reaction to changed circumstances as well, which I think is true for all of these shows.

AS: And I would say that with *The Wire*, that while there were a couple of people here and there who are little more than plot devices, for the most part the show has done a really good job of giving you little clues [as to] why characters are the way they are. When you see Rawls at the gay bar, even if it's for two seconds, it explains so much about the way he carries himself, and how he treats people. Burrell had some scenes toward the end of his run on the show when you realized, "Yeah, he was a hack, but he was kind of made that way by other people."

AJ: Another little example that I want to toss out there that I just loved a lot recently was, whenever you see Lester on a stakeout, he's listening to this old R&B from the age of his youth. It think it's really interesting that you hear very little hip-hop on *The Wire*, but with older characters, you hear R&B music that's very specifically chosen [to match] when that character would have been young—like the guy Omar was on the stakeout with, in that one episode.

MZS: I wondered if there are particular songs that are "stakeout music" for these characters.

AS: I like that in one of the recent episodes, you find out that Bunk's ringtone is Lou Rawls' "You'll Never Find Another Love Like Mine."

AJ: I didn't pick up on that at all, wow.

AS: *The Sopranos* did great stuff with ringtone music. In the scene where Janice and Ralphie are doing the thing that I refuse to describe, and they're interrupted by Ralphie's ringtone, which is the theme from "Rocky."

MZS: My brother Richard sampled Tony Soprano's ringtone, and now that's his ringtone. And it's a little bit eerie, I have to say. When you hear that go off, you expect that the bullets are gonna start flying at any minute.

AJ: That's a pretty good idea. There's probably some generic phone out there that has it.

"I'm as nimble as a forest creature."

AS: Getting back to what you were saying before, Matt, about language: If we're strictly discussing language, *Deadwood* wins in a walk. I don't think anyone would dispute that Milch is one of the great wordsmiths. There are certainly great turns of phrase on the other shows—Marlo's "My name is my name" thing, from the most recent episode.

MZS: And I will say there is a certain rhythm to *The Wire* that is easily overlooked, because it is a show that is so much about the plot and what happens next and the decisions that people make. But yeah, there is a lovely rhythm to what at least some of the characters say to each other.

AS: But I mean, you listen to some of those *Deadwood* lines, and it's—

MZS: In fact— *[removes folded sheet from shirt pocket]*

AS: Oh, and he's got the piece of paper.

MZS: I brought a couple here. Like this one: Francis Wolcott, the monologue from the episode "Something Very Expensive," which contains the massacre sequence, when he's walking through the streets, and he says:

"Past hope. Past kindness or consideration. Past justice. Past satisfaction. Past warmth or cold or comfort. Past love. But past surprise? What an endlessly unfolding tedium life would then become."

MZS: It's just beautiful. It's just beautiful!

AS: Yeah.

AJ: It's really great stuff.

MZS: There's a lot of lines like that in there. And there are so many moments in *Deadwood* that absolutely emotionally wrecked me. Wrecked me. And there are a few moments in *The Sopranos* that did that for me, more in *The Wire*, but *Deadwood*...I was making a list of the episodes that just wiped me out emotionally, and actually, more often than not there was a scene or scenes that did that. Particularly the death of Wild Bill and the funeral of Wild Bill and the trial surrounding that; the Season [One] finale when Bullock fishes his badge out of the mud; "A Lie Agreed Upon," Parts One and Two, which opened season two, and "Sold Under Sin" and "Something Very Expensive." And then Season Three: "Leviathan [Smiles]" and "Unauthorized Cinnamon," which I think is the greatest *Deadwood* episode of all time. This moment in the season two finale, I guess—I'm sorry, season one, when Jewel and Doc Cochran are dancing together in the saloon, and she says, "Say 'I'm as nimble as a forest creature.'" And he says, "You're as nimble as a forest creature." And then she says, "No, say it about *yourself*." And he says, "I'm as nimble as a forest creature." Lovely. Lovely!

And that *Deadwood* had the courage to go there—to be that open in the way that it expressed emotion—stands it head and shoulders above everything.

AS: Now, I love *Deadwood*. I don't think any scenes on that show affected me emotionally nearly as much as some of the ones that I'm gonna rattle off now from *The Wire*.

MZS: Okay.

AS: The death of Wallace. D'Angelo then calling after Stringer to ask where Wallace is. Carver walking down the corridor as Randy calls after him, asking, "You gonna help me, Sgt. Carver? You gonna help me?"

MZS: Oh, that was horrible. I mean, in a good way.

AS: Yes. Bubbles' speech in the most recent episode that we've just been talking about. There's another scene at the very end with Michael and Dukie which is possibly the most devastating thing I've ever watched.

MZS: Actually, I would add to that [list], a couple of episodes ago, the scene between McNulty and his squeeze—

AS: Beadie.

MZS: Yeah. Oh my God, that was horrible.

AS: This show messes me up. I've watched it a few times, and my wife doesn't watch it but she's sitting there with me and I start getting upset, and she says, "Why are you watching this?"

MZS: Yeah. Yeah.

AS: Because it makes me feel like that!

MZS: Roger Ebert had a great line, I wish I could remember in what review it was, but he said when people ask him if a movie is a downer or depressing, he says that no movie that is true to itself is depressing to him.

AS: Yeah.

AJ: That's a great line.

MZS: And I'm paraphrasing. But even if the characters are being unimaginably cruel to each other, if what happens is so grossly unfair that you just can't stand it, if it seems like it's the thing that *ought* to happen in that story, then it was elating to him rather than depressing. And I feel the same way.

AS: Andrew, *The Sopranos* is a more cynical show, but I'd imagine that there were some moments that affected you.

AJ: Absolutely, yeah. The first one that comes to mind is when Tony comes home and finds AJ in the middle of of the pathetic suicide attempt—

AS: Oh my God. Yeah.

AJ: It's just really, really rough stuff, and it showed just how much Tony loved him. I really think there's a lot of scenes [like that] on *The Sopranos*, but they seem to be a little more small, because you're left a little bit more to figure out what's going on inside the characters' heads. I'm thinking of another [scene] very early on, early in the run of the first or second season, where during one of his many drug-related fuck-ups, Christopher is given a "shit or get off the pot" ultimatum by Tony, and at the end of the episode, he's sitting outside Tony's house smoking a cigarette thinking about which way he's gonna go, and then he goes back inside. There aren't as many showy speeches. Oftentimes it's left to you to figure out what's going on inside the characters' heads. The first episode where everybody really realized, "Hey, this is a great show" was "College," from the first season, which was one of the [episodes] that first did that to any serious extent.

MZS: That was the episode where a lot of people got on the train and never got off.

AS: Yeah.

AJ: That episode, exactly.

MZS: There were episodes like that, I think, for all of these shows. [For *Deadwood*], it was the shooting of Wild Bill and that whole sequence with his assassin running through the streets with that music playing— which was actually a cue used in *The Insider* where [Jeffrey Wigand] drives to the courthouse. Just overwhelming. I felt a little bit lightheaded the first time I saw that. I couldn't believe how big it was—how emotionally big and how physically big it was.

AS: And you've got the one guy coming in with the [severed] Indian head that nobody cares about because Wild Bill's just been killed.

AJ: That's wild, yeah. With *The Sopranos* there are a handful of those moments that you think of as really big moments in the show, that *are* really big and bloody, one of the most notable being the climax of the second season—

MZS: I was just gonna bring this up!

AJ: —when Janice kills Richie Aprile, right, and then they have to dispose of the body. In many ways, [the killing is] a shock. But it's the prolonged disposal of the body, and the detail that Christopher and—is it Furio, I think?—

AS: Furio, yeah, with the meat grinder—

AJ:—Furio have to deal with, the nuts and bolts of it, which I find really fascinating. Beyond that, though, so many of the really big moments on the show are small, quiet things. There's very little dialogue in the scene at the end of—I think it's the end of the third season? The one where Tony and Carmela split up temporarily—

AS: The end of the fourth season.

AJ: There's very little dialogue in that scene, and I think it's because [the writers are] trusting, to an extent, that [viewers] have been through similar situations so that they can project onto that. In real life, when you're in those situations, they're pretty quiet, too, because you don't really know what to do or to say. When I was in that situation with my parents, in AJ Soprano's shoes, I certainly didn't know what to say or do.

MZS: I was thinking also of the end of season two, which I just watched again recently. I was up late at night—which is often the case with me—and I called up some *Sopranos* episodes. I wanted to see which ones they had up [at HBO] On Demand, and it was a lot of stuff from season two, and I ended up watching most of season two over the course of a couple weeks. I was surprised by how well it hung together. Certainly the rhythm was different from season one or season six, which had more peaks—

AS: Yes.

MZS: —but in a weird way, it was almost a preparation for the second half of Season Six, because it was sort of a long, slow whimper. And when you get to the end with Big Pussy on the boat, now, talk about an emotionally devastating, complicated exchange—

AS: Yeah.

MZS:—when he is in the boat, and first he's in denial, and then there's sort of a pathetic desperation to him, and there's there's almost a dignity —

AS: Yeah.

MZS:—like he rouses himself and decides to face his fate like a man. And then Tony twists the knife on him when he's telling that raunchy sexual anecdote, and Tony says, "That never happened to you, did it?"

AS: Yeah.

MZS: Even at the moment of his death, [Tony]'s not gonna give Pussy anything.

Laying Pipe

AJ: Of course, now I'm thinking about all the parallels between that and the scene with Paulie on the boat that we were talking about. That's one of the wonderful things about *The Sopranos*, if I can hijack this for a sec—that, maybe because it ran longer than the other two shows, it was able to be a little bit more successful with oblique references to things, and also, with its length, it was able to do some really great self-contained episodes within the context of the big picture. *The Wire* was always a pretty strictly serialized show, with nothing too self-contained in it. *Sopranos* did some great, more or less self-contained episodes about Christopher. One [episode that], maybe because of my own personal circumstances, had a really deep effect on me would be the episode with Johnny Sack early in the last season where Sidney Pollack is the guest star. It was pretty much of a self-contained episode while fitting in very well with all of the themes of the series, and [it] worked beautifully. That's one of those things that speaks to TV as a unique medium. If it were a novel, you wouldn't be able to have this sort of self-contained episode about a guy like that. Or in a film.

MZS: It is sort of midway between a novel and a short story a lot of the time. At least, it has that liberty if it wants to take it.

AS: The interesting thing about *The Sopranos* is, for the most part—if not entirely—the episodes that people remember as the classics had very little to do with anything else going on [in the season]. "Pine Barrens" has nothing to do with anything.

MZS: That's true.

AS: "College" is largely self-contained. Whereas the format of *The Wire*—and to a lesser extent, *Deadwood*—didn't really allow for that. It's just that they're telling one story, where *The Sopranos* was telling one story but had time for these digressions which were often the most rewarding parts.

AJ: Also, I was gonna say really quickly in response to that, when I watched the whole series back-to-back, a lot of the serialized stuff that seemed really slow to me the first time around seemed a lot more interesting and compelling while watching the whole series together. All of the stuff about Little Carmine and the Esplanade and all that stuff, which seemed like pretty slow going and "When's this gonna build up to something?" the first time around, the second time around the serialization seemed a lot smoother.

MZS: That's another quality that these series have in common: they withstand repeat viewings. There is enormous pleasure to be had watching it the first time and not knowing what's going to happen. But then you can go back and appreciate and see foreshadowing that maybe you didn't notice before.

AS: One of the smartest things somebody pointed out to me about this latest *Wire* episode: Marlo gives the whole, big "My name is my name" speech, and someone then pointed out that way back in season two, when Vondas and the Greek are getting out of town, Vondas explains that Nick knows his name, but "My name is not my name."

MZS: Exactly.

AS: They're laying pipe all the way through, and I know *Deadwood*'s doing that, too.

MZS: The continuity people on those shows must have had whip marks in their backs. It's unbelievable how much they remember, and the little things that they can pull out and build on further down the line.

AJ: One weakness, perhaps, compared to the other two—if you want to call it a weakness—you could tell at a couple of points that they didn't know where they were going all the way through, in that from-day-one, direct sense. I'm sure you guys have probably interviewed David Chase more times than I have—I've only talked to him once for about 20 some-odd minutes—one of the things that surprised and impressed me the most, [and that] I thought about in my own experience with the show, was when Chase was talking about how much the show was about being a parent, and about how he pegged so much to the ages of Robert Iler and Jamie-Lynn Sigler [and] the gaps between seasons [and] making sure that the continuity reflected exactly where they would be at that stage in their lives. This was global attention that he paid to what some people would say was a secondary aspect of the show, the kids. [You'd think that the first level was] the mob level, then Tony and Carmela, with the kids being maybe the third level of the show.

MZS: I thought the evolution of Meadow was fascinating. It was like when you cut down a tree and you can see the concentric rings that indicate the different phases of growth that it went through. That's how precise it was with Meadow.

AJ: Her final fate is, in some ways, one of the more *Wire*-esque aspects of the show—that element that she's going to allegedly become this lawyer fighting discrimination against Italian-Americans. Everybody knows what that really means.

AS: Yeah. She can't get out. No one can get out.

MZS: How fatalistic are each of these shows? That's one question worth asking. To what degree can you escape your destiny, according to each show? Do you have a destiny, and can you escape it?

AS: Well, *The Sopranos* makes it pretty clear that escaping is impossible. I mean, that's what the entire show is about. *The Wire*, less so, but it shows that escaping is very, very hard.

MZS: Well, that line of Tony's on *The Sopranos*, "There's two ways a guy like me can go out—dead, or in prison"—that works, I think, figuratively as well as literally: that either your life is destroyed by an attempt to change your fundamental nature, or you end up in the prison of whoever you were all this time.

AS: And I can see you being more disposed toward *Deadwood* because that's by far the most optimistic show of the three.

MZS: It is. And it sounds funny to say that, because it's such a nasty show. It's so profane and bloody and sexually explicit and everything. But ultimately I feel that it is a life-affirming series, in terms of believing in the potential of every human being.

AJ: [That's] one of the things I found really interesting that maybe didn't come through as fully as it could have because of its early ending—when you look up the historical record and see that Seth Bullock lived to be, like, eighty years old and was one of Teddy Roosevelt's best friends, and all of this amazing stuff about the career that he had after the years of the show.

External Factors

MZS: Let's say a word about the context surrounding these shows—external factors that might have affected how they were made. I bring this up because probably the main argument that people would lodge against *Deadwood* being the greatest of these shows is that it ended on an unsatisfying note, and there was a lot of stuff in season three that felt incomplete, that felt like it was raised and then not followed through on. And of course, my defense against that is that a lot of that stuff was groundwork that was being laid as the first half of, essentially, a two-season arc—

AS: Yeah.

MZS: —that there was supposed to be a fourth season, and knowing how carefully they laid out every single detail in seasons one and two, I find it inconceivable that they would have pursued so many blind alleys in season three.

AS: But I've followed Milch's career very closely for a long time, and the man is a genius, and he does amazing things, but he does have this tendency to go down blind alleys a lot. And I think even in seasons one and two, there are certain points—and I'm gonna be hard-pressed to cite examples right now—where I felt like, towards the end of the season, not everything was coming together as well as it might have. Milch has always been much better at beginnings than at endings.

MZS: I disagree with that, because I think the finale of season one and the finale of season two were maybe the best season finales that I've ever seen on any show. But again, to kind of return to this point, the fact is, when we talk about *Deadwood*, if this were a movie, it would be *The Magnificent Ambersons* or *Major Dundee* or another movie that was essentially taken out of the creator's hands before he had a chance to really properly complete it. That's interesting because for *The Wire* I think, to a lesser extent, that's also true. Weren't there originally supposed to be more episodes [in season five], or did [Simon] hope that there would be more?

AS: Well, actually, I talked to Simon about this the other day, and he said if he'd wanted to do more episodes this season, they would have let him, and they decided after they beat out all the stories that they could do it in ten, ten-and-a-half, and that anything additional they did might have just been redundant.

MZS: Interesting.

AJ: A lot of people felt that the first part of this season felt really rushed. I did not feel that way.

MZS: Yeah. Yeah.

AJ: Although it's interesting: I forgot that it was ten episodes when I was watching it. I watched the first seven of the season assuming that it would go twelve or thirteen, and then after seeing the first seven, I read the press materials and was reminded, "Oh, shit—it's only ten episodes. Well, this is gonna end pretty quick."

MZS: But then, they are painting in broader brush strokes in season five than they had in previous seasons. And I think there are a lot of things that happen that are dependent on our knowledge of what happened in Seasons One through Four, so that there doesn't need to be as much setup—there's more payoff, not as much setup.

Curveballs

AJ: This is a total digression, but I found it interesting the sort of audiences that the shows have found. Reading forums like the HBO boards or Television Without Pity and other places, it's perfectly understandable that *The Wire* would have a very large African-American fan base, just because of all the characters and stuff. But it also kind of makes you realize, by contrast, just how overwhelmingly white the audiences of the other shows are. I found it interesting to read a lot of the online discussion by black viewers and realize just how much discussion online of what's on TV comes from an upper-middle-class, white perspective.

MZS: Right. Right.

AJ: In one of these discussions, a former Baltimore street corner drug dealer is posting on the *New York Times*'s discussion [boards]. Black people from across the social spectrum's perspective on the show has been really fascinating to me. For one thing, it's sort of a testament to what a good reporter someone like Simon is. Most of the writers of that show are white, and black audiences don't seem to notice or care because the characters are so well-rendered. A lot of those discussions speak to just how right Simon gets it, and to what many people have said: that all of these great black actors are going to have a hard time finding work after the show—

MZS: —or at least parts that are as rich as the ones they have on *The Wire*.

AS: Yeah. I mean, Andre Royo was on *Terminator* the other day, and that's a complete waste of him.

AJ: It's a waste of him, but it's a better show than I thought it would be.

MZS: But actually, you know what, though? I was thinking about that, and I was thinking about the sorts of careers that a lot of these actors on *Deadwood* and *The Sopranos* and *The Wire* have had, and [how] even a lot of the most interesting parts that some of them have had have not been as interesting as the ones they had on those shows.

AS: Well, yeah.

MZS: And I would be, frankly, stunned if, as great an actor as Ian McShane is, he ever did anything that was as demanding and as complex as what he did on *Deadwood*. Same thing for Gandolfini. And there are even smaller players I think that's true of as well. Molly Parker, you know, my God, look at all the things she got to do. When is she going to be able to do all those things again?

AS: A lot of that comes from the fact that these people were doing series, and now they're trying to move on to movies, and no movie part will ever be as complex as Tony Soprano or Al Swearengen or Bubbles.

MZS: Is that an inherent strength of the medium, then, as opposed to movies?

AS: Yeah.

MZS: Yeah.

AJ: And another thing about that is [series] will give opportunities like that to actors that have been around. McShane had a really, really long career in England. Some stuff about his career I'd forgotten about or wasn't even really aware of—that he was on *Dallas* for a couple of seasons in the '80s, you know—

MZS: My God, I'd forgotten about that. Did he have a Texas accent?

AJ: I don't know. I think he was playing a British guy with an exaggerated British accent. I was reading some interview where he was talking about hanging out with Frank Sinatra in Vegas in the mid-'70s. He's been around for a long time, and he gets the role of a lifetime this way. Molly Parker did tons and tons and tons of stuff in Canada before she [got] this role that lets her do [all] that. With film, you already have to have a certain level of celebrity to get somewhere, and with TV, it really is more about the talent, or it's much more about who's right for the role… No one ever accused Steven Van Zandt of being the world's greatest actor, but he's a lot of fun to watch as an actor.

MZS: That's true. It seems like there's a little more room to throw some curveballs, casting-wise.

AS: On *The Sopranos*, Tony Sirico, Steven Schirippa, some of the others—I don't know that they can give you a lot more than they gave you on *The Sopranos*, but for that show, they were perfect.

AJ: Yeah, yeah, yeah.

MZS: I'll never forget going to the premiere of season two of *The Sopranos* at Radio City Music Hall. I took an editor from metro who wanted to tag along, and so we went together. Tony Sirico walked in before the thing was gonna start, and he had an entourage with him, and they were all dressed in unbelievably expensive, flashy suits, just like him. And there was a guy who was at his right hand all the time, and he was this absolutely enormous guy. He was probably six four, six five, maybe taller. Looked like, just, a hulk, like Ivan Drago from *Rocky IV*. This editor, who was sitting next to me, said, "Oh, my God." And I said, "What?" And he said, "That guy. You see that guy with Tony Sirico?" And I said, "Yeah." And he said, "I can't believe they let that guy out." I said, "What did he do?" "He beat a guy to death in a bar like five or six years ago. He's not supposed to be out of prison. I can't believe he's out." Y'know, like, "Don't make any sudden moves around this guy."

AS: *The Wire* certainly has a lot of guys like that involved. Snoop (Felicia Pearson)—her criminal history is well-documented. Deacon Melvin is played by Melvin Williams, who was the basis for Avon Barksdale. There's a lot of that. The real-life Omar ended up playing Omar's sidekick toward the end of the series.

MZS: Have there been any shows that are comparable in scope to the shows we're talking about here, before this? And if not, why? Was it just circumstantial?

AS: I think being on HBO and having the freedom that HBO provides, and then having these three very talented guys named David working on them—

MZS: Yeah, that's interesting, isn't it?

AS: I'm thinking of changing my name.

AJ: I was thinking about this the other day. I'm getting ready to write a long review of the first several hours of the *John Adams*, which I'm loving, and realizing, "We're looking at the HBO knob-gobblers club here, aren't we?"

AS: Yeah.

MZS: Yeah, that's true. I've watched the first three of *John Adams* as well, and—

AS: I haven't seen any of it, don't spoil it for me, I don't wanna know how it ends!

MZS: Adams gets whacked.

AS: Dammit!

MZS: On a boat.

AS: But if you look at *Homicide*, which is the closest thing to a direct ancestor of *The Wire*—

MZS: *Hill Street Blues*—

AS: —but I'm saying, both of those shows are great, great shows, but they're chalk drawings and *The Wire* is a painting.

MZS: Yeah. And you had Bruce Weitz having to call people "dirtbag" and "hairball" because they couldn't use profanity on *Hill Street*.

AJ: A big influence—and I just watched it again last year, after having almost forgotten about it because it had a short, short run—was Paul Haggis' CBS show from the '90s, *EZ Streets*—

AS: *EZ Streets*, yeah. I love *EZ Streets*.

AJ: There was a real sense, like on *The Sopranos*, of this past that ties back into—and I dunno, it felt like it took place in this really complex and developed world. That and *Hill Street Blues*. There were only a few shows that really gave you that sense before the HBO series of the late '90s came along...It's fascinating—one show I talk to people all the time about who are like, "I loved that!", [even though] at the time it didn't seem to have enormous critical respect, was *Deep Space Nine*, which had a sense that felt a bit like *Deadwood* to me. You felt you were seeing a really small slice of a really big picture. Unlike the other *Star Trek* shows, you felt like there was a lot of stuff going on beyond this tiny place where the characters were.

MZS: I've been very impressed with *Battlestar Galactica* in that respect—with how hardcore it is, and how kind of pay cable it seems. I can't believe some of the places that they go on there, in terms of content, and that fact that it really is an adult series. It's not for children.

AS: HBO certainly spawned a lot of these great shows. *Mad Men* on AMC. *The Shield*, to some extent, on FX. Because of what *Oz* and *The Sopranos* and the rest of these shows did, the rest of cable is starting to catch up.

AJ: But HBO really is still The Standard. I had missed the last few episodes that FX showed of *The Riches*, and it's coming back for its second season right now, so I was going back and looking at the last couple of episodes of the first season. There's this one scene where Eddie Izzard's character snorts a whole bunch of crystal meth and is realizing just how expensive his family's lifestyle is, and how much money he has to put together, and then he's screaming at Minnie Driver on the phone, "Do you know how much money we're spending on HBO?" They just have to acknowledge it, almost. You've talked about FX being kind of the HBO Lite—

MZS: It's interesting some of the different lessons that these cable networks seem to have drawn [from the success of HBO series]. For FX, it's what I call the "Oh, shit!" factor—that the appeal of HBO shows is when you're watching them and somebody does something *totally crazy* and the audience goes, "Oh, shit!"

AS: You were supposed to stuff your mouth with food when you said that.

MZS: I was, that's right!

AS: But you ate all your bacon already.

MZS: I know!

AS: Couldn't wait.

Ending or Beginning

MZS: Well, is this the beginning of something, or is this the end of something?

AS: I don't know. The problem with *The Sopranos* was that it was so good, but also so popular that I think it made people think it was possible to replicate that success on a regular basis. I think one of the reasons *Deadwood* got cancelled, because it was never gonna bring ratings close to what *The Sopranos* brought.

MZS: And yet, all things considered I think it was the second or the third highest rated show that they had, consistently.

AS: Yeah.

AJ: Another thing about *Deadwood*, too, is that it had to be a lot more expensive than anything shot in contemporary—

AS: And also the fact that Milch is constantly writing and rewriting and tearing things apart and starting over.

AJ: It would be like the budget problems that [NBC] had with Aaron Sorkin on *The West Wing* times five, probably.

MZS: I ask this because I was re-watching some episodes from season one of *Deadwood* not too long ago, and at the beginning of the DVD they have a little trailer celebrating HBO. And this was, I guess, 2004, maybe, late 2004, when the first season came out on DVD. And in there were all these shows that were in rotation on HBO: they had *Sex and the City, Six Feet Under, The Sopranos, Deadwood* and *The Wire*—

AS: —yeah—

MZS: —at the same time!

AS: Yes.

MZS: They were all in production at the same time!

AJ: And *Curb Your Enthusiasm*. Don't forget about *Curb Your Enthusiasm*.

MZS: And *Curb Your Enthusiasm*, yeah. And I felt like I was looking at—this is like the lost continent of Atlantis here.

AS: Yeah.

MZS: You know? Is it gone?

AS: You know, all it takes is for another one to come around and be a hit. But it's gonna be hard.

AJ: Shows like *Tell Me You Love Me* and *In Treatment* seem like they're going in a slightly different direction. It seems like almost [the] pursuit of a very different audience. They're shows that I like quite well. Anytime that you get shows that I consider intelligent—

MZS: But they're not shows that make me put my four-year old son to bed early.

AJ: No, they're not. But perhaps they are more female-skewing shows than they're male-skewing shows. That's one possibility.

MZS: I suppose that's possible. But then again, I have a lot of female friends who love series television, and they're not into those shows as much as they were into *The Sopranos* or *Deadwood*.

AJ: Oh, I know. And I totally got my mom, who's in her mid-'60s, into *Deadwood*, which I did not at all expect would happen. And she just became obsessed with it. Making calls like that is hard. It seems like right now, Showtime is kind of chugging along [with] the HBO model to a certain extent. I'm not really too crazy about any of their shows, except for *Brotherhood*, which ironically is the one that people say is a *Sopranos* rip-off, but I think it has a little bit more of *The Wire* in it. It owes a bit to both—

MZS: I was gonna say, *Sopranos* plus *The Wire*.

AJ: I think a show like *Dexter* emphasizes how fundamentally gimmicky they are in some ways. I don't know if it was a salute to it or a jab at it, depending, on that last episode of *The Wire*.

MZS: I felt like it was a jab.

AJ: I kind of took it that way, too.

AS: Have any of us convinced the others of the rightness of our cause here?

MZS: Not really, but only because I do think—and I keep emphasizing this in comments sections of articles at *The House Next Door*—that ultimately these things come down to who you are and what you believe—

AS: Yeah—

MZS: —and what sort of world you think we live in, or ought to live in. And everybody's a little different in that regard, and different works of art speak to us differently.

AJ: That's absolutely true. It really did kind of bum me out when that one commenter sort of said that he thought I was sort of...

AS: —insulting *The Wire*—

AJ: —by saying it wasn't the best show ever, you know. Well, I don't know. I was sort of grasping for a snappy lede. But just because you love one show doesn't mean you can't really love another. In my response, I hope I was sort of able to put it in terms that articulated my viewpoint by comparing it to bands, and how I might just say my favorite band of all time would be The Velvet Underground, the second favorite would be The Rolling Stones, but their influence is equal, their importance is equal. It really just comes down to your world view and what things you respond to on a personal level, but you can still acknowledge both of them as being equally great. And there are times when you want one, there are times when you want the other.

AS: Between us, I think Matt and I have written one or two, it not three doctoral theses on *The Sopranos*, and yet here we are—we're both arguing for two of the other shows—

MZS: —yeah, yeah—

AS: —but it doesn't make me love *The Sopranos* any less.

MZS: No, certainly not. Certainly not. Well, I think that ought to do it.

AS: Yeah.

MZS: Thanks, everybody.

AJ: Thank you, and hopefully all of this will be understandable.

AS: Yes.

More Valuable Than Sex: Risky Business
BY ANDREW JOHNSTON ON AUGUST 5, 2008

One day during the long lazy summer of 1983, I found myself at a matinee of *Mr. Mom* and saw a trailer that featured a kid in his underwear lip-synching Bob Seger and a quick glimpse of unshaven teen saying "I've got a trig midterm tomorrow and I'm being chased by Guido the Killer Pimp!" The former got me curious, the latter made damn sure I was at Charlottesville,

Va.'s now-defunct Barracks Road Theater (where I'd seen my first-ever movie, Disney's *Song of the South*, in 1972) the night *Risky Business* opened.

Most of the teen sex movies of the early 1980s had less to do with what it was like to be a teenager in the 1980s than they did with what it was like to be a teenager in the 1950s and '60s, the era when the folks who made them had grown up. The genre was stuck in the long shadow of *American Graffiti* and *Happy Days*, and filmmakers were acting under the assumption that there was no reason kids born when LBJ was in office wouldn't identify with the worldview of the almighty Boomers. The most notable exception up to that point was *Fast Times at Ridgemont High*, a movie short on characters I could identify with. (Even in 1982, it was obvious that Judge Reinhold was practically pushing 30.) The trailer for *Risky Business* suggested I was in for something different; what that was I could never have anticipated.

As much as I loved them, teen sex comedies didn't exactly make me feel good about being the kind of kid I was in 1983, the year I turned 15. They all took place in a world where smart and sexually inexperienced kids (i.e., guys like me) were always laughably pathetic, and rich ones (me again) were universally evil and arrogant. Here, finally, was a movie that didn't pass judgment on those qualities. In the opening scene, our hero Joel Goodson recounts a dream in which he's riding his bike home through his affluent neighborhood and winds up inside a neighbor's house where a nubile girl invites him to join her in the shower, a dream that turns into a nightmare when the shower stall turns into a classroom full of his peers taking the SAT, for which he's three hours late. How could I not identify with the guy?

Joel may be good-looking, but fundamentally, he's all nerd. Much as the scene where Joel pours himself a tumbler of Chivas with a splash of coke to wash down the TV dinner he eats by candlelight is a nerdy approximation of adulthood, the scene everyone remembers—in which he lip-synchs Bob Seger's "Old Time Rock and Roll" while prancing around in his skivvies—is an equally clueless approximation of rebellion. Like the great iconic characters, Joel's a bit of a blank slate, all the better for the audience to project images of themselves onto. He's not defined by what he is (rich, handsome) but by what he's not: not as studly as his pal Glenn, not as cool as Miles (a disheveled iconoclast who's on his way to Harvard while the clean-cut Joel faces an uncertain future), and not as geeky as Barry, who doesn't even know that "bonking" and "fucking" are the same thing.

The trappings of Joel's life are such that he could be seen by neckless future fratboys as a reflection of themselves—a success waiting to happen— but he's also one of the few screen teens of the '80s who's ever shown doing actual homework. Dominated by his wildly materialistic parents and surrounded by peers with a much clearer sense of their future place in the world (or at least the illusion of such a sense), Joel was, beneath his looks, what millions of naïve and confused kids saw themselves as: a smart, well-meaning type looking for a road map to guide them toward something approximating maturity through a world they didn't feel like they belonged in. Tom Cruise, the actor who played him, was born Thomas C. Mapother on July 3, 1962, giving him six years on me—a yawning chronological chasm when you're 15. But Joel Goodson was born on May 5, 1966 (per the birthday card his grandparents attached to the savings bond he liberates from a safe-deposit box to pay for his sexual initiation with a prostitute)—a more bridgeable two years and twelve days older than I— and the first time I saw everything turn out OK for this schnook who has nightmares about showing up three hours late for his SAT, who can't even masturbate in peace without the specter of parental authority invading his head, I felt like someone had handed me the map I'd been looking for since the second my balls dropped.

Risky Business' status as the film that made Tom Cruise Tom Cruise overshadows its status in the teen-movie pantheon, but there's an emotional reality to it that puts the arguably-more-celebrated films of John Hughes to shame. Hughes set his movies in a made-up Chicago suburb, Shermer, but *Business* takes place in the real-life community of Glencoe, IL, and that fact—combined with the way the film acknowledges that Joel and his peers are uncommonly wealthy instead of acting as if everyone lives the way they do—provides the story with a grounding in reality that's absent from most of the Hughes oeuvre. And while *Business* is a movie that commodifies sex, it's also a film that acknowledges a truth Hollywood seldom articulates—that sex is actually something that scares and confuses teenage boys. After the dream, Joel plays poker with his friends and tells them about the time he chickened out on a chance to lose his virginity, a common experience that real-life guys cop to even less often than they acknowledge choking the chicken. Joel's confession leads Miles to offer a piece of advice destined to loom forever in the collective subconscious of my generation: "Sometimes," he says, "Ya gotta say 'What the fuck', " driving the point home by adding "If you can't say it, you can't do it."

When Joel's parents leave town for a few days, he follows his buddy's advice in baby-step increments, dipping into the family liquor cabinet, screwing around with his dad's precious equalizer and taking the old man's Porsche out for a joyride. "That's a good start," says Miles, who forces his friend to take things to the next level by calling a prostitute for Joel, then swallowing the newspaper ad with her phone number so Joel can't wimp out. The prostitute, Jackie, turns out to be a black transsexual—and when Joel balks at her arrival, she resolves the situation under the customer-is-always-right doctrine ("When you're buying a TV, you don't get Sony if you want RCA") by passing him the number of a hooker named Lana, saying, "It's what you want. It's what every white boy off the lake wants."

And was she ever! As Lana, Rebecca De Mornay seemed a Platonic ideal of which Jack Jouett Middle School's precocious Shifflet girls were a mere shadow, the perfect embodiment of a brand of pragmatic sexual confidence I'd never seen in a girl who didn't live in a trailer park. After Joel has the sexual initiation of his (and my) dreams (she rides him like a mechanical bull on his dad's La-Z-Boy, as the American flag fades to static on a TV in the background), Lana displays a money-hungry, all-business attitude the next day that briefly villainizes her before her secrets are revealed: She ran away from home, we learn, because her stepfather wouldn't stop coming onto her. Her vulnerable state led her to become the virtual slave of her pimp, Guido, and the rest of the movie becomes a romantic fantasy about her and Joel liberating each other from their respective prisons. One scene in particular made me buy into this fantasy with a vengeance: After driving his father's Porsche into Lake Michigan and getting suspended from school, Joel, at the end of his rope, runs to Chicago for a shoulder to cry on. As the camera swirls around Lana and the broken, defeated Joel during an extended hug, it's made clear that a real, intimate connection with someone you can turn to in your darkest hour is more valuable than mere sex—a downright subversive notion in an era loaded with movies about hormone-crazed maniacs desperate to lose their virginity by any means necessary. And while that may be true, I was too entranced by the moment to pay attention to a key detail: the revelation that sexual pragmatism I found so attractive in her (and, by extension, the Shifflet girls) was a direct result of her stepfather's endless attempts to get into her pants. I became convinced that if I could save a girl like her from a life of exploitation, she could save me from my miserable family life—without realizing, of course, just how damaged such girls often are.

Which is how I wound up spending the next seven years looking for Lana.

Friday Night Lights

Friday Night Lights Recap: Season 2, Episode 1, "Last Days of Summer"
BY ANDREW JOHNSTON ON OCTOBER 6, 2007

They did it.

My visit to the set of *Friday Night Lights* (documented via a lengthy transcript of my conversation with Kyle Chandler and Connie Britton that you'll find here [*Time Out New York* TV section] left me with little reason to worry about the series becoming a different show when it returned for season two, but a nagging voice in my head kept making me fear that in the interest of newbie accessibility, the show would dumb itself down or ease up on the poetic, wordless moments responsible for some of the series' greatest feats of characterization. True, the Landry-Tyra plot that has provoked much controversy does pose some potentially thorny issues, which I'll come to in due time, but for the most part, "Last Days of Summer" is the best and most artful season premiere of a returning show since "Guy Walks Into a Psychiatrist's Office", the episode that began season two of *The Sopranos,* aired in January 2000.

It's very apt that "Summer" begins with an unidentified Panther player jumping into a swimming pool, since the episode throws us in the deep end from the word go. It's not plot that the episode leads with, but character: the stalemate in Matt and Julie's relationship and Julie's new affection for "the Swede", is all explained via economical edits, zooms and camera moves before anyone has opened his or her mouth. And the instant the characters start speaking and we get Landry's brilliant "What Would Riggins Do?" line, the characters are speaking in their true authentic voices. Then we get the note perfect spat between Julie and Tami which leads into a breathtaking childbirth scene (set to Wilco's "Muzzle of Bees", which bookends the episode) and before you know it we've been completely enveloped by the universe of Dillon. There are a lot of reasons why I love *Friday Night Lights,* and its ability to draw you into a fully believably fictional reality with a genuine sense of life going on beyond the frame—a tricky task at which, besides *FNL,* only *The Sopranos* and *The Wire* have really succeeded at in recent years.

"Last Days of Summer" could not have been an easy episode to write:

"State", the April season finale, was clearly intended to provide maximum closure in case it turned out to be the last episode of the series. "State" is a darn fine episode, but the Panthers' championship win felt a little too Hollywood—a loss might have offered a purer reflection of the "being a man means turning defeat into victory" speech that Coach Taylor delivers at halftime. On the other hand, of course, ending with a defeat would have been a real downer of a way to end the season (and, I'll admit, while I wanted them to lose for reasons of narrative authenticity, I appreciated the victory a lot in context: *FNL* has provided me with a great deal of strength and inspiration ever since I began wrestling with some severe health problems not long before the series began, and "State" aired the night before I entered the hospital for surgery followed by what turned out to be an eleven-day stay during which Coach's halftime speech played itself back in my head many times. And while the impasse between Coach and Tami about his college coaching job created a conflict that could carry the series into a second season, Tami's pregnancy gave the Taylors a happy ending.

To be frank, I was extremely dubious about the Taylors having another kid: Unless an actress' real-life pregnancy is being written into a show, which was not the case here, adding a kid is something that's often done when writers have no idea what to do with a female character anymore and figure that motherhood would provide a convenient excuse to shove her aside. I couldn't believe that the *FNL* writers could have painted themselves into that corner with a character as rich and vibrant as Tami, and I could not have been happier about getting proven wrong.

Tami's nonchalance about letting her belly flop around in public while Julie cringes is a hilarious, perfectly-pitched moment that allows for a masterful transition to the birth scene and Coach's scramble to get there on time. The sequence, in which the characters leave the talking to Jeff Tweedy, reminds us how deeply Coach and Tami love one another while subtly establishing the extent of Coach's loneliness in Austin.

I was dreading the possibility of Tami having a son, which would have been the cliché thing to have happen. The kid's gender wouldn't really be a big deal either way, since if the show was to run for seven seasons, the kid would just be six at the end. But having a girl reinforces the dichotomy of Coach's life, which is evenly divided between all-male and all-female environments. His protectiveness of Julie shows Coach could never neglect a daughter but having a son would undoubtedly weaken the paternal devotion to his players' well-being that makes him so good at what he does (a point that receives major attention next week). The few scenes we see of Tami in hands-on mothering mode make it instantly evident that instead of being punted to the sidelines by motherhood, the presence of Gracie is going to create daily new challenges that will put her to one of the tests of personal strength that all *FNL* characters must face at some point.

If Coach has been in Austin for eight months, he must have left Dillon almost immediately after the events of "State": The Texas high school football championship generally occurs during the week between Christmas and New Year's Day, and "Last Days of Summer" obviously takes place in August. One certainly assumes (and hopes!) the Taylors haven't gone that long without seeing each other. If Coach had only come back to Dillon for quick weekend trips when he only saw the family (or if they'd all met up at family reunion-ish events in other locations with relatives we hadn't met yet), it makes sense that he wouldn't have seen Grandma Saracen, Buddy Garrity, etc., since leaving town. His reunions with them allowed for the smooth insertion of necessary exposition (about the new coach's rejiggering of the offense and Buddy's continuing run of ill fortune) as well as some beautiful emotional moments (the supermarket run-in with Matt and his grandma is just delightful).

The most emotionally intense scenes of all, though, are those between Coach and Julie. My friend Jared Sapolin has compared the tensions in their relationships to the occasional feuds that break out between Rory and

Lorelai Gilmore, which in his book is the highest of praise. But except for Luke, Amy Sherman-Palladino isn't very good at writing characters who aren't good at saying what they really think, so the most explosive and heart-rending Lorelai scenes, sort of like those on the Marshall Herskovitz-Edward Zwick relationship dramas that I love just as dearly, are prone to occasionally coming across as overly pat and writerly, without the rough edges that makes the parent-child showdowns so believable (last year, I contemplated pitching a House Next Door piece about *FNL* that would have borrowed a title from Van Morrison, "Inarticulate Speech of the Heart", but I never got around to it). The escalating tension that culminates in Coach tempering his gruff side and telling her that no one will love her less for leaving Matt produces a scene that's intensely real, and the prospect of Coach being torn between his devotion to Julie and his paternal interest in Matt is full of terrific dramatic potential.

The big scene between Riggins and Lyla felt as scripted as the Coach/Julie scenes felt real, but not in a bad way—here, we did get a dash of *Gilmore Girls*esque wit, which Taylor Kitsch and Minka Kelly put a nicely organic spin on. I like the idea of bringing these two back together—at a certain level, it seems like a matter of necessity: With Tyra now preoccupied with Landry, Rig needs some kind of love interest. But Lyla's embrace of Jesus—a move that feels really right—could have some very interesting effects on Riggins' struggle with his self-destructive impulses (If Rig and Lyla don't become an official couple, it'd be interesting to see what would happen if Lyla hooked up with Smash, the most committed Christian among the principal characters).

And finally we come to the Landry/Tyra situation. I agree with those who feel it's a potential bad sign for the series' creative direction, but if there's any show like this that could make such a story work, it's *FNL*. I was a lot more convinced by Jason Katims than Alan Sepinwall was about the potential it offers for a really intimate and interesting story about Landry's family, but the potential for a melodramatic meltdown is impossible to deny. It didn't help matters that Landry's attack on the stalker was reshot and the version that wound up on the air was different and more brutal than that on the critics' screener. The survival of the stalker (what I'd initially been betting on) or a dismissal of charges via self-defense now seem a lot less likely. Alan's arguments against the scene are so compelling that I kind of feel like a pussy for not letting it turn me off the show…but when the attack is followed by something like the second "Muzzle of Bees" sequence, with the unbelievably moving shot of Coach contemplating his newborn daughter and cradling her in his hands (and the rueful final shot of the Panthers' field from the air), I'm just helpless. Long story short: For now, I reserve judgment.

Some quick hits:

The world of Dillon is so convincing that it's always jarring when actors one recognizes from elsewhere show up. This was the case tonight when Chris Mulkey turned up as the new coach. He has a million and one credits to his name, but to me (and, I suspect, to many who read this site) he'll always be Hank Jennings, Norma Jenning's ex-con ex-husband on *Twin Peaks*. Hank was one of *Peaks'* least developed characters, but Mulkey always made it seem seem as if we knew more about him than we did. I doubt he'll be sticking around for very long on *FNL*, but it certainly seems as if he's going to do the same with his character here. And if a recognizable actor was going to be cast as Landry's father, they could have done much, much worse than Glenn Morshower. A Texan by birth, he's an extremely well-traveled character actor with a resume packed with several dozen generic military and police officer roles over the last two decades. He became a major fan favorite on *24* as Secret Service agent Aaron Pierce, a man whose sense of decency and devotion to the constitution saved President David Palmer from getting tossed overboard by his cabinet in season two in addition to making him a key player in the fall of President Charles Logan. Both story arcs—in particular the latter, in which Pierce had an intense but chaste flirtation with First Lady Martha Logan (Jean

Smart, in a guest run that has already become legendary)—proved him to be an actor of great subtlety and sensitivity, and his few scenes in the next two episodes make me incredibly eager to see how his talents are tapped by the series. He can be seen ever so briefly in "Last Days of Summer", having his photo taken with another Panther player before we cut to a nanosecond shot of a wincing Landry.

I'm a little divided about the new credits sequence, which adds a more explicitly jubilant note (by acknowledging the championship win) but also seems just a little too energetic. The flow of the original credits created a tremendously effective mood and captured the heart of the series in a way that the new credits just don't quite match. They only fall short by a tiny bit, but the effect just isn't the same. Optimist that I am, I'm going to assume I'll get used to them rather than reading them as a metaphor for how the flavor of the series might change.

Friday Night Lights Recap: Season 2, Episode 2, "Bad Ideas"
BY ANDREW JOHNSTON ON OCTOBER 13, 2007

Cynical fans of *Friday Night Lights* may argue that the title of season two's second episode describes the writers' actions as well as the characters': Exiling Coach Taylor to Austin, sticking Landry on the team, bringing the stalker back, having Landry kill him…all bad ideas. On the other hand, if *FNL* is going to do stories like this, they're being done about as well as they possibly could be.

Coach and Tami spend the entire episode apart, and the glimpse we get of his neo-bachelor life in Austin isn't exactly comforting. When Tami advises him to succeed by making himself indispensable, she's describing his role at home. Making himself indispensable at TMU certainly isn't an option, as Coach's story line with Antwone illustrates that the college game operates under completely different rules than those he's accustomed to. Back home, where only a small percentage of the players will make it to college ball, let alone the NFL, football is "preparation for the rest of your life," per a slogan on the wall of the Panther locker room. In Austin, it's how guys like Antwone stay in shape as they bide their time waiting for an eventual payday while the coaches are lazy babysitters distracted by their own agendas. When Coach's boss says "you must have been a hell of a high school coach," I think Coach Taylor realizes that his main role in Austin is going to be delivering the same speech to the same board over and over again, vouching on behalf of players who'll revert to divahood as soon as the hearing is over, making Coach lose a little more of his soul every time.

Coach might not have come to this realization were he escorting a player less smart than Antwone, who's quick to call him out on the idiocy of wasting his time with the TMU team when he has a newborn daughter who needs his attention. Coach and Tami's shared stubbornness brings out the best in each other when they're together, but apart, neither can see the forest for the trees. Glenn, the science teacher pinch-hitting for Tami, is a great foil for her feisty nature, but when while we initially take her side when Glenn drops by and makes a snarky remark about her messy house, things change when she visits Glenn at the school: We see her through his eyes, and only by getting an outside perspective on Tami do we realize how ridiculously overextended she is. Walking however many miles with a newborn when it's 105 out is just not something a sane person does, though she does a heck of a job of trying to rationalize it.

Of all the characters on *FNL*, no one is a bigger poster child for the overextended than Matt Saracen, who this week is both callously dumped by Julie and made increasingly aware that his skills will be underused on the gridiron so long as Coach MacGregor is running the Panthers. Matt gets some nominal relief in the form of Carlotta the nurse, whose arrival results in scenes that make Matt's grandmother once again come off as a benign version of Livia Soprano. Carlotta's presence is something that could go either way—on the one hand, it frees Matt from endlessly repeating his season one story arc ad infinitum, and it also provides the show with a much-needed continuing Latino presence. On the other, there's something undeniably sitcom-ish about the whole setup, and that doesn't fit very well with the series' established tone (I'm also less than enthused about the prospect of her turning into a love interest for Matt). Next week's episode provides some reassurance that the writers know what they're doing with her, but no-one can be blamed for having reservations based on "Bad Ideas".

The Tyra/Landry scenes, I'm pleased to report, are about as good as they could be—which is to say, they don't redeem the storyline (not yet), but neither are they an embarrassment. Landry's one scene with his father is brief, but it's enough to give us a pretty good snapshot of their relationship: Landry isn't Bobby Hill, nor is his father Hank, but Officer Clarke clearly doesn't understand Landry completely, and the vibe between them can't help but evoke the loving but awkward relationship between Arlen's top propane salesman and his only son. It's inevitable that Landry's father will get sucked into the vortex of last week's events, and what we see of their relationship this week and next continues to make me cautiously optimistic that the writers will successfully navigate the characters out of the mess they're in (though the earlier it happens in the season, the better). As far as things that might complicate a potential ongoing relationship between Landry and Tyra are concerned, I'll take a pudgy C-list rally girl over a dead stalker any day of the week.

Although Landry's admission of being well and truly in love with Tyra seems awfully late in coming given how much time they seem to have spent hanging out between seasons, I'm glad he was quick to show some backbone when she accused him of not being sufficiently manly under the circumstances. It led to the most effective scene the storyline has yet yielded, in which she says she wishes she'd killed the stalker herself and Landry says she should be glad she didn't. The writers are at least making an honest effort to address the kind of guilt that someone with Landry's innate nobility would feel under the circumstances, and the scene also raises the possibility that the moral quandary might prove to Landry and Tyra that they aren't right for each other, which—if that's the case—might have taken them much longer for them to realize had the stalker not died. I'm not trying to defend the dead stalker storyline, mind you, but rather saying that if it has to be done at all, I'm just glad it's being treaded with due moral seriousness and relative complexity.

As far as Jason's interest in experimental stem-cell surgery is concerned, the fact that the notion occurs to him in an episode with the particular title that this one has is something that pretty much speaks for itself. I'd be pretty worried about the potential storyline if I wasn't reasonably confident that his interest in such an obvious quack treatment is a red herring.

The final major story line in this weeks's episode, and the most heart-rending, belongs to Buddy Garrity, who finds himself suffering the consequences of at least two decades' worth of bad ideas. Buddy's drunken reenactment of his glory days as a Panther is an incredibly sad scene which shows just how misguided he is: Buddy obviously thought he'd be OK without his family as long as he had the Panthers, but this week he learned that he needs the team a hell of a lot more than they need him. His drunken collapse at the pep rally provided a handy (and relatively organic) excuse for Riggins and Lyla to share a moment, in addition to raising the possibility that Buddy is what Tim could become if he's not careful. I expect Tim and Buddy to be redeemed in tandem over the course of the season, but I don't expect it to happen without complications. It seems more than likely that Coach Taylor's return to the helm of the Panthers is going to be linked to Buddy's attempts to reestablish himself as Mr. Panther Football; the big question, then, is whether any bargain Coach makes in the process will turn out to be a Faustian one.

Friday Night Lights Recap: Season 2, Episode 3, "Are You Ready for Friday Night?"
BY ANDREW JOHNSTON ON OCTOBER 22, 2007

The divisive Landry-Tyra plot line recedes into the background for a week as the Panthers take to the gridiron at last for their first game of the 2007 season. The long run-up to said game retroactively draws attention to how there's undeniably been some spinning of wheels in the first two episodes of *FNL's* second season, and tonight's episode continues the trend. I really loved "Last Days of Summer", and I think that anyone who considers "Bad Ideas" a shark jumper is being premature, but this week's episode—by no means a bad one—makes it hard to deny that the writers are still in housekeeping mode as they continue dealing with the consequences of having had to make sure that last season's "State" could have served, if necessary, as a series finale as well as a season-ender.

Sending Coach Eric Taylor (Kyle Chandler) to the new job in Austin was a good move from a character development POV in terms of how it gives us a really solid look at why he's a great high school football coach rather than a great football coach, period—he excels at a kind of mentorship that doesn't work in the more corporate world of college ball. But while I really liked his scenes with Antwone last week (as well as his reluctance this week at being forced to cut an underperforming player), his separation from the Panthers and Tami (Connie Britton) has gone on a bit long. I'm sure these early S2 episodes will flow more smoothly when DVDs of the whole second season are out there, and the Matt-Smash tension (more about that below) offers a couple of ways for the writers to unseat Coach McGregor without too much difficulty. But the juxtaposition of Coach's plot with the rest of the current story lines makes it seem pretty transparent that the writers are spending a lot of time moving around furniture.

Case in point: Jason Street's (Scott Porter) interest in the experimental stem-cell surgery, which I'm pretty sure is just a device to get Jason and Riggins (Taylor Kitsch) on a road trip together which will (I hope!) make Riggins a little more mature and leave Jason in a position where he can better focus on becoming the terrific coach we all know he can be (on the subject of Jason, it would have been nice if the writers threw in a line saying he got his GED over the summer or something like that—as of now, I believe he's technically a high school dropout). It probably didn't need to take so long to get them on the road, though by the same token it allowed us to get some pretty interesting scenes with Riggins and Lyla, which proved that Riggins isn't purely self-destructive: He knows he needs something beyond football (and three-ways) to give his life meaning, but in Dillon, there just ain't too many options.

The tension between Tami and Julie (Aimee Teegarden) has been another interesting repercussion of Coach's stint in Austin, and I'm pleased with how unafraid the writers have been to make Julie legitimately unsympathetic. In time, there will probably be a big teary scene in which Julie, her cheeks streaming with tears, turns to Tami for support with a jam she's in, but for the time being it's interesting to see the writers make her as cold as they have (as in the scene where she calls Gracie "your baby"). It'd be a shame if the writers overplayed stuff like the scene where we see the Swede and his buddies smoking pot—Julie's smart enough that I'd like to think that seeing her new beau's friends be stupid and boring while they're high would be enough to keep her away from drugs.

After making an ass of himself while drunk last week, it seems a stretch in some ways for Buddy (Brad Leland) to actually start to get somewhere with a Machiavellian plot to unseat Coach McGregor and bring back Coach Taylor, though it helps that Coach Taylor wasn't around to see Buddy at his worst (and that Riggins, for obvious reasons, is more likely than many people to cut Buddy a break. Their mutual sympathy, of course, sets up the episode's funniest line: "I've seen you play hung over many times, and you've always performed like a champion!"). The preview for next week's episode suggests that Buddy's plan might not go so smoothly, and while that adds some believability to the story line, it of course also poses the prospect of us having to wait even longer for Coach Taylor to be back where he should be.

At the beginning of the episode, when Coach McGregor calls Jason Street "coach", I was hoping the writers would muddy the McGregor story line by having his respect for Jason sort of cancel out his dick-itude towards Riggins and Matt, making him seem like something less than a complete jerk. "Coach" has often seemed like a religious title on *FNL*, and it's clearly a big deal for Jason when McGregor calls him that…so having him turn around and call Jason "the team mascot" seems like an unnecessarily obvious way to make us dislike McGregor (and an unnecessarily obvious second motive for Jason to go on a road trip). McGregor's embrace of a running offense is also a strike against him due to the way Matt has been built up as a viewer identification figure, and on this front we get some welcome ambiguity. Smash has a point when he says that, as a senior who's being recruited, he's earned his time in the spotlight. However, McGregor lacks the paternal instinct to ensure that Smash's ego doesn't run amok given his new role…so while the Panthers win their first game, the fight between Smash and Matt, and the ensuing lack of team cohesion, suggests that McGregor's coaching strategy is penny wise but pound foolish. But while I found this situation highly believable, I was dubious that nobody pointed at Jason as an example of the folly of building an offense around a single player.

My favorite scenes in the episode involved Landry and his father, which is kind of a mixed blessing—Glenn Morshower plays the character beautifully, and in just a few fleeting moments of screen time we get a vivid sense of how he loves his son but doesn't really understand him, and how he's thrilled that Landry has a girlfriend but is also scared that his son will get burned and is eager, above all, to protect Landry (this extends to Landry's role on the team—he's aware that at a certain level Landry has taken up football to impress him, and he's flattered by it, but also rightly concerned for the kid's physical well-being given his lack of athletic experience). But as good as Morshower is and as admirably subtle as his scenes are, the only reason he's on the show is because of a plot line that has the potential to really screw things up. As I said before, I'm reserving judgement where the story line about the killing is concerned, and if the promo for the next episode is even remotely accurate, it seems we won't have to wait very long to find out if the benefit of the doubt has been earned.

After having cited medical reasons for the delay of a recent *Mad Men* recap, I want to reassure anyone wondering about the delay of this week's *FNL* analysis that health issues had nothing to do with the hold-up: Blame falls upon the failure of my Macbook Pro power adapter and an apparent nationwide shortage that made it impossible to score a replacement. Then, once I scared up another computer, my dog unplugged it from the wall when the recap was half written (after 15 years of writing professionally, you'd think I'd be better about saving documents by now). Despite the annoyance factor, it should go without saying that I don't love my dog any less for it.

Friday Night Lights Recap: Season 2, Episode 4, "Backfire"
BY ANDREW JOHNSTON ON OCTOBER 27, 2007

A better title for "Backfire" might have been "Blowback" or "Fallout", as the episode has more to do with the consequences of plans not working out, as opposed to the actual failure—and even then, not all of the plans collapse and not all of the consequences are negative. While not one of *FNL*'s strongest-ever episodes, it still had a lot of what made me and others fall in love with the series and shows that while some unpopular storylines are still in play, the writers nonetheless have a firm hand on the rudder and know where they're going.

It's rare to see a Panther game at the top of an episode, and perhaps rarer still for one to take up so little screen time. It's also rare to see the team get its asses completely nailed to the wall, though it did happen once or twice last season. Matt Saracen—the center of the show for many viewers—didn't get a lot of screen time this week, but his on-the-field frustration with Smash, and with Coach MacGregor's tactics, was pure Matt. What we've seen of Jason Street's coaching technique has me convinced the Panthers wouldn't have won State if he'd gone injured—he's good at motivating a team and being a leader, but he simply doesn't have the strategic grasp of the game that Matt does. Matt's insight into the mechanics of football has done a lot to compensate for his relatively scrawny body and lack of experience, and one would think that letting him serve as field commander while making Smash the sparkplug would be an obvious winning strategy. It's an obvious winning strategy that MacGregor ignores, out of willfulness or lack of vision, and that ignorance soon costs him his job.

It's been obvious since the beginning that the people of Dillon have no patience with coaches who can't bring the Ws, and the combination of a humiliating loss with the embarrassing public conflict between Matt and Smash gives the Powers that Be a pretty convenient excuse to give MacGregor the bum's rush. While that was a dramatic necessity, I still had a little trouble buying it because of how quickly Buddy seems to have been restored to his role as Dillon's football czar after his public humiliation in "Bad Ideas". I can't help thinking this would have been a good excuse to bring back Dillon's long-unseen lesbian mayor, who seemed at least as football savvy as Buddy and perhaps even smoother as a dealmaker (actually, maybe the last bit isn't really saying much).

A big theme this week is the finality of decisions—at several points, characters are told there's no going back after they cross a certain line. One of the most memorable instances is the scene where Coach Taylor quits his job at TMU. The TMU head coach has been a great bit character, and I was pleased to see him get a strong sendoff via the scene where he tells

Coach to consider his actions closely and that Coach Taylor's transition plan is bullshit as far as he's concerned. Coach Taylor has to choose what he stands for and while he gets the Panther job back by walking away from TMU, undoubtedly, it seemed very clear to me that he was choosing Julie and Tami first and foremost.

I was less skeptical than some about Jason's "miracle surgery" plot, because I thought there was some real potential in him going on the road with Riggins. The *Y Tu Mama Tambien* homage that we got was enjoyable, though there were certain logical quibbles—how did Jason get his hands on $10,000 in cash (even if it was from the settlement over his injury, wouldn't his parents control the funds?) And how can Riggins miss class and practice for a week without getting in incredibly deep shit? Maybe there's some wiggle room there, due to the chaos surrounding the coach's job (and, given the amount of time they appear to spend down there, a bye week for the team happens in the middle of the episode). It seems the resolution of this plot will hinge on Lyla entering the picture, and I'm hard pressed to think of a bad scene to date involving the Lyla/Rig/Street combo, one of the series' most effective combinations of characters, so I look forward to seeing where things go next week.

Speaking of Lyla, I was genuinely pleased to see her money where her mouth is as a Christian by attempting to minister, however awkwardly, to the lads in juvie. As a lifelong agnostic who has nonetheless always deeply admired the teachings attributed to Jesus, I've always been frustrated by Christians who talk the talk but don't walk the walk. The way Buddy seized the occasion to score points with his estranged daughter by hiring her protégé to work in the parts department at his dealership was an interesting case of unintended consequences and one that sets up some interesting future possibilities in terms of the relationship between Buddy and his daughter (though it'd be disappointing if they went in the most obvious direction possible with a story about the parolee being accused of embezzlement, vandalism or what have you at Buddy's dealership.

My favorite parts of the episode, by far, involved the still rocky relationship between Julie and Tami. I can see how, to some people, the sight of all those empty beer cans outside Anton's house, and the sight of the bong on his coffee table, might seem to scare Julie off given her relatively little experience with drugs and alcohol. What actually happens is far more subtle, and far more emotionally authentic. The last thing Julie wants is to become her mother, and her visit to Anton makes her realize that if she hooked up with Anton, she'd be taking a pretty huge step toward making the same mistakes that Tami once did and toward becoming a very similar person. If she gets back together with Matt, I dare say she's going to be even more careful than before about attempting to ensure that the two of them don't relive her parent's lives. What Matt might have to say about this is food for thought indeed.

At last we come to Landry and Tyra, whose controversial story line seems to be rapidly heading to a close. It certainly seems awfully tidy for the cops to essentially dismiss the idea of seriously investigating the death of her would-be rapist simply because he has outstanding felony warrants in other states, but it's by no means unbelievable—especially when you have someone like Landry's father working on the inside. It's telling that the shoulder patch on his uniform identifes him as a "peace officer"—in a city like New York, where police shootings of suspects seems to stoke the fires of racial tension about once a year, the phrase has a whiff or Orwellian doublespeak to it. In a place like Dillon, it sounds aspirational, hinting at the kind of American utopia the residents want it to be. It also speaks to the primary mission of cops in towns with low crime rates—just doing everything they can to keep things going smoothly. Sometimes this involves the Sheriff Andy Taylor brand of police work, locking up drunks and settling disputes between neighbors, and, well sometimes it involves covering up an anger-driven vigilante killing that the DA would probably classify as manslaughter. I've really liked Glenn Morshower in every scene we've seen him in as Landry's father, even though there haven't been that many of them yet, and the clash between him and Tyra hinted at in the trailer for next week's episode certainly seems like a fairly promising way to wrap up the story line while keeping dramatic tension in the air and creating an opportunity to explore the depth of his feelings for Landry. I'm not crazy about the storyline in general, but, as I've said, at least it's being done as well as possible under the circumstances—and "Backfire" provides enough substance, I dare say, to make that statement without coming across as a straw-grasping apologist.

MacGregor's final scene again hits on the theme of unintended consequences, and reminds us that Coach Taylor was a surprisingly passive player in the events that resulted in his return to Dillon, which were primarily engineered by Buddy. Buddy is the one who screwed MacGregor, and the unintended consequences are both the damage to MacGregor's personal life and his transformation into a personal enemy of Coach Taylor. While I would imagine there may well be other head coaching jobs open in the middle of the season in towns that have as little taste for losing as Dillon does, it'd be a shame if the scene was intended to set up a decisive late season encounter a la the return of Ray "Voodoo" Tatum in last year's finale (which never quite made sense to me seeing as, in his last appearance before "State", we were told Voodoo's school in Louisiana had reopened— so how'd he wind up in the Texas championship game?). After the events of the past year, Coach Taylor probably deserves to be haunted by a reminder of the domino effect that our decisions can have on other peoples' lives, but giving him the opportunity to defeat that personal demon in the flesh 20 episodes from now would really just be a bit too much.

Friday Night Lights Recap: Season 2, Episode 5, "Let's Get It On"
BY ANDREW JOHNSTON ON NOVEMBER 5, 2007

With Coach Taylor back where he belongs, at home with Tami and at the helm of the Panthers, *Friday Night Lights* serves up its most season one-line

Season Two episode yet. I've generally liked the episodes that followed "Last Days of Summer", but not since then has there been an episode that really felt like *Friday Night Lights*. Let's get it on indeed.

At a certain level, "Let's Get It On" is a housekeeping episode, one of those where it occasionally seems like there's a list of narrative necessities from which the writers are checking off items: "Deal with fallout from Julie ditching the Swede". "Give Landry his 'Weasley is our King' moment", etc. On some series, such episodes can ironically grind things to a halt instead of moving the plot forward, but that wasn't the case here—in every instance, we were rewarded with scenes that were true to the characters as well as to the spirit of the show.

I was especially pleased to see Matt stand up for himself in the aftermath of his rapprochement with Julie. I've always enjoyed how Landry is far more confident with women than Matt, even though Matt's QB1 status arguably makes him the most desirable guy in town, and while it's entirely logical for him to be a little apprehensive about reconnecting with Julie after getting burned by her, I didn't expect him to be quite so up front about it. Until Matt mentioned it at the dinner with Smash and Coach, it didn't occur to me that Matt might feel betrayed by both Julie and Coach for the same reasons. Between his frustration with the Taylors and lingering angst from his diminished role on the team during Coach MacGregor's brief tenure, Matt had every reason to be pissed off, and I liked seeing him *be* pissed off—during similar situations in the past, viewers have been clued into his feelings via slightly exposition-heavy conversations with Landry, and this felt more organic. Matt's been a little underused thus far this season, and I hope his emergence as a slightly more aggressive character will be accompanied by a story line independent of the situation with his grandma's caregiver. His "all fours" comeback to Smash was hilarious, and also just homoerotic enough that I'm surprised it wasn't shot down by NBC's Standards and Practices department.

The scenes with Riggins, Lyla and Street in Mexico exemplified the punchy, vibrant filmmaking technique that distinguishes *FNL* on the technical plane, and after a couple of visually flat episodes I was pleased to see the series display a visual flair that receded a bit after "Last Days of Summer". Like many, I'm glad that Jason's obsession with experimental surgery has played itself out, and while the symbolic suicide and rebirth was a little grandiose, that's also kind of what Jason Street is all about. As I suspect is the case with a great many male viewers, the characters I've always identified with the most are Matt and Landry—guys who identify with golden-boy jocks don't often go on to become film or TV critics. However, as the first season progressed, I had to deal with some serious health issues which turned my life upside down in ways that made it very easy to relate to Street's adjustment to life in a wheelchair. Jason's drama-queen approach to his disability may seem repetitive at times, but his behavior is totally consistent with his age. His struggles are one of the main venues through which the show has explored the meaning of the "Clear Eyes, Full Hearts, Can't Lose" motto—the philosophy that, with the right approach to life, victory can be found in defeat—and we were overdue for a reiteration of that theme, which is one of *FNL*'s core elements (and one that hadn't received much attention yet this season). I was fairly certain Jason's present story arc would end on such a note, and very glad that the ending was not an entirely happy one (*Y Tu Mama Tambien* was invoked even more blatantly this week than last, with the neat twist of Jason's disability making a menage à trois impossible, regardless of whether or not Lyla would have taken part in one).

My first time through the episode, I wasn't too thrilled about the Coach/Tami story, which felt more like a deliberate comic relief plot than anything we've ever gotten from the series. It was probably Mac McGill's involvement that influenced my thinking—his advice to Coach underscored how odd it seemed for our man to not know how to handle his situation, no matter how long it had been since Tami last had a kid— the Taylors just know each other too well. It also seemed odd that no reference was made to the Taylors' separation while Coach was in Austin, which would have also had a serious effect on Coach and Tami's sex life. Chandler and Britton played the hell out of the scenes, though, and the breakfast vignette offered a fleeting glimpse at the self-doubt that Coach sometimes displays around the edges (when he says "I'm a man taking care of his wife," he almost seems like an actor explaining his character's motivations), which I've always found to me among his most interesting qualities. And if the writers made a slight misstep by underestimating the Taylors' level of intimacy, they were spot on with the understated portrayal of one of Coach's key qualities: The way he sees through the metaphorical baggage and macho mythology of football and sees it as a game that one should have fun playing, a point nicely made by the scrimmage in which everyone trades positions.

Finally, we come to the Landry/Tyra saga, which, well, I won't say I've defended it in the past, but I have said it's an area where the writers deserve the benefit of the doubt. I'm officially glad I did so: For the first time, the plot really worked, in part because we saw it through the eyes of Officer Chad Clarke. Glenn Morshower really hit one out of the park, displaying all the qualities that endeared him to *24* fans and making it seem as if we know more about the character than is actually the case at this point. While the raw facts about indecent exposure charges and whatnot would make it easy for him to judge Tyra, he doesn't seem to—I suspect he's seen enough domestic abuse in his days on the force to know that the bad girl rep isn't necessarily her fault. It's clear that his chief consideration is protecting Landry, not because he sees Tyra as a bad influence, but because he's afraid of his son becoming a collateral casualty to her unresolved issues. He's obviously way ahead of his colleagues where the investigation is concerned, and he's obviously going to be the key figure in the resolution of the crisis. It seems the story will come to a head in the following episode (though with NBC's famous promo monkeys, you just never know), and while I might have once hoped the writers would just get this one over with and move along, I'm now genuinely eager to see how things play out.

Friday Night Lights Recap: Season 2, Episode 6, "How Did I Get Here?"
BY ANDREW JOHNSTON ON NOVEMBER 10, 2007

Since I began doing *Friday Night Lights* recaps, I've generally avoided taking the temperature of fan/critical response to an episode before sitting down to write each week (though it's been unavoidable to an extent when I've run late), so I sort of feel like I'm going out on a limb by saying that "How Did I Get Here?" is an exemplary episode, one that ranks with the best from season one. It restores faith in the series not by rejecting the plot elements that have piled up over the first five episodes or by rehashing fan favorite season one devices, but rather by recapturing the unique voice that seduced us all last year, then using it to go deeper. Simply put, "How Did I Get Here?" is the kind of episode that distinguishes great TV shows from those that are just pretty good.

On *Gilmore Girls*, the difference between an A episode and a merely passable one often came down to whether it was written by Amy Sherman-Palladino (and/or her husband/collaborator Daniel Palladino) or a freelancer. *FNL* at it its best involves a synergy between the writers, camera operators, directors, editors and actors (who are required to do much more real acting than on any other present network drama). "How Did I Get Here?" isn't a perfect episode (the token acknowledgement of "Green is Universal" felt shoved in, but that may just be because of the surrounding campaign—people who see it for the first time on DVD next year may not even notice) but it gave me everything I could want from an episode of *FNL* as well as a few things I didn't realize were needed.

In the teaser, when Jason Street asks himself what he's doing with his life as he stands (so to speak) at the verge of 19, his words at first struck me as an example of his tendency to succumb to self-pity: "Dude," I thought,

"You're a guy in a wheelchair who didn't graduate from high school and doesn't have a GED—but you're an assistant coach to the defending state champion football team. There are dozens of guys your age who've come back in chairs from Iraq who'd give anything for what you have."

But lo and behold, Jason's angst proved to be a much-needed reminder of something it's easy to forget about Dillon because of *FNL*'s tight focus on the characters: At the end of the day, the series takes place in a one-horse town where a lot of people live lives of quiet desperation because they couldn't find a way out. By setting FNL in a fictional town, the creators glossed over a key element of H.G. Bissinger's book that would admittedly be extremely difficult to illustrate on TV: How the oil business boom-and-bust cycle has taken a fearsome economic toll on Odessa, TX in real life over and over again. Having Dillon, and not the wheelchair, be the trap that Jason really wants to escape is a hell of a big step for the character, especially since having him on the sidelines as Coach Taylor's protégé made so much narrative sense. It would have been tidy for Street to become a coach after losing the ability to play, and it would have been an easy way for the producers to keep using him to illustrate the theme of turning loss into victory, but life isn't tidy and the easiest solution isn't always the best one. Street's gift of his memorabilia to Coach came across as a real sign of maturity, and Coach's response, despite its echoes of "I coulda-shoulda done more!" moments from Schindler's List and Dead Poets Society, was completely consistent with the emphasis that Taylor has always placed on mentorship, not winning, as the most important part of being a coach.

Equally moving was the Jason/Lyla scene that preceded Street's conversation with Coach. His decision to turn to her for advice because she's the only person he knows who's successfully changed their life felt just right in light of their history, and Lyla showed how truly she loves him (as a person, if no longer romantically) by resisting the chance to shill for Jesus and giving him the hard truth: The only way to change your life is just to do it. Yeah, it sounds like a cliché, but it's a piece of advice that slices through all excuses—certainly, it's the only advice I'd ever give someone who wanted to give up drugs or alcohol or to leave a bad relationship. Its simplicity, I think, typifies the lack of rhetorical frills that helps make *FNL* so believable, even when it's delivering a message (heck, *especially* then).

Jason's decision to take a new path was, as usual, just one of several elements that gave the episode's title its relevance. I'd been suspecting for a while that the circumstances of Coach's return to the Panthers wouldn't be entirely rosy, and the revelation that he's getting screwed on his salary bore that out. I've been in a roughly similar professional situation before—taking a step to the next rung of the career ladder and eventually realizing it wasn't quite the right thing to do—and even if going back to your roots brings happiness, it's never unconditional. The writers would have been derelict in their commitment to realism if there had been no negative consequences to Coach returning to Dillon. After winning the state championship and winding up with less money, more professional responsibility (the athletic director gig, which, I just realized, gives them an excuse to tell stories that take place after the end of football season) and the burden of another mouth to feed, Eric Taylor has every right to ask how he got where he is.

The titular question applies to Riggins in a big way as well, as I was glad to see that Coach didn't want to cut him any slack for running off to Mexico. Some people have said that Riggins has regressed as a character between seasons, but I think any decrease in his maturity is really the result of him not knowing what it is he really wants, much as Jason didn't either before tonight's episode. Being kicked off the team puts him in a position where he needs to learn the answer to that question stat, and the process by which he does so is going to be crucial to the prospect of a third season: For *FNL* to retain its realism moving forward, Panthers are gonna have to graduate and be replaced, and keeping Riggins on the show by having him fail a year is one of the worst things the writers could do. I think they're aware of the need to move forward judiciously, as evidenced by the superb use of Smash this week. He wasn't at the center of any major story lines, but we know him well enough by now that his behavior made perfect sense. He's serving his own interests by seeking to bring Tim back on board, true, but it's also a sign that he's realizing the importance of the "C" on his jersey, and of being the man of the house for his mom and sister. His scenes were a welcome reminder of Gaius Charles' talent, and I look forward to a story line from Smash's POV in the very near future.

The more I write about this episode, the more impressed I am with the amount of characterization that was packed in. There's a lot to be said about what happened with Matt, Julie and Tami this week, and if I addressed all of it I'd be writing all day (my hope is that posting this recap in a relatively timely manner will lead to a more active comments section and allow me to make further points in dialogue with you, dear reader). Instead, I'd like to quickly acknowledge a few moments I loved that reflected this week's theme—Landry, clueless as to why Tyra dumped him and pining for her, she understandably starts to move on with life; Julie realizing the mistake she made by letting Matt go; Tami blowing up at her sister after being teased with a laundry list of things she can't do because of her responsibilities—and skip forward to that which is probably sparking the most conversation about this episode, which is of course Landry's scenes with his father.

After going back and forth in my mind many times about the Landry-kills-the-rapist plot, I've decided that "How Did I Get Here?" fulfills Jason Katims' "wait and see" advice to fans in his conversation with Alan Sepinwall several weeks ago. A lot of Chad Clarke's actions here don't seem to make sense if you think about them—while there may be no more physical evidence linking Landry to the killing, the DMV would still know the family owned the right kind of vehicle unless Officer Clarke had a means of expunging the database, for one thing—I'm pretty sure Landry knows his dad's actions are illogical, and that knowledge gives great emotional force to the scene where Landry is following his dad to the pit where they burn the car. Landry is fully aware that his dad could well be pissing away a 20+ year career in law enforcement by covering for his son, and until now, I don't think Landry realized his father loved him enough to do something like that. It may be reading a lot into the scene, but as the illustrious Sars pointed out last week, Jesse Plemons is "a master of the slow-dawning on the face," and that makes it easier than is often the case with TV to do a certain amount of projecting (okay, call it fanwank if you want to). Perhaps it was because of visual echoes to a film I love dearly, Sean Penn's directorial debut *The Indian Runner*, but I was absolutely riveted by the scene. As soon as Landry began tailing his father, he must have known his dad was intent on destroying the GMC wagon; still, the "I can't believe this shit is happening" look on his face gave everything an unexpected—and very effective—air of suspense. I'd hoped that tonight's episode would wrap up the story line, but the loose ends his dad leaves behind make that seem unlikely. Even so, the plot was handled so effectively this week that, to my great surprise, it's now fine by me if we haven't seen the last of it.

Friday Night Lights Recap: Season 2, Episode 7, "Pantherama!"
BY ANDREW JOHNSTON ON NOVEMBER 19, 2007

"Pantherama!" is a perfectly serviceable episode of *Friday Night Lights*, accompanied though it may be by a faint whiff of filler. On DVD, it'll probably seamlessly bridge the episodes before, and feel kind of like a transitional segment in a long novel, with the pace slowed a bit to let the audience exhale after Chad Clarke's ominous torching of the car last week. And while it's now clear that the saga of Landry/his dad/the killing/etc is going to cover two more episodes, those tired of it can take comfort in the emergence tonight of what I think has the potential to be one of *FNL*'s best-ever story arcs. I'll get to that in due course; for now, lets's go to the videotape.

Given Smash's elevation to captain, his vital role in the MacGregorization of the Panther offense and his head-butting with Matt, he's received surprisingly little screen time this season, so tonight's focus on the running back was very much overdue. Certainly, we saw signs of the "old" Smash—the way he instinctively slides into horndog mode when the cheerleader shows up as he's talking to the recruiter—but he's obviously grown up a lot. He has a much better idea of what it means to provide for his family via football now—if he doesn't want to go to the historically black school on an academic scholarship, it's not because he covets the material perks of a big school or winces at the prospect of playing for a 2-9 team.

Smash is smart enough to know he's not that smart: He'd have to bust his ass pretty hard to keep his grades high enough to hold onto that academic scholarship, and once he was done with school, his moneymaking opportunities wouldn't be that hot—sure, he could still make it to the NFL. Lots of players from historically black colleges and universities do (the New York Giants' Michael Strahan, for one) but they often have a hard time of it in the draft because the uneven competition in football at the HBCU level provides few opportunities for coaches to size up their skills in action against known Division I quantities. Material greed is influencing Smash to some degree here, make no mistake, but Smash knows what he has to do if he wants to provide for his mama—a woman who, on the other hand, seems so flattered by the academic recruiter's pitch that she's willfully blind to the potential downsides. The best things she could do in this situation, of course, is to enlist Coach Taylor's help in sorting everything out, and his agreement to do so promises to develop the coaching-as-surrogate-fatherhood aspect of football on the series, one of my favorite *FNL* elements and one that we haven't had much of lately due to Matt's increasing independence and the chaos surrounding the coaching transition.

This week's episode made me do a lot of thinking about Matt. A hookup with Carlotta is something we could all see coming from a mile away (the same can be said of a number of things in the episode, come to think of it), and things with Lauren continue to move fast. It's no surprise the ladies are taking more of an interest in him now that he's the QB of the frakking defending state champions; what's startling is that he isn't more of a big deal. The people of Dillon continue to treat Smash and Riggins like rock stars, while Matt, for the most part, keeps being Matt. It'd be tiresome to see him face temptation in every episode, but what we've seen of Dillon's football culture makes me think that the issue of his ego could be getting a little more play. If he's not swaggering, he's definitely a bit more confident—the laid-back smile he flashes around both the girls, which they can't see, is hugely winning. I can't help wondering to a degree if the smile is more a reflection of Zach Gilford's personality than it is of Matt's. No matter what, it reminded me of the young Paul Newman in his less sulky roles and reminded me that Gilford has a particular kind of good looks/charisma combo more common to '60s/'70s leading men than to those of today, and it of course makes me eager to see him in some feature film roles (why can't I help suspecting that in either 2008 or 2009, we'll have a Sundance competition slate with *FNL* alumni in three quarters of the films?).

As to the inevitable question—Lauren vs. Carlotta—I'm with the latter all the way, and not just because their chemistry is more believable. Lauren's automotive advice to Matt is spectacularly bad—I suspect there has never been a worse time than the present to buy an old Dodge Dart. I drove a '72 Dart for most of my college days in the late '80s, which were not coincidentally the only time in my adult life when gas was consistently available at around $1 a gallon. After Saddam Hussein's invasion of Kuwait, gas went through the roof and the Dart became one of the least appropriate cars a jobless college student could have. On his Alamo Freeze salary, and with no small amount of grandma-related expenses to cover, Matt would have been a hell of a lot better going for a 10-year-old Toyota in today's $3-a-gallon world. And if the guy with the bad dye job knocked $200 off the price because Matt's QB1, you have to wonder what he was asking in the first place—in 1987, my Dart was just $600.

Julie was pretty annoying this week, leading me to believe that Matt's definitely much better off without her. Her story with the new journalism teacher moved *way* too fast and should probably have been spread over a couple of episodes. Her article came together way too quickly, and weirdly came across as part op-ed, part feature—we really should have seen her do more reporting on it. Tami's suspicion of the new teacher seemed a bit extreme at this early a point, causing me to wonder if he reminds her of a situation in her past. On the heel of the Swede situation, it seems a little soon to have Julie repeat another of her mom's high school mistakes.

There was actually a lot to chuckle about in the journalism storyline. The 250-word movie review made me laugh, because it takes a lot of experience to write a good one at that length—it's a lot smarter to teach kids how to write, period, before one starts teaching them to write short. As an alumnus of Columbia's journalism program, Noah's pride in having gone there gave me a healthy laugh, especially since few people still have an ego like his when they graduate from there (and if he did, a year of gruntwork at the Milwaukee paper would have robbed him of any remaining illusions). The shout-out to the *Journal-Sentinel* was a neat in-joke for Columbia grads, as j-school professor/Pulitzer Prizes head honcho Sig Gissler was formerly the editor of the Sentinel, one of two papers that merged in 1995 to form the MJ-C.

I really enjoyed all of Riggins' scenes with Tyra, even if the situation that took him to her house—Billy's relationship with the older woman—strikes me as wildly unbelievable—Billy's just a little too crass and dumb, I think, to interest the woman we met last year—that is, unless Dillon is "really" short on eligible men. With the focus of the Santiago plot shifting to Buddy Garrity, the redemption-of-Riggins arc could get a little dissolute if the writers aren't careful—but I like seeing Tim and Tyra interact as friendly exes, and I can easily see him influencing her toward the conclusion that Landry is the guy for her, regardless of what his dad says.

The Pantherama event itself was pretty dopey, especially since the Tyra and Lyla "let's put on a show" sequence was dominated by generic background Panthers we've seldom seen before—it can be hard to swallow the need to put guys like Landry and Santiago on the team when so many previously-unseen players are capable of emerging from the woodwork on a moment's notice (another puzzler—if Tami found out she was pregnant in December and gave birth to Gracie in August, she couldn't have missed more than three weeks or so of school if we're only two games into the season—so why does everyone act like she's been gone for months?). Thankfully Matt and Smash were involved in the event itself; still, the amount of time devoted to it really did seem like an attempt to pad the episode (though it was all basically made worthwhile by Tami strong-arming Lyla and Tyra into managing the entertainment, an absolutely classic Tami moment.

As to the potentially brilliant story arc I referred to at the top...it may be premature, but I think the plot with Buddy and Santiago could shape up to be one of *FNL*'s defining stories. Brad Leland is one of the show's least-heralded good actors, chiefly because he's so good at making Buddy so dislikable. He steps it up a notch in the scenes where he talks about what a great foster dad he'd make, making it transparent that in reality, Buddy's approaching the situation as one might approach adopting a dog. He's getting in way over his head here, and none of it would be half as interesting if the writers weren't defying expectations with Santiago, making him a smart kid who got pretty good grades before his family situation got out of control rather than a mere Latino gang punk. The kid has a real nobility to him, and while the line about him never having had a real bed before was corny as hell, it sure worked. Add Tami and Coach's vested interests in Santiago to the mix and you've got an arc that could run all season and provide god knows how much meaty material for the show's two deepest and most beloved characters as well as one who could only benefit from more depth (Buddy) and a hugely promising newcomer (albeit more promising as a character than as a player at this point). Let's just hope the writers' strike doesn't fuck it all up.

Although the preview over the end credits was for Episode 2.9, "Confession", the episode of December 7, there's still 2/8. "Seeing Other People" (I had to check to make sure it wasn't a rerun—for some reason that totally sounds like an S1 title) coming up on November 30. In the meantime, here's wishing everyone a spectacular holiday meal with the people they most want to be with.

Friday Night Lights Recap: Season 2, Episode 8, "Seeing Other People"
BY ANDREW JOHNSTON ON DECEMBER 1, 2007

"Seeing Other People", like "Pantherama!" before it, is a midseason episode with something of a holding pattern feel to it, and which places a much heavier emphasis on character than plot. Yet despite the absence of Santiago, the most intriguing character to join the show this season, "People" was the better episode by far. This week's installment featured some of the richest and most intense scenes between Coach and Tami in awhile, yet though the performances of Kyle Chandler and Connie Britton are among *FNL*'s most reliable elements, what really impressed me this week was the filmmaking. Last season, much was made of how the series' editing style in early episodes put off some viewers, and the distinctive visual style was indeed somewhat toned down as a sop to mainstream viewers. "People" was hardly avant garde, but the scenes between Matt and Carlotta had an intense intimacy to them that wouldn't have come through if the series wasn't committed to visual storytelling in a way that few TV dramas are.

We begin with something many viewers have been begging for since early in the first season: A Panther game in which the outcome, for once, is *not* determined at the last minute. As many have noted, you'd expect a state championship team to have at least a couple of one-sided blowouts over the course of a season…but here, it's the Panthers who get their butts whipped. One might expect Coach Taylor to be a little upset about experiencing such a brutal defeat so soon after returning to Dillon, but he's rapidly distracted by his marital situation, much as Smash is distracted by his recruiting visit to a notorious party school.

As the title suggests, this week's episode is all about the relationships, a focus that's established before the end of the teaser. After Lauren invites Matt to stay over and he defers in the interest of tucking in Grandma Saracen, I half expected him to say "…but I can sneak out and be back here in half an hour, baby!". Instead, when he gets home, it's clear he deferred because of his interest in Carlotta, who promptly shoots him down. As the "open relationship" scene later makes clear, Matt's confidence around women now exceeds his actual level of experience, which is a classic recipe for trouble, and he soon learns the hard way that if you expect a woman to give you credit for something (in this case, for blowing off Lauren), it's almost certain that she won't.

If it wasn't for the tenderness of the Matt and Carlotta scenes—which reminded me of David Gordon Green's *All the Real Girls*—everything with Matt and Smash this week would have come a little too close to *Varsity Blues* territory. Certainly, Smash getting chased out of the dorm in his boxers was a scene that could have come from any number of teen movies. I was amused that Matt was the one he asked to bail his ass out of trouble, and pleasantly surprised that Matt resisted the urge to twist the knife, allowing the scene to evolve into an organic bonding moment between them. In their scenes at the Alamo Freeze, Smash has usually been the alpha dog socially (despite Matt's status as the more senior employee), and after the antagonism between the two that erupted after Coach McGregor began giving Smash more of the spotlight, I'm really enjoying seeing them relate as something resembling peers for pretty much the first time ever.

The real drama this week centered on the Taylors, and after the recent jokiness about Coach's desire to get "back in the saddle" following Gracie's birth, I enjoyed seeing their marriage get treated seriously once again. We've seen Coach and Tami fight before, but never to the point of him getting exiled to the couch for the night. From the moment he was introduced, Glenn was too transparent a dweeb for Coach to logically envy him—or at least, that's how it seemed. The reason for his envy—that he missed being her best friend—struck me as incredibly poignant and very apt in light of what we've seen of their relationship. The strong, believable friendship component has always been the most compelling thing about their marriage—they're one of the few couples on TV who seem like real partners, as well as one of the few who it's easy to buy as a couple that have actually been together for 18 years or so, and for Coach to acknowledge how much it means to him to be the guy who cracks Tami up made for a really striking moment of vulnerability on his part. Just as touching, in a totally different way, was the bit where Tami talks about needing a night out and he immediately offers up a date-night scenario so fully developed that it's obvious he'd been waiting ages for an opportunity to toss it out there. If there's ever been another couple on TV who constitute a better advertisement for marriage than the Taylors, I sure can't think of them.

Yet while the Taylors seem plenty healthy as a couple, Tami's tirade directed at Noah was the latest of several occasions this season on which she's come across as somewhat less than stable. It was disappointing when she told Noah—who, for all his arrogance, is clearly focused on Julie's best interests—that she could have him fired, and funny when she said she could have Coach kick his ass. But when she said she could have him sent to prison, she went way over the line. I mean sure, recommending the dreadful *A Prayer For Owen Meany* over a superior work such as *The Hotel New Hampshire* is a shame, but it's certainly not criminal.

Tami's actions were exaggerated by the time they got back to Julie, but even so Julie's response didn't seem that out of line to me—and I say this as someone who's found Julie to have pretty much become an insufferable bitch this season. Julie saw Tami's attack on Noah as an attack on her, and, as with the Swede, Tami's sense of righteousness kept her from seeing how her actions would come off in Julie's eyes. It seems pretty clear to me that the mother-daughter feud will be one of the season's major story lines, and I'm hoping it doesn't take long for the plot to yield some good material for Jessalyn Gilsig, who's terrific at playing characters like Shelly and who has so far been criminally underused since her arrival on *FNL*.

Riggins' scenes with his ultracrass housemate struck me as lame, needless comic relief until it became apparent that the result would be his return to the Panther lineup. I didn't expect him to be back on the team so soon, but I'm glad it worked out this way—too many story lines have been drawn out longer than necessary this season, for one thing; for another, his apology to his teammates was a really terrific scene. Riggins' tendency to refer to Jason as "Six" in Mexico always struck me as a little odd (he never did that last season, did he?), so I was glad the writers provided some continuity by having him refer to the other players by their numbers. While his comments to the benchwarmer were funny and poignant, they also underscored Landry's absence from the practice scene, since in light of last season's tutoring and Riggins's previous insight into the Landry-Tyra relationship, he surely would have had something to say to the guy.

As to Landry, the whole bit with the rapist's brother seeking to apologize to Tyra seemed like a fairly contrived way to push the character down a path he was already on. Landry's discomfort with his father's actions would seem to make his confession inevitable. When he met with the rapist's brother and kept reiterating that the guy was beyond redemption, Landry was obviously trying to justify the killing to himself, even though we've seen him display a level of guilt which suggests he's already long past that stage. The only really interesting thing about it was how, as an apparent only child, Landry was unable to relate to the guy's desire to reconcile his brother's cruelty with the support he'd offered his sibling.

By the time Landry got around to talking to Lyla, he seemed almost too casual about the burden he was carrying, and their scene would have frustrated me completely were it not for the casual way he talked about trying to be a good Christian, which struck me as a fine example of the way the series normalizes religion and makes it seem like an organic part of the characters' lives. At the same time, if Landry holds such beliefs, it seems unlikely that he'd need Lyla to give him a push, especially since the preview for next week suggests that he feels a deep need to be punished for his actions regardless of how they're interpreted by the authorities. It seemed odd two weeks ago that NBC would have shown a trailer for next week's "Confession" in lieu of one for "Seeing Other People", and the final scene, which felt tacked on, came off as an attempt to justify that trailer by having the tail wag the dog. Some people may consider what NBC did to be a classic example of promo monkeys going too far with the spoilers, but look at it this way—by emphasizing the confession, which we all knew was coming anyway, the network made it possible for a lot of strong moments in "Seeing Other People" to take us by surprise.

Friday Night Lights Recap: Season 2, Episode 9, "The Confession"
BY ANDREW JOHNSTON ON DECEMBER 10, 2007

Somewhat surprisingly in light of the title (to say nothing of the avalanche of network hype), Landry's admission of guilt occupied a relatively small chunk of "The Confession". That's too bad, since it offered us by far the best scenes of the episode. There were some fine moments in the other story lines—most notably the biggest, loudest Julie v. Tami throwdown yet—but some seriously false notes in Jason Street and Tim Riggins' stories kept this from ranking among the upper tier of *Friday Night Lights* episodes.

If I feel as if Landry's plot deserved more time, it's because the shortage of it kept Jesse Plemons and Glenn Morshower from having more scenes.

The story wouldn't work at all if Plemons wasn't such a fantastic actor who puts across so much more than is in the script. Given the self defense/ defense of another aspect (and, well, the fact that they're all in Texas), Landry's chances of being prosecuted were pretty infinitesimal. Add his status as the son of a lawman and those chances are basically nil. Landry should be smart enough to realize that (and so should his dad, come to think of it), and his failure-or refusal-to do so, says a lot about him. Landry would probably be just as haunted if he was a soldier who'd killed a man on the battlefield—for him, taking a life is just not something done even remotely lightly. Landry's insistence on being punished for his actions is all there in the script, but it wouldn't surprise me if it's not terribly convincing on the page. Plemons played the scene as if Landry had gone over everything in his head enough times to have effectively brainwashed himself, and when he decides to play along with his father and the attorney, I got the sense that he did so not because he'd been convinced his actions were justifiable but because if he went to prison, he'd be extending his punishment to his parents and Tyra, none of whom remotely deserve to be hurt by his actions. The story line may have been resolved, but the look in Landry's eyes in the final shot implies he'll be carrying the burden with him for the rest of his days.

After being MIA for two weeks, Jason Street returns with what may very well be the dumbest plot point *FNL* has ever asked the audience to swallow. In light of Dillon's apparent size, the likelihood of the town having more than maybe two women with profiles on the dating site for wheelchair fetishists is pretty slim...so it completely destroys suspension of disbelief to have one of them be a chick with a jones for water sports who has apparently never even heard of Street before. I could maybe buy it in a town of a couple hundred thousand people, but Dillon has consistently been portrayed as a city that can't have more than 60,000 residents max. Off the top of my head, I can think of a dozen ways they could have set Jason up with the waitress (and, more importantly, have engineered circumstances to make him Herc's roomie) that didn't require such an inane stab at comedy.

Speaking of comedy, the scene where Matt and Carlotta are interrupted by Grandma Saracen could have been quite nearly as bad if it hadn't been played and cut in a way that made it feel really true to the characters instead of coming across like an *American Pie* outtake. The same can be said of the scene where Smash gets ready to give Carlotta the full treatment only to learn that she came into the Alamo Freeze looking for Matt. *FNL* doesn't do comic relief very often, but when the writers go for it, it only really works when it plays off well-established characterization.

I was sure we'd seen the last of Riggins' crazy-roomie story line and had mixed feelings about seeing it turn up again. I expected Riggins to wind up living with the Taylors back during the first season and was surprised to see it happen now. The development makes more sense at this point, attached as it is to the continuing story of his struggle to rejoin the team. I'm really glad that Coach is still making Riggins work for his spot on the team, but it doesn't seem quite right to have the story line lashed to the roomie action, which plays as if the writers can't quite decide if they want to elicit comedy or suspense. I liked the scene where the roommate menacingly stalks Riggins at the gymnastics meet, but after seeing how long Landry's story line got dragged out, I'm really wary of this one taking way too much time to resolve (to say nothing of the potential for cheesy melodrama created by the roomie's instability and drug use—with Landry's story line finally over and done, it's way too soon for the writers to be covering even remotely similar territory). Santiago and Buddy's story line continues to be one of season two's stronger elements, though the odor of *Good Will Hunting* during Santiago's big scene in the pickup truck was perhaps a little too strong. I didn't expect things to work out as well for him and the Panthers as they did on the gridiron, and the game was one of the better football sequences that the show has served up in awhile. Otherwise, the most notable scene in the episode that I haven't covered yet was the latest Julie-Tami dust up, their most spectacular and entertaining yet. It was a great showcase scene for Connie Britton, though it also had the unintentional effect of pointing out the degree to which Coach Taylor has been somewhat shunted to the sidelines and rendered a little more passive as a character in the weeks since he's returned to Dillon from Austin (if nothing else, it would have been nice to tie him in to Landry's story line and let Kyle Chandler have a scene or two with Morshower, since the effects of Landry's confession etc. on his involvement with the Panthers has largely been glossed over). Going into the writers' strike, *FNL* had more episodes in the can than many other scripted dramas—15 of the 22 episodes ordered for the season have been shot. That means there are six episodes to come, which I expect to be rolling out during February sweeps at the latest. The creators of the show obviously realize that Kyle Chandler is one of their greatest assets; that being the case, I very much hope to see him take a more proactive role in the series when it returns in 2008.

Friday Night Lights Recap: Season 2, Episode 10, "There Goes the Neighborhood"
BY ANDREW JOHNSTON ON JANUARY 4, 2008

The concept of the "good jumping on point" episode means less and less in this age of downloads (legal and otherwise) and rapid-turnaround DVD releases, but "There Goes the Neighborhood" is nonetheless an episode that functions as such ideally. It's not one of the finest *FNL* episodes ever, but it strikes a terrific balance between Taylor family drama, heartfelt high school soapiness and actual football (so what if it's a bye week?). All told, it's one of the best episodes of the second season yet because, in many ways, it feels so casual.

Which is not to say that nothing of note happens. Certainly, the tornado (*FNL*'s first big visual-effects shot, as far as I can recall) gave the NBC Promo Monkeys plenty to work with, and the resurrection of Mrs. Garrity's post-Buddy relationship definitely seems like a story the writers will milk for awhile. What I enjoyed most about the episode was the exposure it gave Tim Riggins, and how Tim's activities gave us a chance to see a new side of Coach Taylor. For the last few weeks, it's often felt that we were seeing Coach more from the outside than before. If an actor less talented than Kyle Chandler was dealing with the exact same scripts (impossible, of course, since the creative team is writing for him specifically), he'd probably come off as too much of a cypher. There's only one moment where it feels like we really get a look at the "inner" Eric Taylor here—when he tells Tami he likes how having Riggins around helps even the gender teams (with Gracie and Shelly around, he's now outnumbered 4:1!)—but we see plenty of classic elements of his personality, most notably his emphasis on formality (when he greets the Laribee team) and his ferocious protectiveness (when he pulls Riggins off Julie, of course, but perhaps more notably when he pulls the Laribee coach off of Rig).

I have some mild reservations about where Riggins' storyline is going (on the basis of next week's episode, which I've already seen), but no matter what, I'm really looking forward to seeing Taylor Kitsch step up as an actor. In his scenes around the Taylor house this week—and in his interactions with Julie in particular—Kitsch seems more relaxed than usual, and spends a lot of time flashing a sincere, laid-back smile. The presence he emits is even more notable given his relative shortage of lines this week. He's definitely graduated to the Zach Gilford/Gaius Charles level, leaving Scott Porter even further in the dust than before.

Some of the stuff involving the Laribee Lions confused me—it's one thing to have thirty or forty-odd football players sharing a school's athletic facilities, but having several dozen more students sitting in on classes and whatnot seems like an enormous burden on Dillon High's infrastructure. In the real world, I'd expect the Laribee players might get bussed in after their last class; however, if they weren't around all day, we wouldn't have had the Dillon-Laribee melee, an enormously enjoyable scene made more so by how clear it is that the actors and extras involved all appear to be having the time of their lives.

The melee is motivated, of course, by Landry's attempt to reheat things with Tyra now that everything with the killing has been laid to rest, and I was pretty impressed, at least at first, with how that was handled: Tyra totally seems like the kind of gal who'd be interested in a guy like Landry as long as she couldn't have him but who would get cold feet as soon as the obstacles to a relationship disappeared. I don't necessarily have a problem with her explanation—that her feelings for Landry are so strong that she doesn't know how to process them—but it does seem like a bit of a stretch for her to have the self-awareness required to explain them to Landry so lucidly (and while she clearly doesn't care much about having a bad rep at school at this point, she should have known that going out with the Laribee player would make her an instant pariah—in fact, I'm surprised she didn't catch a hell of a lot more grief for it).

Although Lyla has had no shortage of scenes this season, very few have been at home, so the writers haven't had many chances to bring us up to speed on the progress of her mother's new relationship. Naturally, Pam Garrity's impending marriage creates ample dramatic possibilities for Buddy—some of which are tapped into tonight—but the impact of Buddy's desperation was muted for me by the continuity issues raised by his account of the relationship to Eric. Given the massive disparity in physical attractiveness (and the apparent disparity in age), I'd always assumed that Pam was a younger trophy wife who Buddy had picked up after he had already become a rich guy and local power broker. During Buddy's drunken recollections of his glory days earlier this season, we learned he was a Panther star in the late '70s, thirty years ago. That'd put him near 50 today, which seems reasonable, but there's no way in hell she's old enough to have gone to high school with him (Merrilee McCommas, who plays Pam, is 36 in real life, while Brad Leland is 53).

Julie continues to show her bitch side this week, which is no small achievement considering her lack of scenes with Matt and the MIA Adam. I liked the casual portrayal of a house party heavy on underage drinking, though if there was a scene explaining how she got there, I must have blinked and missed it. Riggins' rescue of her gave us a nice look at his innate decency and shored up the surrogate-sibling bond between them that I'm really digging. Unfortunately, it also set up Coach's misinterpretation of their relationship, a situation I found far too trite and predictable—or would have, at least, if Chandler's anger wasn't so convincing. Coach was, of course, all the more pissed because it wasn't just any guy he "caught" Julie with, and his anger would have seemed painfully clichéd if not for Chandler (or at least if Coach hadn't stuck up for Riggins just a few hours earlier). Then again, clichés exist for a reason—there isn't a father alive who'd be happy to catch his daughter in such a situation. One of the signs of a really good TV show is when we're reminded of the emotional truth that created the whole catalog of narrative clichés in the first place, and on that count *FNL* succeeds here as always.

Friday Night Lights Recap: Season 2, Episode 11, "Jumping the Gun"
BY ANDREW JOHNSTON ON JANUARY 12, 2008

Perhaps in part because "Jumping the Gun" is one of the few episodes this season that I've had the opportunity to see twice before writing about it (meaning I had more time for things to pop out at me), this weeks's installment of *Friday Night Lights* seemed particularly meaty. Although lots of characters turn up incidentally, the script keeps a tight focus on three of the series' central figures—Coach Taylor, Smash Williams and Tim

Riggins—and the exclusion of Matt, Landry, Jason, Tyra, etc., allows for a somewhat deeper exploration of the issues du jour.

The transition from the February letter-of-intent for seniors being recruited for college ball to the verbal-commitment paradigm is a good thing for *FNL*-because the season covers the period between August/September and December, we otherwise would have no clue where Smash would wind up before the series came back without him for season three (assuming, of course, that a third season is in the cards). Smash's vetting of the schools, and his ultimate decision, answer a lingering question about his new girlfriend Noelle: I'd been wondering if perhaps she was a sleeper agent for Miami Southern, the school at which her brother plays, who was trying to steer Smash there. Instead, her intense grilling of the recruiters (and her clear joy at Smash's decision to play at TMU) suggests she could be more like Lyla in the days before Jason's injury—not quite a gold digger, but nonetheless eager to follow her man on his road to glory. If not smarter than Lyla, though, she certainly has more perspective—she seems like the kind of gal who'd major in business or pre-law and would be sure to have a contingency plan for her future. As a former cheerleader with a good head on her shoulders, she'd certainly do damn well for herself as a pharmaceutical sales rep.

I'd been inclined to think that Mama Smash's disdain for Noelle had to do with a general lack of enthusiasm for her son dating a white woman—she was none too thrilled when he briefly hooked up with Tyra last season—but "Jumping the Gun" left me convinced that the real reason was Noelle's laserlike focus on the pro career she thought Smash was pursuing with a little too much vigor. Now that the hatchet has been buried all around and Smash is TMU-bound, I expect to see Mama Smash and Noelle get along with each other much better in future episodes. I've always been impressed by Liz Mikel as Mama Smash, and this week's episode gave her particularly strong material. I look forward to seeing a lot more of her as we learn more about just why Smash's commitment to TMU constitutes having jumped the gun.

The title, naturally, also applies to Coach's confrontation with Shelly, which came a little too early for Tami's liking. I can't see too many viewers taking Tami's side here: Between the "borrowed" blouse, the broken eggs and the hair dryer—and that's just this week—no-one can blame a guy (especially a guy like Coach) for gently steering her toward the door. (When Coach pops in the game tape and finds an episode of *The Office* on it, I have to wonder if it was chosen because, like *FNL*, it's owned and produced by NBC Universal or if one of the *FNL* producers sees *The Office* as embodying the kind of TV that Coach wouldn't like or "get"—last season, it's the show Julie and Matt were watching when he was nonplussed about Matt coming over). And while I understand that it's hard for the writers to come up with enough Tyra-at-work scenes to fulfill the minimum number of Applebee's plugs agreed to in the product placement deal, come on, Tami—if your sister is volunteering to pick up the tab, go ahead and milk her for a meal at a better restaurant! Tami may not be fond of extracting payback so directly; still, I was impressed by the attention to detail shown by having her pointedly wearing the "too sexy" shirt when she has lunch with Shelly at the end of the episode.

With the game out of the way and their coach headed for the unemployment line, it's a safe bet that we've seen the last of the Laribee Lions story arc. Both my viewings of the episode were via a rough cut disc provided by NBC with a fair amount of temp audio, and the game sequence provided an interesting look at how the plot of an episode can change on its way to the air. In the version I saw, the announcer—his lines clearly being read by someone who was hanging around the studio rather than the actor whose voice was ultimately used—delivers exactly the same description of the situation going into the final play that we hear in the broadcast version of the episode. However, the scoreboard shows Dillon leading 45-43, as opposed to being down by 5 as per the announcer. I'd expected that in the final version, the narration would change to reflect that Dillon was trying to hold on to a slim lead rather than aiming for a late comeback, but that wasn't so: Instead, every shot of the 45-43 scoreboard was replaced by one of a 38-43 scoreboard—something that would have been a lot harder for the producers to fix than the narration, especially in the shot that shows Matt running in front of the scoreboard. I thought that even though Riggins was clearly about to score a TD that would have put Dillon over the top either way when the Laribee coach runs onto the field, the score might have been changed to 45-43 because the writers didn't like the idea of Dillon winning a game only because of interference by the opposing coach.

Finally, we come to the Riggins story. It seemed pretty cruel of Coach Taylor to kick Rig to the curb when he found him sleeping in the locker room, and that was just the first of many bitter pills Tim had to swallow this week, others including his encounter with the MILF next door, his discovery that Billy is in worse financial straits than realized and, of course, the abortive TD. I suspect that nothing hurt Tim more, however, than having Coach Taylor praise him for being honorable just seconds after he and Billy have returned from stealing $3K from the meth dealer while picking up Tim's stuff. I'm glad the confusion over the situation with Julie has been laid to rest (by swooping in to 'fess up just as Coach and Tami are kissing and making up over the Shelly situation, Julie incidentally shows an impressive gift for being able to discern the perfect moment to deliver bad news to her father while suffering minimal consequences), but I have mixed feelings about the heist. On the one hand, Tim really should know better by now; on the other, the story line obviously stands to reinforce the surrogate fatherhood vibe between Coach and Riggins that I've been enjoying more with each passing week. Two concluding observations on the Riggins situation: 1) Why isn't he being recruited even a quarter as aggressively as Smash? Sure, he's missed games and has a checkered rep, but his grades and test scores can't be any worse than Smash's, and we've seen him score so many TDs that there would have to be some school—a third-tier party school, at least—that would offer him a scholarship. 2) Hey, Tim and Billy? If you steal $3000, use $2K to pay the mortgage and are at a loss for something to do with the remaining $1,000, here's a thought—*save it for next month's payment!*

Friday Night Lights Recap: Season 2, Episode 12, "Who Do You Think You Are?"
BY ANDREW JOHNSTON ON JANUARY 19, 2008

Compared to a lot of fans and commentators, I think I've been pretty charitable toward the second season of *Friday Night Lights,* but charity has its limits: "Who Do You Think You Are?" is a flat-out clunker, a trite, soapy episode that's easily the worst of the season to date and in the running for the lamest-ever episode of the series.

All of this week's main plot lines came off as almost unbelievably contrived. I'm the first to admit I don't know much about child development, but it seems far, far too early for the Taylors to be thinking about dropping Gracie off at daycare. Given the inherent chronology of the season—the Texas state championship takes place the week between Christmas and New Year's—it isn't even Thanksgiving yet on the show, meaning Gracie is, at a maximum, three months old. The whole separation-anxiety plot just felt like a flimsy excuse to generate tension between Coach and Tami over the issue of whether she should keep working outside the house. Coach, as has been clear since the beginning, is nothing if not stubborn, but his stubbornness here—amped up by Mac McGill, the last person from whom Coach should take relationship advice (other than Buddy, perhaps) was exaggerated to a degree that made him seem almost unrecognizable.

Carlotta's departure from Dillon was so abrupt and so under-explained that it almost certainly has to be the first step in a plan by the writers to bring Matt and Julie back together—but now that Julie has been turned into such a complete bitch, does anyone want that to happen anymore? The only good things to come from the plot were the really funny, natural-feeling scene where Matt admitted to Landry that he and Carlotta were an item and the affecting scene where Matt admits the extent of his feelings for her.

FNL has been extremely shrewd with its use of recognizable guest stars, and at first I was thrilled to see *Veronica Mars*' Francis Capra turn up as Santiago's old pal (Capra, by the way, suffers from a medical condition of some sort that's being treated with steroids, which first caused the severe acne that started to show up during the third season of *Mars* and which has now apparently caused him to put on some weight). Soon, however, it became apparent that Capra was stuck in a true eye-roller of a plot that the writers were milking for comedy one second and for pathos the next. Buddy's paranoia about leaving his valued possessions at home was entirely justified, and his decision to drag them back home so as not to offend Santiago was just silly, especially since it was obvious from the beginning that his gut impulse was going to be on the money and it wasn't going to be a Racism Is Bad story.

Lyla's Christian-radio plot was similarly frustrating—the call-in show felt completely bogus (for a program called "I Was A Teenage Christian", they certainly didn't talk about religion very much) and the oral sex question felt like something a writer thought a Texas teen would ask rather than the kind of question that would actually get thrown out there in real life. Riggins' prank call—which led to the two-second return of Jason Street, MIA for the past few weeks—merely served to set up what felt like the 40th time Riggins and Lyla have gone around the block dealing with the same issues. And could Lyla and her dweeby cohost have any less chemistry?

Most annoying of all was the plot about Smash and Noelle. Where to start? Noelle's parents and Mama Smash are unbelievably stupid if they think ordering their kids to break up is going to do anything other than strengthen their bond and make them want to spend even more time together. Mama Smash has legitimate reasons for disapproving of the relationship that have nothing to do with racism, but Noelle's parents seem completely out to lunch—they themselves don't seem to be racists, otherwise they wouldn't bond so easily with Mama Smash, and their fear that racism will cause problems for Smash and Noelle as a couple completely overlooks the fact that Smash is a future college football star who has already been on magazine covers and national TV before even graduating from high school. He's one of the most recognizable and revered guys in Dillon, and it struck me as ludicrous that the yahoos at the movie theater didn't recognize him and didn't promptly shut the fuck up when they realized who they were dealing with. Obviously, as a white guy, I may not be entirely qualified to address the topic, since racism exists in places and contexts in which liberal whites like myself never expect to find it, and there could well be star African-American high school football players out there who find this story to be 100% realistic. Nonetheless, I feel I'm both qualified and justified to say that within the context of *Friday Night Lights*, it felt like a total crock.

On the subject of things that feel like a total crock, I have great respect for *The New York Times'* Virginia Heffernan as a television critic, but her column in this week's *New York Times Magazine*, in which she says that *FNL*'s low ratings are the result of it not being a series that can be turned into a franchise with "online extensions" makes little sense to me. *FNL* has a thriving online community, as the show's TWoP fanbase proves, and using stuff like a series' volume of fanfic as an index of its success totally overlooks sitcoms—there isn't exactly a lot of *Curb Your Enthusiasm* or *30 Rock* fanfic out there, yet no-one uses that to argue that the shows are failing to connect with a mass audience. Neither is a network's willingness to merchandise a show an inherent sign of its health—the *CSI* comic book, spinoff novels and video games, for example, didn't start coming out until well after the original series was an established blockbuster. It's possible that I'm somehow misinterpreting Heffernan's thesis, but her column nonetheless left me scratching my head.

Friday Night Lights Recap: Season 2, Episode 13, "Humble Pie"
BY ANDREW JOHNSTON ON JANUARY 26, 2008

On the heels of the season's biggest turkey, *Friday Night Lights* makes a notable return to form with an episode that sees a number of storylines converging as the writers' plan for the rest of the season starts to come into focus. The big question, of course, is whether that plan will come to fruition—or, rather, will *FNL*'s second season have 22 episodes or 15? It all comes down to how things work out with the WGA strike, of course, and it's increasingly clear that if the strike doesn't end soon, few dramas will have ended the season with more balls in the air.

At the center of "Humble Pie" is Smash Williams, whose dilemma is the main reference point of the title. Hauled off in cuffs from his own house, days after his beatdown of the race-baiting assholes, Smash is advised by his attorney to deliver a public apology to the racist dickwads—confessing to his actions in public, oddly, before a deal with the DA has apparently been signed. The Smash-baiters offer our first real glimpse of a country club-fratboy element in Dillon, a town where few wealthy citizens apart from Buddy Garrity have ever received much screen time. The presence of these assholes suddenly makes Dillon seem a lot less idyllic (it also seems odd that the jerks would get to air their side on TV—using a racially-charged word like "thug" no less—before a "react quote" from Smash was already in the can), and given the nature of the controversy, it's surprising that no-one apart from his fellow Panthers has Smash's back. Where's the minister at the Williams' family's church? Where's the Dillon chapter of the NAACP? Aggravating questions aside, the one promising development to emerge from the story line is that we finally have a continuing plot arc—can the Panthers make it to the playoffs without Smash?—revolving around what happens on the gridiron.

This week's title is one of the series' most literal—indeed, it might be a little too on the nose—insofar as it also applies to the activities of Lyla, Tyra, Jason and Riggins. For her part, Tyra comes to realize that Landry is just too good of a guy to go unclaimed, as Dillon's own Enid Coleslaw (with a little bit of Lane Kim thrown in), Jean, emerges as the gal who's clearly right for him—or at least a lot better suited for our lad. Lyla, meanwhile, comes clean about her past with Riggins to Chris, her new born-again beau (where Chris is concerned, it's time for your faithful correspondent to eat some humble pie himself—as a devoted *Gilmore Girls* fan, I'm hugely embarrassed at my failure to recognize Matt Czuchry last week—he looked familiar as hell, but his combed, eerily helmet-like coiff threw me off compared to Logan Huntzberger's customarily unkempt locks. Still, I should have recognized that voice anywhere).

Jason's plot left me divided—on the one hand, it was a lot of fun watching him get eaten alive by the other sales associates at Buddy Garrity's dealership, who see Jason's dual status as a football hero and a quadriplegic as a huge threat to their commissions. Jason's sale to the chronic browser was also a good example of the triumph-over-adversity motif that's central to *FNL*, and one of the rare cases where the theme is addressed in a self-contained, single-episode storyline. On the other, there were some annoying continuity issues—it was just a few episodes ago, after all, that we saw Jason walk away from his job as Coach Taylor's assistant because he wanted to make his own way in the world. Granted, Jason has the excuse of financial hardship, but it seems odd for him to accept a job from Buddy of all people so quickly thereafter. And as for Buddy, while he understandably sees dollar signs when thinking about Jason's potential as a salesman, he seems overly charitable given the bad blood between him and Jason that resulted from the ill-fated Jason/Lyla engagement, the story line that brought Buddy as close as he's ever come to flat-out black-hat villainy.

For awhile now, Tim Riggins has seemed to be going around in circles, so having him straight up tell Lyla that he loves her gave him some welcome forward momentum…even if, unsurprisingly, he was spurned by her. Rig can be proud, but he ain't dumb—thankfully, he's quick to accept the $3000 that Lyla offers him to repay the meth heads, who I sincerely hope we've seen the last of. Some people may balk at Lyla having easy access to such a sum, but it made plenty of sense to me—Buddy is obviously a pretty wealthy guy, and Lyla is nothing if not spoiled by him. I have no trouble imagining an off-camera scene where she got him to cough up the cash in about two seconds flat (heck, it's entirely possible she told him what the money was for—if so, he probably saw it as an investment in the Panthers returning to the playoffs).

On a lot of other shows, "Tami becomes the girls' volleyball coach and Tyra joins the team" would be a dumb one-week plotline, and while it's a story that doesn't arrive without issues—on top of Gracie and her guidance-counselor duties, it's an awful lot for Tami to be taking on—like many *FNL* plots, it works far better than it has any reason to, both because of the writing and the cinematic energy of the practice sequence and the game (why the heck is Riggins hanging around during the practice, anyway?). The volleyball plot is the one story line that generally stayed clear of the "humble pie" theme, in the apparent interest of building toward a future payoff—a payoff that may never arrive if the season ends after just two more episodes.

Friday Night Lights Recap: Season 2, Episode 14, "Leave No One Behind"
BY ANDREW JOHNSTON ON FEBRUARY 3, 2008

No matter what happens next week, no matter what sort of inadvertent cliffhanger *Friday Night Lights* fans are handed as a result of the WGA strike, I think it's safe to describe "Leave No One Behind" as a vintage episode. For me, certainly, it exemplified almost everything that made me a fan during the first season—and, more than that, almost everything which made the series a significant source of personal inspiration during some very hard times. With the series' future unclear after next week, I'm just glad we were able to get one more such episode before what could very well be the end.

At least after spending a few minutes on Google, I've been unable to verify whether the phrase "Leave No Man Behind" originated as the tag line for *Black Hawk Down* or if it was a military slogan before Ridley Scott's 2000 film. Regardless, it obviously wasn't just for PC reasons that the title was rendered in a gender-neutral form: While several characters are rescued from emotional quagmires during the episode, others are indeed left behind, and they aren't all male. But we'll deal with that in due course.

Early in the episode, Coach Taylor meets with the Panthers and gives a speech very similar to the halftime talk that fired up the team to come from behind and win the championship last year in "State": "It's about more than just football—it's about adversity and how we stand up to it. What we are gonna do is we're gonna work, we're gonna adjust, and we're gonna work some more. We're gonna take adversity and turn it into an asset."

It's a speech you can boil down to six words he doesn't say here, but which Smash does at the end of the episode—"Clear Eyes, Full Hearts, Can't Lose"—and I'm helpless before any episode of *Friday Night Lights* which ends with that slogan. The first season of the show began a few weeks after I returned to work from a hiatus occasioned by cancer surgery, and over the course of the season I had a pretty rough time adjusting to the juxtaposition of work and chemotherapy as well as adjusting to life with a colostomy bag (a temporary situation reversed by another operation several months later). Throughout the year, Coach Taylor's message about turning the negative into the positive was immensely valuable to me, in particular because of how vividly it was illustrated by the story lines involving Jason, Smash and Matt and how the Panther slogan never seemed like something to which mere lip service was being paid—it was a credo the characters lived by every week, and one I adopted as my own (at least as something to aspire to, because lord knows it's a lot easier to just feel sorry for yourself sometimes). The 2007 football season hasn't been any easier for the Panthers, yet this time around, the motto never seemed as relevant as it did tonight.

It's a particularly rough week for Matt Saracen, who's buckling under the stress of caring for his grandmother even before she has the fall that sends her to the hospital by the end of the episode. When we first see her, she's sufficiently out of it as to be confusing the smell of eggs with that of sausage. After Matt leaves, he learns of Smash's suspension on the radio just as a cloud of steam erupts from the radiator of the Dodge Dart I knew he shouldn't have bought. It's a somewhat clumsy visual metaphor, but Matt deserves what he gets for spending that much money on a nearly-40-year-old gas guzzler.

At the team meeting, before Coach tears into his speech, we see another example of the Matt/Smash tension I found so enjoyable in the earlier episodes of the season—being a sarcastic dick, dare I say it, brings out Zach Gilford's best as an actor. That made Matt's exploration of the dark side more entertaining than it should have been, I dare say, though the sight of Riggins constantly egging him on, seeing how far he could make Matt go and using that as an excuse to descend to ever lower depths himself, was plenty depressing as far as Riggins' own progress goes.

I always love a good Grandma Saracen/Coach Taylor scene, and the one at the hospital was a huge treat—her warmth and enthusiasm whenever she comes in contact with Coach is always palpable through the screen. It's a quality that's cleverly exploited here in that it lowers our guard in advance of the scene where Coach drags Matt into the shower (a scene which parallels the Tami/Julie dustup I'll get to shortly) and tells him to shape the fuck up. Matt's response reminds us that he's just a kid: "You left me for a better job. Your daughter left me for a better guy. Carlotta left me for Guatemala. My dad left me for a damn war. What's wrong with me?" Sure, it's a *Good Will Hunting* moment, and I have no doubt that more than a few viewers rolled their eyes. But clichés are true for a reason, and if you've ever had abandonment issues, it's hard not to be moved by the scene and to feel that Matt is one hell of a lucky guy to have someone like Coach Taylor there for him.

And after everything that Smash has been through, he's a lucky guy to have a mother as steadfast as Mama Smash, who refuses to drop the "I Told You So" bomb when her son's gravy train goes hurtling off the rails. Her encouragement provides another echo of the team motto, motivating Smash to give one hell of a pep talk of his own to the Panthers, who take to the field determined to transform adversity into an asset—and, by necessity, leaving behind Smash, who instantly turns into a crying wreck in an incredibly moving final scene.

As I said before, Julie's plot largely parallels Matt's, and those who picked up on her envy of Tami's attention to the volleyball squad last week—something I missed—turn out to be right on the money. Much as in the later Coach/Matt scene, Tami gives her daughter a blistering lecture before abruptly realizing she's the one who's really in the wrong. In real life, I can't imagine Tami having much success at persuading the license bureau dude to let Julie take the test late—not unless it she did a lot more eyelash batting and skin-flashing—but her success here made for a sweet scene indeed courtesy of Connie Britton's inexhaustible reservoir of brassy charm.

Aside from Smash, the person most obviously left behind is, of course, Jean, who I'm sure is entirely right when she tells Landry that he's making a big mistake. I was very impressed by Jean's bluntness when she asks Tyra if she's a friend or a rival, in a scene made all the funnier by the height difference between the two girls (I think Jean was sitting down in all of her scenes with Tyra last week; this time, we see that her eyes are about as far off the ground as Tyra's breasts). Caught off guard by the question, Tyra gives Jean her blessing, and instantly comes to regret it. Throughout the episode, Tyra's behavior seems to support the "she only wants what she can't have" theory vis-à-vis her relationship to Landry, as opposed to the "he's just too much of a geek for her" theory (which Landry himself subscribes to).

When Tyra seeks advice from her mom about the issue, her mom's blunt words—"When haven't I competed with another gal for a guy? I like the chase. I like the challenge. I like to win"—are words she clearly should have taken as a warning. Instead, she seems to take them as a license to aggressively pursue Landry. While he first gives her the treatment she deserves outside the movie theater, he soon reveals the extent of his weakness by dumping Jean (in a scene that, the more I think of it, reminds me quite a bit of John Malkovich's brilliant "It's beyond my control" kiss-off in *Dangerous Liaisons*) before running off to join Tyra. Much as I like the guy—how *can't* you like a guy who's torn as to whether *Jaws* is a better date movie than *Star Trek: The Wrath of Khan*?—I really want to see him learn his lesson after breaking Jean's heart—if that didn't happen, this wouldn't be *Friday Night Lights*. The way things stand now, however, there might not be enough time left for us to ever find out what happens next.

A few miscellaneous notes: In the past, Dillon's nebulous location has been described as "West Central Texas", however in the DMV scene, the reality of the Austin locations collides with the series' fictional world when we see that Dillon is on US Route 183, which has its northern terminus at Presho, SD and which ends at Refugio, TX, just above the Gulf of Mexico. The entire Texas portion is in the eastern third of the state, including Austin, where it intersects with Interstate 35.

I'm sure Austinites can identify exactly which branch of the Alamo Drafthouse Cinemas Landry and Jean go to for their screening of *Jaws* (is it the same theater where Matt and Julie saw *Eragon* last year?), but since the Alamo has become a chain encompassing Houston, San Antonio and Katy as well as Austin, it's not out of the question for there to be a Dillon branch of the Drafthouse on Earth *FNL* (or, if Dillon is really in "West Central Texas", for them to have driven to the San Antonio theater). Of course—this is where the geek in me comes out—this means that Coach Taylor, Lyla Garrity and Tami's high school boyfriend who we meet next week all exist in the same universe as a Kyle Chandler, a Minka Kelly and a Peter Berg, as the first two have cameos in *The Kingdom* while the latter directed the film. Naturally, the Drafthouse could have just been showing the Lars von Trier miniseries...

In the scene at Coach's office, a quick shot of his PC reveals that he's using Windows Vista at work. I'd like to think that Coach would be discerning enough to be a Mac user, and perhaps he is at home—at school, he's of course at the mercy of the school district's IT department. Given that we've seen evidence of Dillon High functioning on a very tight budget, I'm surprised the district decided to make the leap from XP—I'm sure they got a good deal on an educational site license for Vista, but the additional hardware and support costs sort of seem like a needless extravagant expenditure.

Finally, I gotta say I feel pretty bad for any surviving members of the 1958 and 1962 state champion Panther teams who still live in the Dillon area—their victories are acknowledged by plaques in the locker room but are left off the scoreboard, which mentions no Panther championships prior to 1966. The nine district championships won by the Panthers leave no room for any earlier district titles, but since only six of those nine teams went on to win State, there's plenty of room on the right side of the board for acknowledgment of their success.

Incidentally, the scoreboard confirms that the year of Buddy Garrity's state championship season was in 1978 (all we knew before is that Jimmy Carter was President at the time) and that prior to last season, the most recent Panther state championship was in 1998. The 55-game win streak mentioned on the board presumably took place in 1978-81, when they won four consecutive district titles. Can that be reconciled with them only winning State twice in that period? There are some questions that, in order to be answered, require a level of research more obsessive than even I am capable of…and this is one of them.

Friday Night Lights Recap: Season 2, Episode 15, "May the Best Man Win"
BY ANDREW JOHNSTON ON FEBRUARY 9, 2008

Until we know for sure whether the 15th episode of *Friday Night Lights'* second season will turn out to be the last, there really isn't much to say about "May the Best Man Win". The episode resolves one major continuing story line—the crisis enveloping the future career of "Smash" Williams—and does so in style. The other ongoing stories, and the new ones that are introduced, are considerably less promising, but past experience has shown us that you can't really judge an *FNL* storyline until you see how it plays out—which largely leaves us in limbo.

I consider Jason Street's date with the pee girl to be one of the series' absolute low points, so I was considerably less than enthused by the return of the waitress who rescued him from her—the writers would have been much better advised to bring back the tattoo artist from last season if they wanted to reconnect Jason with a girl from his past. Of course, given the time since their last encounter, the creative team would have had to jump through hoops galore to get her pregnant relative to their last encounter— heck, any kid they conceived would be as old as Gracie by now. I don't recall there being that much to suggest Street had sex with the waitress, but that could be because I was barely considering the possibility in light of Jason's condition.

In principle, I'm not against a story involving Jason becoming a father, but in this context it leaves a lot to be desired. For one thing, this happens just after he lands the job at Buddy Garrity's dealership, and we haven't had the chance to see him settle in to the job or to watch him really take stock of how it stacks up to what he wants from life. And while Jason tells the waitress that he wants nothing more than to be a father, I don't think we've really heard him say so before, so it totally comes from out of the blue. And a lot of the surrounding circumstances just felt like sloppy writing—after the circumstances of Coach and Jason's last encounter, their lunch at Applebee's seemed too random, and too casual—and lord knows there's no reason on Earth why Coach wouldn't know Jason's age offhand. The reminder that Street is 19 reiterated that Scott Porter—at 27, the oldest of the young actors on the show—is probably too old to be playing Street, and there are also issues with having the waitress be 19. If that's her age, then why wasn't she a Dillon High classmate of Street's (okay, maybe she went to the nearest outlying high school). Having her be a few years older would have worked better, unless the writers felt that they'd gone to the well too many times with Dillon kids and older love interests after the stories involving Carlotta, the Swede, Adam, Chris (Lyla's Christian beau) and Riggins' neighbor (incidentally, I noticed that the actress playing the waitress has the same one-eye-higher-than-the-other thing going on that Shannen Dougherty does—is there an exact name for that condition?).

Running down the rest of the stories, I have to say that while I like the idea of Riggins going to church regularly—especially if he discovered that he likes it, and that his motives have nothing to do with recapturing Lyla's heart—giving him a sports-talk show at the Christian station is just a dumb idea. His discussion on the air of the game that Dillon plays this week made me realize that we aren't told the outcome of last week's game (if we are, I totally missed it)...and, given what a complete blow-out this week's is, it really makes me wonder why everyone was freaking out about how hard it would be for the Panthers to make the playoffs without Smash. And while it was nice of Matt to let Landry score a TD, wasn't Landry hobbling around last week as a result of having tripped over something? I guess he could have recovered in time, but an explanatory line of dialogue couldn't have hurt. (On the subject of Landry, I thought his bragging about bedroom action with Tyra was quite out of character—it would have been a lot more true to form for him to acknowledge that he was getting some, then say "a gentleman doesn't go into details" instead of acting as naïve as he did around Matt).

I'd thought Peter Berg's guest appearance might be a sign that the creative team's early start on the season gave them enough perspective in terms of the WGA strike deadline to have planned this week's episode as a possible finale (when I visited the set in early August, the season's seventh episode was in production at a time when many other series were just shooting their third or fourth). I guess I'm just too symbolism-oriented by nature, as there wasn't anything terribly valedictory about the series creators' appearance as Tami's high school boyfriend. Coach's irritation towards him and general lack of patience was totally in character—but, like some of what the coach at the historically black college says about their friendship, the encounter raises a number of thorny chronological/continuity questions about how long the Taylors have been in Dillon, where else Coach has worked, etc., etc. I'm probably thinking about all this way too much, but if you're the kind of person who spent way too much time as a teenager trying to resolve internal contradictions in comic book timelines, it's hard not to get distracted by such minutae.

In the whole episode, there was only one scene that really stood out as a superior *FNL* moment: The sequence in which Noelle prepares Smash for the meeting at Alabama—a scene that removes any doubt about the sincerity of her feelings for him—and the ensuing conversation with the coach. The Alabama coach projects a decency that makes it immediately clear that he probably would have stood by Smash had he made a commitment to play for the Crimson Tide, and the look on Gaius Charles' face as Smash gradually realizes this further proves that, next to Zach Gilford, he's the best of the younger actors on the show. The coach's concluding "Tell your mom I say hi" may gild the lily somewhat, but it's also the kind of thing you just know he'd say in real life under the circumstances (one thing did bug me, however—if Smash and Noelle were supposed to be at the actual Alabama campus in that scene—and, if for the sake of argument, Dillon is located at the same coordinates as its real-life counterpart, Odessa TX—then they would have had to drive 939 miles to get there!). If the second season of *Friday Night Lights* is allowed to play itself out, we can only hope that, when the series returns, the still-unresolved storylines are wrapped up by means of moments as sincere and affecting.

The Wire

Proposition Joe: The Art of the Deal
BY ANDREW JOHNSTON ON SEPTEMBER 6, 2006

"Charlie Stollers just sold dope. No profile, no street rep. Just buy for a dollar, sell for two."—"Proposition" Joe Stewart

Apart from state Sen. Clay "she-iiiiiiit" Davis, "Proposition" Joe Stewart is the only character on *The Wire* with something resembling a catchphrase: "I got a proposition for you." Prop Joe, as played by Robert F. Chew, is friendly as can be when trying to coax Stringer Bell or Marlo Stanfield to do his bidding; but to viewers with an omniscient view of David Simon's Baltimore, the look in the fat man's eye constantly reminds us that while the West Side boys play the game from the gut, Joe is always thinking at least five moves ahead.

Joe made his first appearance on *The Wire* in a cheap suit that made him look more like a civil servant than a crimelord, coaching the East Side's best in an annual basketball showdown against a West Side team fielded by Stringer Bell and Avon Barksdale. Both teams had ringers on the court—Avon was fielding a junior college prospect while Joe had recruited a pro baller from an Italian team—and the Barksdale gang seemed to have a shot at breaking their losing streak. But after persuading Avon to raise the stakes on their bet, Prop Joe called a second ringer off the bench, an unassuming short guy with dazzling fake-out skills that gave the East Side its third consecutive victory in the grudge match.

Joe's Br'er Rabbit tactics gave way to a more complex brand of strategy in season two after Avon Barksdale's imprisonment left Stringer in charge of the towers. While Joe and Stringer both prefer to avoid violence in order to stay off police radar, the big guy is in many ways the anti-String. While Bell pours his money into real estate development and dreams of pursuing political power, Joe is content to use a dingy appliance store as his headquarters. Stringer's quest for legitimacy gets him fleeced by the sleazy Clay Davis, while Joe's belief in crime as an honorable profession allows him to grow rich doing business with international gangsters like the Greek.

In season two, Joe persuades String to cut a deal behind Avon's back by telling the story of a West Side player from the '60s who made a fortune and retired because of his success at remaining anonymous and lulling the police into complacency. ("Want to know what kills more police than bullets and liquor?" Joe asks String. "Boredom. They just can't handle that shit.") As much as Joe would like to emulate Charlie Stollers, it's not an option; he needs to deal with the lightning rods like the Barksdales and Stanfield to secure the territory without which he can't get his product on the streets, and many in his raucous family—most notably his nephew Cheese—have been seduced by the flashy side of the gangsta life. "I got motherfucking nephews and in-laws fucking all my shit up all the time, and it ain't like I can pop a cap in their ass and not hear about it Thanksgiving time," he rants to his Russian suppliers. (In all fairness, however, Cheese's lack of discretion helps Joe discover that the cops are stepping up their wiretap operations in season three.)

Joe is a good 10 years older than the rest of the street figures we've met on *The Wire*, and though he's unquestionably a survivor, he's might be the last of his kind. The "co-op" approach to the drug trade that he persuades Stringer and his peers to adopt is eminently practical. "For a cold-ass crew of gangsters, y'all carried it out like Republicans and shit," Joe says approvingly. But it has little appeal to a generation of players who see slinging rock as a means of fulfilling power fantasies rather than as a business. In a less violent culture, the co-op model could be a success, but only in a situation where de facto, off-the-books decriminalization à la "Bunny" Colvin's Hamsterdam was prevalent enough to make turf wars a nonissue. If full-blown legalization was to occur, entrepreneurs at Joe's level would surely be swept away as soon as the Wal-Marts and Phillip Morrises figured out how to get a piece of the action.

Joe sees himself as a businessman first, and he does take his actual business seriously, repairing and reselling toasters for puny sums of money Avon wouldn't bend down to pick up. But he's all criminal; he may avoid violence personally, but his business model depends on manipulating others into spilling blood to serve his interests. The use to which Joe puts his fierce intelligence brings to mind a line from the titular leader's narration in Spike Lee's *Malcolm X*: "Cats that hung together trying to find a little security, to find an answer, found nothing. Cats that might have probed space or cured cancer—Hell, West Indian Archie might have been a mathematical genius—all victims of the American social order." It's a bit of a stretch to call Joe a potential Rhodes scholar thwarted by the system (if anyone on the series deserves that description, it's D'Angelo Barksdale), but his brains could certainly serve better causes. And the close calls he's experienced over three seasons prove that if he has a weakness, it's that he's not quite as smart as he thinks he is.

Like Bubbles, Joe is based on an actual person of the same name, and the real Proposition Joe's preference for negotiation over violence could not keep him from getting gunned down in a Baltimore nightclub in 1984. Of course, that doesn't necessarily mean the fictional Joe will meet the same fate: Although many storylines are based on cases journalist-turned-screenwriter David Simon reported (and which cop-turned-screenwriter Ed Burns investigated), Simon has been very clear about the lack of one-to-one plot parallels between the series and the historical record. "Some of these events actually occurred, and a few others were rumored to have occurred," Simon writes in his introduction to the companion book *The Wire: Truth Be Told*. "But many of the events did not occur, and perhaps the only distinction worth making is that all of them *could* have happened [emphasis added]." Joe may still get backed into a corner, but the big guy seems smart enough to talk his way out and get back to business as usual.

The Wire Recap: Season 5, Episode 1, "More with Less"
BY ANDREW JOHNSTON ON JANUARY 7, 2008

It's my pleasure, dear readers, to welcome you to *The House Next Door*'s coverage of the final season of *The Wire*. Having been asked to recap the conclusion of perhaps the most substantial TV drama ever (only *The Sopranos* comes close) is a privilege—the equivalent of writing, in the Victorian era, weekly assessments of the closing installments of Charles Dickens' *A Tale of Two Cities* or Anthony Trollope's *Can You Forgive Her?* as they were serialized. *The Wire* is not an easy show to write about in this context. I've seen two-thirds of this season's episodes, and unlike many other serialized dramas, episode-to-episode continuity on this one is so tight that it becomes hard to separate one chapter from the next. Rest assured that I'll avoid all spoilers for as-yet-unaired episodes in my recaps and will keep my focus on the installment at hand. Any speculation about future events will be just that.

Notwithstanding the numerous references to Chris and Snoop's accumulated corpses having been discovered "last year" in the abandoned rowhouses, it's pretty clear that about 15 months have passed since season four ended with "Final Grades", in which the discovery of the bodies in late December 2006 took the air out of an apparent decline in the city's murder rate. "More with Less" begins in March, 2008, under ironic circumstances—the shoddy state of Baltimore's schools, documented in great detail in Season Four, has led Baltimore's mayor, Tommy Carcetti, to divert every possible cent toward education, leaving the police department gasping for air.

While *The Wire* has a long history of presenting us with sympathetic criminals—Proposition Joe, Stringer Bell, D'Angelo Barksdale and so on—there has never been a doubt that, at the end of the day, it's the police who are generally in the right. Series creator David Simon challenges this belief in the opening scene by having Bunk Moreland, Ed Norris and Jay Landsman, three of the most consistently engaging cops, extract a confession via the sort of underhanded tactics that Simon documented in his book *Homicide: A Year on the Killing Streets*, but which were seldom used on the TV version because they would have made it hard to root for Frank Pendleton, Tim Bayliss et al. Indeed, Simon goes so far as to have Bunk paraphrase Adolf Hitler, who wrote in *Mein Kampf* that:

"The great masses of the people in the very bottom of their hearts tend to be corrupted rather than consciously and purposely evil, and that, therefore, in view of the primitive simplicity of their minds they more easily fall a victim to a big lie than to a little one...Such a falsehood will never enter their heads and they will not be able to believe in the possibility of such monstrous effrontery and infamous misrepresentation in others."

It's a scene that's as chilling as it is entertaining, though it also features one of *The Wire*'s rare diversions into the realm of the "overclose": Norris' statement that "Americans are a stupid people by and large—we pretty much believe whatever we're told", an observation that also echoes the Führer. However, Simon isn't attempting to demonize the cops—if he was, the perp who "Professor" Landsman hooks up to the copier wouldn't be such a dullard. Given the role that the media plays in this season, Bunk and Norris' observations serve as a declaration of a theme that we can expect to see reflected in all of the season's storylines.

Also entertaining yet depressing is the return of Jimmy McNulty's alcoholic "McNutty" persona, which has given us some of the series' funniest and most memorable moments (such as the vice sting mentioned by Dozerman, which took place during the second season). McNulty's return to uniform duty (and his decision to shack up with Beady) at the end of Season Three seemed like a sincere conversion, but I don't think McNulty's tumble from the wagon represents creative backsliding on Simon's part (or an attempt to placate fans who complained about McNulty's diminished role during Season Four): The bureaucratic obstacles he faces in his quest to bring Marlo, Chris and Snoop to justice could drive anyone to drink.

On a similar note, while it's ostensibly a positive development to see that Bubbles is now clean and sober—and has apparently been so for more than a year—his circumstances are hardly uplifting. He's living with a sister who still doesn't trust him, and he faces temptation on every corner he passes on his way home at night. While *The Wire* is one of the most plot-dense series, the secret to its success is the ease with which it enables us to think of the characters as real people. Bubbles, having been based on a real-life addict and stoolie by the same name, has always been especially vivid (for which the astonishing Andre Royo deserves as much credit as Simon and his fellow writers), and the grim particulars of his situation make it hard to celebrate his sobriety as a triumph. No reference is made to Bubbles having accidentally killed Sherrod with the hot shot last season, but it's clear that the only reason Bubs is staying clean is because of the massive guilt he feels for having accidentally taken the life of his protégé.

Quite nearly as disheartening are the glimpses we catch of Michael and Dukie, who have apparently been absorbed into Marlo's drug business past the point of no return (though Michael is obviously shielding Dukie to the best of his ability). Despite his tutelage under Marlo, Chris and Snoop,

Michael still has traces of a soul, and it will be very interesting to see how he chooses to play the game—he's clearly smarter than Marlo (who's no dummy, but whose intelligence definitely has its limits), and at this point he could grow up to be a nonviolent, negotiation-oriented player à la Prop Joe or String as easily as he could fit the ruthless mold of Marlo or Avon Barksdale.

Marlo may be more inclined to use lethal force than Prop Joe, but he's still all business, as we see when he pulls a fast one on one of his retail dealers to get a better split for himself, as well as when he dupes the cops into thinking he's having a tryst at a motel when he's in fact attending a meeting of Prop Joe's co-op. Indeed, Marlo may be taking on more business than he can handle—in addition to running the west side and obviously plotting to replace Prop Joe as Baltimore's top wholesaler (hence Chris's trip to the courthouse to look up the file on Sergei Malatov, the Russian McNulty put away in Season Two, who has ties to Joe's supplier, "the Greek"), he still has to avoid the investigation into Chris and Snoop's murder spree. And then there's the little matter of seeking revenge on Omar.

What Marlo doesn't have the perspective to realize is how close he is to complete victory: With the two forces that are ostensibly intended to be the most powerful defenders of the public interest—law enforcement and the local press—both reeling from budget cuts, he's like a fox scoping out a henhouse that he has no way of realizing is unguarded. His actions at the co-op meeting suggest that while he's on the verge of attaining massive power, he has absolutely no clue how to use that power effectively. If he makes a premature attempt at controlling the game without a mentor or consiglieri as canny as Joe, String or Butchie in his corner, Marlo stands an excellent chance of becoming his own worst enemy.

Each season of *The Wire* has introduced us to a different Baltimore institution, and for the final season Simon has chosen the *Sun*, where he spent twelve years as a reporter. Our POV character is city editor Gus

Haynes, played by Clark Johnson, who was so brilliant on *Homicide* as detective Meldrick Lewis. Johnson has had an illustrious career as a TV director in the years since *Homicide* ended its run (in addition to having helmed the very first episode of *The Wire* in 2002, he also directed the series finale), and it's a treat to see him act again. The strong parallels between the situations at police HQ and at the *Sun* offices make it clear that Simon has an almost evangelical belief in the press as a guardian of the public, and the picture he paints of the current state of the industry is by no means a pretty one. Every time the paper tries to save money by, say, making do without a transit reporter, it takes a step further away from its mission to "comfort the afflicted and afflict the comfortable", as an industry maxim puts it. Newspapering is about the kind of fleet-footed analysis that exposes the city council president's quid pro quo with the drug dealer/titty bar impressario at the last second. Unfortunately, defending the public interest isn't customarily a path to bigtime profitability, as we see when the *Sun's* head honcho mandates that any coverage of race at the University of Maryland should reach a predetermined conclusion (intriguingly, the scene represents a thinly-veiled jab at legendary newspaperman Gene Roberts, who, like the "Gene Robbins" referred to in the episode, is a former editor of the *Philadelphia Inquirer* who is presently a professor of journalism at U-Md.).

Although Haynes only turns up at the episode's halfway point, his blend of cynicism and passion and his commitment to his profession instantly establish him as a classic *Wire* character, and it's a constant joy to see him interact with the remaining *Sun* lifers who have yet to take buyouts (many of whom, I understand, are played by former *Sun* colleagues of Simon's, much as officers such as Western District commander Dennis Mello are played by former real life Baltimore cops). Simon has said that once season five of *The Wire* has concluded, he'll have said all he has to say about Baltimore, law enforcement and every other subject the series has touched on. It's too bad he feels that way, as a series built around Haynes would pretty much instantly become the best-ever TV drama about the newspaper world, leaving *Lou Grant* et al. far behind in the dust. Still, ten episodes involving the fictionalized *Sun* are much better than nothing, and by weaving the press into his grand urban tapestry, Simon ensures that the richest portrait of city life in the medium's history is now all the more complete.

The Wire Recap: Season 5, Episode 2, "Unconfirmed Reports"
BY ANDREW JOHNSTON ON JANUARY 13, 2008

By the end of "Unconfirmed Reports", all of the pieces for *The Wire*'s final season are on the board, and it becomes possible to get a pretty good idea of where things are heading: Avon Barksdale offers us a clean, concise summary of Marlo's master plan, the "big lie" promised in the opening scene of the season begins to emerge, and David Simon's critique of the Baltimore Sun grows even sharper. It's a dense, rich episode with many intensely raw moments, and one which shows that Simon & Co. have a good handle on the pace of this accelerated season (three episodes shorter than seasons one and four and two episodes shorter than seasons two and three).

We begin with one of the most powerful and realistic depictions of a 12-step meeting that I've ever seen in film or television, in which an attractive female addict testifies that any list one makes of things he or she won't do to get high turns into a list of things they will do as soon as the inner addict takes charge. It's a lesson Bubbles is no doubt familiar with, but one he shrugs off as he takes to the podium, urged by his sponsor Walon to share during the meeting's closing minutes. Bubbles uses the opportunity to joke about his addiction before going to the brink of addressing how he accidentally killed Sherrod, then abruptly pulling back. "I don't feel nothing!," Bubbles proclaims indignantly as he storms away after the meeting. "That was never the problem!," Walon yells after him, and he's entirely right.

Lester Freamon emerges as perhaps the closest thing to a David Simon stand-in as he spins the Clay Davis probe into a sort of unified field theory of urban corruption, hinting that this season could turn out to be *The Wire*'s own *Chinatown* depending on how far Simon chooses to go. Right after we see Freamon explain it all to Sydnor, we're treated to Marlo laying out his own nearly as expansive agenda to Chris and Snoop, essentially handing them a to-kill list. The scenes that result, later in the episode, are a much-needed reminder that in addition to being incredibly vicious, Chris and Snoop are a hell of a lot fucking smarter than they look. In his meeting with his F.B.I. contact, McNulty is as confident as can be that he can pin the killings on Chris and Snoop in just a couple of weeks given the right resources, but I'm inclined to think he's drastically underestimating them and that he'd be totally screwed even if the feds gave him a blank check.

At the *Sun,* we see Gus Haynes in a meeting in which the paper's self-important executive editor James Whiting and his smarmy lieutenant Thomas Klebanow lay plans for an education series that seems intended more to impress Pulitzer judges than to actually change anything in Baltimore. Somewhat ironically, what Whiting proposes sounds sort of like what *The Wire*'s fourth season would have been like if it was intended more to impress Emmy voters than to reflect what Simon and Ed Burns have learned about the city's schools from their years in the trenches. Whiting's comments to the effect of "if you leave everything in, soon you've got nothing" could speak to TV writing insofar as if one leaves in all the "dramatic" elements of a script—romantic subplots, comic relief, etc—a writer can be left with no room left to deliver an actual message.

In interviews, Simon has talked fairly specifically about the Pulitzer-generating "Philadelphia model"—inspired by the work of Gene Roberts, the template for Whiting's pal "Gene Robbins"—which was imported to the *Sun* by Bill Marimow and John Carroll, the apparent inspirations for

Whiting and Klebanow. Simon's comments made it seem as though he considered this model the key to the paper's decline. However, in his letter to *Slate*'s TV Club last week, Simon mentions (but doesn't name—perhaps for legal reasons?) a *Sun* reporter who committed a number of Jayson Blair style fabrications on Marimow and Carroll's watch, who they were warned about but failed to discipline. The sequence in which Scott Templeton is sent to write a color piece on the Orioles' opening-day game and returns with the story of the wheelchair-bound "E.J." seems to make it pretty obvious that Templeton is being established as a stand-in for that reporter. The Simon-Marimow-Carroll feud has been documented all over the place in enough articles to make one's head spin; notable ones include this Columbia Journalism Review cover story [https://archives.cjr.org/cover_story/secrets_of_the_city.php?page=all] and this Esquire piece by Simon [https://www.esquire.com/news-politics/a4115/david-simon-0308/]. Maybe it's just me, but the intensity of Marimow and Carroll's defenders and their tendency to describe Simon as someone unnaturally obsessed with the situation only makes me more inclined to take Simon's side (of course, Simon's track record with *The Wire* also has more than a little to do with it).

It's too bad that HBO chose to advertise the return of Avon Barksdale, as advance word of his appearance kind of takes the edge off of a spectacular entrance that more than befits his villainy—seriously, it's right up there with Darth Vader boarding the blockade runner in pursuit of the Death Star plans. Wood Harris makes the most of his minimal screen time with some killer line readings ("Fuck all them East Side bitches! That's just the way I feel about it. I got nothing but love in my heart for West Side niggas, nothing but love—of course, you know, I got to have my taste too..."). It's a great cameo by a character I was thrilled to see again but don't expect to see after this, though anything's possible. My only regret is that we didn't get to see Marlo deliver the $100,000 tribute to Brianna before his meeting with Sergei.

From the "ask and ye shall receive" department, we get a pretty decent shot of Lester Freamon walking toward the camera at the end of the episode (as he enters his office and speaks with Rhonda Pearlman), which would seem to lay to rest A. McCann's doubts about Clarke Peters' physical capabilities (Peter's gait seems a little strange in the scene outside the diner, but he seems to be moving around just fine in the office scene, which is shot from a much better angle). Lester has neat character moments throughout the episode, most notably when he's listening to vintage R&B on his stakeout while reading a magazine about his beloved miniatures. If there's one character on the show who I wish we had the time to learn a lot more about before the series leaves the air, it's him.

It's to Simon's credit that we don't see Chris and Snoop's massacre of Junebug and his family and associates; when you're dealing with that many bodies, it's creepier to see the aftermath rather than the crime itself unless you go the "found footage" route, as John McNaughton did with Henry and Otis's home invasion in *Henry: Portrait of a Serial Killer*. The one kill we see Snoop rack up is more than disturbing enough. Michael is clearly in way the hell over his head, and given the incompetence of the kid who joins Chris and Snoop on the drive by, you can tell they're grateful to have a protégé with some semblance of a brain. Of course, Michael's conclusion that the killing is ultimately pointless proves that he's smarter than his erstwhile mentors, and, as I said last week, if Michael emerges as a major player over time, he's definitely going to be more of a Prop Joe or a Stringer Bell than an Avon or a Marlo. We didn't need the scene where he chooses not to shoot the kid in order to reach that conclusion, but even Shakespeare played to the cheap seats every now and then.

The Wire Recap: Season 5, Episode 3, "Not for Attribution"
BY ANDREW JOHNSTON ON JANUARY 21, 2008

I don't deny it: *The Wire* didn't quite float my boat when I saw the first broadcast of the first episode in the Summer of 2002. Like many, I only became obsessed with the show on DVD, meaning I absorbed Seasons 1-4 by watching them in batches of two to five episodes. Because of my press ties, I received all of Season Four in advance in the summer of 2006, just as the Season Three DVDs became available; when I learned I was heading into the hospital and wouldn't be able to watch TV for a while, I raced against time to watch the two seasons in just over a week. I offer these details to explain how my reaction to *The Wire* may differ from that of someone who watches the show week by week. If such a viewer finds an episode like last week's "Unconfirmed Reports" uncommonly preachy, it'll leave a bad taste for a full week. Viewed back-to-back, however, the preachiness seems a minor digression which fades into the background once the plot kicks back in. "Not For Attribution" is a serious plot episode, one that as such is likely to leave the "Unconfirmed Reports" naysayers pleased that the show is back on track. For folks in the press like myself, who received copies of the first seven episodes of the season from HBO, the soapbox moments felt like necessary context, at least when an episode like this week's falls hard on the heels of the speechifying.

In my write-up of "More With Less", I said I found the return of "McNutty" to be somewhat depressing after seeing Jimmy McNulty display some measure of personal growth over the course of seasons Three and Four. When first watching the episode, I thought perhaps David Simon was folding under pressure from fans who found a sober McNulty boring and wanted to see him in his out-of-control mode a few more times before the series packed it in. However, "Not For Attribution" and last week's "Unconfirmed Reports" make it clear that "McNutty" is key to the story David Simon wants to tell—a sober McNulty would never come up with his crazy scheme to get his bosses to pay attention to the deaths of homeless men, and even if he did come up with the scheme, no way in hell would he be capable of acting on it without a healthy quantity of Jameson's coursing through his veins.

"Not For Attribution", then, basically picks up where "Reports" left off, with the inebriated McNulty forging evidence and Bunk Moreland being apoplectic with dismay. McNulty may be an alcoholic tail-chaser, but he's by no means a dummy—doctoring old evidence to make it appear that the killer has been active for awhile is a very shrewd way to keep people from noticing how closely connected he is to the case, thereby solving the problem pointed out by Toadmonster in his comment on my write-up of last week's episode: If every body McNulty catches is related to the bogus killer, wouldn't people quickly grow suspicious? The way things stand now, it's a little less likely to be the case.

In an inspired stroke, McNulty retroactively inserts the killer's "trademark"—a red ribbon tied around a victim's wrist—into a report written by Ray Cole, the homicide detective who died between seasons two and three who was played by Robert F. Colesberry, one of the series' executive producers, who died in early 2004. The photo of Cole that we saw at his wake has long been a staple of *The Wire*'s credits sequence, and invoking him now is both a nice way to salute Colesberry once more as the series enters its final stretch and a much more organic way of having McNulty pull off his scam than it would have been for him to doctor the case files of a dead or retired detective who had never been mentioned on the series.

McNulty's big lie helps make "Not For Attribution" one of *The Wire*'s funniest episodes, and leaves little doubt that David Simon intends to beef up the series' satirical side as it heads into the sunset. Comedy is generated by other sources too, such as Marlo Stansfield's naivete (more about that shortly), but the bulk of the laughs come from Bunk's exasperation with McNulty's plan. The masterstroke moment, of course, comes when Bunk calls upon Lester Freamon to talk some sense into McNulty—a decision that at first seems as though it will pay off ("Shit like this actually goes through your fucking brain?!" Bunk asks incredulously), but which backfires when Freamon offers to help McNulty pull it off. With Freamon on his side, McNulty's chances of success are now about a thousand times higher than before, and it's a treat to catch a glimpse of a more playful Freamon channeling his frustration (and, of course, his formidable intellect) into the scheme.

The police and city hall plots connect with the activities at the *Sun* this week, early enough in the season to help forestall the "College Fiction Workshop 101" vibe that Virgil P complained about in his comment last week. Scott Templeton obviously has a major role to play in the future; given that, I was very happy to see Alma Gutierrez take on a more prominent role, as I really like her perspective as a newspaper newbie. As always, the episode title is relevant to the action in several different ways, though its primary importance is related to McNulty's manipulation of Alma and Norman Wilson planting the story about Ervin Burrell being thrown under the bus by Carcetti. I could easily devote another thousand words to the Burrell/Rawls/Daniels/Carcetti/Green situation, which is totally in my wheelhouse. I've always been intrigued by office politics in the world of law enforcement; Daniels' rise feels like something Simon has been planning for a long time, and I love it when a story that has been developed gradually over the course of several seasons suddenly clicks into place. Daniels's now-ex-wife is a character I've always loved to hate on account of her iciness, and I loved the scene where she advises her former husband to forego promotion lest Burrell unleash the dirt we've long known he has on Daniels. Compared to the other major storylines, this one is still simmering on a low flame, but I can't wait to see how it effects the other stories when it finally reaches a boil.

The scene at the *Sun* where Whiting tells the staff that the *Sun* is closing its Beijing, Moscow, Jerusalem, Johannesburg and London bureaus is striking in terms of its timing—while the real life paper's London and Beijing bureaus closed in 2005, the actual *Sun* only shuttered its Moscow bureau on December 19, 2007. The scene was not without a certain personal resonance for me, as my uncle Oswald L. Johnston Jr., a longtime international correspondent (he spent most of his career at *The Los Angeles Times* and retired after taking a buyout in 1992) got his first break as an overseas reporter when he was hired as the *Sun*'s man in Rome in the mid-'60s. Ozzie wasn't at the *Sun* for a particularly long spell before going to the *LA Times*, but it was sobering to hear his accounts of management behavior at Times Mirror (then-owner of the *LAT* and the *Sun*) at the time of his retirement, just as I was resolving to break into the field—and that was before the Internet began to threaten the newspaper business.

Indeed, Simon lets the *Sun* stuff get a little sentimental this week as a line is drawn between those who really live for journalism (the old timers, plus Alma Gutierrez) and those without a true passion for the business (Scott Templeton). Templeton's sneering dismissal of Roger as "dead wood" showed that while he's ingratiated himself with management, he's fundamentally a stranger to the true culture of the paper, otherwise he'd know that Roger is the kind of guy who could tell you everything about Cedric Daniels except his shoe size. Roger and Gus's accounts of what drew them to the business are certainly misty-eyed, but in an entirely believable way. Anyone who's spent much time around reporters can tell you that while they're generally stereotyped as a crusty, cynical bunch, newsmen (and -women) as a whole are a very romantic lot, for good reason: no one would work so hard for so many hours a week for so little pay if they didn't truly believe they were part of an enterprise with the power to change the world for the better.

One final note on the *Sun*: I'd long assumed that when *Wire* characters referred to "the *Sun* papers", the plural was a Baltimore quirk. Even though the term isn't explained this week, a light bulb nonetheless went off over my head as I realized why *Wire* Baltimorons use the "s": Until September 15, 1995, there was a separate evening edition, so the *Sun* was in fact two newspapers. More than a dozen years have passed since then, but the habit of thinking of the *Sun* as a two-paper institution apparently lives on.

The Wire's street characters were busy as ever this week. Marlo contiunes to move forward with his scheme to replace Prop Joe as Baltimore's biggest wholesaler, and although he has brains, balls and the town's most coldhearted killers on his side, it's increasingly apparent that his naivete could be his Achilles heel. "It ain't easy civilizing this motherfucker," Joe sighs after Marlo insists on visiting the offshore bank where he's deposited his funds in the apparent belief that if he can't see and hold his money, it doesn't exist. Marlo's jaunt to the islands follows another tremendously funny bit of business when he attempts to bribe Vondas into doing business with him rather than Joe. After Vondas rejects his cash because it's literally dirty, Marlo, in an incredible display of chutzpah, goes to Joe to get a load of crisp replacement bills. Joe is obviously aware that Marlo is a potential threat, and in teaching the younger dealer the finer points of money laundering, he displays his familiarity with the time-honored "keep your friends close and your enemies closer" strategy. For all his insight into Marlo, Joe seems to underestimate just how eager Marlo is to extract bloody revenge on Omar. Cheese's back-channel dealings with Marlo don't bode well for Joe, may be too devoted to neutrality for his own good.

Marlo too, however, may be underestimating an enemy. He dispatches Chris and Snoop to kill Butchie in the hope of luring Omar back to Baltimore, but we all know that Omar is someone you really don't want to piss off. After what happened in Season Three when Stringer Bell made an attempt on Omar's life in violation of the Sunday truce, there's no doubt that when Omar returns to Baltimore, he's gonna come out swinging hard. Omar's island hideout seems idyllic at first glance, but the sight of a busted toilet in the alleyway outside his house (as well as the state of his kitchen) makes it clear that he isn't exactly living it up on the lam. Weather notwithstanding, going back to Baltimore could represent a step up in his surroundings.

There's still a lot I haven't gotten to, so in the interest of expediency I'm going to give the short shrift to Michael, Dukie and Clay Davis, whose scenes this week, fascinating though they may be, are more about laying groundwork for future developments than anything else. Michael was reticent in describing Chris and Snoop's massacre at June Bug's house to Dukie, though of course he wasn't an actual eyewitness to the killings. Nonetheless, it was believable—and very affecting—for him to respond to the bloody murders by trying to be a normal kid for a day and going to Six Flags with Dukie. After their day at the amusement park, the stark contrast presented by Michael's return to his corner hit me like a bucket of cold water. The biggest unanswered question about the season at this point is just what role Michael and Dukie will ultimately play, and right now your guess is as good as mine. As for Davis…jeez, I actually felt myself feeling kinda sorry for the poor guy, whose back is very much against the wall now (although the scene where Rhonda Pearlman grills his driver on the stand kept me from feeling too much sympathy). He's smart enough, I dare say, that he'd only try and cut a deal with Carcetti if he was really desperate, as otherwise I expect he'd give Carcetti a little more credit for his intelligence. The bit where Carcetti shuts him down by saying that he'd already know about it if the ministers had a problem with Daniels was entertaining, but also somewhat sad given Davis' utter helplessness.

Two final points: I've always loved ? and the Mysterians' "96 Tears", one of the great garage rock anthems, and I loved the scene where McNulty stumbles out of the bathroom as it blares on the jukebox and flirts with the blonde he'll soon do from behind on the hood of his car. For all the wisecracks we've heard McNulty and others make about "the Western District way" over the years, few scenes have said as much about the debauched nature of Baltimore's police culture as McNulty flashing his badge to the uniform cops who quickly drive off after catching him in flagrante. And although James Whiting broke out his "more with less" line once again this week, his belief in clean narratives above all wasn't reiterated in the *Sun* scenes. Even so, it was evoked by the scene where Syndor is baby sitting the grand jurors and we hear the prosecutors talk about streamlining the account of Clay Davis' misdeeds so that the jurors don't get "lost in the details". Journalism and the law, it's obvious, are forces that Simon believes are intended to protect the people; the sight of their agents patronizing the folks they're supposed to be defending (which is exactly what happens when facts arrive so packaged and predigested) is among the most stinging examples *The Wire* has offered of urban America's slow-motion collapse.

The Wire Recap: Season 5, Episode 4, "Transitions"
BY ANDREW JOHNSTON ON JANUARY 28, 2008

"Transitions" is what I think of a true "fan's episode" of *The Wire*: From beginning to end, it's jammed with scenes that exemplify everything people watch the show for—rich character interaction, crisp dialogue, dry humor, righteously indignant muckraking and complex wheels-within-wheels plotting. It's also the kind of episode that can only be done at this point in a season, when there's still time for events to play out in all manner of ways before groundwork has to be laid for the finale. Such episodes often fall a little too early to feature seismic, game-changing events, but that's definitely not the case here.

The title refers, of course, to the journalistic art of the seamless segue from one paragraph to another—and while, like most of the season's titles, this one comes from the vocabulary of journalese, the episode itself somewhat ironically has less *Sun* action than the three that preceded it. At least it seems to—this week's events on the streets, at city hall, in police HQ and at the Western District station house represent the culmination of so much long-term plot and character development spanning several seasons that the *Sun* scenes can't help seeming like weak sauce by comparison.

The two principal transitions, of course, are Rawls' temporary elevation to the commissioner's office (with Daniels taking over as Deputy Commissioner for Operations for a few months of grooming before being handed the top job) and Marlo's coup against Proposition Joe, which both makes Marlo the king of the East Side and leaves "the Greek" with no choice but to do business with him. I'm sure a substet of *Wire* fans will float the theory that it's actually Marlo, and not Joe, who takes a bullet in the final scene, but that's wishful thinking. I mean, come on—is David Simon that cheap? The second that next week's "React Quotes" hits HBO On Demand (where it should do better than usual thanks to viewers who don't want to be forced to choose between *The Wire* and next week's Super Bowl), the theory will deservedly die quickly.

Spooked by his ex-wife's concern about the dirt in Burrell's possession, Daniels goes to the commissioner to swear that he had nothing to do with the effort to oust him. Before Burrell has the chance to use the incriminating evidence—which apparently proves that Daniels was part of a corrupt Eastern District drug squad during his early days on the force—he's persuaded by council president Nerese Campbell to go quietly and accept a cushy private sector job that will pay him just as much, if not more than he was making as Baltimore's top cop. It's a blatant bribe, one that is somehow bizarrely legal, much as the loan that allows Rhonda Pearlman to nail Clay Davis with the "head shot"—something "every kid with a starter home" does, as Lester Freamon points out—is bizarrely illegal.

There's a great shot toward the end of the episode of Daniels smiling with satisfaction as he visits his new office, but his happiness would naturally be short lived if he knew that Campbell now has the dossier, which he presumably believes to be out of circulation as a result of Burrell's failure to use it. It's a pretty safe bet that we haven't seen the last of the folder—but with no other viable African-American candidates for the commissioner's office in sight, expect Campbell to use it as a means of keeping Daniels in line rather than getting him out of the way.

In the wake of Butchie's death last week, we learn a little more about his background—apparently he wasn't born blind but rather lost his sight to a bullet shortly after he took to playing the game. Joe, who knows everyone remotely connected to the drug trade—he really is a classic center-of-the-web intelligence broker, like Conan Doyle's Mycroft Holmes or George R. R. Martin's Littlefinger—appears to be the only one of the current players (apart from Omar, of course), visits the gangsta florist we've seen before and purchases a flower arrangement accompanied by a message that could double as a dying curse hurled toward Marlo: "Woe to them that call evil good and good evil" (that's Isaiah 5:20, in case you were wondering). Joe, as we learn in his ensuing conversation with Slim Charles, is well aware that Cheese is in business with Marlo behind his back, but he claims to be wary about taking premature action against members of his own family. Instead of moving directly, Joe tells Slim he's going to take a few steps back until the Omar-Marlo feud settles down, allowing Cheese to run his business in the meantime—implicitly putting Cheese in Omar's line of fire. When Omar later demands that Slim take him to Joe, Slim swears up and down that Joe had no complicity in Butchie's death. Cheese's name is not mentioned (Slim may not know that Cheese steered Snoop and Chris toward Butchie), but Joe's unfaithful nephew is nonetheless now at least #4 on Omar's revenge list, and ought to be looking over his shoulder at all times—at least unless, God forbid, Marlo & Co. somehow manage to take care of Omar first.

Joe doesn't really sign his own death warrant until the next co-op meeting, at which he rules against Cheese and in favor of Hungry Man in a territorial dispute (in a great continuity touch, the strip-club owner who cut the shady deal with Nerese Campbell in "More With Less" identifies himself and tells some of his side of the story at the co-op meeting). The scenes that follow are among the most powerful depictions of treachery and gangland justice in the annals of filmed crime drama, up there with Fredo Corleone's inadvertent betrayal of his brother (and Michael's subsequent revenge) in *The Godfather Part II* and the execution of Tommy DeVito in

GoodFellas when he thinks he's about to be made. As the meeting breaks up, there's a great shot of Joe and Marlo facing each other in profile, with Joe's massive gut symbolizing the distance between them. "You need to focus a bit more on working with people," Joe tells Marlo, before the younger dealer walks away with a sneer on his face.

Even so, Joe continues his mentorship of Marlo by setting him up as Maury Levy's newest client—and, in a great display of what makes Joe *Joe,* we see him bond with Herc over their mutual contempt for Earvin Burrell, who was a year ahead of Joe in high school. Even as Joe continues his efforts to reshape Marlo in his own image, Marlo continues to move against him by having Chris and Snoop offer Hungry Man as a gift to Cheese, one that more or less literally comes tied with a bow (for his part, Hungry Man reacts the way any of us would to getting shanghaied by Chris and Snoop: "Man already shit himself, and we ain't even get started yet," Snoop marvels with a laugh. "Get a gift, give a gift," Chris counsels Cheese, essentially sealing Joe's fate.

When Marlo and his lieutenants visit Joe at home in the final scene, Marlo delivers a line that's both a withering dismissal of Joe's patronage and a clear-eyed assessment of his own character: "I wasn't made to play the son." Indeed, when Marlo arrived on *The Wire*, he was already a fully-formed evil, and his ability to hold sway over volatile personalities such as Snoop and Chris stands as ultimate proof that he's a natural-born leader. Up to his literal dying breath, Joe attempts to bargain his way out of trouble; in response, Marlo offers perhaps the most chilling display of his charisma yet as he coaxes Joe into accepting death without resistance.

Another arguable transition—a much more subtle one—is the continued growth of Ellis Carver into a stand-up officer and, more than likely, Daniels' spiritual successor. At the top of the episode, the man with the worst haircut on television, Western District patrolman Anthony Colicchio, attempts to bust Michael and his corner boys, only to walk into a trap: The bag in which he expects to find Michael's package turns out to be full of dog pooh. Michael (wearing an all-too-apt "Ghetto University" t-shirt) and his pals may not be holding, but they still succeed in pissing off Colicchio enough to haul them down to the station house under arrest for harassment.

Carver (who you'll recall made a futile attempt to take Randy Wagstaff under his wing last season and spare the lad from foster care) sides with Michael and will have nothing of it. "I've seen some stupid shit in my day, but even by Western standards this rates a whole new category!", Carver barks, before announcing his intent to bring charges against Colicchio over the incident. Carver's decision displeases his old pal Herc, but he sticks to his guns. In addition to showing his continued evolution as a man and a police officer, the incident could also be construed as marking another stage in the transition of the Baltimore Police into being an African-American-controlled institution (a transition that, in the *Wire* universe at least, has been taking place from the top down). To Colicchio, Michael & Co. are "fucking yos", but a black cop like Carver is able to see their behavior for what it is, which is just boys being boys (though Michael proves he's further along the road to manhood than his baby face suggests when his crackhead mom asks for help finding work and he tells her he's not going to pay her to be his mother).

At the *Sun*, Scott Templeton displays his work ethic (or lack thereof) by going to interview for a Metro job at the Washington *Post* while Alma Gutierrez busts her ass doing real reporting to help the *Sun* get the scoop on Burrell's ouster. The *Sun* gets that story, but budget cuts on the courtroom front result in them losing out on the perp walk that Rhonda Pearlman sets up for Clay Davis. All of Davis's scenes are fantastic and a testament to Isaiah Whitlock Jr.'s brilliance as an actor. The Davis who shows up to testify, deeply humbled, is a man we've never seen before, and it's breathtaking to watch Whitlock as Davis first takes the stand, inspecting the evidence against him as if the paper was contaminated with Ebola, and then turning on the Clay Davis persona we all know the second he steps in front of the cameras that are waiting for him outside the courthouse. *The Wire*'s criminal failure to receive any Emmy nominations for season four makes it extremely unlikely that the television academy will recognize Whitlock, but I'd argue that few actors on The Wire are more deserving (though of course there are strong cases to be made for André Royo, Michael Kenneth Williams, Robert F. Chew and Wendell Pierce— hell, you could fill the all the Supporting Actor slots twice over with *Wire* regulars and still leave out a ton of amazing actors).

This week's opening quote is attributed to Scott Templeton, in reference to his failure to get hired at the *Post,* but it could just as easily apply to how it's a buyer's market out there for Templeton's bullshit, as well as for the lie McNulty is peddling. The "buyer's market" line is also delivered by Lester's old partner (still stuck on patrol as a result of getting screwed over by Rawls, we're told), who Lester has surprisingly little difficulty persuading to provide him and McNulty with access to a fresh corpse. The bogus serial killer may be McNulty's baby, but Lester takes point on the matter this week, persuading McNulty to visit a homeless camp in search of potential "witnesses" in the hope of creating an alibi that will keep anyone from suspecting that the killer is a fake. McNulty's enthusiasm for the scam remains undiminished, as we see when he carves defensive wounds into the fingertips of the "victim". Indeed, the glee with which he tells Beadie about the case almost makes it seem as if McNulty is starting to believe his own lies. Rather than the hoax, I'd say the definitive proof of how unhinged McNulty has become is his increasingly voluntary estrangement of Beadie, a woman who is clearly one of the best things to ever happen to him. Beadie's speech about how she never believed the "McNutty" stories until he fell off the wagon is, however, unfortunately tin-eared and well below *The Wire*'s usual standards (as well as unworthy of Amy Ryan's formidable talent). Given the amount of awesomeness that David Simon and Edward Burns cram into this incredibly dense episode, though, I'll gladly forgive them for whiffing one measly scene.

With so much of the blog punditry about this season centering on the *Sun* storyline and the debate over whether David Simon's treatment of the paper comes down to sour grapes (you know it's getting out of hand when the Brits start chiming in), it's refreshing to have come across a source of discussion that's 100% free of *Sun*-related content: Sudhir Venkatesh's weekly accounts for *The New York Times' Freakonomics* blog of watching the show with a group of fellows who have actually played the game. Venkatesh has assembled a gallery of real characters alright, but half the fun comes from the censorship the transcript goes through to meet the *Times'* standards . "But white folks [who write the series] always love to keep these uppity [characters] alive," says Orlando, a retired Brooklyn gang member, speaking of Prop Joe during the roundtable on "More With Less". Some of Venkatesh's reportage is so colorful ("I knew that f——t would come back," Flavor rejoiced, beer spilling down his arm. "Get his a——, Omar. Get Marlo, that little b——ch.") that at least one commenter over there has accused him of pulling a Stephen Glass/Jayson Blair (or Scott Templeton, if you will) maneuver. To my mind, that's high praise—because as I see it, a reporter can't be charged with making shit up unless he's doing a really good job.

In the latest of the many essays that he's been publishing in lieu of interviews, David Simon describes a season two dust-up with then-Mayor Martin O'Malley, who was threatening to rescind the series' permits to film in the city after he was displeased (as the *Sun*'s Jay Spry would diplomatically cast it) with the first season. The timing is interesting insofar as the encounter may have influenced the creation or characterization of Carcetti, a transparent O'Malley analogue who made his first appearance during the third season. In the piece, Simon mentions the real people behind a number of other characters, but in this case he leaves it to his readers to make the connection themselves.

The Wire Recap: Season 5, Episode 5, "React Quotes"

BY ANDREW JOHNSTON ON FEBRUARY 4, 2008

"Just 'cause they're in the street doesn't mean they lack opinions"—Haynes

At this point, I doubt many folks would disagree if I described the narrative momentum of *The Wire*'s fifth season as freight train-esque. "React Quotes" is jam-packed with incident, and while (as the title suggests) much of the action is in response to things that have gone down before, there are just as many new developments which propel us into the second half of the season on a mighty head of steam.

We begin in the park, where Marlo has taken to meeting Vondas at the bench where he and Joe held their conferences in years past. Vondas, ever the pragmatist, says a few words to mourn Joe's passing before initiating Marlo into his world by giving him a cellphone he can use for an apparently secure means of communication. (Surveillance ops long since stopped being the central theme, or even the central organizing device, of *The Wire*, but it's still odd to have a show with that name where there isn't some wire-tapping going on, and a good bit of what follows is devoted to once again turning Lester Freamon into someone who spends way too many hours in a dank storage room filled with electronic equipment.) Taking over that spot on the bench next to Vondas is almost enough to cement Marlo's status as top dog, but his ascent won't be complete until Omar has been dispensed with. Last season, Marlo's rise through the ranks was in many ways invisible, as those who stood in his way vanished without a trace, their bodies only turning up months later in the rowhouses. This year, Chris and Snoop have been leaving their victims where they fall, as a means of setting an example of what those who cross Marlo can expect. Kima found all of the corpses at Junebug's house in situ, and as Alma tells Gus Haynes at the *Sun*, one Joe Stewart was found dead in his living room, while the body of one Nathaniel Mantz was found in a back alley garage (some of the folks discussing the episode in Alan Sepinwall's On Demand thread speculated that the third victim, the domestic homicide, was Bodie's grandmother, but I heard the last name as "Bogusz," not "Broadus", and apparently the HBO closed-captioner went with "Boguss"). Are Chris and Snoop certain their guns are untraceable, or are they getting sloppy? I'd say the answer lies somewhere in the middle.

This week's episode was written by David Mills, who adapted David Simon's *The Corner* for HBO and who has also written memorable episodes of *Homicide* and *NYPD Blue*. This is only his second *Wire* (following on "Soft Eyes", Season Four's second episode), and he has a grand old time playing in Simon and Burns' sandbox, tossing out line after line of dialogue that is intensely colorful yet always true to character for whomever is saying it. Case in point: Tommy Carcetti. "How does it feel, Clay? Not much fun on the ass end, is it?," the boy-faced mayor crows as he sees a TV report on the indictment of everyone's favorite state senator. Norman Wilson, canny as ever, is quick to advise him that "you don't dance on Clay's grave until you're sure the motherfucker's dead." A lot could yet go wrong for Rupert Bond and his risky plan to prosecute Davis at the local level, but his show for the cameras is enough to persuade Carcetti that Bond is worth cultivating as a potential heir—because no matter what, he certainly wouldn't make a worse mayor than Nerese Campbell would.

Earlier, when Chris and Marlo left the park to prepare to hunt Omar, Chris said he needed to go home to say he might not be back for awhile. I expected we were going to see that Chris lives with his mom, but in retrospect I realize that might have been too much of a reprise of the situation with Omar and his grandmother. Instead, it seems, Chris is shacked up with a girlfriend with whom he has two kids. It's a humanizing touch, to an extent, but it also makes him seem like even more of a monster for being able to come home and be an affectionate dad after a long day of shooting people in the head and covering their corpses in lime.

Chris and Snoop's next stop is the offices of Maury Levy, where Chris's behavior suggests that they've been committing their crimes while using a car registered in his girlfriend's name. Levy counsels them to use a car registered to some random schmuck, in addition to providing counsel vis-a-vis Chris' gun arrest last season. On the way out the door, Marlo gives Levy his cellphone number. Not knowing of the trick Vondas showed Marlo, Levy says that if Marlo is talking on a cell, "Joe gave him to us just in time," causing him to cackle at the prospect of the massive billings that would result from Marlo's arrest.

Shortly thereafter, at the *Sun*, Alma tells Scott Templeton that she has a police source on the serial killer story, and the two go off to meet McNulty. Since the beginning of the season, fans have been predicting that Templeton's story would converge with McNulty's, but I expect few predicted exactly how it would happen. McNulty tells the reporters that the killer is a sexual fetishist, but it's instantly obvious that he hasn't thought things through. Grasping at straws as he tries to come up with enough half-assed specifics to sell the story to Alma and Templeton, he basically accepts a how-to-manufacture-a-news-story lesson from Templeton in order to re-purpose the "facts" about the killer in a media-friendly package. The scene's humor is underplayed to the point of near-invisibility, but it's there, and it represents some of the first real evidence to back up David Simon's claim that this will turn out to be *The Wire*'s most "*Strangelove*-ian" season.

Having played a role in convincing Burrell to go quietly last week, Nerese now turns her attention to Clay Davis, who comes into her office angrily insisting that he won't go down alone. As proof that Davis isn't fucking around, he unleashes something we've waited four and a half episodes for: His trademark *Sheeeeeeeeeeeeiiiiiiiiiiit*, probably the longest such exclamation he's ever dropped. Davis must have dirt on Campbell, though, otherwise she wouldn't take such pains to convince him to (if necessary) take a hit and accept a brief prison term so he might fight another day.

If patriotism is the first refuge of a scoundrel, I've always felt that ethnic pride can only be inches behind it. In the tradition of such scandal-plagued real-life politicians as former Newark mayor Sharpe James and former D.C. mayor Marion Barry, Davis teams up with Carcetti's predecessor, Clarence Royce, to play the Afrocentrism card, arguing that he's being set up by a white-dominated media that's determined to keep blacks from attaining too much power. That said, Royce takes pains to tell Davis—through the clenched teeth of a Cheshire-cat smile—that if the state senator can't retain some degree of plausible deniability regarding corruption charges, he's well and truly fucked.

After sharing a byline on the first serial killer story, it seems Templeton is out to claim the follow-up for himself. Looking to interview the homeless, he visits the Catholic Workers soup kitchen where Bubbles volunteers, and is nonplussed to discover that most of the folks there aren't actually homeless but rather "working poor". This allows for a smooth segue to Bubbles, who we see in the kitchen washing dishes. The shelter supervisor wants Bubs to serve meals instead, and Bubbles declines. After he visits Walon at work, we realize why: Bubs is convinced he has HIV from years of sharing needles and exposing himself to risk god knows how many other ways. Walon takes Bubbles for a test, and the negative result knocks our old friend for a loop. He obviously wanted to be positive—or felt he deserved to be—as punishment for years of sinning in general, and particularly for leaving the hot shot where Sherrod could get it. Realizing he's not facing a death sentence, I expect the stakes in Bubs' battle to stay sober will rise as he flounders for something to hold onto, something to live for.

Back at Homicide, McNulty learns from Landsman that the bosses have approved unlimited OT on the homeless case for two detectives—McNulty and Kima. Horrified, Bunk drags McNulty into his "office", the interrogation room, and says that if his scam is going to take a real detective off a real case (the massacre at Junebug's house), then McNulty has truly taken his scheme way the fuck too far. McNulty clearly hoped that Freamon would be his partner in the investigation, and he quickly enters damage control mode, telling Kima to use the OT to work the Junebug case while he handles the serial killer on his own for a spell.

You'd think this would be enough to scare McNulty into caution; instead, it just makes him more rash. By this point, Herc has used his access to Levy's office to obtain Marlo's cell number, which he passed to Carver who in turn gave it to Freamon. The two detectives come up with their ballsiest scheme yet: Stage a fake call from the killer on a pay phone, use that as an excuse to get a wiretap—and then put Marlo's number and not the pay phone number on the request form. McNulty goes to the *Sun* after learning from Landsman that the paper has apparently received a call from the killer. Templeton has just served up a bogus story about a homeless family living in fear of the killer, but that's not enough for him. His decision to manufacture the call plays out on his face as he's approached by the tweedy reporter with whom he's supposed to tag team an education piece, something he clearly anticipates about as much as a colonoscopy. After he says the killer told him to expect a total of 12 victims—and provides a lame response to McNulty's query about how and why the killer reached him on his cellphone—McNulty picks up the ball and runs with it, saying he was called from the same area as Templeton and that the killer also mentioned the number 12.

Now that Templeton and McNulty are locked into a spiral of codependence that's more elaborate and intense than either man can imagine, McNulty and Lester proceed with the wiretap, and the episode ends with Lester intercepting a cryptic signal off of Marlo's phone. In various On Demand threads, I've seen a lot of guesses as to the nature of the signal, few of them right—which surprises me, since the trick that Vondas showed Marlo is both incredibly simple and, when you think about it, incredibly obvious. If people are going nuts trying to figure it out, though, who am I to spoil the fun?

You know it's a good episode when I'm this far into the recap and haven't even gotten to the stuff sure to spark the most conversation. In scenes sprinkled throughout the episode, Omar mounts a long and meticulous stake out at the apartment of Monk, an underling of Marlo's who has been set up as a sacrificial pawn. Omar's long, patient wait parallels Lester's stake outs, while Marlo's manipulation of Monk has very strong echoes of the way Nerese wraps Burrell and Clay Davis around her finger. The episode comes to an intense climax—one of the most intense the series has ever given us—when Omar's plot collides with the one major story line I haven't yet discussed.

Early in the episode, Dukie gets his ass kicked after a (much younger) corner kid lobs a soda bottle at his head (when Dukie tries to defend himself, older boys are quick to intervene on his assailant's behalf). This leads Michael to take Dukie to Cutty's gym for a lesson in self-defense (strangely, it seems Dukie and Cutty somehow never met during season four or during the 15-month gap before season 5). In a hugely poignant scene, Cutty tells Dukie that "not everything come down to how you carry it in the street. I mean, it do come down to that if you're gonna be in the street, but that's not the only way to be." When Dukie replies "out here it is", Cutty retorts that "the world is bigger than that, at least that's what they tell me." So, Dukie asks, "How do you get from here to the rest of the world?" Cutty sighs and says "I wish I knew".

Cutty tells Dukie that if he's not suited for the corner or the ring, he has "other skills," a point also made by Michael in the scene where Dukie asks him for a shooting lesson. The scene shows us just how far he's traveled down the road to being a merciless motherfucker, nailing targets with impressive skill and telling Dukie, like a sage from a Samurai movie, that one should never draw one's weapon unless you're well and truly ready to use it.

Even though Michael, like Cutty, urges Dukie to concentrate on his intellectual abilities, I was terrified at first that Michael drags Dukie into the line of fire—during the epic shoot-out that goes down when Omar storms into Monk's apartment, falling into the trap that Chris has carefully laid for him, you can briefly see someone taking one of Omar's bullets in the kneecap. The scene is so shadowy that at first, I couldn't be entirely sure it wasn't Dukie. Subsequent inspection, much to my relief, proved otherwise.

Even without Dukie in danger, the shootout is pretty goddamned pulse-pounding. After subjecting us to the deaths of Butchie and Prop Joe these past two weeks, for Omar to fall next would be more than any fan could take. But Omar lives to fight another day, or so it appears—it's not entirely realistic that he could survive a leap through a window at that height, but neither is such a thing unprecedented. Even if you consider it a stretch, don't forget that we're talking about the one character on the series to exude a sort of reality-distortion field that allows him to be more myth than man. Omar has been called the ghetto Batman before; a more accurate comparison might be to Marvel's Punisher, given Batman's code against killing and his rejection of firearms, but I wouldn't want to insult Omar by comparing him to a mook like Frank Castle (in a fight between the two, my money would be on the man with the scar). No matter who Omar reminds you of, there's no denying that his legend can only grow on the heels of what is surely the most daring escape in a long career filled with close calls.

A few miscellaneous notes: When Clay Davis makes his first radio appearance, he's visiting an actual African-American talk station in Baltimore, WOLB 1010AM, "where information is power!" (per the slogan on the studio banner). The DJ interviewing Davis is Larry Young, the station's morning drivetime host. The station on which Davis makes his second radio appearance is unspecified, but I'd be willing to bet it's a real life station too.

To my relief, Amy Ryan was put to much better use this week in the scene where Beadie visits Bunk at Homicide to talk about McNulty's travails. In a handful of scenes, we got to do some pretty serious catching up on McNulty's personal life, via a return visit from his kids (holy cow have they grown!) and his ex wife Elena. Since she only made one appearance last season and it's been so long since I watched any *Wire* episodes earlier than that, I'd completely forgotten the character was played by Callie Thorne. After four seasons of watching her torment Denis Leary as Sheila Keefe on *Rescue Me*, seeing her turn up here was almost as distracting as Dominic West showing up in a loincloth in *300*. Almost.

The Wire Recap: Season 5, Episode 6, "The Dickensian Aspect"
BY ANDREW JOHNSTON ON FEBRUARY 11, 2008

"If you have a problem with this, I understand completely."—Lester Freamon With each successive episode of *The Wire*'s final season, it seems, fans have become more firmly split into two camps: Those who think the show is as fine as ever, and those who are frustrated by what they perceive as a mounting lack of realism. Beginning with "The Dickensian Aspect", I expect that schism to start growing even wider. For my part, I'm with the "same as it ever was" gang and am caught up in the story David Simon is telling, which—if the sixth and seventh episodes of the season are any guide of what to expect from the last three—will grow increasingly satirical by the week.

For a couple of seconds, Simon fucks with our heads by teasingly suggesting that Omar's body is being dragged away from the apartment building from which he leapt in "React Quotes". When we see Marlo's footsoldiers pounding the pavement and canvassing E.R.s, however, it's soon apparent that Omar indeed made his escape. "That's some Spider-Man shit there," Marlo says to Chris as he looks up at the balcony. "We missed our shot. Now he's gonna be at us."

Marlo doesn't seem especially pissed at Chris, which is perfectly logical—nobody can deny that Chris, Snoop and Michael did everything they could have. Exactly how Omar survived his leap is not made clear, but his broken leg suggests he hit the ground rather than grabbing onto another balcony or windowsill and pulling himself inside the building. Unless he was able to lock that storage room from the inside, though, it seems like a big stretch for Marlo's lackeys to have skipped it in their search (he's also in there an awful long time before he bandages his leg and hobbles off on his erzatz crutch).

Down at Homicide, Bunk is more livid than ever about McNulty's scam after his trip to the *Sun* in the previous episode. "That asshole's making up his own shit," a smiling McNulty says of Templeton. But while McNulty is pleased as can be at how successful his big lie has become, he gets the first inkling that things have gone too far when he decides to put more pressure on the top brass by staging another "killing" and learns that because of the hype around the serial killer, any DOA call to Homicide (who, as we've seen, check out DOAs that are obvious non-murders, in order to eliminate the possibility) results in an instant media circus. In response, he comes up with a way to stage a killing without a dead body.

Seeing a drooling, spastic homeless man by the side of the road, McNulty pulls him off the street and slips $100 in his jacket (on the basis that it can't be a kidnapping if the "victim" gets paid) and takes him off to see Lester, with whom he arranges the next stage of the con: Shooting footage of the bum with the camera on a clean cellphone, then dragging the guy down I-95 to Richmond and parking him in a shelter there along with an ID card saying he's from Cleveland rather than Baltimore. It's crazy, sure, but not any less crazy than anything else McNulty has done (still, I wish they'd come up with a more subtle way to let us know McNulty was in Richmond rather than slapping the city's name all over the door of the shelter). At the *Sun*, Whiting and Klebanow are predictably as pleased as can be with Templeton's latest article about the serial killer, and Templeton is so busy eating it up that he's caught off guard when Whiting asks him what's next. He comes up with the idea of spending a night with the homeless, a gimmick he hopes will fulfill Whiting's wish for coverage that reflects "the Dickensian aspect of the homeless".

Very little of what Templeton experiences can be described as "Dickensian", but the adjective certainly fits the episode as a whole as connections are drawn between scattered plotlines in ways that some may find credibility-stretching, but which are appropriate if you're one of those (like me) who has always seen the series in literary terms and believes a certain amount of license comes with the territory. One might argue that the most Dickensian moment in the entire series comes when Bunk, in his back-to-square-one investigation of the rowhouse bodies, is led to the grim institution that is now home to Randy Wagstaff, who he pledges not to arrest out of respect for "that crazy motherfucker Pryzbelewski." Last season, Randy was the most playful and charming of the four boys we spent the year with, and the one who best fit the profile of a lovable street kid out of *Oliver Twist*. A year later, he's grown far more than Michael or Dukie, and his spirit has been broken by his time in the foster home, perhaps because he feels abandoned by Carver. "Why don't you promise to get me out of here?," he asks Bunk. "That's what y'all do, ain't it—lie to dumb-ass niggas?" As Randy barges out of the room, he ferociously body-checks another kid on the stairs, giving us a grim example of the behavior he's had to adopt in order to survive.

Bunk's investigation next leads him to Michael's mother, who at last clues him in to the connection between her son and Marlo and Chris, giving Bunk the first real lead on the rowhouse bodies in ages. Now that he's starting to get enough evidence to make the case, a new question comes to the forefront: Can he do so before McNulty's scam is exposed?

Lester's willingness to go along with McNulty has been criticized by some viewers, and the scene in which he tells Sydnor about the wire tap on Marlo kinda-sorta plays like an attempt at preemptively addressing some of that criticism with the line about how he's run "out of time and patience". McNulty is pleased to have Sydnor in the loop on the Marlo front, but he's not quite ready to trust him with the truth about the serial killer, though Sydnor's query about ties between Marlo and the homeless killer means McNulty may soon have no choice.

A lot of people expected the New Day Co-Op to bite the dust last week, but Joe's organization managed to get a brief reprieve. As the members convene, we learn that Marlo, somewhat surprisingly, isn't yet their number one suspect in Joe's death. Whoever has the hook-up, they agree, will be the one who offed Joe. When Marlo takes charge of the meeting, he shocks everyone by claiming responsibility for the deaths of Joe and Hungry Man. It's soon clear he's being entirely disengenuous, as he goes on to explain that he's responsible because he inadvertently led Omar to them. He then puts a stiff bounty on Omar's head: $100,000 if he's captured alive, $250K if he's dead. Usually, of course, it's a live capture that yields a bigger reward, but Marlo is no fool— he's a lot, lot safer having someone else kill Omar for him if at all possible. However, right after Marlo dangles the prize money in front of Baltimore's assembled dealers, he foolishly alienates them by announcing a spike in the cost of his package. Marlo may have youth and power on his side, but the other dealers have numbers and experience on theirs, and Marlo's completely out to lunch if he's not taking the possibility of mutiny into account.

Omar reveals something of a new side of himself as he makes his next moves: He's never seemed to show much awareness of his status as a street legend, but here, he shrewdly takes advantage of his rep to start boxing Marlo in. By chipping away at Marlo with small raids, he ensures that as many people as possible hear his message—"Omar thinks Marlo is too much of a pussy to face him in the street"—thereby giving Marlo no choice but to personally participate in a standoff. If Marlo doesn't, he'll have no credibility left and will surely be pushed aside by his rivals, resulting in him going down in history as the William Henry Harrison (or Pope John Paul I) of Baltimore crimelords. Even before Omar blows up the SUV, Marlo's crew are quaking in their boots—Chris is terrified of Omar going after his family, completely forgetting about Omar's well-known policy of sparing civilians at all times.

I look forward to reading reactions to "The Dickensian Aspect" from commentators who've been dogpiling on the *Sun* storyline, since the newspaper action has never been as even-handed as it is this week. Yes, Gus is given more reason than ever to suspect that Templeton is up to no good as another lie is revealed: When reporting the story about the woman who died of the seafood allergy a few episodes back, Templeton allowed himself to be duped by her sister, issuing an appeal for scholarship donations for the dead woman's kids, all of which went straight into the dead woman's pocket. On the other hand, despite all the reasons we're given to hate Templeton this week (including his self-congratulatory appearance on Nancy Grace's show), his encounter with the homeless veteran allows us to see that he's actually capable of being an excellent writer and reporter when he actually does his job and refrains from just making shit up.

The biggest surprise—and the biggest mystery—is the issue of Prop Joe's leak within the State's Attorney's office. Joe had made cryptic hints in the past which suggested that he had an inside source; now that he's dead and the leak is confirmed, it'll be interesting to see where the plot goes given the near-complete lack of suspects—before this season, Rhonda Pearlman is pretty much the only character we've met from the SA's office, and chances are good it isn't her. Rupert Bond expresses dismay at the leak and seems initially confused when Pearlman shows him the evidence, but given the shortage of viable candidates for the mole, he can't be ruled out. I don't think it's inconceivable that the leak is someone we haven't met yet—some people might think that was "cheating", but I don't.

However, it's worth noting that at some point in the last couple of days, HBO added a character from the SA's office to the roster of "The Law" characters on the network's website: Grad Jury Prosecutor Gary DiPasquale, played by Gary D'Addario. As an older white guy (he's at least 55), D'Addario isn't Suspect #1, but if there's one thing we've learned from

The Wire it's that no one is beyond corruption. (Also added to "The Law" roster: Detective Vernon Holley, played by Brian Anthony Wilson, and Officer Michael Santangelo, played by Michael Salconi. Added to "The Paper" over the weekend was *Sun* Regional Affairs editor Rebecca Corbett, played by Kara Quick.)

Finally, I was disappointed to find Simon & Co. screwing up series continuity—and demanding a lot of fanwanking from viewers who want everything to make sense—by providing a chronology of recent Baltimore mayors that leaves no room for Clarence Royce. When Carcetti is dedicating the construction project, he mentions a chain of predecessors that includes Thomas L. J. D'Alesandro III (mayor from 1967-71 and the older brother of current Speaker of the House Nancy Pelosi; he's appeared as himself in a cameo in—I believe—Season 4), William Donald Schaefer (1971-87), Kurt L. Schmoke (1987-1999; he's also been on *The Wire*) and Martin J. O'Malley (1999-2007). The problem, of course, is that O'Malley is the real-life model for Carcetti (much as Nerese Campbell is an apparent counterpart to present real-life mayor Sheila Dixon), and *The Wire*'s fictional timeline, including several years with Royce as Mayor, began in 2002.

Fanwanking this one isn't actually that hard—if the IMDb is correct that Royce made his first appearance in the first episode of Season 3, it's possible that on Earth-*Wire*, O'Malley was mayor from 1999-2003 and ran for governor four years earlier than he did in reality. However, the very existence of O'Malley in the world of *The Wire* is problematic since during seasons three and four we're repeatedly told what a big deal it is for a white guy to become mayor at this point in time. It's stuff like this that make one realize how smart Aaron Sorkin was when he initiated a policy on *The West Wing* (a policy scuttled by his successors) of never mentioning a real-life president after Dwight Eisenhower.

ANDREW JOHNSTON

The Wire Recap: Season 5, Episode 7, "Took"
BY ANDREW JOHNSTON ON FEBRUARY 18, 2008

"They don't teach it in law school."—Pearlman

The Wire is usually pretty good about not talking down to its audience, but early in "Took" there's a scene in which Lester Freamon goes over the whole scheme involving the tap on Marlo's cellphone and that on the phone of the "homeless killer" in which he and McNulty are pretty much telling each other stuff they already know. It's a little annoying, and while I'm generally a big fan of Richard Price, I think it's a scene that other *Wire* writers (David Simon and Edward Burns, for example) might not have made so obvious: Price is perhaps more used to writing for a general audience than for a cadre of obsessives; here he seems to be erring on the side of safety. It's the one scene that feels like a clunker in an otherwise fine episode that ratchets the momentum up even further, yet manages to end on one of the most peaceful and introspective moments in the series' run.

When McNulty calls Scott Templeton to fuck with the reporter's head, pretending to be the killer he's invented, it seems the game may be over for a second when *Homicide*'s Vernon Holley intercepts the call. It's soon clear that McNulty intended for the call to be recorded at Homicide; even so, it's the first of several moments in "Took" in which the house of cards seems about to crash down on McNulty. At the *Sun*, when he meets with Klebanow, Haynes and Templeton once again, McNulty is peppered with questions from Haynes that leave him scrambling for quick answers and suggest that the city editor would see right through McNulty if he wasn't so distracted by his problems with Templeton. When McNulty and Rhonda Pearlman meet with Judge Phelan again, the jurist observes that the killings coincided with the tough-on-crime governor gearing up for a reelection campaign. "You may want to check the governor's alibi," Phelan says, making a wisecrack which reminds us that there are a lot of

- 346 -

smart folks in Simon's Baltimore, and for every three people who accept McNulty's scam at face value, there's going to be at least one who can immediately tell that things don't add up.

Clay Davis has always seemed like someone whose success is due more to his mouth than his brain, but honey-tongued loquaciousness means little without smarts to back it up. Badly hurting for cash, Davis shows his intelligence by persuading one of Baltimore's top attorneys to represent him for well below his usual fee, pointing out that the publicity he'd get for representing Davis would be worth well more than his billable hours. Davis's trial is one of a number of scenes in "Took" that feel like "*The Wire*'s greatest hits": The limo driver's testimony (and, to a lesser extent, that of Davis himself) echoes Omar's moment on the stand in Season Two, one of the funniest scenes in the series' history.

Even though Davis makes a fool of himself on camera by quoting from *"Pro-mee-thus" Bound* by "Uh-silly-us", there are only 12 people he really has to impress, and they presumably lack access to TV. The limo driver mentions misdeeds of Davis' that fall outside the purview of the trial, as the judge is quick to point out; but by keeping the case's focus ultra-tight, she makes it that much easier for Davis to work his magic on the jury (comprised of 10 African-Americans, one Asian woman and one white man). The incident garners Quote of the Week honors for Pearlman; her observation that they don't teach this shit in law school is nothing if not an understatement.

McNulty's success with the ruse, meanwhile, certainly seems to be going to his head, as he uses the case as an opportunity to become everybody's new best friend, throwing handfuls of overtime at his fellow cops in a manner that recalls Clarence "Bumpy" Johnson throwing Thanksgiving turkeys to a Harlem crowd at the beginning of *American Gangster*. McNulty is so transparently happy to be able to play the role of OT Fairy for his fellow officers that you have to think it's only a matter of time until they realize how suspiciously unshaken he is by the supposedly disturbing case he's investigating.

Of course, McNulty won't evade punishment if Bunk has anything to say about it. Everyone's favorite Homicide curmudgeon repeatedly gets in the grills of McNulty and Freamon this week, railing harder than ever against them for diverting resources from real cases such as Kima's triple homicide (which, via an informant's leak, she has tied to Chris and Snoop). After Carver hauls in Michael Lee (who, in another reference to episodes past, gets to deliver McNulty's immortal "What the fuck did I do?" line), Bunk, following up on his re-investigation of the rowhouse murders, presses Michael to give up Snoop and Chris. Later, back on the street, Michael finds himself in the middle of Omar's latest attempt to intimidate Marlo into a public confrontation. In the eyes of most, Michael is still "just a kid", but he knows all too well that he's descended far enough down the dark path for Omar to have no qualms about killing him, and he thanks his lucky stars (as well he should) that he wasn't recognized from the shoot-out at Monk's apartment.

One might argue that the scene in which Gus Haynes gives a bunch of pointers to *Sun* reporter Mike Fletcher is a time-waster—Gus's credibility as a journalist has been long-since proven with the audience—but it's still nice to see evidence of how good he is at what he does. His insights into Fletcher's story and what the younger reporter needs to do to hone his craft lend extra credence to his sincere praise for Scott Templeton last week—as well as to his criticism of Templeton for going too far this time with his "To Walk Among Them" story, which makes the homeless sound like extraterrestrials.

Haynes' level-headed *Sun* colleague Rebecca Corbett, who has also previously displayed suspicion of Templeton, again takes Haynes' side, but that means nothing when Klebanow decides to pull rank and run Templeton's story unchanged. While most of this week's allusions to the past harken back to earlier seasons, this week we get parallels to scenes from just a week ago as Fletcher spends time with the homeless (and the non-homeless Bubbles) himself, in what seems like an honest, "this-is-the-right-way-to-do-it" version of Templeton's night under the freeway. If

Templeton had interacted with Bubbles, the beloved addict would surely have been reduced to a lurid stereotype in the resulting story; Fletcher, one expects, is much more likely to treat him as a human being.

In the past, there have been amusing parallels between McNulty and Kima as, once the pressure of the job ruptured her relationship with her partner Cheryl, Kima herself took to drinking and skirt-chasing. This week, Kima reenacts one of the all-time classic *Wire* scenes when, upon getting to spend a weekend with her son, she buys an Ikea bed and has a hell of a time trying to cobble the damn thing together while under the influence, a task that severely tried McNulty's patience when he took a shot at it back in (I believe) Season Two. Kima's struggle to turn a pile of particle board into something usable gives way to a wonderful final scene in which she lulls her son to sleep with a ghetto version of *Goodnight Moon*. It's a peaceful, deeply moving moment— and, given the pace of events, probably one of the last tranquil moments that anyone on *The Wire* will experience for quite some time.

A couple of observations: Price and Simon throw a huge spanner into the works as far as continuity geeks like me are concerned by giving a cameo to none other than Richard Belzer, Detective Munch of *Homicide: Life on the Street* and *Law & Order: SVU* fame. Although Belzer identifies himself as a former bar owner—and Munch co-owned a tavern on *Homicide*—I'm inclined to think he's not reprising the role. For one thing, he shares the frame with Clark Johnson, who of course played one of Munch's co-workers, Meldrick Lewis, on *Homicide*.

For another, if he is playing Munch, he'd theoretically be connecting *The Wire* to the same continuity as a vast array of other series, few of which seem like they take place in the same world: In addition to *Homicide* and *SVU*, Munch has appeared on the original *L&O*, *The X-Files*, *The Beat* (UPN's short-lived 2000 series about uniformed NYPD patrolmen, starring Mark Ruffalo), *L&O Trial by Jury*, *Paris enquetes criminells* (the French remake of *L&O Criminal Intent*, starring Vincent Perez as a Gallic version of Vincent D'Onofrio's character) and even *Arrested Development* and *Sesame Street*! Through various other crossovers, these series can be linked to *The Simpsons, Chicago Hope* and the ultimate crossover magnet, *St. Elsewhere*, which, via the notorious Tommy Westphall Hypothesis, theoretically takes place in the same universe as *Buffy the Vampire Slayer, Seinfeld, Walker Texas Ranger, Fresh Prince of Bel Air, I Love Lucy* and *Mayberry RFD*. Given some contradictions between *Homicide* and *SVU* where Munch's biography is concerned, it's possible to argue that the *Homicide* Munch and the *L&O* Munch are different characters in different universes (even though the *Homicide* Munch has appeared on the *L&O* shows, one of whom grew up in Pikesville, MD, the other in New York. Yes, it's enough to make your head spin, but such is the nature of obsessive TV fandom. In any event, my position is that *The Wire* takes place in its own universe, with no ties to *Homicide* or any other series.

The lawyer representing Clay Davis, Billy Murphy, is a real-life defense attorney, one of the city's finest, as well as a member of the city's black aristocracy (his great-grandfather founded the *Baltimore Afro-American*, a legendary black newspaper that's popped up in the background on *The Wire* once or twice). In the biography on his website, Murphy describes a philosophy that leaves no doubt as to why he was Clay Davis' first choice: "I look at it this way—a trial lawyer who isn't able to use the full spectrum of techniques has arbitrarily limited himself. If a trial judge pushes you, you've got to push back. I used to say that my client is a child of God and everybody else is a son of a bitch."

The Wire Recap: Season 5, Episode 8, "Clarifications"
BY ANDREW JOHNSTON ON FEBRUARY 25, 2008

It's just a lie"—Terry

In "Clarifications", one of the most seismic events *of The* Wire's entire run—you know what I'm talking about—is treated surprisingly casually and accorded less build-up than the deaths of a zillion other characters over the years. Perhaps more than any other incident this season, the death of Omar calls attention to the delicate balancing act David Simon has assigned himself.

Other HBO series that have been allowed to run their full course—*Six Feet Under* and *The Sopranos*—also generally featured season-long story arcs, but theirs were customarily looser than those on *The Wire*, making it easier for creators to provide closure on several seasons of continuity while simultaneously wrapping up the business at hand. The extent to which the fake serial killer plot has polarized *The Wire*'s fan base suggests that even if Simon has a satisfying ending to the current story up his sleeve, some fans will complain that he didn't pay enough attention to resolving the big picture. On the other hand, if the final two episodes dwell heavily on tying up loose ends and escorting characters to their final fates while ending the current story arc in a somewhat perfunctory manner, half the audience could walk away feeling as if they'd spent a whole season having their chains jerked.

When commentators compared *The Wire* to fiction, they often pick the sprawling, society-spanning novels of Charles Dickens and Anthony Trollope as their reference points. But the technique of giving each season its own theme has a more immediate antecedent, series crime fiction, and it may be useful to look at *The Wire* through that lens. The shift in tone between Season Five and its predecessors has attracted a lot of criticism, but such shifts are fairly common between volumes of, say, Ed McBain's 87th Precinct mysteries (where the vibe could be more serious or less depending on which regular cast served as a given book's protagonist) or George Pelecanos' Dimitri Karras/Marcus Clay novels, where the atmosphere fluctuated depending on the year the novel was set and how old the characters were at the time (this is also the case with Walter Moseley's Easy Rawlins mysteries). Of course, none of the above examples have as much inter-series continuity as *The Wire*. Simon may not be venturing into unexplored territory as *The Wire* closes, but he is trying to do the sort of alpha/omega reconciliation that can make or break the reputation of a writer—or a series.

"Clarifications" is concerned first and foremost with resolving the story at hand, and at that level it's surely one of the season's best episodes. But there are also lots of character florishes that subtly point toward the series' ultimate resolution, making it an episode worth reappraising after we see how everything finally plays out.

Despite the earnest intentions behind McNulty's scam, he's often appeared to be having the time of his life as he manufactures evidence and dupes his bosses. This week, however, the chickens come home to roost. So far, we've mostly seen him dealing with peers and subordinates during his investigation, never having to deal with anyone who ranks higher than Jay Landsman, who has never seemed terribly concerned with the particulars of murders as long as the clearance rate is high enough to keep him out of trouble. As the episode begins, McNulty is being grilled by the full departmental brass, including Rawls and Daniels, and it's soon clear the heat may be more than he can take. "I'm all for a little kinky shit every now and then…", says Rawls, whose colleagues might not laugh so hard at the wisecrack if they knew of the bars he frequents. Rawls is an asshole no matter how you slice it, but the scene also reminds us that he's a damn good cop and, potentially, a more effective commissioner than Daniels might be. Baltimore's black power brokers would balk at a white commissioner, we've been told more than once, but incumbency is a strong weapon, and I wouldn't be surprised to see him hold onto the job as the series ends—though of course it all depends on how and when he learns the truth about McNulty, and what he chooses to do about it.

The frustration that Dukie displayed when asking Cutty how to escape his situation has solidified into rigid determination, as we learn when we see him doggedly looking for work. Dukie's visit to a sneaker store leads to the return of a familiar face: Bodie's old running mate Poot, who claims to have gone straight because he just got tired of life on the corners (he conveniently neglects to mention that he's done time in Jessup since his last appearance). Poot says he'd like to help Dukie but couldn't hire him even if there was an opening because he's just too young for the job, then hilariously suggests that Dukie resume slinging rock until he's old enough for legit employment. That might deter a lesser kid, but Dukie keeps forging on until he gets what could be the lowest-level gig in town, helping an old-school junkman who collects scrap metal in a horse-drawn cart. As we saw with the end of Season Three and with Namond's fate at the end of Season Four, Simon isn't above handing out happy endings when he feels like it, and I sure as heck hope Dukie survives Episode 60 with his dignity intact—if not, his perseverance could end up seeming an exercise in audience manipulation rather than an example of a determination we would all do well to emulate.

It's been fascinating to see (and attempt to predict) how various characters respond to McNulty's ruse when they learn the truth about it. I was sure he was going to spill the beans to Carver when he approaches him at the Western for help getting the manpower Lester needs to go after Marlo. Certainly, Carver is among those I'd expect to react the most negatively to the hoax. If the ruse ends the careers of McNulty, Freamon and others (as seems very likely), at least there's a competent crop of successors waiting in the wings. We've already seen Carver display strong leadership this season, but it was a treat to see Syndor in action as a field general. He's clearly turning into the cop that Lester could have been if he hadn't been exiled to the pawn show division for all those years. In any event, given the well-documented parallels between Kima and McNulty, I didn't expect her to react quite so vehemently to the truth, though I suppose her famous diligence should have tipped me off. Lester's indulgence counts for a lot, but with Bunk, Kima and Beadie all lined up against him, I wouldn't be at all surprised to see McNulty pull the plug on his scam early in the next episode and then spend the remainder of the series trying to get the genie back in the bottle.

Tommy Carcetti is usually portrayed as a pretty sharp guy, but it was colossally stupid of him to only visit white politicians in Prince George's County, and even dumber of Norman Wilson to have let him do so: According to Wikipedia, the population of PG County was 62.7% African-American as of 2005, and with a percentage like that you can be sure that black folks have been the dominant ethnic group there for many years now. It's a mistake that would have been inconceivable in real life but which makes sense as a plot device to force Carcetti into bed with Clay Davis and Nerese Campbell. The payoff is one of my favorite *Wire* moments ever: Carcetti telling Davis, "It scares me to think what damage you could do with two votes on the liquor board." Davis laughs his ass off in response, but the mayor obviously wasn't kidding.

I'm going to skip over the issue of the intriguing scene in which Lester Freamon blackmails Davis—as well as, basically, everything that goes down at the *Sun*—because so much of it is setup for the last two episodes and is relatively hard to evaluate independently. This leaves us, of course, with the most discussion-worthy element of the episode, the death of Omar Little. There are many thematic ways to interpret his unglamorous death, including the possibility that it's a critique, a la David Chase, of audience bloodlust. I don't think that's the case: For all its grit, *The Wire* has always been much more inclined than *The Sopranos* to give viewers what they want. As noted in this comments thread, his death evokes the killings of Jesse James and "Wild" Bill Hickok in ways that speak to the underlying nature of the entire series.

At first, I was a little annoyed that Omar's death slipped through the cracks at the *Sun* in the same way that the killings of Prop Joe and Hungry Man did—yeah, I thought, we get it, the point's been made: the folks at the *Sun*, even Gus, have no clue what's really happening in Baltimore. Upon further reflection, this made me realize something interesting: Simon admirably resisted the temptation to add a stand-in for himself to the fictional *Sun* staff—if he had, there would have been a reporter who knew full well what Omar's death meant (in the behind-the-scenes book *The Wire: Truth Be Told*, Simon described the struggle he experienced when he fought his bosses—successfully—to be allowed to publish an obituary for the real-life Bubbles). The episode ends with a curious scene in which the medical examiner switches the tag on Omar's body with that of another corpse (which sort of looks like it could be the body of prosecutor Gary DiPasquale). The scene plays as if the ME isn't quite sure that the body is Omar's and is trying to verify his ID somehow; as I pointed out in a comment predating this recap, the tag clearly gives Omar's age as 47, a flat-out impossibility that contradicts the statement earlier in the episode that he's supposed to be 34. It could just have been a production goof (one exacerbated by how long the director let the shot linger), but I couldn't help thinking about what deeper meaning there could be to the authorities having contradictory info about Omar on file.

The first thing that came to mind is the possibility that the contradiction is supposed to indicate Omar's metamorphosis from a man into a legend, a transformation made obvious long ago when we saw kids arguing for the right to "be" him in their game of cops and robbers (or vigilantes and dealers, rather). We haven't seen much evidence yet of Prop Joe undergoing a similar transformation, but it's not hard to see it happening if Marlo's business strategies inspire nostalgia for a more peaceful time. Over the course of *The Wire*'s run, as we've seen the destructive effects of "progress" on the urban middle class in all manner of ways, the series has been described by many as a eulogy for a dying way of life.

But what Simon could be doing—which sounds very similar but isn't quite the same thing—is illustrating the process by which the present becomes history and history becomes myth. Much as the culture of the camp on *Deadwood* is so different from our own as to make that series sometimes seem like it took place on another planet rather than merely in another time period, the Baltimore of 2002-08 is going to seem so different to the Marylanders of 2064 as to appear legitimately alien. Calling *The Wire* an elegy implies that the passage of everything it depicts is worthy of mourning, and that's clearly not the case. Simon's brand of storytelling is so close up that this might take a few years to become apparent, but *The Wire* just might be the equivalent of a series that, by focusing on forgotten people and mundane events, illustrates how the decadent pre-revolutionary French state began turning into the unrecognizable industrial nation that it had become by the end of the 20th century.

The Wire Recap: Season 5, Episode 9, "Late Editions"
BY ANDREW JOHNSTON ON MARCH 3, 2008

Is the best episode ever of the best TV drama ever QED the best single TV episode of all time? That's not a philosophical conundrum I face where "Late Editions" is concerned, since my pick for the best series of all time is *The Sopranos*. Those who believe *The Wire* to be the finest series in the history of the medium, however, are going to spend a lot of time debating the question, since after two viewings it's pretty clear that "Late Editions" is *The Wire*'s single best episode. I'm in a position to say this since I've been fortunate enough to see the series finale—which isn't to say that *The Wire*'s final episode is a disappointment, just that it's not as good as "Late Editions." Obviously, a lot of "Editions" serves to set up the finale, but the two episodes are not so tightly connected that "Editions" can't be discussed separately, and without fear of spoiling the series finale.

As a big fan of George Pelecanos, I was thrilled to see his name attached to the teleplay credit for "Editions"; of the acclaimed crime novelist trio that has contributed scripts to *The Wire* (the others being Richard Price and Dennis Lehane), Pelecanos has always been my favorite, and his particular gift for dialogue is in evidence throughout the episode. We begin with Lester Freamon contemplating the clock code that Sydnor cracked last week, a code that quickly leads the younger cop to a spot in the boondocks where Marlo's crew is about to take delivery on an enormous shipment of pure heroin. In the first of many great scenes that Lester scores—in a lot of ways, this is really his episode—he goes to Daniels and says he's been investigating Marlo using resources from the Clay Davis case. I'm sure I'm not the only person who thought Lester was going to come 100% clean and reveal the truth about the serial killer, perhaps taking all the "credit" for the scam in order to spare McNulty. Instead, he leaves Daniels with the impression that he's done nothing seriously inappropriate, and Daniels quickly signs off on the arrest of Marlo and his gang (Snoop, however, is able to avoid arrest because she's at Levy's office at the time of the sweep). Of all the great throwaway moments in the episode, one of my favorites is one of the most simple: The "uh-oh" tone of voice with which Pearlman asks "why?" when Daniels asks her if she's sitting down before (off-camera) telling her that Marlo's about to fall.

Marlo's arrest is one of the few developments that doesn't turn out to be too good to be true: No sooner does Dukie turn up than we see him being pressed into stealing scrap by the junkman who hired him last week (a literal junkman, as we learn at the very end). Daniels' new job proves to be equally problematic when his balls are put in a vise by Carcetti's chief of staff Michael Steintorf, who demands that he and Rawls cook the crime stats to produce a 10% drop in violent crime—or else. The situation makes Daniels the first of several characters who are faced with a choice between staying true to themselves or repeating the decisions that formed the fate of another. Daniels therefore stands at the brink of becoming the next Burrell, much as Michael, per Snoop's final speech, is poised to inherit Omar's mantle. Lester, generally a relatively sober fellow (though by no means a teetotaler), celebrates Marlo's arrest by stepping into Bunk's traditional role as McNulty's drinking buddy.

Lester has always been the cop most inclined to see the big picture where the drug trade is concerned, so I was a little surprised by the suggestion that he had never before considered the role that Baltimore's sketchier defense attorneys play in financing the business. The scene where Davis spells it all out for him, however, is classic. His blackmailing of Davis turns out to be the ultimate extension of his plan to use anti-Davis resources to take down Marlo, and it leads to the intriguing revelation that the courthouse leak is a level above Prop Joe: Levy bought the leaked documents before turning around and selling them to Joe. Still, the coolest part of the scene comes when Pelecanos goes into the realm of "fan service" by having Davis reminisce about how he scammed Stringer Bell.

I was dearly hoping for a return appearance by Bunny Colvin and Namond Brice before the end of the season, and their visit didn't disappoint. Namond's participation in a debate tournament, describing how little the U.S. is doing to combat the spread of HIV in Africa, shows that Bunny is as effective a foster father as one would expect him to be—and given the precariousness of Dukie's position at the end of the episode, it's damn nice to see that at least one of the kids from Season Four is unquestionably on the right path. Carcetti's apology to Bunny for how he handled Hamsterdam didn't seem quite in character for the mayor (or at least didn't seem fully motivated), but so be it.

What I loved the most about the episode—and which motivated me above all to proclaim it the best *Wire* ever—are the episode's two big speeches: Marlo's monologue in jail and Bubbles' speech from the podium at the NA meeting. Marlo has seldom so much as raised his voice in the past, so it was fascinating not just to watch him lose his cool but to see what could make him do so. Omar, it seems, had more insight into Marlo's psyche than was apparent at the time—if Snoop hadn't kept her boss from learning that Omar was calling him out, Marlo would have most likely fallen to him. Marlo's seething anger at his name being taken in vain allows Jamie Hector—already a very intense actor—to display a fury we hadn't seen before, and it's mesmerizing. Bubbles' speech was arresting for different reasons—essentially, it's the climax of a character arc that began in his very first appearance, and it's hard to imagine a better final outcome for him. It was genius of Pelecanos and Simon to keep Bubbles' moment of doubt offscreen—even before he started to tell the story, it was clear he didn't fall off the wagon that day, but that made me no less inclined to pump my fist in the air when he said that he didn't get high when he couldn't contact anyone else in the group.

The least progress toward a final resolution came on the *Sun* front, where Gus expanded his investigation of Templeton's manufactured quotes and stories but little else happened. As a result, I'm going to keep most of my thoughts on the newspaper story line on ice until the finale airs, since so much of this episode's *Sun* action is pure set-up. And little enough happened with McNulty that I'm going to refrain from diving into his activities as well.

I'll wrap things up by asking a question that left me stumped after both my viewings of the episode, and which also left our illustrious host and publisher scratching his head: Why does Herc tell Levy that the cops are running a wire on Marlo? Under the circumstances—with no evident leak in Marlo's gang to serve as the source of the clock code, nor with there being any good reason for the police to even have Marlo's number—doesn't that come awfully close to self-incrimination?

The Wire Recap: Season 5, Episode 10, "-30-"
BY ANDREW JOHNSTON ON MARCH 10, 2008

The moment it was announced that the Baltimore *Sun* would factor into the final season of *The Wire*, it should have been obvious that the series would end with an episode called "-30-". In addition to being the slug used inside the business to mark the end of a news article (Wikipedia tells us it's an Arabic-numeral conversion of "XXX", which was used to signify the end of telegrams during the Civil War), it's also the name of a 1959 film directed by and starring Jack Webb that I've never seen but which, according to one of my journalism-school instructors (a very Gus Haynes-like guy, come to think of it) is a bottomless trove of sentimental clichés about the newspaper trade—and a film that reporters love to watch in large groups and mock the bejeezus out of when they're all liquored up.

Some people, I dare say, will claim that *The Wire*'s final episode offers as unrealistic a picture of the news biz as Webb's movie, and I'll admit that basically none of the *Sun* action worked for me at all. That being the case, I was relieved and pleasantly surprised that the *Sun* played a relatively small role in the episode when both the title and the opening quote (from the paper's most celebrated alumnus, speaking about his profession) invoke the world of journalism. For the most part, "-30-" is devoted to resolving the story of McNulty's fake serial killer and to the business of steering the characters toward the rest of their lives, and it succeeds admirably at both.

It didn't occur to me until my second time through the episode, but one of the main reasons why "-30-" works so well is its narrow focus: With most of the Omar/Marlo/Snoop/Chris plot business out of the way, the satirical tone that David Simon has been aiming for all season in McNulty's plot came across more clearly than ever before. I'm really glad: Several weeks ago, I predicted that McNulty would more or less skate as a matter of bureaucratic necessity, but the seemingly-universal consensus that the story could only end with McNulty going to jail had left me worried that the ending I predicted would be one it'd be hard for Simon to sell to the audience. Clearing the decks accomplishes this, in addition to giving the whole episode a welcome sense of cohesion by ensuring that what's left of the Marlo plot is more tightly connected to the other stories than everything involving his gang has been thus far this season. Indeed, the only stuff that really feels extraneous are the scenes featuring Bubbles, Michael and Dukie, which, while very fine, largely revisit the territory covered in last week's episode and make many of the same points, often less elegantly. While I liked the relaxed pace of "-30-", there's little doubt that it could easily have been converted into a regular-length episode without losing much of its substance.

The episode gets rolling with one of Aiden Gillien's funniest-ever scenes—which, given the number of spectacular tantrums we've seen Carcetti pitch since he's been on the show, is saying a lot. Between episodes,

Rawls, Norman Wilson and Mike Steintorf were apparently clued in to the truth by Daniels and Pearlman, sparing us a bunch of potentially repetitive scenes and increasing the impact of Carcetti's reaction by cutting right to it. The scene is only slightly marred by a detour into the dreaded land of the Overclose (something that happens three or four times in the episode) when Wilson observes that McNulty was doing the same thing that Carcetti's team was by using the homeless issue to (hopefully) vault him to Annapolis. Like Rawls, intriguingly, Wilson seems convinced that the scam was all about the OT and not about putting away Marlo.

Be that as it may, Carcetti having posed for the cameras with the drugs and money seized last week is, more than anything, what motivates the cover-up: Having nothing come of the bust would not only keep Carcetti from becoming governor but it would make him a national laughing stock to boot (at least that's how it seems as the episode begins—ultimately, the bust basically does go up in smoke and Carcetti emerges just fine).

Daniels knows that McNulty and Freamon are good police, but despite his years of experience with them, he's not at all inclined to cut them slack over the scam. It seems pretty clear this is because the scam genuinely offends his sense of decency. Pearlman, however, is only really incensed when it becomes clear how much she stands to lose if the truth comes out. When she crosses paths with Lester, however, she doesn't have the chance to blow her stack at him before he lets her know that Gary DiPasquale has copped to being the courthouse rat. I thought DiPasquale surrendered to Lester a little too easily, which—like the lack of other plausible suspects who could have been behind the leak—made this aspect of the plot feel a little undercooked.

The cover-up finally clicks into place when Steintorf and Rawls have a conversation setting up what Wilson calls a "road to Damascus" moment for Rawls. I'm sure I can't be the only *Wire* fan who thought Steintorf would prevail by letting Rawls know he's seen him in gay bars; indeed, we see Rawls checking out a woman at the beginning of their conversation, presumably as a knee-jerk ass-covering maneuver. Instead, Steintorf offers to broker Rawls' appointment as the head of Maryland's state police if he'll play along. Since Rawls is no dummy, he swiftly agrees—doing so not only ensures his future but also guarantees that Daniels, and not he, will take the fall if everything goes south.

I couldn't help being amused by Dukie's encounter with Marcia Donnelly, the assistant principal of his old school, since I had something similar happen to me in high school—as a kid, you don't realize just how many students people like her deal with, so it's easy to assume you'll be recognized when you go back to your old school, and it can be confusing and disappointing when you're not. While she doesn't recognize Dukie, that's not a problem when Prez makes his farewell appearance. To my surprise, I had a muted, mixed response to seeing him—it's hard to tell if he's become a good teacher since season four, or if he's just turned into someone who knows how the system works and has resigned himself to it. If the latter is the case, he's not so jaded that he's unwilling to give Dukie the money he asks for.

I was dearly hoping that Dukie would sign up for the GED course for real, and hugely disappointed when he didn't. I might not have responded that way on my first viewing had I been watching the episode on a bigger TV—the set I watched it on made it hard to see the wear and tear on his face. After Prez drops him off and his boss, amazed at Dukie's success, observes that "teacher must love your black ass", I of course knew Dukie was doomed (he withholds $150, but it's pretty frakking obvious that money ain't going toward the course). By the way, I hope Simon's excessive symbolism w/r/t Dukie's new employer and companion is a coincidence or accident: Not only is he a junkman, but *he owns a goddamn horse!*

When Templeton makes his attempt at extending the serial killer's run, setting up the confrontation in which McNulty cops to being the one who called him, Matt and I (we watched the episode together) both found ourselves wondering if the episode was going to into a realm of satire even darker than we thought possible by having McNulty frame the reporter for the non-murders. Certainly, that would completely cement the Alan Sepinwall school of thought about McNulty having crossed into bad guy territory when he shanghaied the homeless man to Richmond. Personally, I would have been delighted if Simon had gone there—it would have given Templeton his just desserts (in a manner, granted, that would be grossly disproportionate to his sins), and it would have been a huge display of creative balls. When it first occurred to me that McNulty might escape unpunished because everyone above him has so much to lose, I envisioned the level of satire being ratched up to the *Network* level, and having McNulty railroad Templeton would have fit with that perfectly. Instead, it's the copycat killer who gets framed—though not really, since he did kill two people. Although McNulty has their blood on his hands (assuming they wouldn't have died if the hoax wasn't in effect), the resolution is a bit on the tidy side—and, unfortunately, it allows for the heavy-handed final resolution of the *Sun* plot.

Almost everything about the end of the *Sun* story left me dubious and frustrated. As we discussed the episode afterwards, Matt said that Gus getting punished for his accusations against Templeton is the kind of thing that happens in the real world all the time. Presumably he wasn't fired because his union would have raised a stink; still, demoting him to the copy desk seems like a punishment better suited to the military or to high school than to the professional world. Obviously, Gus's claims would instantly be proven true if a powerful figure outside the paper who'd been burned was willing to step forward. Conveniently, Daniels and McNulty have both been forced to resign at this point (and the city official who came off as being smarter than he is thanks to Templeton certainly wouldn't dis him), so apart from the homeless veteran, the only people with reason to suspect Templeton all work at the paper.

What this means, then, is that every single person we've met who's on Gus' side and who has doubts about Templeton—including the Metro,

Regional Affairs and State editors, who are all at least Gus' equal on the masthead and some of whom may be above him on the food chain— *every single one of them is a wuss who's so scared of losing his or her job that they're willing to let Gus take the fall.* This isn't an implausible scenario, but it does conflict with the established characterizations of a number of *Sun* characters, most notably Regional Affairs editor Rebecca Corbett. In my decade-plus as a professional journalist, I've seen a lot of people compromise their principles in order to stay employed, but never have I seen so many people compromise so much. At the risk of seeming terminally naïve, I have to ask if things are really that much worse in the newspaper world than they are in the magazine biz (and now that I've raised the question, I'm sure more than one person will provide evidence in the comments below that yes, things are that bad). The story obviously ended the way it did because of the point that Simon (pictured above in a blink-and-you'll-miss-him Hitchcock-style cameo this episode) wanted to make. Surely, after the episode is over, Alma's going to write her way out of Carroll County, Gus will triumphantly reclaim his old job, and Whiting, Klebanow and Templeton will all have to make like Janet Cooke and return their prizes...*right?* My desperate longing for that to be so just proves how good Simon is at creating believable characters of a sort you don't often see on TV; much of that believability is based on observations Simon could only make if he was the kind of reporter whose excellence this season sentimentalizes.

A one-hour cut of "-30-" probably wouldn't have room for as many Maury Levy scenes, and I really wish we'd gotten more of him throughout the series after seeing him prove his smarts by deducing what's wrong with the case against Marlo. While he's fundamentally a scumbag and we've seen him salivating over the billable hours he can rack up when his clients do dumb things, he's a straight shooter insofar as we've never seen him proactively rip off his clients. When he takes Marlo to meet the room full of power brokers, I initially assumed he was going to do to

REMEMBERING A.J.

Marlo what Clay Davis did to Stringer Bell, but his conduct in the scene left me convinced that he was legitimately trying to help Marlo invest his money. Levy doesn't need to rip off Marlo: As he points out to Herc, having gotten Marlo off the hook is going to guarantee him more new business than he can handle, and there's never going to be a shortage of dealers in Baltimore—as Cheese points out to Slim Charles et al., it's the kind of town where anyone who sells drugs and doesn't have $900,000 lying around basically has to be a complete idiot (and was it just me or was Cheese's final exit, in the middle of a pretentious speech, reminiscent of Samuel L. Jackson's death scene in *Deep Blue Sea*?).

Of the scenes wrapping up plots that were already basically wrapped up last week, Marlo's coda was the only one that felt both interesting and necessary. After learning in "Late Editions" that Omar was calling him out, he felt a burning need to assert his alpha-dog bona fides, and while he's surely relieved to have skated, being forced out of the game is a very bitter pill for him to swallow. At that cocktail party with Levy, he's uncomfortable as hell and can instantly see it's a world he'll never belong to. When he goes onto the street looking for a fight and confronts the corner boys trading stories about Omar (his death has now been mythologized to the level of the gunfight at the OK Corral), he's further emasculated when they dismiss him as a pussy because he's wearing a suit. When Marlo asks "Do you know who I am?", it's clear that nothing is more important to him than responding to Omar's use of his name, even though Omar's out of the picture. When Chris shot Prop Joe a few weeks ago, Matt observed that the look on Marlo's face was akin to a kid torturing an animal who thinking "that's interesting—I didn't think it'd react that way", and when Marlo sustains a bloody arm wound and shows no sign of pain, he reacts similarly—as if he's thinking "that's interesting—I didn't think it'd feel like this." (On the subject of Omar's death, even as the myth of his theatrical demise grows, we see detective Michael Crutchfield taking Kenard into custody for the shooting. Obviously Kenard is too young to serve serious time, but the case is nonetheless officially closed and the ID of Omar's killer is a matter of public record, at least unless Kenard's age causes the file to be sealed. I don't think it's a stretch to speculate that people on the street would dismiss the truth as a conspiracy theory if they heard it).

Much of the last 20 minutes was unapologetic fan service, which in this case was by no means a bad thing. McNulty isn't as original or complex a character as Omar, D'Angelo Barksdale and other creations of Simon's, but thanks to Dominic West's charisma, he's become one of the most memorable and engaging characters in the history of the medium, and Jay Landsman's speech at the "wake" is a wonderful tribute to him, one which truly captures everything that makes McNulty the rogue we love. The wake revealed that with 30 years on the force, Lester 's going to get his pension, while McNulty, with just 13 years under his belt, has no such luck. I've assumed Lester to presently be in his mid-50s (Clarke Peters will shortly turn 56), and his tenure together with his age bolster my belief that he's a college graduate, which I suspect would have been rare for any rookie cop in the mid-'70s regardless of race. Dominic West is 39 this year, and if that's McNulty's age too, I think it's safe to assume that after high school, he might have spent time in the military and then fucked around for a few years before joining the force. If he continued his education past high school, I'm inclined to believe he either got a two-year community college degree or went to a less-than-great four-year school and dropped out.

The long concluding sequence veered into oversell territory again with Michael's stick up scene, though that may be excusable since his transformation into the "new Omar" was less telegraphed than Dukie's metamorphosis into the Bubbles of his generation. Still, something about it seemed almost comic-booky, as if Omar's mantle was something that gets passed around like the superhero IDs that get passed from one generation to the next in the DC Universe (I've long since lost track of how many DC heroes have used the name Starman, for instance), which seems ever so slightly to make Omar seem less unique. Similarly, Dukie's shooting-up scene in the montage retroactively stole some power from his heartbreaking final exchange with Michael last week.

Bubbles' final scenes also felt a little redundant after his stunning turn at the NA podium last week, but upon further reflection they do offer some substance—it was moving to see him sit down at the dinner table with his sister and niece after all the shit his sis has made him eat, and we also got a better sense of his physical transformation. Andre Royo looks fantastic with the short 'fro he sports here, and his body language also vividly expresses how far Bubs has come. I also really liked his last scene with Walon, in which they contemplate the quote from Kafka, a writer neither of them has actually read. And while I'm sure there must be an example from an earlier season that's slipping my mind, I almost wonder if the scene was the first time that we've actually seen someone chowing down on a crab on this set-in-Maryland series.

Throughout the montage it was hard not to be reminded of the end of Season Three, when Simon took a shot at wrapping things up so as to provide closure in the event of a premature cancellation. Apart from the examples cited above, Simon is about as generous with the happy endings as he was then: Carcetti becomes governor, Rawls gets to lead the state police, Lester gets to enjoy a peaceful retirement with Shardene (who I was thrilled to see again), McNulty appears to settle down with Beadie, Ricardo Hendrix and Slim Charles take over the connect (and presumably revert to a business model akin to the New Day Co-Op), Pearlman rises to the bench, Nerese Campbell becomes mayor…and, best of all, Stan Valcek becomes the commissioner of police. The sequence also features the return of Wee-Bay, who appears to hit it off famously in prison with Chris, the member of Marlo's organization who takes the hardest blow (by the way, earlier in the episode there's a bit of a continuity error with Chris's previous bust—Levy says it happened in 2004, which would put it during Season Three, not Season Four).

The sequence reprises Blind Boys of Alabama's cover of Tom Waits' "Way Down in the Hole" that played under the opening credits of Season One. It's interesting to think about the song in the context of this final montage as opposed to the series' traditionally downbeat credits sequences. I've been a big Waits fan since high school and purchased *Franks Wild Years* (the album that introduced "Way Down in the Hole") the week it was released in 1987, less than a month before I first left home for college. Even so, I never got around to properly figuring out the story behind the song cycle (billed on the album as "un operachi romantico in two acts"), which originated as a Steppenwolf Theater production directed by Gary Sinise that ran in Chicago and Off Broadway in New York in the summer of 1986.

It turns out that "Way Down in the Hole" was an outtake from the play, a song that never found its way into the musical-theater piece and got shoehorned onto the album. In the program book for the concert tour which followed the release of the album (the tour more or less documented in *Big Time*), Waits offered the flimsiest context for the song: "Checkerboard Lounge gospel. Here, Frank has thrown in with a berserk evangelist." At the amazingly thorough website The Tom Waits Library, the annotated lyrics to each song are accompanied by a list of known covers. Most of the songs on *Franks Wild Years* can claim five or six recorded covers; "Way Down in the Hole" has 22 and counting.

It's not hard to see why it's been so enduring: The fearsome energy of Waits' original studio version lets it work for secular listeners as a slam-bang snapshot of a world on the brink, the particulars of the words reach out to an entirely different audience. The lyrics—unvarnished Pentecostal propaganda, an appeal to embrace Jesus or suffer the consequences, to live clean or else—have an appeal that crosses racial and class boundaries. Many of the covers listed are by Christian artists, a large portion of them African-American.

The Wire's cultural mash-ups have been both surprising and convincing (what other show would devise circumstances in which a bunch of black men would sing the Pogues?), and the series' bona fides with African-American viewers have probably done a lot to turn the Waits song into a gospel standard. The imagery that accompanies it here, however, is much different from what we usually get in the show's opening credits. Superficially, the montage can be read as saying "...and so life goes on for the characters you've been following over five seasons." But when images of happiness—Lester and Shardene's domestic bliss, for example—are cheek by jowl with Herc's further descent into corruption and Carcetti's ascent on the basis of untold lies, the lyrics' of Waits song lend the montage a different cast. It becomes more like the one that ended *The Sopranos'* second season, which intercut scenes of seedy porn stores and street corner addicts with Tony's lavish graduation bash for Meadow. We may like knowing that Lester went unpunished and Daniels and Pearlman's relationship survived the scandal and that their careers continued to flourish; as characters, they are more sympathetic than not, and therefore, to an extent, our surrogates, the people we root for. But you know what? Like Carcetti, Rawls and everyone else, they paid heed to temptation and failed to walk the straight and narrow track (to paraphrase the lyrics), so they're all going to hell (Bubbles, of course, earns a bye as the only one who actually follows the advice of the lyrics).

The sequence flirts with self-indulgence until the very end, when it shifts gears from scenes of *Wire* characters to shots of average Baltimore people living their daily lives. It's one of the few times in the series when Baltimore comes across as a thriving organism rather than a dying one, and I'd be lying if I didn't say I found it rather exhilarating. As the episode ended, I told Matt that I was sure the haters would compare the last half hour to *The Return of the King* and say that Simon, like Peter Jackson, served up a few endings too many (for the record, I've always defended Jackson on this count). Only when I took a break for a grocery run in the middle of writing this column did it occur to me that McNulty's final line ("Let's go home") is not far off from the very last line of *The Lord of the Rings* both on page and onscreen, delivered by Sam Gamgee ("Well, I'm back"). The 150 miles from Baltimore to Richmond are a hell of a lot less than the trek from the Shire to Mordor, and McNulty, unlike Sam, has one last leg of the journey in front of him as *The Wire* ends. Still, those shots of ordinary people at the end of the long montage represent one of the few times on the series when Baltimore is presented as a place that someone could legitimately miss and could honestly look forward to seeing again. That, more than the muckraking and social commentary, could be the one thing about *The Wire* that tells us the most about who David Simon really is.

As of the end of the preceding paragraph, this column was scraping up against the 3500-word mark, and there are still plenty of observations about the episode that I haven't gotten around to making yet. So as not to exhaust the patience of my readers—and so that I don't stay up all night writing another 3500 words—I'm going to bring this to a close. I'd like to thank everyone who's been reading my recaps all season, especially those who've taken part in the discussions in the blog comments here. In addition to calling me out on errors I have no excuse for, you have provided endless food for thought. Your lively comments also forced me to make sure I brought my "A" game every time I sat down at the keyboard and made me feel like a schmuck when I didn't. I'd also like to thank Keith Uhlich for the peerless technical assistance he's provided on all my recapping endeavors at *The House Next Door,* as well as the people at HBO who have done so much to make my job and my recapping duties a hell of a lot easier than they might be otherwise. It should also go without saying that I'd like to thank David Simon, Richard Price, George Pelecanos, Dennis Lehane and everyone else who's written an episode of *The Wire* for creating such a brilliant piece of collaborative art. Last, but most certainly not least, I'd like to thank Matt for inviting me to write weekly columns about a landmark show's final season.

Andrew Johnston is the television critic for Time Out New York. *To read a transcript of Andrew, Matt Zoller Seitz and Alan Sepinwall debating the relative merits of* The Wire, The Sopranos *and* Deadwood, *see* David vs. David vs. David.

Mad Men

Mad Men Recap: Season 1, Episode 1, "Smoke Gets in Your Eyes"
BY ANDREW JOHNSTON ON JULY 20, 2007

It's a little uncommon for *The House Next Door* to recap a series from the very beginning—thus far, it's only been done with *John from Cincinnati*— but Matthew Weiner's *Mad Men* is really something special: After seeing the first four episodes at least twice each, I'm as hopelessly infatuated as I was when I got seduced by *The Sopranos* and *Buffy the Vampire Slayer* during their first seasons back in the late '90s—yes, it's *that* good. So yeah, I'll be dissecting the travails of Don Draper and his Sterling Cooper Advertising colleagues every Friday for the next 13 weeks, in the process offering those entranced by the series a place to discuss it (as I write this, Television Without Pity had yet to devote a thread to it). If you missed the premiere, be aware that mild spoilers follow—so look away if you want to approach the series *tabula rasa*, but do come back after catching one of AMC's rebroadcasts (the series is also available on iTunes).

Matthew Weiner wrote "Smoke Gets In Your Eyes" in 1999 as a spec script when he was a staff writer on Ted Danson's sitcom *Becker* who was eager to make the leap into drama. It somehow crossed David Chase's desk; as a result, Weiner became a key creative player on *The Sopranos*, writing or cowriting a number of seminal episodes (among them "Unidentified Black Males", "The Test Dream", "Kennedy and Heidi" and "The Blue Comet"). Yet, terrific though *Mad Men*'s pilot may be, there are ways in which it's clearly the work of a less mature writer than the Weiner beloved by *Sopranos* fans—of the first four episodes, it's the only one to make ironic jokes at the expense of the era in which it's set. Such gags seem a bit like showboating by a writer eager for attention, but they're forgivable in light of how substantial the episode is as a whole. The series' main influences are evident from the word go: Weiner has obviously seen *The Apartment* and *Sweet Smell of Success* several dozen times. It's equally clear that he's a big fan of Cheever and Updike—Our protagonist, Don Draper (Jon Hamm) has the same opacity to him that often characterizes the leading men in their stories.

The lack of exposition in the pilot is one of its most seductive qualities—the little we learn about Don (he's brilliant but impatient as hell and does not suffer fools gladly, and there are hints that traumatic battlefield experiences in either WWII or Korea did a lot to shape his personality) makes us eager to know more, and the subsequent episodes make it obvious that Weiner & Co. are going to take their sweet time about revealing what makes him tick. There's no equivalent to Tony Soprano's sessions with Dr. Melfi to let us know what's going on inside his head; indeed, the thesis that drinking served the same function in the 1950s that antidepressants and talk therapy do today is shaping up to be one of the major themes of the series. It also takes awhile for the relationships between some characters to become clear—only from reading the press kit did I discover that Don's boss Roger Sterling (John Slattery) is the son of one of the agency's cofounders, a man who died at a very early age (we learn a tiny bit about this in the brilliant fourth episode, which provides our second glimpse of the agency's other namesake, Bert Cooper, an eccentric played to perfection by Robert Morse—who, appropriately enough, created the role of J. Pierrepont Finch in *How To Succeed in Business Without Really Trying*).

Social anthropology is one of Weiner's main concerns—we're dropped into this world and allowed to draw our own conclusions about it, as was generally the case with *The Sopranos* (at least before Chase began his meta-critique of audience bloodlust). This is especially effective in relation to the depiction of gender roles via Peggy (Elisabeth Moss), whose ignorance of her effect on men plays a big role in next week's episode.

The cynic in me wondered if the use of Lucky Strikes in the episode was a backdoor advertising strategy—an extension of Don's end-run around the ban on marketing cigarettes as "healthy"—until I learned from Wikipedia that Luckies disappeared from the U.S. market last year. Don's invention of the "It's Toasted!" tagline is one of the few major anachronisms (the phrase began appearing in Lucky Strike ads in 1917; if Weiner wanted to be scrupulously accurate, he could have had Don coin the early-'60s TV ad slogan "Lucky Strike separates the men from the boys....but not from the girls"), and the use of a real-world brand poses some thorny creative issues. Fake brands are a long tradition in film and TV satires of the ad world, including many of the works that inspired Weiner. Using a real product adds verisimilitude, but creates the possibility Weiner and his writers could get lazy and make a corny period campaign for a well-known product a weekly staple. And though Don and his team work on print ads for Right Guard deodorant next week (and Bethlehem Steel in episode four), the products so far serve the plot rather than vice versa (it's pretty clear that Weiner is going to go fictional whenever a Sterling Cooper campaign factors into an ongoing story arc, as with Rachel Menken and her department store).

As Nancy Franklin's review of *Mad Men* in *The New Yorker* reminds us, the "office movie" was a major genre in the late '50s and early '60s, and if Weiner just wanted to pay tribute to it, Don could have worked in any number of fields. Advertising has a particular association with the culture of the three-martini lunch, however, and it points us toward what appears to me the major theme of the series: Frustration. Following one of the best-known clichés about ad men, both Don and Paul (Michael Gladis) have unfinished novels in the hopper and, as Don memorably says in the fourth episode, Sterling Cooper is home to "more failed artists and intellectuals than the Third Reich." In coming episodes, the theme of frustration expands to encompass the relentless conformity of suburban-housewife culture as well as the awkward relationship between Pete Campbell (Vincent Kartheiser) and his his aristocratic parents. Per the calendar on the wall of the gynecologist Peggy visits, "Smoke Gets In Your Eyes" takes place in March of 1960. We're about six or seven years away from when America's collective frustration came to a boil; in the first episode of his remarkable series, Weiner turns on the gas, lights a match and places his characters on top of a long, slow flame.

Selected comments:

Matt Zoller Seitz • Also, Jon Hamm is a real find. I don't recall seeing him in anything before, at least not with this much screen time. He reminds me a bit of Rock Hudson in "Seconds" and Paul Newman in "From the Terrace." He's dashing and confident, but there's something quite damaged about him.

Matt Zoller Seitz • Glad you're going to be writing about this show each week. It's fascinating, not just for its hard, at time opaque quality -- with a few exceptions, alluded to by Noel above, Weiner just lets the characters exist in their time and place without throwing us little cover-your-ass references to let us know that the people who made the show aren't borderline Neanderthals like their characters. They are who they are, and America is what it was.

At first it seems like Don is being set up as an audience surrogate, an anachronistic beacon of "sensitivity," in the scene where he gets outraged over a junior coworker's sexist piggery towards his new secretary. But later in the episode we realize that it's probably more about defending his turf as an employee, and demanding the deference he believes he's earned, than showing everybody how enlightened he is. (In the scenes with the department store boss, a woman, he shows that he does not play well with the opposite gender, particularly when they're on equal social footing.)

A potentially great show. It reminds me a little bit of the early seasons of "M*A*S*H," before the actors became producers and decided to reform the major characters and make them as sensitive and suffering as possible. Weiner's ad men are prisoners of their gender, their time and place and their mile-deep insecurities. I look forward to learning more about them, and I'm jealous that you've seen more episodes.

Mad Men Recap: Season 1, Episode 2, "Ladies' Room"
BY ANDREW JOHNSTON ON JULY 27, 2007

AMC's press mailing of the *Mad Men* pilot included a note asking critics not to reveal Don Draper's "secret" to readers. Naturally, on my first viewing, I kept wondering what the heck the secret would be. Don's response when Roger Sterling asked him if he'd ever hired any Jews ("Not on my watch!") had me inclined to think Don was a member of the tribe who was "passing" as a WASP, and that may yet be the case given the mysterious origins that are referred to in the opening scene of "Ladies' Room" (the way he compares himself to Moses in the opening scene could certainly be construed as a hint in that direction). Of course, AMC was referring to Don being married with kids ("I saw that coming a hundred miles away," my ex-girlfriend said, and I probably should have as well), and the heavy emphasis on Betty Draper (January Jones) in the second episode reveals a good bit more about where the series is going.

"Ladies' Room" evokes *The Sopranos*, where *Mad Men* creator Matthew Weiner made his bones as a dramatic writer, in a number of ways: Simply by merit of being a housewife—and a woman whose comfortable lifestyle is the result of her husband's morally dubious career path—Betty is, obviously, the series' closest analogue to Carmela Soprano; inevitably, her behind-the-wheel panic attack (and subsequent treatment by a psychiatrist) also brings Carmela's husband to mind. But there's also a more subtle influence: As was often the case on *The Sopranos*, the episode title has a number of meanings—both

Betty and Sterling Cooper's newest secretary, Peggy, spend time in literal ladies' rooms, but the title could just as easily refer to the kitchen where Betty trades gossip with her neighbor, or to the psychiatrist's office (since therapy is clearly seen by Don et al. as something that's only for women), Don's mistress' apartment (where she makes the rules), and the Sterling Cooper steno pool (governed by a complex all-female pecking order that Peggy is clueless about, in part because she has little concept of her effect on men until the end of the episode, notwithstanding her tryst with Pete Campbell last week).

The housewife whose personality is smothered by suburban peer pressure is, of course, one of the biggest clichés there is. I'm inclined to think, however, that what's stifling Betty isn't suburbia per se but rather her marriage to Don, who clearly sees emotional repression as both a virtue and one of the main reasons alcohol exists ("Maybe your wife is just a better drinker," Don tells Roger after his boss says he probably knows more about Betty than he does about his own spouse). We'll obviously get to know Betty better in the weeks to come; in some respects, the most important thing about her plot tonight was simply that it reveals she'll be having her own major story arcs as the series progresses and that the action won't unfold strictly from the POV of Sterling Cooper employees.

Insofar as doings at SC are concerned, one of the most interesting aspects of "Ladies' Room" is how it presents Don as seriously emasculated. To be sure, he's the alpha dog where Pete, Paul, Salvatore et al. are concerned, but he quickly rolls over when Bert Cooper (one of my very favorite characters on *Mad Men*, even though he only has two brief scenes in the first four episodes) orders him to develop an advertising strategy for Richard Nixon, whether the GOP's 1960 presidential candidate likes it or not. Similarly, Don unblinkingly follows Roger's example vis-à-vis his boss' philosophy that women's problems are something you deal with by paying other men to handle the situation. One could even argue that Betty has Don by the short and curlies merely because she's capable of making him ask what women want.

That age-old question is raised in the scene where Don's team presents their Right Guard ideas, a scene that will surely strike some as laden with irony that plays to the cheap seats. I don't see it that way: Right Guard was introduced in real life right around the time *Mad Men* takes place, and the ideas that Don is pitched seem exactly like the sort of thing that real ad guys would have come up with then. Similarly, there's nothing eye-rolling about Peggy's discussion of her salary—to dismiss that scene as audience pandering is to say that nobody in 1960 ever talked about money (likewise, the bathroom attendant's line about decreasing purse sizes threatening her livelihood is by no means unrealistic given the way actual trends were going at the time). Having period characters comment on the world around them isn't necessarily equivalent to making jokes at their expense or urging viewers to congratulate themselves for living in a more "advanced" era.

One difference between today and 1960 (and between 1960 and the late sixties) that the pilot skipped over, but which surfaces this week, is how the *Mad Men* era is one of the last times in American social history when younger men strived to appear older rather than vice versa. The main vehicle for this observation is Paul, who the episode establishes as another of my favorite characters. Weiner et al. are clearly taking advantage of Michael Gladis' astonishing resemblance to the young Orson Welles, and it works like gangbusters (I thought Gladis might have been asked to gain weight to emphasize the resemblance, but friends who saw him onstage a couple of years ago tell me he had a fairly pudgy face even then; I forgot to ask them if his voice was as Wellesian as it is here...and man, do I wish I could have found a photo of Gladis smoking that pipe!). We don't spend a lot of time with him, and even then we mostly see a façade he's mounting to hopefully score points with Peggy, but there are plenty of throwaway lines that make me love the guy—his affection for radio (pretty obviously a tribute to Welles), his mortified reaction to Peggy's disdain for science fiction and his thinly-veiled contempt for his job all really make me want to see an episode devoted to him. Given that Weiner & Co. are already writing to Gladis' strengths just two episodes into the series, it seems inevitable that he'll get some time in the spotlight—but not until after Don receives heavy scrutiny next week, and Pete Campbell the week after that.

Mad Men Recap: Season 1, Episode 3, "Marriage of Figaro"
BY ANDREW JOHNSTON ON AUGUST 4, 2007

"Draper? Who knows anything about that guy. No-one's ever lifted that rock. He could be Batman for all we know."—Harry Crane

"Marriage of Figaro" begins with a bombshell revelation, albeit one that's been hinted at somewhat: Don Draper probably isn't Don Draper after all. No dialog in the episode rules out the possibility that Richard Whitman's old buddy has mistaken Don for someone else, but Don's behavior, beginning with glazed grouchiness (which tellingly causes him to miss the conductor's bemused reaction to the VW ad) and culminating in a marathon drinking binge that goes a long way toward alienating his wife Betty, it's clear that ol' Larry was on the money.

My first viewing of "Marriage of Figaro" (which I saw out of sequence, as the screener was sent out after the one for next week's stunning "New Amsterdam") led me to dismiss it as the series' weakest to date, but the next day I was haunted by the way Don's frustration leads him to reach out to Rachel Menken and then further wall himself off from his family after she spurns him. I watched it again that day, and again the day after that. If it's not my favorite episode of the series, it's still the one I find the most complex and sophisticated. There's very little plot here—the episode is far more concerned with letting viewers exist in Don and Betty's world (with a couple of excellent tangential moments involving Harry and Pete). The Asian-family prank that gets played on Pete is a fascinating bit for a number of reasons—the glib use of now-frowned-upon terminology ("orientals", "chinamen" etc.) is creepy enough, but instead of seeming like an opportunity to congratulate themselves for being advanced, the whole thing seems genuinely alien since it's impossible to tell why everybody thinks it's supposed to be funny.

Don's ability to come up with the funniest one-liner about the Asians when he's at his most pissed-off ("I'm still waiting on my shirts") speaks volumes about his intelligence, and—at the risk of entering cultural-stereotype land—there's a dark Borscht-belt tinge to it that lends ammunition to Don's-a-closet-Jew theorists (ditto his "Maybe I should stop paying you!" crack to Paul last week. Even if Don's not a secret Jew, his rooftop flirtation with Rachel Menken is nonetheless an example of the "real" Don—who may not even be Richard Whitman—taking a baby step toward opening up and suffering a painful rebuff for his effort.

The episode really kicks into gear when Don begins his bender while building a playhouse as a birthday present for his daughter. By my count, Don knocks back at least five beers, at least one mint julep and at least one healthy tumbler of bourbon over the course of the day. That's a hell of a lot of alcohol by any standard, but it's by no means out of the question for a truly experienced drinker. Don doesn't get so bombed simply so he can tolerate building the playhouse—rather, it seems pretty obvious that he's drinking to suppress the real him that began to emerge when he was recognized on the train. The dark humor of the sequence obscures, at least on an initial viewing, some of the additional hints about Don's past that are revealed: His comfort with manual labor certainly hints at working-class origins (and/or having done plenty of shit work in his military days), as does the hilarious scene where he takes a leak and finds himself unable to wipe up without disrupting Betty's meticulous organization of the bathroom. An unexpected side effect of this is the extra virility that comes through—Betty and her friend suddenly see Don as a sex object once his rough side begins to surface. Not until my fourth viewing of the episode did I realize that we actually see the exact moment our protagonist resumes the role of Donald Draper: It's when he slips Betty his beer and exchanges it for a mint julep.

The scenes with the Drapers' friends and neighbors during the birthday party are among *Mad Men*'s most frightening examples of retrograde behavior to date. The assumption that new neighbor Helen Bishop's divorcee status QED makes her a slut is expressed by the braying men and whispering women alike in cringe-inducing terms (we're also treated to an especially creepy example of casual anti-Semitism). The swelling bile comes to a head when gap-toothed neighbor Jack delivers a brutal slap to someone elses' kid…for the crime of spilling a drink. You truly can't blame our man for getting so hammered—it's the only way he can tolerate the people he has to surround himself with as a requirement of the role he's playing.

The title of the episode is something of a puzzler. At one point during the party, a radio is tuned to a broadcast of the eponymous Mozart opera, which I'm afraid I'm not familiar with. The closest parallel to the episode that Wikipedia's plot summary offers up is the motif of unknown identity—Figaro, like Don, was a foundling, though the barber-turned-valet learns who his parents are in the opera. Whatever the nature of Don's true identity is, it's something he's labored mightily to escape, and because of how closely Matthew Weiner and Jon Hamm are playing their cards where Don is concerned, it's a shock to see the ultraconfident pitchman at the brink of suicide during his meandering birthday-cake run. When he belatedly returns with a dog for his daughter, the first time I saw the episode, half-asleep at 2 am, I reached the weird conclusion that he'd gone into the city for an offscreen tryst with Rachel Menken and returned with one of the denizens of her rooftop kennel, which of course makes no sense (among other things, the dogs are totally different breeds). The dog, obviously, is a stray Don picks up in order to save face with his daughter, and it works like gangbusters. Our protagonist may be pretty damned good at selling cigarettes and toothpaste, but there's no product he's better at pushing than Donald Francis Draper.

Mad Men Recap: Season 1, Episode 4, "New Amsterdam"
BY ANDREW JOHNSTON ON AUGUST 10, 2007

"There's a Pete Campbell at every agency out there"—Bert Cooper

With "New Amsterdam," *Mad Men* enters the realm of bona fide tragedy via the most unlikely of avenues—a story about Pete Cooper, who heretofore came across as a superficial asshole with more ambition than brains. Well, he's still a superficial asshole with more ambition than brains, but now we know why.

When Pete tries to ditch his wife, Trudy (Alison Brie), when she arrives at Sterling Cooper for a lunch date, the scene stands in marked contrast to his apparently sincere confession of an almost mystic transformation that swept over him while exchanging marriage vows. He's got good reasons for his moderately less enthusiastic view of married life: The woman who last week asked what meal he wanted waiting for him at home is a spoiled daddy's girl who sees no value in the importance Pete places on work, and who promptly sends him on a demeaning mission to beg his father for money to purchase the Park Avenue apartment she covets.

The scene with Pete's parents reveals where Pete's work ethic comes from. He was born rich, to be sure, but not as rich as he might have been had his grandfather played his hand differently. His parents still run with a wealthy society crowd, but they're obviously bitter about being merely very rich instead of having the gobsmacking Sultan of Brunei-level fortune that Pete's dad clearly expected to enjoy upon marrying into the Dyckman dynasty. And Pete, who has a job his father either doesn't understand or, more likely, is wildly envious of, is the person upon whom his father vents all of his frustrations. The full impact of Pete's dad's devastating closing line—"We gave you everything. We gave you your name. What have you done with it?"—takes awhile to become apparent: As surnames go, "Campbell" doesn't seem to carry any more baggage than a moniker like

Murphy, Jones or Davis. The weight of the name that was actually being referred to is something I'll address below in a sec.

In *Mad Men*'s first three episodes, Pete's aggressive tactics seemed to stem simply from wanting Don's job. As the scenes with his parents and in-laws reveal, though, Sterling Cooper is the only place in Pete's life where he can really be a man—or so he thinks. He's desperate to be respected for his intrinsic qualities; he certainly fancies himself a smart and creative guy. But he is doomed to always and forever be seen as a Dykman, and to be prized only for the connections his name brings. When Pete and his "cousins" take the Bethlehem Steel client out for a night on the town, we realize that Pete literally is a pimp and procurer—and, awful as it seems, that his father was actually right about what Pete does (notwithstanding his overly harsh "no job for a white man" crack). Pete realizes why Sterling Cooper has hired him. "You people tell me that I'm good with people," he says, "which is strange because I've never heard that before." But he obviously has no sense of his true importance to the agency, otherwise he wouldn't act as if getting fired is basically the end of the world (these scenes are a tremendous testament to Vincent Kartheiser's acting chops—by reading his face, you can visualize the scenarios running through Pete's mind about what will happen when he gets home).

The last act of "New Amsterdam" contains what are probably my favorite *Mad Men* scenes to date—Don and Roger's meeting with Bert Cooper, whose casual display of power is as deeply chilling as it is entertaining to watch, and Don's subsequent conversation with Roger over cocktails. The former includes one of the episodes' two most brilliant lines, "Some people have no confidence in this country"—though it means little without context or the benefit of Robert Morse's delivery. The other immortal line, Don's quip about Sterling Cooper having more failed artists and intellectuals than the Third Reich, speaks for itself. It's not like Don's given nothing to do in this episode, but these scenes—in which Don displays surprising candor by first voicing his discomfort with the notion that Pete is more important to Sterling Cooper than he is, and then by proving he has Roger Sterling's number with his withering "maybe I'm not as comfortable being powerless as you are" quip—are definitely his most proactive. Like the scene when Betty returns home to find him sleeping, with a rough sketch of the revised Bethlehem Steel campaign on the nightstand, they serve as welcome and believable reminders that Don is incredibly smart and incredibly good at his job. Pete doesn't envy Don's power or paycheck; it's the respect that Don commands because of his intelligence and skills which Pete covets, and which he'll never have. The look on Pete's face in the final scene proves that he has just enough self-awareness to realize that he'll forever be a prisoner of his relatively feeble intellect and (as the woman on the co-op board proves yet again) his formerly gilded name.

A few random notes:

I really, really hope that the use of *The Button-Down Mind of Bob Newhart* is not an anachronism. I haven't been able to find an exact release date for it—some online sources say 1/1/60, but I suspect that's a generic placeholder 1960 date. The album reached #1 on Billboard's pop chart on 5/16/60, but it didn't debut at number one—otherwise, the reference books would probably say so. In a forthcoming episode, a reference is made to Adolf Eichmann having been captured by Mossad agents "last week". Eichmann was apprehended on 5/11/60, so unless the Newhart album really did debut at #1, it would presumably have been out for awhile in late April/early May, which is when "New Amsterdam" apparently takes place (this lines up nicely with Pete's parents having just put their boat in the water after a winter in drydock, as well as the tarps on the furniture—presumably they're returning to a residence they left vacant over the winter, or are packing up a residence they intend to leave vacant for the summer).

The scene in which Pete and his wife tour the apartment and she says it's listed at $32,000 but could be had for $30,000 may seem like a groaner, but it's actually incredibly accurate. In the late 1950s, several dozen enormous white-brick apartment buildings (just like the one in the exterior shot) went up in Manhattan, just as the migration of Manhattanites to the suburbs was kicking into high gear. As a result, for awhile real estate was, as unbelievable as it seems now, a buyer's market in Manhattan; as a *New Yorker* article on the subject revealed several years ago, the developers of the white-brick behemoths were forced to compete for occupants with incentives such as free cars or two years' free rent on a five-year lease. Pete's comment about making just $75 a week might also seem like a rib-nudger, but anyone who's read *The Operator*, Tom King's biography of David Geffen, knows that 1960s salaries were typically expressed in dollars per week (I'm not sure when the paradigm shift to per annum took place), and that junior executives in media-related fields really did make that little back then.

It's impossible for me to say enough good things about John Slattery's performance as Roger Sterling. Slattery, in my opinion, is far and away the most gifted actor on the series, and Sterling the most interesting character (yes, even moreso than Don). While it's clear that Don has never seen Roger deploy the particular management gimmick he uses to scare Pete into line, it's equally evident that this is by no means the first time he's used it. The tactic also provides us with our first glimpse of how Roger's military experience influenced him; the only way he could have learned how to dress Pete down that way would have been by close observation of a drill instructor. There's also a hint of his military in the tremendous scene with Don where he waxes philosophical about his love affair with alcohol. "My generation, we drink because it's good, because we deserve it. We drink because it's what men do," he says. "You're all so busy licking an imaginary wound." Don, showing his hand ever so slightly, replies that "some of them aren't so imaginary." The stuff that Roger went through in order to feel deserving of the bottle—as well as Don's wounds—are topics that will naturally be addressed in the weeks to come.

Finally, I can't remember the last time I saw a woman peeing on television. The scene where she's interrupted by Glen Bishop (apparently played by Matthew Weiner's son!) is pretty jarring, not only because Betty is shown doing something that usually only men are shown doing on TV, but also because of her perfect housewife exterior that she labors so hard to keep up. The sight of June Cleaver or Laura Petrie taking a leak would be only slightly more shocking.

And is Glen gonna grow up to be one seriously fucked-up teenager or what?

Mad Men Recap: Season 1, Episode 5, "5G"
BY ANDREW JOHNSTON ON AUGUST 17, 2007

"Donald Draper? What kind of name is that?"—Adam Whitman

That explosion you just heard was the sound of the skulls of several hundred *Mad Men* fans erupting, *Scanners*-style, from the stress of trying to make chronological sense of Don Draper's life given what we learn of his past in "5G". We'll deal with the continuity issues in due course, but suffice it to say that, pending future revelations, a whole lotta fanwank is required. But first, on to the story itself....

"5G" makes it official: Don Draper, in a past life (almost literally, since he apparently faked his own death) was Dick Whitman. "It's not me," Don tells Adam Whitman (Jay Paulson), the sad-sack janitor who turns up at Sterling Cooper after seeing a photo in *Advertising Age* of the man who used to be his older brother. Indeed, while many viewers over at Television Without Pity have been quick to conclude that Don is a cold, cold guy on the basis of his treatment of Adam, I'm inclined to think that his behavior is more the result of cognitive dissonance. Dick Whitman's transformation into Donald Draper is so complete that, as we saw in "Marriage of Figaro", the tiniest crack in the facade is enough to send him on a huge bender. In "5G", the gig is very close to being up—both because of Adam's arrival and because Peggy learns of Don's affair with Midge and then reveals it to Joan (Christina Hendricks), which she really shouldn't have done. Even if Adam never appears again, Peggy's knowledge that Don was up to something when he slipped out for lunch—knowledge Don is entirely ignorant of—will surely have consequences down the line.

Once again, because of Don's lack of a Jennifer Melfi figure—or even a good friend—it's impossible to tell what's going on in his head after Adam surfaces. This, of course, makes it possible for viewers to assume that Don's going to shoot his brother (technically, they're half-brothers, as this week's episode strongly implies and next week's makes clear). Certainly, there are few reasons to doubt that Don has the intestinal fortitude required of a killer—it would come as no surprise to learn that he's killed men on the battlefield—he's also smart enough to know that he'd never get away with the cold-blooded murder of Adam in a flophouse where dozens of fellow occupants would hear a gunshot. There's the slightest twinge of actual affection in the brothers' embrace in room 5G, which probably comes more from their status as mutual survivors of what was presumably a very brutal household than it does from any blood tie.

So much of what happens to Don in "5G" hinges on information that has yet to be revealed that it's premature to evaluate the episode within the context of the series. Even so, the story works surprisingly well as a self-contained piece—like "Marriage of Figaro", it provides strong evidence of the influence of short-story writers—most specifically John Updike and John Cheever—on the direction of the show. On the subject of short stories, the B plot about Ken Cosgrove (Aaron Stanton) being published in *The Atlantic Monthly* is a gem. Ken is the junior executive about whom we've learned the least, so the fact that he's a writer—and a productive one—is as surprising to us as it is to Pete Cooper and Paul Kinsey. Pete's reaction—he's envious enough to seriously consider pimping his wife to her ex-fiance to get published—builds on "New Amsterdam" in interesting ways. It's possible to read Pete's reaction as the result of entitlement, but probably more accurate to take it as additional evidence of a burning desire to make it on his own and prove himself to his father (who reads *The Atlantic*), even if doing so requires stooping to extreme sleaziness. Paul's response is funnier, and makes me love the character even more. He clearly fancies himself the smartest guy—and the most frustrated artiste—among the ranks of the junior execs, and it's equally obvious that his high opinion of himself isn't based on any actual work (Don's probably on the money about Paul with his amendment to Roger's crack about everyone at the agency having a very small percentage of an unfinished novel in their desks). And lord almighty, does his story about that night with those "negroes" in Jersey City sound terrible or what? His I-can't-believe-I-said-that-out-loud reaction to Ken's description of his two (!) novels ("Those don't even sound stupid!") is one of the series' funniest moments to date, and it—along with incidents in the next two episodes—helps an important aspect of the series come into focus. My friend Charles B. François has always maintained that *The Sopranos* was, above all, a comedy of manners, and it's increasingly obvious that this is the case with *Mad Men* as well.

Some miscellaneous points:

Continuity-wise, the big issue with "5G" is reconciling the amount of time Don would need to rise to his position at Sterling Cooper with him having joined the army at seventeen or eighteen (I'm going to go out on a limb and assume he voluntarily enlisted as a means of leaving home) and being a veteran of the Korean War rather than WWII. It only makes sense if you figure Don spent a fair amount of time in the service, (which isn't a huge stretch if he indeed signed up as a means of escape). Figure he enlisted in mid-late 1946 after reaching the age when he could do so, then was sent to Korea pretty early in the conflict—while still Richard Whitman— and then, after seeing a fair amount of action and getting wounded, was honorably discharged as Donald Draper before the end of 1950. I'm imagining a scenario in which he was the only survivor of a patrol that got wiped out and who, before being rescued, donned (no pun intended) the uniform of a dead—and considerably more privileged—comrade. If the real Don Draper already had a college degree, this could give him nine years in the trenches at SC, which seems about right—though of course the unanswered question of how much of Don's résumé has been spun out of whole cloth gives Matthew Weiner a fair amount of wiggle room. I didn't see last week's behind-the-scenes segment, but some fans were apparently annoyed that Weiner and/or Jon Hamm offered up the "spoiler" that Don is an orphan. That may turn out to be a vicious tease—yes, Don Draper may be an orphan (it'd certainly have made his identity easier to steal), but Richard Whitman obviously lived with his stepmother until he was around 18, and his biological father was in the picture until he was at least 10 (his presumed age at the time of Adam's birth). For this to work, Don would be around 33 and Adam 23, which doesn't quite jibe with the actors' apparent ages (I read somewhere that Hamm is 36; Jay Paulson looks more like he's in his late 20s), but we'll pretty much have to live with it.

The sum that Don gave Adam—$5000—gives the episode title a neat double meaning (in addition to the room number, it's shorthand for "five grand"), and in today's money that comes out to about $33,000 and change. It was also the average annual US salary then, and it's not too far removed from that of today (the most recent median number I can find is around $43K; factor in differences and buying power and it probably all evens out). Of course, Don's ability to produce the money nicely dovetails with the thinking behind the Liberty Capital "executive private" account that serves as "5G"'s Product of the Week. His inclination to keep that much cash lying around suggests it might have been a personal safety net for him to hightail it on if his secret was exposed—or, like his beer drinking in "Marriage of Figaro", it could be read as a sign of the culture he grew up in (a child of the depression might have a gut distrust of banks that wouldn't be there for someone who grew up as privileged as, say, Roger Sterling did).

Finally, the choice of *The Atlantic* as the magazine with Ken's story resonated with me on a personal note, since a few years ago I was dumbstruck upon learning that my father had published a poem in the magazine right around that time (well, in '64 or '65). Dad downplayed his accomplishment when I made the discovery ("they just put it in this section where they ran light verse and stuff, it was a funny piece and not a 'serious' poem", etc), but it nonetheless completely changed the way I think about him. That one-off publication in *The Atlantic* was the end as well as the beginning of Robert C. Johnston's professional literary career; Kenneth Cosgrove, I'm assuming, will ultimately prove to be somewhat more successful.

Mad Men Recap: Season 1, Episode 6, "Babylon"
BY ANDREW JOHNSTON ON AUGUST 23, 2007

"Babylon" is probably *Mad Men*'s most entertaining episode to date, but it's also the most frustrating installment in the series so far. On the one hand, it's loaded with absolutely priceless lines of dialogue and does a lot to further our understanding of several characters and relationships. On the other, it takes too many of its jokes a little too far, resulting in the largest amount of annoyingly obvious period jokes since the pilot.

The episode begins with an intriguing coda to last week's episode: Don Draper slips on the stairs and hits his head, resulting in a brief flashback to the day his brother Adam was born in the 1920s. At first glance, it seems to recall the numerous flashbacks to Tony Soprano's childhood that *The Sopranos* offered over the years, but there's a key difference—the flashbacks in "Down Neck" and other episodes were often shown from a relatively objective POV rather than being filtered through Tony's memory. Here, however, Don Draper and his younger self seem to make eye contact through time. It's a hallucination, obviously, but it's also a very effective way to convey the uneasiness of his relationship with the past and the degree to which the events of "5G" continue to haunt him, his apparent ultra-stoicism last week.

After this emotionally tense scene, "Babylon"'s comic streak becomes evident when Don and Betty's discussion of Rona Jaffe's 1958 novel *The Best of Everything* and its 1959 screen adaptation results in Don obliviously claiming that Salvatore's affection for Joan Crawford constitutes evidence of the screen legend's sustained beauty. The meta nature of the line makes it a bit of a groaner, but it's also so funny and effective in context that it's hard to begrudge Weiner the joke (the same goes for an anachronism I'll get to way down below).

In any event, the discussion of Crawford leads Betty to revisit her mother's death, resulting in one of the series' rawest marital scenes to date. Don waves away his wife's melancholy mood, saying that "mourning is just extended self-pity" and then bringing up a pygmy tribe he read about that brewed their ancestors' ashes into beer—a beautiful metaphor for the way he relates to his past, per his binge in "Marriage of Figaro".

At Sterling Cooper, the focus shifts to Roger Sterling, who continues to be the series' richest character. Sterling's wife, Mona (Talia Balsam) makes a crack about how her husband's grey hair makes him look older than he is, a joke that sort of breaks the fourth wall—many people assume that John Slattery is around 50, but he just turned 44 or 45 (depending on whether one believes Wikipedia versus the IMDb) on August 13—indeed, he's at least a year younger than George Clooney, the ex-husband of Balsam, Slattery's real-life spouse.

The interplay between Joan and Sterling's family at the office, followed by the masterfully-staged revelation of Sterling's affair with the queen of the steno pool, is one of the series' most elegant and intriguing sequences yet (and it gives a whole new level of meaning to Joan's "5G" quip about Don, unlike most of the men at Sterling Cooper, being handsome enough to snare a mistress outside the office). Her remark here about how "food that close to a bed reminds me of a hospital" hints at events which may have shaped her, and she has enough great moments in this episode to make me seriously hope that she continues to be a major player.

When Joan tells Roger that she knows as much about men as he does about advertising, she's incriminating the hell out of herself in light of how Sterling's insight into the business has been another source of many of the series' best lines (this week: "They always say that", in response to the Israeli official's remark that her ideal tourist would make as much as Don does). As in Don's bedroom scene with Betty earlier, there's a jokey reference to women as the equivalent of cars that can be traded in forr new models. While that's unfortunately true where the wives and mistresses of the rich and powerful are concerned, the wisecrack is undercut by Joan's frank description of the sense of power she derives from stringing along multiple sugar daddies. The advent of serious feminism is still a few years off, yet Joan is hardly the only woman who enjoys a significant amount of control over the men in their lives.

Salvatore's priceless remark about Israel's most marketable quality being the local tendency toward extreme attractiveness sets up the reintroduction of Rachel Mencken when Don asks for her unvarnished insights into the Israeli mindframe. It may seem like a flimsy excuse to have lunch with her, as Don is obviously still attracted to her, but it also speaks to the cultural-sponge sensibility that makes him so good at his job. Rachel maintains the upper hand throughout the encounter both because she has knowledge Don wants and because she plays her emotional cards so close to the vest. This leads to the breathtaking scene where she reveals her feelings for Don in a phone conversation with her sister. It's an incredibly well-written and acted scene that may just be one of the most realistic depictions of the way siblings relate to each other that I've ever seen in film or television. The scene ends with a blistering assessment of the social rules that bind the characters of *Mad Men* as tightly as the codes that govern the lives of those in *Pride & Prejudice*. "It's 1960, we don't live in a shtetl, we can marry for love," her sister argues to Rachel. "I'm not sure people do that anymore" is the solemn reply.

Matthew Weiner definitely overplays his hand in the sequence where the Sterling Cooper secretaries serve as an impromptu lipstick focus group while the men literally watch from the peanut gallery (Pete Campbell even brings a snack!). One secretary's bleating remark that brainstorming sounds like something difficult is inches over the foul line—it's hard to believe that any woman could have such a low opinion of her faculties when she's got the example of Joan walking around in front of her daily.

Joan's covert manipulation of the focus group and titillation of Roger through the glass marks another display of her power, which we soon learn is something she guards jealously when we see her patronizing the hell out of Peggy when relaying the message that Fred Rumsen (a terrific new character played by Joel Murray) is intrigued by Peggy's potential as a copywriter. At first glance, Rumsen seems like he might be the biggest lush at Sterling Cooper (no small achievement), but he's soon revealed as someone whose clear-eyed view of the business rivals that of Roger Sterling. Rumsen's put-down of Ken is classic; ditto the way he uses one of Salvatore's snarky quips as the jumping-off point for an impassioned—and convincing—explanation of why Peggy might be an advertising natural. Unfortunately, Weiner once again gilds the lily by ending with Rumsen's too-far-over-the-top observation that observing Peggy's insight was "like watching a dog play the piano."

The wave of verbal wit crests in the episode's climactic sequence, the delicious war of words between Don and Roy, the bohemian poseur with whom Midge is apparently also involved. Midge displays her power by goading the two, then sitting back and watching the sparks fly, and the lads don't fail to put on an impressive show. The montage that follows as the beatnik poets at the club hand the stage to a corny folksinger, like the wisecracks which cross the line, is annoyingly on the nose (and the song just doesn't seem right for a 1960 folkie, though that may just be me), but it's redeemed by the haunting final shot of Roger and Joan in front of the hotel after their latest tryst. Ultimately, we see, Joan's power at the office and in the boudoir means little if she can't be seen with Roger in public. And while the liaison may provide Roger with relief from a miserable marriage, the inherent nature of the relationship means that relief will forever be superficial and short-lived. As broad as "Babylon" is at times, it ends on a note that beautifully demonstrates the level of insight that makes *Mad Men* so special.

Some insanely nerdy historical points:

"Babylon" is by far the most specifically dated episode of *Mad Men*—since Mother's Day is the second Sunday in May, the opening scene therefore takes place on May 8, 1960. During Don and Rachel's lunch at the Pierre, she makes reference to Adolf Eichmann having been apprehended in Argentina by Israeli agents "last week". Eichmann was captured on May 11, 1960, but was held in a safe house for ten days before he was flown to Israel. David Ben-Gurion made Eichmann's capture public on May 23 and it first made the New York *Times* the following day.

For Rachel's statement to be correct, three weeks would need to pass in the middle of the episode, placing their lunch during the week of May 30-June 3. Even then, a scan of the *Times'* online archive suggests that Israeli authorities were vague about the specifics of the capture for quite some time: On May 26, the Paper of Record ran a three-inch unbylined item commenting on a story in the Israeli press, which reached the conclusion that "the implication of this dispatch, which was subject to Israeli censorship, was that Eichmann was kidnapped in Brazil or Argentina." Not until June 2 was Argentina specifically identified by the *Times* as the locale of Eichmann's capture, via an AP story which tantalizingly only cites anonymous "reliable sources" as the basis of an extremely detailed account of Eichmann's life on the lam. This would push us into the week of June 6-11 1960, two weeks after the capture first made the news and a full month past Mother's Day. Instead of delving further into pretzel logic to justify Rachel's line, it's probably best to just conclude that Matthew Weiner screwed up.

The use of *The Best of Everything* is a bit off, as Rona Jaffe's novel was published in 1958 and the screen version was released in October, 1959. The references to *Exodus*, however, are chronologically accurate, as the Leon Uris novel, published in 1958, was still a bestseller two years later and reached the screen in December of 1960. Unfortunately, the funniest and most stinging line of the whole episode—Joan's invocation of Marshall McLuhan—is unfortunately an anachronism. *Understanding Media: The Extensions of Man*, in which the great Canadian cultural theorist coined the phrase "the medium is the message", was published in 1964.

Mad Men Recap: Season 1, Episode 7, "Red in the Face"
BY ANDREW JOHNSTON ON AUGUST 31, 2007

Mad Men continues to bring the funny with an episode that furthers the exploration of Roger Sterling's personality that began last week in addition to showing us a previously unseen side of Don Draper. His possessive, macho reaction to Roger's drunken pass at Betty is consistent with the Don of previous episodes, but his revenge prank reveals a more playful sense of humor than the tendency toward dry, dark wit with which we've become familiar.

But while Roger is used as a source of comedy more than once (the scene where Don provides him with driving tips from the doorway is one of the series' funniest), there are just as many scenes—if not more—that present him as a fairly pathetic figure. His unsuccessful attempt to schedule a last-minute tryst with Joan shows him longing for his youth ("I could put on my whites and we can pretend it's V-J Day"), but even then his youth probably wasn't all that—his naval heroism in the Pacific, revealed this week, falls short of his father's WWI exploits, and he apparently went through childhood with the demeaning nickname "Peanut" (a nickname Bert Cooper still uses on occasion). No wonder, then, that he takes comfort in the privileges that come with having one's name on the building.

Status and privilege play a big role in the episode. Even notwithstanding the era's more permissive attitude toward driving under the influence, I'm sure some people will be disappointed in Don's failure to keep Roger from getting behind the wheel after their massive binge, but Don has a zillion reasons to let Roger get behind the wheel. Above and beyond the being angry at Roger for putting the moves on Betty, there's the simple fact that Roger's his boss—an imperious one, as we see when he takes pleasure in yanking Pete Campbell's chain by calling him "Paul"—and Roger wouldn't have taken kindly to any attempt to keep him from driving. Then there's the spite motive: Because Roger cozied up to Betty, there's a level at which Don couldn't care less if Roger has an accident.

Don's actions against Pete Campbell in "New Amsterdam" showed him to be a very rash guy when angered, so the subtlety of his plot against Roger is a little bit unexpected but very, very impressive. All Don did was adopt the same deferential position he did at the beginning of the episode and the rest took care of itself (well, yeah, he bribed the elevator operator and then had to walk up all those stairs himself, but still). The dividends are significant: In addition to punishing Roger for scamming on Betty, the prank will presumably spare Don from working on the Nixon campaign (something he obviously wasn't eager to do) and, by extension, spare him from having to work closely with Pete. Roger becomes the only conceivable scapegoat for the loss of the Nixon campaign, but he's also the one person Bert Cooper is least likely to punish. It's really kind of brilliant.

Pete Campbell's subplot about the chip and dip raises the intriguing possibility that Pete is basically the guy Roger was 20 years ago. Yes, Pete tried to get proactive about manipulating Trudy in "5G", but here, he's back to the thoroughly emasculated position he was in at the end of "New Amsterdam", and her offscreen hectoring of him very much evokes what we can infer about the marriage of Roger and Mona Sterling (at least before the war made Roger more resigned and cynical). After "New Amsterdam", there was a fair amount of fan speculation that Pete would try to turn his premarital one-nighter with Peggy into an ongoing affair as a means of compensating for his emasculation at home. After last week, talk turned to the possibility that this would be accompanied by Pete taking credit for her copywriting. Pete and Peggy's first scene certainly seems to suggest this, but I think it's a little too obvious a development. The odd bonding between them that we see in their last scene together made me think of another possibility: What if they join forces to advance each others' position at the agency? Now that we've passed the halfway point of the season (sad but true), it seems pretty obvious that the narrative momentum will increase and the connections between characters will get tighter and more complicated by the week. In more concise terms, we'll find out soon enough.

Miscellaneous points:

Pete's acquisition of the rifle and his horsing around with it makes a nice callback to the hunting theme of the story that wound up in *Boy's Life* back in "5G". It's a nicely metaphorical obsession for him to have, since hunting is regarded in so many cultures as a means of proving one's manhood, and being his own man is obviously Pete's most burning desire. It's a goal that means so much to him that he'll happily take shortcuts to achieve it, and this, I suspect, will be his undoing on more than one occasion in the episodes (and seasons—I wish!) to come.

The details we get about Roger's father's WWI service are sketchy, but I'm inclined to think the elder Sterling survived the incident in the trenches, which—here's where the chronology gets tricky again—presumably took place before Roger was born (because let's face it, I can't see a rich guy with a kid being drafted to serve in the war—or, rather, I can't see a guy like that not being able to get out of the draft, unless of course he was as eager to get away from his wife as Roger is from Mona.

Being against smoking doesn't usually make someone seem Machiavellian and evil, but so it is with Bert Cooper, whose chiding of Roger weirdly makes Sterling Cooper's senior namesake seem that much more slimy. His anecdote about Hitler and Chamberlain is absolutely brilliant, however, and while it's probably too good to be true, I really wish it was. I've attempted to verify it on Google, but without success. If any readers know more about this, I'd appreciate it if you could lay out the details in a comment below, and I suspect others would be just as grateful as I.

Mad Men Recap: Season 1, Episode 8, "The Hobo Code"
BY ANDREW JOHNSTON ON SEPTEMBER 7, 2007

Although I name-checked Todd Haynes' *Far from Heaven* in my initial review of *Mad Men* in *Time Out New York*, I've never really thought of it as a major influence on the series—by and large, Matthew Weiner seems to draw much more inspiration from films and literary works that are actual products of the Eisenhower/Kennedy era and not from period pieces created after the fact. But with "The Hobo Code"—the most polished and, to my mind, the most moving episode of *Mad Men* yet—it's impossible to deny Haynes' influence on Weiner. I don't say so simply because the episode concerns a closeted gay man (Sterling Cooper art director Salvatore Romano, brilliantly portrayed by Bryan Batt) but because of its heartbreaking depiction of self-deception and thwarted desire on several fronts.

"The Hobo Code" also evokes *Far from Heaven* in terms of visual texture—light, shadow and color are used very deliberately, and the camera angles make the episode feel much more like a film than a TV show (and *Mad Men* is already much more cinematic to begin with than most small-screen dramas). All of that is only appropriate given the theme of visual cues and unspoken language that pervades the episode.

I expect the revelations about Don's past to command the most fan attention—yet, as intriguing as they were, I was much more fascinated by the story of the triangle between Salvatore, the visiting client, Elliott

(Paul Keeley) and Lois Sadler (Crista Flanagan), the new Sterling Cooper switchboard operator who falls for the closeted art director. Lois is a woman unlike any we've seen on the series thus far—like Joan, she's proactive and prone to somewhat duplicitous behavior, but her motives and MO are entirely different. Instead of using her sexuality to get what she want, she's like a Jane Austen heroine—incredibly smart, and simultaneously assertive (she's one of the only women we've met on the show who actually pursues what she wants rather than letting it come to her) and neurotic. She's so taken with the message she gets from one set of symbols (the way Salvatore's flamboyance overlaps with the stereotype of a sophisticated continental romeo) that she ignores clues to his sexuality. Joan's remark to the operators about the way she reads signals—"You have voices, I have other things"—underscores the extent to which Lois' attraction is driven entirely by her (mis)interpretation of signals gleaned from eavesdropping on conversations between Salvatore and his mother.

Salvatore, meanwhile, knows exactly what's going on with her—the "Oh shit, what am I going to do now?" look on his face as he hangs up the phone after speaking with her is one of the few moments of complete, brutal honesty in the episode. Still, he succumbs to self-deception just as completely as Lois does—he obviously received Elliot's coded message ("When I mentioned the renovation, I didn't know if you heard me," the client says), otherwise he wouldn't have gone to the hotel bar at all. But his evident surprise when Elliot explicitly tries to seduce him proves that he certainly didn't expect things to go that far. The big question about Salvatore up until now has been whether his heterosexual façade is being maintained solely for the benefit of those at Sterling Cooper or if it's an act of self-deception as well; now, it's very clear that the truth is the latter.

"You're loud but you're shy," Elliot tells Salvatore as they finish their meal, which is a massively insightful reading of the art director's personality. Salvatore's bitchiness at work ("You don't need money to dress better than you do, Wayne") is practically a neon sign announcing his sexual orientation, but at the same time he mutes the message by dropping bogus signals that he's straight—signals that, occasionally, make a meta-reference to the theme of coded messages ("The salesman pushed this tie on me for 20 minutes, but I would have bought it right away if I knew it worked," he tells his subordinates Wayne and Marty). Batt, Flanagan and Keeley are all breathtakingly good, and I sincerely hope we haven't seen the last of Lois.

While the aesthetics of the episode invoke Haynes' recreation of the world according to Douglas Sirk, the surprisingly graphic Pete-Peggy sex scene was a notable exception—although the subject matter of *Far from Heaven* would have been off limits in the 1950s, the way it was presented never violated the content rules of the time. Their coupling was remarkable for number of reasons—the contrast between the raw carnality of the act and the intimacy of their whispered exchange after she leaves the office was just insanely sexy, and the encounter set up two moments of magnificent creepiness: The moment where Pete dissects Peggy with his eyes from across the room at P.J. Clarke's and, even better, the scene where he finally shows some backbone in front of Trudy as they converse on the same couch upon which he ravaged Peggy hours earlier. Pete and Peggy's story is less concerned with the theme of unspoken signals than Salvatore's and Don's are, but the motif is still present—Peggy's "mark your man" ad copy for Belle Jolie centers on a sort of code, and while she doesn't mark Pete, he leaves his sign on her via the torn collar which Don is quick to notice.

Finally, we come to Don's story, which gives us an insane amount of stuff to chew on. We first see Don when he's summoned to a solo meeting with Bert Cooper, something that has him spooked until he's handed the bonus check. The scene between them is incredibly fascinating: Much as Salvatore's efforts to maintain his façade nonetheless result in coded signals he unwittingly transmits to Elliot, the behavior required to keep the Don Draper persona going yields signals that Cooper detects and which leads him to believe that he and Don are kindred spirits. When Cooper is able to detect that Don is lying about his familiarity with *Atlas Shrugged*, he explains what he means in words that almost sound like he's talking down to a child. "It's strength—we act different. Unsentimental about all the people who depend on our hard work."

There are strong parallels between the Don/Cooper scene and the dynamite flashback involving young Dick Whitman's encounter with a hobo played by Paul Schulze (a/k/a Father Phil from *The Sopranos* and Ryan Chappelle from *24*). Both Cooper and the hobo consider themselves superior to the rest of the world because they follow a self-centered philosophy, and both offer to teach Don the secret wisdom that elevates them (as they see it) above the rest of the human pack. It seems pretty likely that the effects of Don's encounter with the hobo will be explored further in the weeks to come; the effects of Don's conversation with Cooper, on the other hand, are immediately evident. Don may have not had the time to start reading *Atlas Shrugged* before the meeting with the Belle Jolie clients, but he was obviously empowered by the faith Cooper showed in him. With his amazing "I'm not here to tell you about Jesus..." speech (a monologue worthy of David Mamet), Don wins the Belle Jolie account through sheer manly swagger, which is how he likewise puts Midge's bohemian friends in their place.

The blond beatnik in the fez is presented as a lightweight poseur version of the hobo—he talks the talk vis-à-vis his separation from society, but his wounded reaction to Don's declaration that "the universe is indifferent" shows us that he can't walk the walk. It's hard to tell how much Don does (or doesn't) share Cooper's sense of superiority over humanity at large, but he sure as hell feels superior to Midge's friends—the smug putdown he delivers before breezing undisturbed past the cops, armored by his suit ("*You* can't") is as scathing as they come. As we see in the followng scene with his son, though, Don was deeply rattled by the memories that flooded his mind at Midge's apartment—when he tells Bobby to ask him anything and promises to tell the truth, he's clearly seeking absolution. Bobby's response, unintentionally, shuts down Don as swiftly and mercilessly as

Don shut down the beatnik. Don's lies are a burden he can't easily shrug off, and the last shot of the episode reminds us that the door of his office bears the same coded message that the hobo carved into the gatepost of the Whitman farm: A dishonest man lives here.

Selected comments:

Andrew Johnston • The thing about Don not realizing they were actually in love until he saw the photo worked well insofar as he only made the connection when he saw them through the lens of his career--Hamm sort of mumbles the line and buries it, but Don says something like "I spend all day faking pictures of people being in love, so of course I recognize it". It's a hamfisted point in some ways, but a really interesting one nonetheless.

Andrew Johnston • I hasten to add that credit for inspiring my interpretation of the last shot goes to a woman whose name I do not know, the girlfriend of a coworker (he told me that she made the point during their post-viewing conversation about the episode). I'd meant to make the attribution in the article itself or in a footnote but failed to do so. She has all my thanks for an observation that allowed the whole episode to really click into place in my mind.

Mad Men Recap: Season 1, Episode 9, "Shoot"
BY ANDREW JOHNSTON ON SEPTEMBER 14, 2007

Probably because of how high "The Hobo Code" set the bar (plus the extent to which I was jonesing for new episode of *Mad Men* after almost two weeks—I'd had the luxury of seeing "The Hobo Code" a few days in advance of its broadcast), but "Shoot" struck me as a relative disappointment, even if it still offers plenty to chew on. Despite significantly increasing our understanding of Betty Draper (in addition to further developing Pete, Peggy and Joan), the episode just came across as too much of a standalone thanks to the plot about Don being tempted by an offer to jump ship and join McCann-Ericson.

Maybe I've been spoiled by *Friday Night Lights,* where [spoiler alert for those who haven't seen the whole season] Coach Taylor actually chose to leave the Dillon Panthers for TMU (though we all know that won't last), but it never seemed as if there was any possibility that Don would leave Sterling Cooper—nor was there really a compelling reason for him to. As a result, the only real tension came from his mixed feelings over Betty resuming her modeling career, and because we were denied the chance to hear what he thought about more than one or two aspects of the complex situation, it turned out to be one of the rare times when Jon Hamm's skill at making Don so magnificently inscrutable turned out to work against the material.

The big question, of course, is whether Betty was ever aware that she was only approached about the Coke modeling gig because the McCann posse wanted to snare Don. Certainly, she spent much of the episode in a dream world of sorts, oblivious to the presumed queerness of both Giovanni, the Italian designer who initiated her into modeling, and the McCann art director. Beyond being restless and flattered, though, it's clear Betty took the job in large part to give her mom a Bronx cheer beyond the grave.

Betty's uber-metabolism, which let her eat what she pleased while working as a model in the old days (okay, maybe she was bulimic, but there wasn't any real evidence) is provided with an intriguing parallel by the way Peggy remains intensely sexually desirable to Pete despite her weight gain. A lot of fan speculation on TWoP and elsewhere centered around the possibility of her being pregnant (creating an opening for a back-alley-abortion story line), but much as I was deeply relieved that Matthew Weiner didn't go with the obvious and have Pete take credit for Peggy's copy, I was equally pleased a possible pregnancy was eschewed in favor of a plot thread about her putting on some pounds, which is all the more intriguing for how quotidian (for TV) it seems.

The Peggy-Joan scene was both hugely enjoyable and extremely edifying insofar as it proved just how completely oblivious she's been rendered by her singleminded focus on getting ahead by sleeping around and playing office politics. The notion that Peggy was trying to get close to Paul Kinsey almost had me doing a spit take. As the show moves forward into the '60s, my money is definitely on Peggy, and not Betty, being the main avenue down which the show follows the evolution of feminism.

In Matthew Weiner's *Fresh Air* interview (which I really need to get around to checking out one of these days), he apparently talks about about Sterling Cooper being an agency that "just doesn't get it", and Joan's perplexed response to Peggy's ambition reveals that the not getting it isn't limited to the executives (Salvatore's big line, by the way, was a brilliant simultaneous example of both the not getting it and the "loud but shy" brand of queer behavior that his would-be lover called him on last week).

I'd been inclined to write off the fan argument that Pete is the one guy at SC who does get it, reading his responses to pop culture (his approval of the VW commercial, etc) as him being contrary for the sake of being contrary, and thereby that he just didn't have the brainpower to back up his big talk. I was proven wrong by his brilliant idea of having John F. Kennedy "watch Mamie's funeral" after he recounted the Dartmouth prank to Harry. While I definitely gave Pete insufficient credit for brains, I didn't overestimate his balls, which were proven deficient by the way he let Harry twist in the wind (or so he thought) by hesitating to cop to his idea, which Bert Cooper left the room believing to be mostly Harry's brainstorm. Harry has been a pretty low-profile guy at SC in terms of major business activity, despite the huge size of the media department (displayed when Paul took Peggy on the nickel tour of SC back in "Ladies Room"), so it'll be very interesting to see what effect, if any, this has on his status at the office.

Don's status at the office, of course, is sure to rise in tandem with his salary (that $45,000 a year, by the way, is apparently more than $300K in today's dollars). After giving Adam Whitman $5000 and then signing his bonus over to Midge, Don could certainly use that $5K bump, but money clearly isn't the reason he stayed at SC—he could surely have negotiated his way to $45K or more at McCann. The real issue is whether he stayed at SC because a smaller agency offers him inherent advantages (i.e., it's easier to hide his past at SC), because he wanted to keep Betty from working or because he was pissed off about his wife being used in a ploy to get him to jump ship. A poster at TWoP offers the intriguing theory that Don might have been influenced by the Jackie Kennedy TV spot, if it left him offended by how she was being pimped to boost her husband's prospects.

In any event, Don's confession that he'd have done anything to have a mother like Betty is the episode's most direct reference to Don's past (unless he was being literal when he told Roger he'd once died in the middle of a pitch!), and given that we've seen her complainig about Don's reticence to discuss his past, that confession may be the largest factor behind Betty's decision to abandon modeling and throw herself into motherhood. And does she throw herself into motherhood! I thought the Drapers' creepy neighbor was actually going to kill the dog, setting up a confrontation that would allow us to see Don at his scariest. Never did I expect to see Betty unloading a BB gun at the pigeons in what started out looking like it was going to be an oblique *Sopranos*-esque ending. It's a scene which again proves that *Mad Men* has a much stronger comic element—and that the Drapers' marriage is far stronger than any viewer could have guessed when the show premiered.

Some miscellaneous points:

Not long before *Mad Men* made its debut, there was a minor flap about a potential product placement deal between AMC and the Brown-Forman Corporation, the beverage company that distills Jack Daniel's. The actual deal didn't go through, but AMC apparently decided to include three subtle references to Jack Daniel's over the course of the season as a gesture of thanks to Brown-Forman for all the advertising they buy on the network, rather than as product placement per se. Tonight was the second reference—Fred Rumsen sends a bottle of Jack to Harry and Pete to congratulate them on the Nixon maneuver. Reference No. 1 was back in "Babylon" when Roy and Don ordered Jack Daniel's at the artsy Greenwich Village café. This time, the product wasn't even mentioned by name, but the bottle is instantly recognizable. Surprisingly, the deal didn't prevent a clearly identifiable bottle of Smirnoff, distributed by Brown-Forman's rivals at Diageo, from turning up in "Red in the Face". Chalk one up for historical accuracy: It's been well established that Roger is a vodka man, and Brown-Forman's marquee vodka, Finlandia, didn't arrive in the United States until 1971. While liquor ads are banned on broadcast TV, the FCC seems to have no such policy against plugging liquor brands by name, as Stolichnaya gets a prominent shout-out in the forthcoming premiere of NBC's *Bionic Woman*.

I've been quite outspoken in my championing of John Slattery, but Vincent Kartheiser is really starting to rival him and Jon Hamm as the series' acting MVPs. Kartheiser's demented glee when he explains his anti-JFK plot to Harry is enormously delectable, and while he leaves us with no doubt that Pete is simmering to a boil while Ken and Harry make fun of Peggy's weight, Kartheiser totally doesn't telegraph the attack on Ken, which wouldn't have been a fraction as effective if anyone knew it was coming. More than one fan has commented on Kartheiser's resemblance to Johnny Depp, in particular to Depp in Tim Burton's *Ed Wood*, and it would be pretty great if Kartheiser was able to enjoy a Depp-like career after *Mad Men* has run its course.

Finally, I was pretty stunned when the episode ended with what I believe is the first time *Mad Men* has used a 21st century pop song, or any post-1960 pop song for that matter. The song in question is "The Infanta," from the Decemberists' 2005 album *Picaresque*. Per good ol' Wikipedia, "In the Spanish and former Portuguese monarchies, Infante (masculine) or Infanta (feminine), also anglicized as infant, is the title given to a son or daughter of the reigning King who is not the heir-apparent to the throne." The lyrics describe a ridiculously ornate procession thrown in honor of such a person, and while we know very little about Betty's past at this point, it has been established that (like Grace Kelly, interestingly) she hails from the swanky Main Line suburbs of Philadelphia. Her family may not have the wealth or power for her to be an Infanta per se, but she's certainly received a lot of princess-like treatment from others over the years, and the song's bouncy energy makes it an inspired way to punctuate the scene, regardless of its year of origin.

Selected comment:

Andrew Johnston •
I wrote my review based on the DVD that AMC sent out to the press, which had "The Infanta" playing over the scene where Betty's unloading the BB gun and then over the INSERT CREDITS HERE title card. I assumed the song would be used in the broadcast version (esp since AMC didn't send it out to the press until a day or two before airtime as opposed to a few weeks in advance as has previously been the case). The calendar is obviously catching up with the production schedule. But yeah, I suspect they either couldn't clear "The Infanta" or Weiner decided to go with a different song late in the game.

Mad Men Recap: Season 1, Episode 10, "Long Weekend"
BY ANDREW JOHNSTON ON SEPTEMBER 28, 2007

Mad Men salutes a man who I consider one of the three biggest influences on the series, the great Billy Wilder (the troika is rounded out by Cheever and Updike), with what could be the series' bleakest and most depressing episode. At the very least, it's the episode most heavily saturated by the casual misogyny that makes *The Apartment,* Wilder's magnum opus, as chilling as it is ultimately uplifting. But even Wilder couldn't avoid occasionally succumbing to the temptation to overclose (though not necessarily in *The Apartment*), as TWoP's ever-astute Sars and our equally illustrious host put it, and "The Long Weekend", while largely excellent, unfortunately crosses that line a little more than usual.

We begin with the introduction of Betty's father, who's been mentioned previously in ways that suggest Don isn't a big fan of the guy. Don quickly switches sides, however, when Betty voices her belief that it's a little too soon after her mother's death for her father to have embarked on a new relationship. Don's logic is sound—after 40 years of marriage, his father-in-law lacks the skills to go it alone as a widower—while Betty counters that all he needs is a housekeeper. While it's hard to disagree with Don, his argument helps establish the theme of female subservience ("I live to serve," his father-in-law's girlfriend said a little earlier) that is largely responsible for the episode's intense creepiness.

At Sterling Cooper, we're treated to another screening of ads from the 1960 Presidential campaign. The dismissive response to Kennedy's ad seems like another example of SC being an agency that "just doesn't get it", though at least Don & Co. are smart enough to think that Nixon's ad sucks pretty hard too. Pete's admiration of the Kennedy strategy—"the President as product"—again shows him to be one of the most forward-thinking guys there, but Don's brainstorm—casting the election as a narrative—proves he's even more forward-thinking by anticipating Presidential campaign strategies of the 1980s and beyond. Don's insight is driven by his personal identification with Nixon as a self-made man—for reasons the audience knows about but which no one at Sterling-Cooper does—and while it's intriguing to see the biographical facts about Nixon cast in such a light, it's also the first time the episode veers into "overclose" territory (perhaps more for Don's "he's the Abe Lincoln of California" line than for the parallels to Don's life).

While Don is rightly proud of having bootstrapped himself into his job as Sterling Cooper's creative director, he seems to believe that luck or fate also played a large role—otherwise, he'd probably boast of his roots when Rachel Menken reminds the assembled executives that her father actually started with nothing and says she doubts anyone else in the room can say the same thing (while Don has been cagey about his background to everybody, a humble beginning is nonetheless a component of his adopted identity, per his discussion with Roger and Mona Sterling at the beginning of Ladies Room). Instead, he adopts a position of respect toward Abe Menken, though he also doesn't shy away from delivering one of the forceful pitches that have become his signature (which leads to Mr. Menken's line comparing the agency to a Tsarist ministry, another of the terrific political-historical metaphors that the series does so well. Rachel, having no idea what he's talking about, briefly becomes a surrogate for audience members on whom such references are lost). During his spiel, Rachel displays an impressive poker face as far as her feelings toward Don are concerned, but her father's comment about Don being "too dashing for my taste" implies that he may well have picked up on his daughter's sentiments anyway.

It's with the story concerning Joan's roommate Carol that the episode starts to enter a whole new dimension of creepiness. In their first scene together, when Carol arrives at the agency, Joan is as bitchy to her roomie as she typically is to Peggy and the rest of the steno pool. Her cattiness doesn't seem unjustified: Carol is a veritable catalog of upper-middle-class clichés—before getting fired, she had a stereotypical entry-level publishing gig, and she's living in Manhattan on her parents' dime (hateful as Joan may be, her manipulation of men such as Roger arguably constitutes evidence of greater industriousness). While Carol seems pathetic at first, she proves to be a more complex figure—and a legitimately tragic one—when her exasperation over being fired leads her to admit the extent of her feelings for Joan. Joan shuts her right down with an icy unflappability so complete as to be practically Victorian. Though the particulars are different—the unrequited passion is one-sided—Carol strangely reminded me of Anthony Hopkins in *The Remains of the Day* in this scene, which left me absolutely devastated (of course, it goes without saying that Joan is infinitely bitchier than Emma Thompson's character).

I'm of two minds about the follow-up scene, in which Joan and Carol return to their apartment with the guys they met at the bar. On the one hand, Carol resigning herself to having sex with this creepy, pathetic fat guy pushes the scene further into the realm of tragedy. On the other, as a longtime Manhattan resident, I simply can't believe that they couldn't find better looking guys, or that someone like Joan would in a million years fall for that guy's line. Sure, ubiquitous cellphones are 30-some-odd years off, so Joan can't just call up Ken Cosgrove or Paul Kinsey to see what bar they're at, but it would have been a lot more believable to have Carol experience her humiliation at the hands of a Sterling Cooper junior exec in full on drunken letch mode. The ugliness and stupidity of the men Joan and Carol hooked up with pushed the scene deep into the realm of the "overclose", even if what the scene conveyed about how men treat women as objects—and how women agree to be treated as objects—fed right into the central theme.

This theme is most vividly conveyed, of course, by Don and Roger's plot. I love how Roger is instantly able to tell which set of twins among the four is likely to be the sluttiest (I choose to read it as a coincidence that they're also the least conventionally attractive pair of sisters). The bit where one of the twins observes that "people" (presumably men and only men) always ask them to kiss each other makes it seem as if the girls are on the naïve side, but it soon becomes clear that their cynicism about sex exceeds even Joan's. Then again, it's no wonder they're so jaded given how Roger behaves—it's clear he's far from the first guy they've met who acts this way. Roger's sleaziness gives the lie to his earlier claim that Sterling Cooper is nothing like the insurance firm in *The Apartment*, but his "Dracula" line (and the way he rides Mirabelle like a pony) again constitutes overclose.

I was as surprised as Roger that it was a heart attack which provided his wake-up call—I'd expected cirrhosis or a DUI accident to make him reconsider his lifestyle rather than the ulcer he was banking on. His crisis may strike some viewers as a moralistic example of chickens coming home to roost, but the extent to which Bert Cooper sees Roger's coronary as a threat to the agency's very existence suggests it will have greater meaning where the larger plot is concerned. Roger's crisis unsurprisingly gives John Slattery an opportunity to shine—he's just amazing in the hospital bed scene—but the whole situation nonetheless feels a little forced, and his line about how "I've done everything they told me—drank the cream, ate the butter"—may very well be the series' single most egregious example of heavy-handed irony.

Don's response to Roger's heart attack yields a much more interesting and subtle bit of irony—instead of driving Don to change his own ways, Roger's heart attack leads him to engage in a self-destructive brand of carpe diem. At least that's how Rachel sees it, even though an affair with Don is something she very much wants. At the time, of course, she has no idea that Don is being driven by a strong craving for a kind of intimacy he feels he can't achieve with Betty, but which he seems to feel that she, as a kindred spirit, can provide. Don's final speech, which connects a lot of dots and allows a lot of free-floating facts to coalesce, may also be overclosing at some level, but Jon Hamm makes Don's long-awaited opening-up so convincing and poignant that I'll let Matthew Weiner & Co. off the hook.

A few miscellaneous observations:

This week's episode was particularly notable where geeky continuity-oriented details are concerned. In addition to a callback to the sketchy OB-GYN from the pilot (who apparently offers illicit abortions in addition to prescribing birth control on the sly), Roger's heart attack—and Joan's reaction to it—ties in nicely with Joan's evocative line from "Babylon" about how food near a bed reminds her a little too much of hospitals. Bert Cooper's oblique revelation that he knows of her affair with Roger helps make the point nicely, and suggests that Weiner has found an ingenious way to keep Joan around in future seasons despite her transparent desire to find a rich husband to live off of: Her professional skills are too useful to Cooper for him to let them get squandered. It'll be very interesting to see if Cooper's "don't waste your youth on age" admonition is a warning that stays with her in the long run.

Finally, it wouldn't be an episode of *Mad Men* without at least one easily-avoidable chronological cock-up. Certainly, there are a lot of little details the episode gets right—in 1960, Labor Day indeed fell on September 5, per the memo we get a glimpse of about the office closure. And, according to the IMDb, *The Apartment* had its New York City premiere on June 15, 1960, followed by an L.A. premiere a week later on June 21. It presumably went into general release immediately thereafter, and given how much longer films stayed in theaters 47 years ago, it's by no means out of the question that Roger and his family might just be getting around to seeing the film at the end of August. The IMDB also says that *Psycho,* mentioned by Roger in the same scene, opened on June 16, 1960 (a Thursday, oddly). However, Joan's remark that she looks "somewhere between Doris Day in *Pillow Talk* and Doris Day in *Midnight Lace*" is where the wheels come off the wagon. *Pillow Talk* was a 1959 release, but the now-forgotten *Lace* didn't open until October 13.

Selected comment:

Andrew Johnston

Well, in defense of the series I'll note that this episode actually touched on the theme of "Unauthorized Cinnamon" via Don's speech about being a pallbearer at his aunt's funeral when he was 16. For the most part, Don is passive in this episode, but there's nonetheless a lot of meat to his scenes. The first time I watched the episode, Don's closing speech felt anvilicious as hell, but the second time around, his desire for intimacy became more palpable and Rachel stood out in contrast to Betty, Joan, Carol and the twins as a woman who takes no shit from men. Her behavior is more a case of being her own worst enemy, which is a subtle but important difference.

One note I forgot to make about the timeline of the series: While Don's concluding speech certainly nailed down a lot of facts that had heretofore only been implied, one major point was left unspoken--for the chronology to make sense, Don's father must have died while his stepmother was pregnant with Adam, and she must have likewise hooked up with their "Uncle Mac" before Adam was born. It seems likely that Weiner is on top of this, since the flashback to Adam's birth made it feel as if the scene was taking place in an urban household as opposed to the rural backdrop of "The Hobo Code"...but it's still a potentially sticky point.

What you say about the show working best when it lets the characters just exist totally speaks to how a lot of my favorite scenes are those where we see Pete, Ken, Harry and Paul fucking around and goofing off...while their antics are admittedly used to buttress a lot of thematic points, their scenes are also by and large the least heavy-handed w/r/t social differences between 1960 and today.

Mad Men Recap: Season 1, Episode 11, "Indian Summer"
BY ANDREW JOHNSTON ON OCTOBER 5, 2007

Adam Whitman makes his second—and last—appearance on *Mad Men* in "Indian Summer", checking out of the series at the beginning of an episode that favors plot and narrative momentum over the thematically self-contained brand of storytelling that has prevailed in recent weeks (and which couldn't have been timed better in light of today's humid 86-degree weather). Each of the last few episodes has had more references to earlier ones than the last, and the increasing number of callbacks, combined with the way narrative strands are converging, suggests the season will play fairly differently on DVD.

The package that Adam sends his brother—which presumably contains something other than what's left of the money from "5G", otherwise Adam wouldn't have so much cash on hand when he slips the noose around his neck, is like the gun that Anton Chekov spoke of so memorably—if it shows up in act one, the writer's doing something wrong if the trigger isn't pulled in act three. Pete's acquisition of the package is close enough for government work where Chekov's maxim is concerned—it doesn't give us a climax, but it does end the episode with the series' most significant cliffhanger yet. Pete has the gun in his hand—now, the question is how much damage he can do with it.

For the most part, I've shied away from specific prognostication in these recaps, but it's hard to resist where the next two episodes of *Mad Men* are concerned. Next week's will reveal a lot about what we can expect from the series in future seasons: On *The Sopranos*, where Matthew Weiner earned his stripes, the season's most eventful episode was always the penultimate one, while the finale was usually something of a coda that reflected on the season's preceding twelve installments. Given that the title of next week's show is "Kennedy vs. Nixon", the pattern seems likely to hold. If it is the season's climactic episode, then one of two things will happen: Don will succumb to blackmail and appoint Pete as Sterling Cooper's head of account services, or Bert Cooper will learn that Don Draper came into this world as Richard Whitman.

My personal hunch, fostered by this week's revelation that Bert Cooper isn't just an admirer of Ayn Rand but is apparently a satellite member of her circle of followers, the Collective (though Cooper is significantly older than key Rand devotees such as Alan Greenspan, Nathaniel Branden and Leonard Peikoff, not to mention Rand herself, who was 55 in 1960), is that Cooper's opinion of Don would only rise upon learning just how much of a self-made man Don is. Since we'll have our answers soon enough, I'll refrain from further attempts to divine Weiner's intentions and will return to the episode at hand.

Although Betty and Peggy's shared sexual frustration plays a big role in "Indian Summer," the link feels more coincidental than thematic—Betty's scenes are there to remind us that Don's pursuit of Rachel (and before her, of Midge) is not without consequences at home, while Peggy's feel like groundwork for a later exploration of the changing role of women in an office such as Sterling Cooper. Peggy's increasing role as a copywriter—which gains her more respect from Don, Fred Rumsen and Ken Cosgrove—is paralleled by a plunge in her self-esteem, courtesy of Pete's callous behavior, that leads to her putting on weight (Elisabeth Moss, by the way, deserves kudos for her lack of self-consciousness while wearing the fat suit that simulates Peggy's physical expansion). Peggy initially thinks she's being asked to write about the dubious weight loss device because she's fat, not because she did well with the Belle Jolie account, and the realization that it has more to do with the latter (a little more, at least) clearly gives her an ego boost, as we see from her date with the truck driver. Even so, it also reminds us how naïve she is, via her chirpy conclusion about why people in Manhattan are "better". Nonetheless, the scene at the end where she straps on the vibrating belt is less sad than it is, arguably, a display of an admirable pragmatism that makes me very eager to see what will become of her in future seasons.

Betty, on the other hand, still has a ways to go with sorting out her sexuality. I loved how she kept herself from going through with her potential *Penthouse Forum* scenario with the salesman by telling him Don would probably rather buy an AC from Sears, a comment that aims a howitzer right at his balls (to borrow a phrase from Roger Sterling) by invoking the new model of consumerism that would soon torpedo the door-to-door biz. The specificity with which she invokes his sales pitch while in bed with Don later suggests that, subconsciously, she wanted to let Don know that she has options and could easily stray if she wants to. Don doesn't pick up on this, however, and reads the situation as an attack on the sanctity of "his house". With a lot of men, that would be equivalent to a potential attack on their wife's virtue, but for someone who moved up in the world as Don did, being lord and master of a middle class household probably means a lot more to him (and means different things) than it might for many other men of the era. The scene where Betty tells her friend about the salesman takes the point about men and property a little too far via Francine's observation that her husband would break her arm for letting a salesman into the house, but I'll let it slide since I'm just so relieved that Francine's baby apparently turned out OK despite all of the anvilicious drinking and smoking we saw her do during the pregnancy (although their circumstances are totally different, Francine's bearing as she fired up a Kent in her milk- and sweat-stained housedress couldn't help reminding me of the young Livia Soprano we saw in "Down Neck", who, about 45 miles south of Peggy and Francine, would then be tending to the six- or seven-week-old Tony).

Finally, there's the fate of Roger Sterling to chew on. When Roger arrives at Sterling Cooper, he seems a completely changed man, a development that seems a little too pat to be true. It is: His confession to Joan that she's "the best piece of ass he ever had" brings to mind a certain cliché about old dogs and new tricks. I was pretty dubious about the need to bring in Roger to serve as "both dog and pony," as he puts it, especially in light of "Lucky Strike Sr."'s relatively muted reaction to Roger's second heart attack. Mona Sterling tears into Bert Cooper for being more cynical than she thought was humanly possible, and I'm wondering if perhaps he was even more cynical still: Could he have deliberately been setting up Roger to take a fall in order to more easily persuade clients to accept the necessity of bumping Don up to partner? I certainly wouldn't put it past the guy.

The weekly grab-bag:

I was briefly taken aback by Rachel's sister invoking the name of Robert Morgenthau without specifying who he was (he was mentioned by surname only), which seemed surprising for the time. Morgenthau has been Manhattan's district attorney for more than 30 years, but in 1960 he was still in the private sector, as a partner at the firm of Patterson, Belknap & Webb (now Patterson, Belknap Webb & Tyler). In 1961, JFK appointed him U.S. Attorney for the southern district of New York (the job that made Rudolph Giuliani's career), and he was the Democratic nominee for governor in 1962, losing to Nelson Rockefeller. The Nixon administration forced him out of the Justice Department seven years later, and, following a stint as deputy mayor under John Lindsay and a failed attempt to score the Democratic gubernatorial nod a second time, he became district attorney in 1974. His name isn't mentioned in the lede of a single *New York Times* article in 1960, which suggests that the only way the Menken sisters would know who he was would be if their family did business with Patterson, Belknapp & Webb (at which potential future U.S. Attorney General Michael Mukasey is presently a partner).

The Nixon-Kennedy debate mentioned by Roger was presumably the first of the candidates' four such events, which took place in Chicago on September 26, 1960, about a week to ten days before tonight's episode. Roger must have seen the debate on a TV in his room at the hospital—which seems kind of extravagant for 1960, though as Don points out, "He's rich—they're taking good care of him".

Somewhat to my surprise, the season premiere and ABC press info on the next few episodes of *Desperate Housewives*, it doesn't seem like John Slattery's going to be leaving Fairview anytime soon. Depending on when *Mad Men* wrapped for the season, he must either have been shooting both shows simultaneously or segued from one to the other with no more than a couple of days off in between. Here's hoping the quality of his work on *Mad Men* inspires the *DH* writers to give him better material this year—it pains me to say it, but his long courtship with Eva Longoria last season was one of the dullest patches that series (which, when it's on top of its game, I really like) has ever suffered through.

Mad Men **Recap: Season 1, Episode 12, "Nixon vs. Kennedy"**
BY ANDREW JOHNSTON ON OCTOBER 15, 2007

"I wish I knew more—I bet a lot of people do"— Pete Campbell

Well, after "Nixon vs. Kennedy", just about the only things we don't know about Don Draper are his shoe size and the age at which he lost his virginity. While the wartime flashback felt a little bit as if the writers were checking off items on a list of things that need to have happened (in a manner that reminded me of *Star Wars Episode III: Revenge of the Sith*, oddly enough), the present day action gave us a powerhouse climax to the season.

I was pleased to see that my two main predictions last week were on the money: Bert Cooper was indifferent, if not approving, toward Don having taken an unorthodox path to the top—and, à la *The Sopranos*, the penultimate episode proved to be the most explosive, setting the stage for next week's finale to be more of a denoument. Elements of the episode seemed like examples of what the otaku crowd call "fan service"—the acknowledgement of Michael Gladis's resemblance to Orson Welles, and a long-overdue subplot for Harry Crane—but they felt organic and not like gratuitous winks. It's hard to imagine how a *Mad Men* fan could fail to be thoroughly satisfied, unless he or she is the kind of person who feels it's capable to get too much of a good thing. Certainly, I felt "Nixon vs. Kennedy" to be the best episode in several weeks. Some of the metaphors may have felt obvious, but the show's tendency to "overclose" had nothing to do with it—these metaphors, I realized while digesting my first viewing, speak very much to what I now realize is one of *Mad Men*'s most significant points about how America has changed since 1960, and it's a complicated enough point that Matthew Weiner et al. can be forgiven for using the occasional broad stroke to address it. But we'll get to all that in time.

We begin with the introduction of Herman "Duck" Phillips (Mark Moses), in a scene that proves his caginess as well as offering more delicious evidence of that of Bert Cooper. As Don escorts Duck out of Cooper's office, we get a healthy earful of exposition about him from the junior execs. Duck's "disintegration" and divorce in London after an affair with a woman he met at the British Museum is a scenario that sounds very similar to Don's relationship with Midge if it had played out differently. The juniors, too young to have really had such experiences themselves yet, see Duck as a pathetic case of self-destruction—in particular Pete, whose sense of entitlement is inflamed by his anger at the prospect of someone who fucked up getting a job that "he" deserves. Don's transparent disdain when Pete reiterates his interest in the account services job turns our boy's seething up to 11, and the game is afoot.

Pete, it seems, has been haunted by Don's mystery box since the end of "Indian Summer", and not just for the leverage it gives him—I doubt he'd be losing as much sleep and going through the box so obsessively if it contained photos of, say, Don injecting heroin or having sex with one of Sterling Cooper's black elevator operators. Richard Whitman's self-reinvention as Don Draper and subsequent success at elevating himself from nothing is something Pete's brain is conceptually incapable of rationalizing. To him, the only way someone could pull it off is if they were patently a criminal. Pete's definition of manhood is 180 degrees from Don's: He lives in a world where it's determined by how one fared in the genetic lottery and how good one is at exploiting old-boy-network connections, not on the basis of ingenuity and hard work.

These two paradigms have their first collision when Pete drops the Dick Whitman bombshell and Don responds by playing dumb. Don's body language is clearly intended to intimidate—he hopes he can get Pete to back down simply by establishing himself as a more powerful alpha male. Pete's failure to fold makes it clear that it's not much of an exaggeration to describe the stalemate as being in the league of a clash between the proverbial irresistible force and an immovable object.

Don's visit with Rachel, however, reveals just how much Pete spooked him, in addition to revealing that his machismo and creative intelligence mask a childlike naïveté that emerges in crisis moments, the result, no doubt, of the mistreatment he received from his stepmother (the one area of his past that isn't cleared up by "Nixon vs. Kennedy". When the shit hits the fan, as the Korean war flashback also illustrates, Don's first impulse is to run and to do whatever it takes to get a fresh start with a clean slate. Rachel is entirely correct when she accuses Don of acting like a 15-year-old; fortunately, he's smart enough to listen to what she's saying and process it.

Much as Don has created brilliant ad campaigns as the result of coincidental inspiration at various points during the season, he has an "eureka" moment (off-camera) in which he realizes that Rachel's admonitions contain the key to his problem with Pete: When he blindsided Rachel—and when Pete blindsided him—neither of them had really thought through the consequences of their actions. When Don returns to Sterling Cooper, he goes another round with Pete and we get one of the most explosive scenes of the entire series. In the plainest language possible, each of them tells the other exactly what they've wanted to say about him since episode one but hasn't, and the fireworks are really something to behold.

Despite Don's comparison of Nixon to himself in "Long Weekend", the parallels between the Don-Pete standoff and the Kennedy-Nixon election didn't dawn on me until they were virtually at the door of Bert Cooper's office. When I realized what the writers were up to, it didn't strike me as forced in the least—if these story lines had been introduced maybe two episodes earlier, sure, but the tension in the scene is something that can only result from lots of planning and groundwork, and the confrontation is one that's been inevitable since early in the very first episode. If the standoff with Pete had come at any other time, it's quite possible Don might have caved and given Pete the job he wanted. The outcome of the election, however, changes everything.

The election night focus on the junior execs kept us from seeing Don's immediate response to the election result—what we see instead is his reaction to Bert Cooper informing him of what was then kept from the public but is now generally accepted as fact: That Joe Kennedy colluded with Chicago Mayor Richard J. Daley to deliver Illinois' 27 electoral votes to the Democrats by padding the vote total in Cook County (Illinois' electoral votes alone would not have put Nixon over the top; if he had also carried Texas, also reputed to have been the site of chicanery, its 24 electoral votes would have made him the 35th President of the United States). Believing Kennedy to have won on the basis of privilege and parental interference, Don is fiercely determined to keep the same thing from happening at Sterling Cooper. Kennedy didn't deserve to be president just because his father was a rich, well-connected bootlegger-turned-U.S. ambassador, thinks Don, and Pete doesn't deserve to be head of account services just because he went to Dartmouth and his mother's a Dykman. When Pete asks "You'd rather blow yourself up than make me head of accounts?" (an ironic question in light of the subsequent flashback), Don doesn't hesitate to do so—to back down would be to surrender to a cultural paradigm he opposes with every fiber of his being.

For a few seconds, it appears as if Don's rigid posture and withering stare will intimidate Pete into keeping quiet…but he drops the bomb anyway, and Bert Cooper's response—"Who cares?"—causes one of *Mad Men*'s main points to click into place.

The differences between 1960 and 2007 that *Mad Men* usually dwells on are right there on the surface—drinking, smoking, women's social roles, etc. When Cooper says "this country was built and run by men with worse stories" than what he says Pete made up, he knows what he's talking about: Joe Kennedy's corruption makes JFK, in a sense, a much bigger fraud than Don. But to the world—and, more importantly, to his wealthy peers—Kennedy represents the ultimate triumph of privilege. Yes, the five presidents that followed him —Johnson, Nixon, Ford, Carter and Reagan—were all men of modest beginnings. But our current chief executive (like his father, the 41st president) is a product of the same monied prep school/Ivy League culture that created Pete Campbell.

Kennedy and Nixon, in the context of this episode, represent dueling visions of America that have been dividing our country for more than 200 years: In some ways, the episode could just as well have been called "Jefferson vs. Adams". Implicitly, I believe, Matthew Weiner is saying that the presidency of George W. Bush, a to-the-manor-born, second-generation commander-in-chief who fakes the common touch and somehow persuades poor and middle-class Americans to vote against their best interests and thereby reinforce the culture of privilege, represents the ultimate triumph of inherited power over hard-earned success. Today, Dick Whitman couldn't get away with remaking himself as Don Draper—electronic records and DNA tests obviously complicate things, but the most significant factor is how the cultural changes of the past 47 years have resulted in the extinction of the values that led Cooper to tolerate—indeed, to approve of—Don's means of ascent. And the message I believe we're supposed to take away is that with this paradigm shift, America lost a significant chunk of its national soul.

By all accounts, Marilee Jones was a superb Dean of Admissions at MIT, but when it was revealed last year that she'd faked her academic credentials, her actual job performance was suddenly meaningless and she became a national pariah. David Edmonson, the former head of Radio Shack who resigned in 2006 when his fake résumé was exposed, might not have been the greatest CEO in the world, but there are Wharton grads who have done worse as the head of major companies. The degree to which both were vilified speaks to a fundamental cultural change in a country that was once a place where outcasts could come from a second chance. In the "three strikes" era, could Tim Allen, who spent more than two years in prison for trafficking cocaine, still become a sitcom and movie star? Could Charles S. Dutton, who served time for killing a man in a fight, still gain admission to Yale and go on to win multiple Emmys? Could former career criminal and longtime convict Danny Trejo become a ubiquitous character actor? In all three cases, I'm not inclined to think so.

Obviously fraud is a serious crime, and those who fake medical or legal credentials to get ahead can put the public at serious risk. But in a true meritocracy, the kind of system that Bush seems determine to abolish via his attack on the "death tax" and other measures designed to make the rich richer, smart and capable people can succeed even if they've invented their past. The 19th century political success of unsophisticated figures such as Andrew Jackson and Abraham Lincoln fed a fundamental American myth: That anyone can rise to the top, no matter their origins, if they just work hard enough. It doesn't matter if it's never been completely true— the popular belief that it was true created a spirit of energy and infinite possibility that is reflected in a thousand American movies from the '40s, '50s and early '60s—and very few American movies today. In our more cynical age, thanks to the victories of the John F. Kennedys and George W. Bushes of the world, the more widespread belief that certain doors are closed to those without connections can keep the Dick Whitmans from even making an effort to improve their lives. The damage that such beliefs have inflicted on America is something that, in my opinion, speaks for itself.

Due to the length and the tardiness of this week's recap (the latter the result of technical and medical issues), I'm going to wrap this up without touching on the junior executives and their election night revels (or, unfortunately, on the Korean War flashbacks) though I hope to touch on the behavior of Ken, Paul, Harry et. al. in a general sense when I weigh in on this week's season finale, "The Wheel".

Mad Men Recap: Season 1, Episode 13, "The Wheel"
BY ANDREW JOHNSTON ON OCTOBER 19, 2007

Mad Men ends its first season on one hell of a high note, with what is probably the series' most *Sopranos*-esque episode yet. *Sopranos* seasons generally wrapped up most of the continuing story arcs in the penultimate episode, reserving the finale for a more meditative episode built around the series' central themes, and *Mad Men* has done the same—although in this case, the theme is one that didn't necessarily leap out before as one of Matthew Weiner's central concerns. As my illustrious colleague David Cote said, "who'd have guessed that in the end, it'd be all about family?"

When I learned that the season finale was called "The Wheel", the first thing that came to mind was a relentless forward-moving force crushing everything in its path—a symbol of progress, yes, but the kind of aggressive, dehumanizing progress represented by the fearsome gears in Charlie Chaplin's *Modern Times*. A metaphor for change that happens whether people like it or not. The second association was with the Grateful Dead song the episode shares its title with, which I recalled as being pretty upbeat but has lyrics that are darker and more resigned than I'd remembered (*"The wheel is turning/and you can't slow down/You can't let go/and you can't hold on/You can't let go/and you can't stand still/If the thunder don't get you/then the lightning will"*). As David Dodd says in his annotations to the Dead's lyrics, the wheel is "a potent symbol throughout human history." Of course, wheels go backwards as well as forwards—in space, if not in time—and along those lines, it's the concept of the past as a thing that can be seen but not touched that makes the episode so deeply moving.

The episode begins about three weeks after "Nixon vs. Kennedy", with Don and Betty discussing their plans for Thanksgiving. Despite Don's more sympathetic view of his father-in-law after the events of "Long Weekend", it seems he's less than thrilled about the prospect of spending the holiday in Philadelphia with her family (Betty mentions a brother who I don't believe has come up before). In the past, Don might have wanted to stick around in order to score some time with Midge or Rachel, but when he says his reasons for staying put are professional, there's no reason to doubt him. In his new role as a partner at Sterling Cooper, Don is

"Duck" Phillips' superior, but we soon see that Duck is far more driven and aggressive than Roger Sterling ever was, and Duck's drill instructor-esque treatment of the junior execs makes it imperative for Don to lead by example.

Of course, maintaining a unified front with Duck isn't the only additional responsibility that comes with Don's new role at the agency: Bert Cooper minces no words as he tells Don that things like his tryst with Rachel Menken just won't fly anymore. The issue of Don's fidelity also comes up when Francine tells Betty how she learned that her husband Carlton is having an affair. When Betty deploys the same tactic (calling a frequently-dialed number found in a phone bill) and learns just who Don has been calling late at night, her season-long arc reaches a powerful climax.

I was delighted by the return of freaky young Glen Bishop, who proves himself the only person with whom Betty can be completely candid. Their scene together illustrates the crux of her problem: Don's backchannel conversations with her psychoanalyst are a bigger betrayal than any affair, and there just doesn't seem to be anybody around whom she can just be herself. At her next therapy session, she ingeniously deals with the situation by addressing the one topic her shrink would never in a million years narc about to her husband—her raw, unvarnished thoughts about Don. "He doesn't have a family, he doesn't know what family is," she says. "I feel sorry for him but should be angry at myself for putting up with it." It's a pretty safe bet that her shrink won't be comparing her to an emotionally stunted child again anytime soon.

Betty also makes it clear that while she may not necessarily know the identities of any women Don is sleeping with behind her back, she's certainly not so naïve as to be unaware of his straying, even before Francine came around. Sex with Don, she says, is "sometimes what I want, sometimes obviously what someone else wants." Don's big scene with Rachel last week proved that he can be a surprisingly naïve guy himself at times, and his ignorance of Betty's perceptiveness sets up the episode's chief message, a lesson that both Don and Harry Crane learn the hard way: If you take your family for granted, they'll slip right through your fingers.

Until Don got on the phone with the desk clerk at the hotel, it never occurred to me that Don might be as yet unaware of his brother Adam's suicide. Surely, I figured, Adam had included a note in the package of photos and memorabilia, which he appeared to mail immediately prior to hanging himself. The discovery of Adam's death drives the lesson home for Don, paving the way for the absolutely devastating scene in which he makes his presentation to the clients from Eastman Kodak. As we saw with the Right Guard campaign way back in "Ladies' Room", the period vogue for space-age futurism has a lot of appeal to advertisers, but Don has an almost supernatural gift for being able to see through flavor-of-the-month bullshit and come up with ideas that connect with consumers at a primal, almost subconscious level.

"Technology is a glittering lure, but there is the rare occasion when the public can be engaged at a level beyond flash if they make a sentimental bond with the product," Don tells the clients. As we learn from the heartrending scene that follows, the secret to Don's insight as an adman is that it's not the public he's seeking to engage, but himself—he's so damaged that the only way he can understand his own feelings is through an ad campaign. Nostalgia, he says, is "literally pain from an old wound. A twinge in your heart far more powerful than memory alone." The slide projector, he continues, "isn't a spaceship—it's a time machine. It takes us to a place where we ache to go again." In Don's case, he's talking about a place he's never been, " a place we know we are loved." Immediately thereafter, he realizes he has the potential to build such a place at home in Ossining, and as he rides home alone, silent, in a train full of merry revelers, he clearly resolves to change his ways the second he walks through the door.

When Don tells Betty he's decided to accompany her to Philadelphia for Thanksgiving, it seemed like an ending that was just a little too pat…

so naturally I was pleased by the reveal of the "real" ending, which inverts the conclusion of *The Sopranos*' first season. Tony is able to find the place he knows he's loved when he gets shelter from the storm (to borrow a phrase from Bob Dylan, appropriately enough) at Artie Bucco's restaurant along with Carmela, A.J. and Meadow. Don, however, is left with nothing but an empty house, on the eve of a holiday that's all about connection and togetherness. I'll refrain from quoting the full lyrics of Dylan's "Don't Think Twice, It's All Right" (released in 1963, so it's not period-accurate… not that there's anything wrong with that), but it's a hell of a choice to accompany the ending.

"It ain't no use in turnin' on your light, babe/That light I never knowed," says the narrator of the song, essentially describing what Don has never known, and which Betty offered him, only for Don to bat it away. And, like Don, the narrator *"once loved a woman, a child I'm told"* to whom he *"[gave his] heart, but she wanted my soul."* The song ends with one of Dylan's patented spiteful fuck-you endings, which doesn't really reflect Don's position as "The Wheel" concludes, but there's no disputing the relevance of the first lines of the final verse: *"I'm walkin' down that long, lonesome road, babe/ Where I'm bound, I can't tell."*

We'll find out when *Mad Men* returns in June 2008.

Finally, an overstuffed edition of the weekly grab bag:

Duck Phillips gets a lot of interesting bits of business in this episode. I like that he's so unfiltered as to bluntly ask Don to help him look good his first month on the job. I also like how he turns the screws on Pete by making it obvious to all and sundry that he only scored the Clearasil account via nepotism. And I frakking *love* how he had the class and smarts to let Don's pitch speak for itself ("Good luck at your next meeting"). It was also hugely telling, in light of what we heard last week about how he crashed and burned in London, that he refused Don's offer of a glass of bourbon. A story line about the state of Alcoholics Anonymous in the 1960s and what the culture of recovery was like in the Kennedy era has a huge amount of potential, and I'd love to see Weiner et al. tackle the subject. I really enjoyed Mark Moses' work during the first two seasons of *Desperate Housewives*, and it's very amusing and appropriate to see him joining *Mad Men* just as John Slattery is rejoining *DH*.

Gotta say I was disappointed that Peggy was pregnant after all, as I thought a story about a woman simply getting fat would be much more interesting. Still, the timing is right on the money for her to have gotten knocked up by Pete during their first tryst, before the birth control pills took effect—"Smoke Gets In Your Eyes" took place in March, exactly nine months before Thanksgiving. Her scenes with Ken Cosgrove, which revealed how little she knows about the psychology of her own gender, reinforced my suspicion that she's the main vessel Matthew Weiner will use to explore the evolution of feminism, and I'm now more eager than ever to see what will happen to her (I'm operating under the assumption that she gave the baby away for adoption, by the way).

Bert Cooper's advice to Don at the end of "Nixon vs. Kennedy" suggested that Don might try to cultivate Pete as an ally, but it's pretty obvious that isn't going to happen. I loved how Pete used Don's own words against him, effectively daring him to put up or shut up by bringing in a new client, and how Don responded by not only hitting the ball out of the park with Eastman Kodak but by also making life worse for Pete by promoting Peggy. The indignant look on Vincent Kartheiser's face when Peggy gets the news is beyond classic and makes it more obvious than ever that he's an insanely talented actor.

Since I saw the first two episodes of the new season of *House* via a lo-res, somewhat pixelated DVD-R that Fox sent out, it wasn't until I saw the third episode in HD that I recognized the aggressive young doctor applying for a spot on Greg House's team as Anne Dudek, *Mad Men*'s Francine. Based on her work there, she's a much better actress than I initially assumed.

Pete is emasculated as ever as the season ends, and drunkenly sulking off in a huff isn't going to change anything for him at home. It's also interesting to learn that Trudy's father is a salesman-turned-executive, which suggests he might not be as wealthy as many fans previously assumed. Watching Pete get humiliated over and over was a great source of pleasure throughout the season, so I certainly hope Matthew Weiner doesn't go any easier on him next season.

The gradual development of Ken Cosgrove and Harry Crane has also been a treat, and while we still know very little about them, everything they did and said in this episode just felt right relative to the few facts we have. I've come to be more impressed with Aaron Staton and Rich Sommer with each passing episode and very much hope that the series helps them land plum movie roles during *Mad Men*'s hiatus. And who didn't love seeing Harry in his undies?

Although Matthew Weiner had no problem blatantly rewriting history by having Don coin Lucky Strike's 1917-vintage "It's Toasted!" slogan in 1960 back in "Smoke Gets In Your Eyes", all the slide projector stuff is basically spot on: Eastman Kodak introduced the Carousel 550 projector in 1961, making it entirely reasonable for an ad campaign to be under development in November 1960. I can't find any info on how much the projector cost when it first went in sale, but at the time the original model was discontinued in 1966, it cost $137, or $179.50 with an optional zoom lens model. In today's money, the two projectors would respectively cost $846.23 and $1108.74. And the projector we see at the meeting is indeed the original model.

Unfortunately, Duck Phillips' references to members of the Eastman family being back in the lab doesn't hold water: George Eastman, who founded the company and invented the concept of film on a roll, never married, fathered no children and left his entire estate to the University of Rochester. Wikipedia tells us that during his lifetime, he donated more than $100 million (in early 20th century dollars!) to several colleges, including—very impressive for the time—substantial donations to historically African-American universities, among them the Tuskeegee Institute and the Hampton Institute. In 1932, at the age of 77, he shot himself rather than spend his remaining days in a wheelchair, leaving a suicide note that can only be described as beautifully succinct: "My work is done. Why wait?"

Last but not least, I really love the photos from the wrap party that AMC posted to its web site, in which the cast members really seem to be enjoying themselves and each others' company. In the eleven photos up there, nary a fake smile can be found. It's great to see that the folks responsible for making this remarkable series have what appears to be a strong, legitimate sense of cameraderie, and it makes me anticipate future seasons all the more.

Mad Men Recap: Season 2, Episode 1, "For Those Who Think Young"
BY ANDREW JOHNSTON ON JULY 28, 2008

Welcome, friends, to *The House Next Door*'s recap of the first episode of *Mad Men*'s second season, "For Those Who Think Young." It's been a huge thrill to see the show come out of nowhere to become the buzz program of the past year (as well as a multi-Emmy nominee), but obviously not as big a thrill for the fans as for the cast and the show's creator, Matthew Weiner, who doesn't waste any time on recaps or self-congratulation, instead throwing viewers right into the deep end to the strains of Chubby Checker's "Let's Twist Again" ("...like we did last summer"). In that spirit, let's get right down to business.

I don't think the length of the gap since Season One is ever specified in dialogue, but the broadcast date of Jackie Kennedy's famous TV tour of the White House (February 14, 1962) proves that about 15 months have passed since Betty blew off Don for Thanksgiving at the end of "The Wheel." I may be one of the few serious fans who never asked the question "Why the fuck doesn't Don have a lock on his office?" during Season One, and I got a huge laugh out of the scene up top in which one is installed. Just as overdue is Don's visit to the doctor, who, in a sign of the times, prescribes him the barbiturate Phenobarbital as an anti-anxiety medication. (Though still prescribed as an anti-seizure medication in other countries, it's now primarily used on dogs in the United States, though it remains popular as a suicide drug—it's what Abbie Hoffman O.D.'d on.)

Although we're not told how Don and Betty reconciled after "The Wheel", the presence of a housekeeper at the Draper residence (and the scene of Betty at riding lessons, almost but not quite as much of a bored-housewife cliché as therapy—trust me, I spent my early years in a wealthy suburb in the early '70s) suggests that Don dealt with the situation in large part by opening his checkbook. He wasn't necessarily just being lazy: It's pretty evident throughout the episode that Don is distracted by some intense angst of his own. Unsurprisingly, his opaque personality and Jon Hamm's sublime poker face makes it impossible to determine its exact nature, though at this point fans know Don more than well enough for us to have plenty of fodder for speculation—speculation that'll have to wait until after we cover the action at Sterling Cooper.

Considering his condition when we last saw Roger Sterling, it was pretty startling to see him carrying on as if nothing had happened to him, though I suspect he's not as strong as he's letting on—his banter with Joan implies that his sex life is now pretty vicarious and that, in a variation on the *Breaking the Waves* scenario, he's getting his jollies from her descriptions of her misadventures. Joan herself now seems more intensely focused than ever on "winning" via the acquisition of a powerful husband, which may in part be the cause of her increased bitchiness at SC vis-a-vis the new copier—it's possible she sees herself as being on a "farewell tour" and is letting the other gals in the steno pool get a last, vicious taste of her poison before she moves on to directing her ire at assorted housekeepers, babysitters, maids, doormen, etc. The arrival of Sterling

Cooper's first copier—arguably the payoff of a joke Weiner set up back in the pilot—gives her a golden opportunity to once again make things hard for poor Peggy Olsen.

On the Peggy tip, we soon learn that she vanished from the office for a couple of months after her kid was born, and that her unexplained absence is still a hot discussion topic among the junior execs (surprisingly so, given that she must have been back about a year by now). Peggy and the gang spend most of the day waiting around for Don to show up for a catered meeting; their long lunch (and mediocre pitches afterward) gives us a prolonged glimpse at the laziness and inertia in the SC ranks that Don is always bitching about, and which is one of the reasons why Weiner keeps reminding us in interviews that, despite the immense power of Bert Cooper and the wealth of Roger Sterling, Sterling Cooper remains a C-list agency.

SC's status in the ad world is often explained by Weiner yet seldom reflected on the show. Duck Phillips represents an obvious attempt to do something about it. Last season, you may recall, Duck urged SC to enter big-money fields in which it had no clients—airlines, pharmaceuticals, etc. This year, Duck—clearly being set up as Don's antagonist for the season (so what if Don brought him on board?)—is determined to get ahead of the baby boom (the oldest boomers are just turning 16 in 1962) by bringing younger talent into the agency. Other than Pete, Duck's the only guy at SC with so much as an inkling of how the baby boom will change consumerism. Roger cheerfully goes along with Duck, suggesting that he hopes to play Don and Duck off each other from the outside; naturally, Duck is actually playing Roger and Don against each other, but Roger's just too conceited to pick up on it. In classic Roger style, he goes to Don saying that Bert Cooper, not Duck, is interested in hiring younger folks. Don (who, unlike Roger and Duck, has never been afraid to tell clients what they don't want to hear) sees right through it and has Roger deliver a reply to Duck. When the eagerly-sought newbies, one of Duck's beloved writer-artist teams, present themselves for an interview, they're eager to keep the visit from hitting the ad-world rumor mill, apparently for fear of having their reputation tarnished as a result of dealing with SC.

Betty's post-Bryn Mawr, pre-marriage stint in the modeling world contributed to making her simultaneously worldly and naïve, qualities that converged with awkward results when she and Don encounter Juanita, her former roommate, at the restaurant where Don takes Betty for Valentine's Day. Betty's the only one oblivious to Juanita's obvious status as an escort, or "party girl" as Don coyly puts it. As Francine's evocation of *Butterfield 8* makes clear, this was one of those periodic times in which pop culture contrives to make the high-end sex trade seem like a glamorous way for bored women to fill their time (Luis Buñuel's *Belle de Jour* was still five years away). Combine that fantasy with the overheated/underexercised libido of which Betty spoke last season, and I dare say you're looking at a recipe for disaster. Her flirtation with the idea of trading sex for car help is the start of something that's sure to turn ugly.

Weiner and Co. cleverly use the famous Jackie Kennedy telecast as the jumping-off point for a montage that brings us up to date on a few more of our favorites: Paul ain't the only one with a new beard, and Salvatore's seems just as spunky as Lois but a lot better looking. We get a glimpse of Joan with her doctor boyfriend (in a vignette which lends fuel to my suspicion that she doesn't really enjoy sex at all), while Pete, somewhat unsurprisingly, spends the night on the couch watching a science fiction movie. (His family ain't as rich as they used to be, but surely he could do better by Trudy than a box of chocolates from Schrafft's, the 1962 equivalent of one purchased at Duane Reade.)

The source of Don's quiet unease, as I said before, remains a mystery, but the onscreen evidence hints at intriguing possibilities. Although Dick Whitman succeeded in the business world on his own, he never got the education that the "real" Don Draper did. Last season, "our" Don often chafed when he was judged on his appearance; now, instead, after the bohemian type in the bar tells him he wouldn't understand Frank O'Hara's *Meditations in an Emergency*, rather than make a bitter wisecrack, he goes out and buys a copy. Don's sudden interest in contemporary poetry and his takedown of the guys who continue their lewd banter after a woman enters the elevator suggest an unspoken question: After all these years of playing the role of "Don Draper," has our protagonist realized he doesn't particularly like his character and resolved on a course of self-improvement? And if so, will it distract him enough to make him vulnerable to the machinations of Duck Phillips? All we can do is stay tuned.

Miscellaneous notes: The work of Frank O'Hara and the rest of the New York School poets is one of my literary blind spots, so I did a little reading up on O'Hara in an attempt to decode the significance of the poem used in tonight's episode. The Harvard roommate of Edward Gorey, O'Hara, like Ayn Rand, is someone the *Mad Men* characters might conceivably cross paths with: O'Hara's day job was as a curator at MoMA, which is about a 10 minute walk from the SC offices. Of course, if O'Hara or Rand actually showed up on *Mad Men*, it could send the show careening down a slippery slope toward becoming *The Young Indiana Jones Chronicles*, a fate I'm sure Weiner wants to avoid. (Here's a question for those who know more about the publishing world (or the publishing world in 1962) than I: If the standard info for *Meditations in an Emergency* is "Grove Press; 1957, 1967", does that mean the paperback release trailed the hardcover by a decade (meaning the paperbacks we see in the episode are anachronisms), or does it mean the book went out of print at some point prior to 1967 and was reissued then? Inquiring minds want to know.)

Secondly, I want to put in a very strong endorsement for the Blu-ray edition of *Mad Men*'s first season, which I devoured in about five days before sitting down to watch the season two premiere. The war between Cablevision and Time Warner Cable kept most New Yorkers from being able to see the first season in HD when it was broadcast, and the difference is simply stunning. It ain't just the rich colors and the level of visual detail: The clarity of the sound mix allowed me to catch lines of dialogue (sometimes entire brief speeches) in almost every episode which were inaudible the first time around. I'd seen every Season One episode at least three times before sitting down with the Blu-ray discs, via AMC screeners that occasionally had unfinished visual effects (Don and Rachel's rooftop kiss in "Marriage of Figaro" took place in front of a green screen), it was great to see the episodes in finished form. The downside was that doing so revealed a number of embarrassing contradictions between the final product and my S1 recaps, largely because I assumed all the music on the AMC screeners had been cleared; the Decemberists' "The Infanta," for example, doesn't end "Shoot," as I said in my column about the episode, nor does Hoyt Axton's "Greenback Dollar" conclude "The Hobo Code." While I hope to be able to watch the show in advance this season as well, in cases where a music choice strikes me as notable enough to mention, I plan to check the screener against a digital video recording of the broadcast version before I post my recap in order to prevent this sort of thing from happening again.

Oh, and the person to whom Don mailed his copy of the O'Hara book? $5 says it's Rachel Mencken.

Mad Men Recap: Season 2, Episode 2, "Flight 1"
BY ANDREW JOHNSTON ON AUGUST 4, 2008

As fine as the Don and Betty-centric episodes that began the first season may have been, *Mad Men* didn't really gel for a lot of people until "New Amsterdam", the episode which showed us that Pete Campbell was going to be a legitimately tragic figure and not just a scheming young nemesis for Don Draper. We've seen Pete suffer plenty since then, but not until "Flight 1" has there been an episode that reveals so much about his character. On the heels of the superb "For Those Who Think Young", "Flight 1" suggests that *Mad Men* will be a deeper and more emotionally complex show this season, no small achievement relative to the quality of Season One.

The action begins at a party at Paul Kinsey's apartment in Montclair, NJ, about a week after the previous episode (for reasons we'll come to in a bit, this episode is very easy to date specifically). In season one, Paul's embrace of African-American culture was fairly cringe-inducing (you may recall his short story about hanging out with "negroes" in Hoboken), but it now seems considerably more sincere—about a third of the party guests are black and, of course, we meet Paul's African-American girlfriend, Sheila. This time it's Joan's turn to come off as the clueless white liberal with her crack about how some day Sheila will be able to drive up to her supermarket in a station wagon and be a customer (as a native of the neighborhood, Sheila has of course shopped there many times). Joan's doctor boyfriend surely makes far more money than Paul and is a better catch in all regards, but that doesn't stop her from being jealous, cattily telling Sheila that "when Paul and I were together, the last thing I would have taken him for is open minded". I'm pretty sure Joan's just saying this to jerk Sheila's chain, as I was under the impression that she and Paul were never really "together"—they may have hooked up a few times, but I can't recall anything to suggest that they were ever an honest to goodness couple.

We've seen the Sterling Cooper gang getting drunk together many times, of course, but seldom if ever with their wives and girlfriends in tow, or with so many non-SC folks on hand. As a result, everyone is trying to inflate their importance at the agency—Pete tells Trudy most of them work for him (even if they don't see it that way), Peggy is emphatic about how she works with the SC gang, not for them, and Joan is quick to describe herself as the office manager rather than the head secretary. The only person who doesn't seem to be overselling his accomplishments is Ken, who, surprisingly, doesn't use his *Atlantic Monthly* story (or any subsequent literary success) to impress the chicks as he aggressively hits on woman after woman at the party. The end credits reveal that Salvatore's companion is no mere girlfriend but rather his wife. While it's pretty obvious she's a beard, their shared amusement with Ken's lascivious behavior reveals that they have a close, affectionate relationship—indeed, they arguably seem more sincerely into each other than any other couple on the show—and I look forward to getting a closer look at their relationship later in the season (we also get our first look at Jennifer Crane, who I half expected to remain unseen a la *Frasier*'s Mavis Crane and a zillion other TV characters of note.

After a vignette of Peggy suffering from a mighty hangover, we leap forward a few days to see Roger and Don arriving at SC, where they discover the whole office gathered around a radio. It seems an American Airlines jet taking off from Idlewild plunged into Jamaica Bay, killing all on board. Don quickly moves to yank any Mohawk ads in the pipeline, while Duck Phillips goes another direction: He calls a contact at AA, learns that a new agency may be part of their post-crash spin-control strategy, and tells Roger and Bert Cooper that they need to strike while the iron is hot. Don winces and accuses Duck of acting in poor taste, but Duck holds fast, insisting that advertising is a field where the ends justify the means. Looking on, Bert Cooper is no doubt recalling his S1 advice to Don that he needs to develop a stronger stomach if he wants to be in the kitchen where the sausage gets made.

Next, we see Pete in his office getting a phone call he simply doesn't know how to process. It seems his father was on the plane that went down and Pete, like many people who lose a loved one with no warning whatsoever, can't process the reality of the situation. Don may have been his enemy last year, but Pete also knows in his gut that, aside perhaps from Bert Cooper, Don is the only real grown-up at SC. It's to Don's office that he staggers, then, dispassionately referring to his fathers' death as "the strangest thing" and saying that he has absolutely no idea what people are supposed to do in such situations. "Go home and be with your family,"

Don says. "Is that what you would do?", asks Pete. "Yes," says Don in response. After "The Wheel", I'd like to think he's telling the truth, but I'm not so sure.

At what I assume is the Campbell family's Manhattan apartment, we see Pete and his fat, obnoxious older brother and their wives doing the best to comfort their mother. Pete's brother is seething over the news that their father died broke and that the inheritance he was counting on (along with most of the Dyckman trust) was flushed down the toilet by their dad in the interest of keeping up appearances ("It was all oysters, travel and club memberships," says Pete's brother). Pete never loses too much composure here, in part perhaps because, as we've seen, Trudy ain't exactly poor, and he's basically been guaranteed a free ride by her folks as long as he can deliver the grandkids. We learn nothing about his brother's wife, but he certainly doesn't seem as fortunate. This scene brings up one of my few nitpicks about the episode: Given how thoroughly Eastern the Campbell/Dyckman clan are, it's hard to conceive of a reason for Pete's dad to have been traveling to Los Angeles, a city that (metaphorically, and I suppose literally too) is as far from the WASP establishment as one can go without leaving the United States. A throwaway explanation certainly wouldn't have hurt (it would certainly be ironic if he had been flying to L.A. to make a connection to Palm Springs for a golf tournament).

At the Draper residence, Don finds himself strong-armed into a night of bridge with Peggy, Francine and Carlton, the latter of whom I don't believe we've seen since "Marriage of Figaro". Don uses the card game as an excuse to teach Sally how to mix cocktails, a sight that would probably be deeply disturbing if we saw, say, Roger Sterling teaching her, but which somehow comes off as funny and affectionate when Don does it (that said, I'd still love to see a flash-forward episode in which the adult Sally goes to a therapist and describes everything that Don and Betty did to screw her up!). Carlton has put on more than a few pounds since we (and Don) last saw him, which he attributes to the stress of being unable to please Francine no matter what he does to atone for having stepped out on her. Betty takes the weight gain as a sign of content, and when Don begs to differ, a fight begins to ensue. Don quickly reverses course, telling Betty he'll say whatever he has to in order to ensure they don't fight, but that's not good enough for her, so Don is once again left baffled by his wife's emotions.

The next day at SC, things get ugly again between Joan and Paul when he asks her what she said to Sheila at the party. She tears into him without mercy, saying that there's only one reason he's with Sheila and that his life in Montclair is a poor-little-rich-boy fantasy. He doesn't respond—or can't because he's too angry—when Joan hollers "What part is wrong?" as he storms off. Maybe I'm as naïve as Joan thinks Paul is, but I really don't think she's giving him enough credit. She's just fucking with his head as she's fucked with those of Peggy and Lois before him, and I gotta say it'd be a crying shame if Sheila was left high and dry as a result. In any event, Joan gets a taste of her own medicine later that day when she sees giggling secretaries leaving Peggy's office and discovers a Xerox of her drivers' license posted on the wall, with her age—she's just turned 31—circled in red (today, naturally, it'd be her weight of 140 lbs that would have other women mocking her). If we see someone swiping the license from Joan's purse, I didn't notice it. Peggy seems like a logical suspect for a few seconds, until the scene unexpectedly turns into an unexpected and rather poignant burying-the-hatchet moment between the two women, a situation that is rife with possibilities.

For a lot of people, the big reveal about the fate of Peggy's baby will be remembered as one of the episode's highlights. Personally, I hoped we'd seen the last of the kid, but the scenario that Matthew Weiner has given us—her doctors and the state decided she lacked the mental capacity to make decisions for or about the baby, so the kid was sent to live with Peggy's mom and sister—is at least a plausible one. It's implied that Peggy generally lives at the same apartment she was in last season, only coming by her mom's place for periodic visits, and given what we see of her mom's unpleasant personality, I don't think anyone can blame Peggy for keeping the visits to a minimum. It seems likely that Peggy's story line will ultimately converge with the plot threads concerning Pete and Trudy's efforts to have a kid, and in light of Peggy's baby's living arrangement, it looks like it'll take some pretty fancy narrative footwork to put Pete and the kid in the same room by the end of the season. Here's hoping *Mad Men* doesn't turn into a soap opera in the process.

Traditionally, there have been two ways that Don's emotions get him into trouble: When he opens up to somebody and gets a response he doesn't know how to interpret (see above), and when he suffers a slight that pisses him off so much that he fails to notice vital details because he's too distracted by his fuming. The latter is what happens when he's stewing over being ordered to dump Mohawk as a client and Pete comes by to tell him about his conversation with Duck.

Pete is in a double bind here: It isn't just the WASP culture of reserve that's preventing him from processing his fathers' death but the attitude of the times as well—it's ages before men are supposed to get in touch with their feelings, and sentimental father-son movies like *I Never Sang For My Father* and *Ordinary People* (heck, even *The Life Aquatic with Steve Zissou*) are still decades off. Lacking the capacity for grieving (though it sure ain't like his dad gave him any incentive to develop that capacity), he responds by seeking out a new father figure—which could have been Don Draper if he hadn't been so pissed off about being forced to dump Mohawk Airlines. Duck, however, seems to have picked up on Pete's needs intuitively—while his initial appeal to get Pete to sign off on going after American is certainly tasteless, it's couched in flattery and sweet talk that makes his true motives fairly transparent. As Don's break-up scene with the Mohawk CEO proves, Don may be a drunk who neglects his wife and kids, but at the end of the day he's basically an honorable guy. Duck, it's increasingly apparent, is anything but. By agreeing to pimp out his father's death to help SC land American, Pete becomes the latest member of an anti-Don cabal within SC: Duck, Roger and Pete are all lined up against him. Making matters worse, Don appears too distracted by his personal life to even be aware that something is afoot. With two season two episodes down, it sure doesn't look like he's in for an easy time in the eleven that remain.

Miscellaneous notes: In real life, there was indeed a tickertape parade for John Glenn on March 1, 1962, the same day that an American Airlines Boeing 707 plunged into Jamaica Bay, killing 95 people. However, Don and Roger's dialogue suggesting that the parade was in midtown near the SC office is off base—Glenn's parade took place in the Financial District's "Canyon of Heroes", the customary site of such events (given the source of the actual ticker tape thrown in the parade, it's not like it could have happened in any other part of town). I'm sure I can't be the only viewer who said "huh?" when Roger made his remark about two-way traffic on Fifth Ave., but apparently Fifth Ave. was indeed a two-way thoroughfare until January 14, 1966, when it was converted into a one-way street heading downtown (on the same day, Madison Ave., also previously a two-way street, was designated one-way, uptown only).

The barber shop where Pete had his final conversation with his dad is still in business after close to a century—it's the Paul Molé Barber Shop, on the second floor at 1031 Lexington Ave., between 73rd and 74th Sts. A men's haircut (by appointment only) will set you back $29, which sounds exhorbitant until you think about what women pay to get their hair done. As far as their argument about dogs goes, I think Pete was actually right and Pete's dad (and Trudy) were wrong: The two breeds look very similar, but per Wikipedia at least, French bulldogs have black ears and not brown ones, while the late Andrew Campbell argued otherwise.

I used Google Maps' street view to look up Joan's address, 42 W 12th St., and found a very nice looking residential building whose tenants will no doubt be thrilled to have their building referenced on *Mad Men*. Unlike the Sterling Cooper building's address (285 Madison Ave), this one corresponds to an actual building (speaking of SC and addresses, take a look at www. sterlingcooper.com—I can't believe I never tried it out before).

The final scene of Peggy at church is made all the more ominous by the Latin liturgy, which is a clever period detail: In March 1962, the first sessions of the Vatican II conference were still five months off. In late 1963, the assembled bishops signed off on the Sacrosanctum Concilium (or "Constitution on the Sacred Liturgy"), which encouraged priests to incorporate vernacular languages into the mass. The practice of saying the Mass in English began informally the following year and was officially incorporated into the liturgy by 1969.

Finally, Duck must have more social juice than anyone at SC short of Pete if, as it appears, he has his own membership at the University Club of New York. One of the city's most venerable WASP institutions, the club is situated in a dazzling 9-story McKim, Mead & White building from 1999 located at 54th St. and Fifth Ave (it has a really slick façade that makes it look like the building has three floors instead of nine). Like the Chrysler Builing, it's one of those privately-held architectural landmarks that merely mortal New Yorkers seldom have the opportunity to venture inside. I've been there twice, for a brunch preceding a wedding and for a reception following a memorial service, and its wood-paneled opulence lives up to the hype.

Mad Men Recap: Season 2, Episode 3, "The Benefactor"
BY ANDREW JOHNSTON ON AUGUST 11, 2008

After the fairly ground-shaking events of "Flight 1"—*Pete's Dad dies! We learn the deal with Peggy's baby! Duck emerges as a full-blown Bad Guy!*—I was somewhat surprised to find that "The Benefactor" was basically a standalone with only the tiniest bit of follow-up to the previous episode. But then the more I thought about it, the more I realized something: Almost all of *Mad Men*'s "big" episodes, "Flight 1" included, are basically standalones. This approach is a reversal of the main TV model of the 1990s, and proof of just how much series creator Matthew Weiner learned from working on *The Sopranos*.

I recently absorbed most of *Maps and Legends*, Michael Chabon's collection of critical essays on genre fiction, in addition to rereading Scott McCloud's *Understanding Comics*, so I hope you'll forgive me for getting a bit academic and pin-headed here. Basically, for most of the history of television, dramas were divided into two varieties: Serials (from *Peyton Place* through *Dallas, Dynasty*, etc) and series that were basically collections of short stories about the characters (pretty much every crime/medical/science fiction series you can think of). The main similarity is that in both types of series, the characters never really changed.

Much of this has to do with the nature of the short story, the form that has arguably influenced episodic TV drama more than any other. I'm sure readers of this column will be able to come up with other examples (right now, all I'm coming up with are Ernest Hemingway and John Updike), but sequential short stories following a single protagonist are far less common in the realm of "serious" fiction than in the genre world—and genre fiction characters, like those on TV, are far less likely to experience real change.

In the 1980s, Steven Bochco began to combine the two forms of TV drama, but the process that leads us to *Mad Men* began in the early '90s with the arrival of Chris Carter's *The X-Files* and J. Michael Straczynski's *Babylon 5*. Both presented themselves (the latter more convincingly than the former) as novels for television, with a defined beginning, middle and ending, during which the characters would experience real change and growth. In the interest of luring in casual viewers along the way, Carter and Straczynski established a dichotomy between "mythology" or "arc" episodes—ones which solved lingering mysteries and advanced the larger plot—and entirely self-contained stories. This template was adopted by a zillion other series over the subsequent years (most notably by *Buffy, Angel, Alias, Lost* and *Battlestar Galactica*), and while it resulted in some awfully good TV, this paradigm tended to create a belief among TV fans that self-contained episodes are inherently inferior to continuity-oriented ones (with exceptions: some would argue that as the *X-Files* mythology spun increasingly out of control, its standalones got better and better).

The Sopranos was a highly serialized show from the beginning, and in some ways became more serialized as it went on (for evidence, look no further than the adventures of Vito Spatafore). But with the fifth episode of Season One, "College", it became clear that David Chase was trying something new—coming up with a self-contained TV episode that would change the protagonist in ways that would be evident for the series' entire run. Over the course of *The Sopranos*'s six seasons, Tony, Uncle Jun, Carmela, Dr. Melfi, Bobby Baccalieri and Johnny Sack (in the final season's superb "Stage Five") would all receive such episodes. With each one, *The Sopranos* became less a crime drama and more a portrait of individuals baffled by a changing world—who in turn added up to a community baffled by a changing world. Like light, which can be both particle and wave depending on your viewpoint, *The Sopranos* was both a serial and a collection of shared-universe vignettes, albeit perhaps one closer to Edgar Lee Masters's *Spoon River Anthology* than to Hemingway's Nick Adams stories or any of Updike's story cycles.

Which, finally, brings us to *Mad Men*. In his comments on my write-up of "Flight 1," Matt Seitz praised what Matthew Weiner is doing this season and connected it to *The Sopranos*, but I don't think he gave Weiner enough credit for taking the David Chase approach further than Chase himself ever has. *The Sopranos* launched a golden age in American TV—*Deadwood, The Wire, The Shield*...you know the drill—but most of Chase's acolytes have been content to stick with relatively conventional serial narratives (even if shows such as *The Shield* took the serial in bold new directions by embracing the novel as thoroughly as Chase has the short story). Only Weiner has seen fit to fully embrace Chase's vision and offer a sort of fractal drama—one that contains conventional continuity, to be sure, but also one where the narrative model is layered rather than strictly linear, and in which it takes quite awhile (unlike with *B5* or *The X-Files*, which wore their complexity as a badge of pride) to realize that the whole is more than the sum of its parts.

This has all been a fancy way of saying that *Mad Men* often feels like a collection of short stories about the characters rather than a conventional TV series. Strip away the Peggy material from last week's episode and you're left with a beauty of a short story about Pete, one in which he learns hard lessons that TV characters seldom do. Prune away Betty's activities this week and what remains is an equally fine (and equally resonant) double-helix story about Don and Harry Crane.

As its thesis, "The Benefactor" argues that artists often wind up with the patrons they deserve: Leonardo and Michelangelo got the de Medicis; a mediocre insult comic like Jimmy winds up with Utz Potato Chips. But beyond the theme lies a deeper question: Are Don and Harry artists? As Don famously told us last season, SC is "home to more failed artists and writers than the Third Reich", but despite his jokes about a novel in progress—I've always taken them as jokes, at least—we've seen little evidence of conventional artistic ambition on Don's part. The artform he specializes in isn't making the client (or, ultimately, the consumer) feel what he does, nor is it the simple art of the con. To become the advertising whiz that he is—and to transform himself from Dick Whitman into Don Draper—he had to master the art of the managed expectation. Even those who specialize in such unorthodox art forms occasionally have to suck it up and kiss their patron's ass, and that's what Don does when he takes Jimmy and Bobbi to dinner with "Mr. and Mrs Utz" (a/k/a the Schillings—it can get confusing since at one point "shilling" is used as a verb).

Who is Don's patron in this scenario? It's both Jimmy and the Schillings, to some degree, but ultimately it's SC itself, and Don clearly thinks he deserves a benefactor who better appreciates his talents—otherwise he wouldn't be slinking off to French films in the middle of the day (though by doing so, he's hardly being a slacker—as with reading Frank O'Hara, he's practicing the art of the managed expectation by attempting to acquire a level of broad cultural awareness that one wouldn't typically associate with a suit like him).

Really, Jimmy has it easy—to please his patrons, all he has to do is cough up a simple apology (and while Jimmy may use alcohol and misanthropy to justify his behavior, his instructions to the cameraman make it clear he's enough of a professional to have known what he was doing). Don has to a) sell the Schillings on Jimmy's sincerity, b) manage Jimmy's expectations by letting him think that he's both smarter than Don and has a chance with Betty, and then c) use his masculinity as a literal blunt instrument when Bobbi threatens to use contractual loopholes to exempt her husband from apologizing (Don sliding his fingers into Bobbi may or may not be a basic cable first, but it's certainly the most sexually explicit scene *Mad Men* has offered yet). For her part, Betty has to "merely" string Jimmy along while simultaneously keeping the Schillings charmed. At first, Betty seems nonplussed about the dinner, asking what kind of prop she's supposed to be—a speaking one or a silent one—but in the final scene she's unexpectedly happy. Like her husband, she's just paid her freight by sucking up to the people who pay for her lifestyle—and, like Don, she just did so by managing expectations. The episode ends with something we rarely get from *Mad Men*—a scene in which Don and Betty feel like both a real couple and a real team.

The early scenes at SC dealing with Jimmy's disastrous commercial shoot don't say much about the degree to which Don does or doesn't see himself as an artist, but they *do* suggest that a hell of a lot of his SC cohorts—including Roger, Duck and even Ken "Published Author" Cosgrove—see advertising purely as a business. Of course, as we learned when Paul took Peggy on a tour of the agency back at the start of Season One, the creative and accounts departments are just tiny slices of SC. The biggest department is media, a purely business department and one which thus far has only been represented by Harry Crane. Harry's an outsider in more ways than one among the junior execs—he's the only non-Ivy Leaguer among the lot, and presumably the only Midwesterner. If his department isn't particularly creative, Harry himself is—last year, he co-concieved (with Pete) the plan to lock JFK out of the TV ad market in Chicago, and this time he proves himself fairly visionary by first attempting to help out his friend at CBS and then urging the creation of a TV department at SC (that they don't already have one certifies dinosaur status).

But Harry clearly doesn't have the patron he deserves—if he did, the promotion would have come directly from Bert Cooper instead of being handled by Roger. When Roger offers Harry $225 a week, you just know he'd have given Harry $240 or $250 if he'd come back with a counteroffer instead of meekly ending the negotiations prematurely. Harry's wife, like Betty, takes pride in her husband sticking up for himself, likewise not knowing the whole story. What they both fail to realize about their husbands (as does Bobbi) is that being an artist—and obtaining the patron an artist deserves—requires as much balls as it does talent; while their spouses may not be entirely lacking in testicular fortitude, they haven't mastered the knack of summoning it when it's most needed.

Miscellaneous Notes: Not too much to touch on this time around, though there are some interesting casting notes. I've been a big fan of Patrick Fischler ever since his genius back-to-back bit parts in *Mulholland Drive* and *Ghost World*, so it was a big treat to see him in the meaty role of a second string Rat Packer obviously based in part on Don Rickles (if you don't know Fischler from his movie roles, you surely recognize him from his guest spots on everything from *Girlfriends* and *Veronica Mars* to *Burn Notice* and all three *CSI*s). And while her blond hair was hidden by her riding helmet (and the role, curiously, is not yet on her IMDB page), Betty's equestrian buddy is played by none other than Denise Crosby, a/k/a Lt. Tasha Yar of *Star Trek: The Next Generation*. And while *Mad TV* alumnae Christa Flanagan obviously impressed Weiner—otherwise

Lois wouldn't have resurfaced as Don's secretary before getting fired this week—she had better well turn up elsewhere at SC; if she was fired both in real life as well as on camera, that'd be just too fucking cruel. The return of the Belle Jolie Lipstick executive, too, was a pleasant surprise; I'm sure I can't be the only fan who ID'd him by his voice before we even got a look at his face.

As to the story about the episode of *The Defenders*, most of it is true: As the New York Times reported on April 9, 1962, CBS was left high and dry when the series' three regular sponsors—Brown & Williamson Tobacco, Lever Bros. and Kimberly-Clark (the latter two are mentioned by Harry's friend)—bailed on the abortion-themed episode, which wound up airing as scheduled on April 28, 1962. Since next week's episode spans most of April, everything lines up with the calendar just about perfectly. According to a 1997 Times article about Showtime's, er, abortive 1999 revival of *The Defenders*, the episode was ultimately sponsored by a watch company (unspecified in the article) which bought up all the ad time for pennies on the dollar. Despite the controversy, an article at the Museum of Broadcast Communication says audience response to the episode was 90% positive. *The Defenders* wound up running until 1965 and was later folded into the same continuity as *Boston Legal* (and a zillion other series) when David E. Kelley retconned a guest character played by William Shatner into having been a young Denny Crane. My one question: Did Weiner et al. leave out clips featuring Robert Reed because there were none that fit, or because they didn't want viewers to laugh archly upon getting a glimpse of the young Mike Brady?

Mad Men Recap: Season 2, Episode 4, "Three Sundays"
BY ANDREW JOHNSTON ON AUGUST 18, 2008

A more accurate title for "Three Sundays" might be "Seven Sundays": The episode spans three consecutive Sundays, true, but with two of them we see how the day unfolds from Don and Roger's perspectives as well as Peggy's, and their stories are compelling enough (and sufficiently disconnected from Peggy's) that they don't necessarily deserve to be lumped together by the title. This week's episode is longer on housekeeping than any in Season Two, and it assumes a fair amount of background knowledge of the show, but in the grand *Mad Men* tradition it's nonetheless remarkably self-contained.

I realized this on my second viewing of the episode, when I saw it with my mother (who recently devoured Season One in less than a week and became obsessed with the show but had only seen the first episode of S2 yet) and my stepfather (who had never seen the show before at all but who's planning to watch S1 when my mom gets it from Netflix so she can watch it a second time). I was afraid that my stepfather would come away spoiled for all of S1 and that my mom would learn far too much about what had happened in "Flight One" and "The Benefactor". As an alternative, I suggested we watch a couple more episodes of *Spaced* instead, but she *really* wanted to watch *Mad Men* (and I really needed to see it again for this recap), so the die was cast. To my great surprise, the episode spoiled very little for either of them: While Don's rough childhood plays a big role in things, no reference is made to his transformation from Dick Whitman into Don Draper or to anything else (Adam Whitman, for example) that would require serious explanation on that front. And while he was of course spoiled as to both Peggy's pregnancy and the fate of her baby (my mom was spoiled viz. the latter, unavoidably), Pete's status as the father is never mentioned (ditto the death of Pete's father, despite the large role the American Airlines plot plays this week). In short, while I thought this would be an awkward episode to use as an introduction to the series, it turned out to be a fine jumping-on point.

Since Sunday is the Lord's day, it's only appropriate that church-related scenes and Peggy's friendship with the young Jesuit, Father Gill (Colin Hanks, in a performance I hope brings him a lot more work), gets more screen time than any other story. The smokin' and drinkin' Jesuit has become something of a movie/TV cliché by now—I guess filmmakers feel that showing Padres indulging in the few vices allowed them (and which are often denied to Protestant clergymen) is convenient shorthand for the hypocrisy of the church. In this case, it didn't feel like a cliché, both because of Father Gill's age and because of the time period. I started to groan when Hanks offered Peggy a lift to the subway, but was relieved and intrigued when it became apparent there wasn't going to be a forbidden love angle and that he was interested in Peggy's professional abilities above all.

The version of the episode that AMC sent to the press contains a massive screw-up that makes a mess of the timeline for Roger's story, but it's something that could easily be fixed digitally—if the fix wasn't applied before the episode aired, I sure hope they do it for the DVDs and Blu-Ray discs: At the seafood restaurant where Ken and Pete take the client from Gorton's Seafood (and where Roger meets the escort), the scene begins with a close-up of a chalk board listing the day's specials—and, in giant letters, the date "Monday, April 16". This makes no sense, as his tryst with the escort (played by Marguerite Moreau, who I've had a massive crush on since I grudgingly saw the otherwise-unwatchable *Queen of the Damned* and who I've followed through a zillion canceled series and guest appearances since) takes place on Palm Sunday, April 15, when everyone else at SC is crunching on the American Airlines presentation (am I the only one who wondered why none of the folks working on Sunday—including Bert Cooper—ever stopped to say "Where the hell is Roger, anyway?"). A digital scrub to turn the "16" into a "9" seems like it would be pretty easy; here's deciding Lions Gate and AMC decide to spring for it.

Bobbie Barrett's return (which required remarkably little explanation to my mom—"she's the wife of this celebrity spokesman from last week" covered everything) makes it pretty clear that she's a fairly voracious sexual predator, and her line to Don about "I've been trying to figure out how to not get bored with you" is, by my lights, enough to get Don off the hook for his behavior last week, which some have equated with rape. As I see it, Don sized up Bobbie last week and two steps that he knew would please her but also catch her completely off guard, thus making her readily susceptible to Don's demand that she withdraw the $25,000 price tag she put on Jimmy's apology. What he did was a classic, highly polished (if admittedly ethically questionable) piece of expectation management, which is of course his great specialty. If Bobbie had felt in any way taken advantage of, either financially or sexually, I highly doubt she would visit Don at SC so soon after "The Benefactor". One thing about their encounter seemed odd to me, and it'd be great if someone who knew more about the TV biz and the advertising world in that era could clear it up: Why would Jimmy need to get out of his Utz endorsement contract to do a TV show? Bill Cosby didn't have to stop shilling for Coca-Cola and Jell-O Pudding Pops in order to land *The Cosby Show* two decades hence, and there are plenty of other semi-recent examples of actors who've held onto endorsement contracts when moving from one TV show to another. How strong was the primary-sponsor paradigm by 1962? As far as I can tell, the practice of working the sponsor's name into the title of the show had pretty much dried up by then.

The meatiest drama in the episode comes from the contrast between Betty's anger at what she perceives as Don indulging Bobby and Peggy's sister Anita's envy of how (from her POV) their mom indulges Peggy, allowing her to do whatever she pleases with no consequences (as she says in confession). In Don's case, his motives are pretty simple: He wants Bobby to grow up without experiencing the abuse he endured as a child (I love the moment when Betty asks "Would you be the man you are if your dad didn't spank you?" and Don keeps quiet). In the case of Anita, it's a little more complicated—I think she's envious of Peggy's working-girl life because she's in denial about being the architect of her own misery. She's stuck in what appears to be a loveless marriage to a boor, and while we haven't seen enough of her kids to judge their behavior, I wouldn't be surprised if she saw them as tiny terrors. All of that unhappiness is the result of choices she made, which put her in a situation where whatever talent she has is never going to be recognized (clearly, it's the help Peggy provided Father Gill which got her more steamed than anything else). She may have the potential to be a great writer or artist, but she's never gonna be recognized as more than a housewife. If, as appears to be the case, Peggy's child is being passed off to the world as her sister's third offspring, it would prove that the family sees her as nothing more than a child-rearing machine, thereby rubbing more salt in the wound. Her confession of her envy of Peggy is entirely understandable; what's uncertain is whether she entered the booth intending to rat out Peggy as an unwed mother or if that was something she just blurted out in the heat of the moment. Either way, it drives an immediate stake through the heart of any potential friendship between Peggy and Father Gill, who—disappointingly to me—seems content to accept Anita's story (complete with the BS line about how she "seduced a married man") at face value.

This week's Don/Bobbie scene seems designed to balance out Don's rough treatment of Bobbie last week and shift viewer sympathy back toward Don. But a shoving match with Betty could very well start the whole debate about whether Don committed a form of sexual assault (or had at the very least become difficult to sympathize with) all over again—or reinforce the convictions of those who didn't forgive Don after Bobbie's visit to SC. As I see it, the scene makes Don more sympathetic than ever: The last thing he wants is to behave like his father and perpetuate a cycle of abuse that could fuck up Bobby as much as it did Don himself. When Don shoves Betty, he's out of control, no two ways about it, but he's also giving Betty a glimpse of his father's behavior, without which he couldn't make his point (another wrinkle here is my mother's theory that Betty fundamentally doesn't like Bobby, which makes each of his Dennis the Menace antics sting all the worse). Fundamentally, however, where both Bobby and Sally are concerned,

Don proves himself a more doting father than usual this week, albeit in his own way and to the best of his ability.

The outcome of the American Airlines situation would seem to insulate Don from any short-term threats posed by Duck, as it's hard to argue with the logic of "we hired him to bring new business, not drive away old business." But argue is just what Roger does with his comment that "old business is old business." The scene illustrates some of the key differences between Roger and Don's approach to advertising: for Roger, it's all about the chase, and it gives him the same charge he gets from seducing women (indeed, with his sexual capacity diminished—his run-in with the hooker this week notwithstanding—it's easy to imagine him transferring a lot of that energy into work, further vexing Don in the process). The whole situation also illuminates the fundamental differences between how Duck and Don approach advertising: Duck's intent to let AA choose from amongst three fully designed campaigns suggests a "the customer is always right" mentality, while Don's insistence on bringing a single, unified vision to the table is consistent with what we've seen of his approach to advertising since day one (to a lesser extent, it's an approach Bert Cooper shares). As Cooper said when preparing a team to work on spec for the Nixon campaign, SC knows (or ideally should know) what the client wants better than the client himself does. If Don's strategy is about taking a feeling he feels in response to a product and making the consumer share that feeling, the first step is making damn well sure the client feels it, too.

Duck's moment of menschiness when he reassures the secretary that Bert Cooper won't fire her (which is proven when we see her escort the AA executives into the SC office) is interesting. I have to say I can't see Don acting the same way in that situation (unless maybe he was to share my belief that the gum Cooper stepped in was dropped by Sally). A lot of the time, he's just too impatient, and too prone to getting lost in his head while hashing out ideas, to be considerate of other peoples' feelings in such situations. The big question is, did Duck keep her around out of the goodness of his heart, or is he being a manipulative bastard and slowly assembling a clique of employees that owe him their absolute loyalty?

Miscellaneous Notes: I wouldn't yet rule out the possibility that Don's creative vision and raw charisma won over the AA brass despite the termination of Duck's buddy. To be sure, AA didn't sign on with SC in real life because, well, *Mad Men* is fiction. However, while most of SC's accounts in the first season were products that are now "ghost brands"—products that were formerly household names and still have name recognition yet are no longer sold (Lucky Strike and Bethlehem Steel both qualify, and Kodak hasn't made slide projectors in years), this season the show has featured more and more real-life brands that are still in use. I'd chalk it up to product placement were it not for the fact that the brands have generally been shown in a light that their parent companies surely wouldn't approve of if they'd struck a placement deal. The folks at Gorton's Seafood can't be too pleased with one of their executives being shown gleefully patronizing a hooker, and last week's Jimmy Barrett story didn't exactly make Utz look like the world's greatest potato chips. As for AA, they surely can't be thrilled that *Mad Men* has reminded the world of their 1962 crash, but it's not like they can do much since it's part of the historical record. Point being, it seems that corporate/brand history is one area where Weiner doesn't mind bending the facts a bit (indeed, it may be a necessity) so anything could happen.

Most ultra-fancy restaurants in New York are open six days a week and take either Sunday or Monday as a day off, but in the past two episodes *MM* characters have patronized Lutèce on both Sunday and Monday. Can any reader more knowledgeable about New York in the '60s than I tell me if the restaurant was open 7 days after all, or if they took the day off at a more random point in the week (say, Monday or Tuesday)? Of course, it could just be a mistake...

The visual device of using the church programs to establish the passage of time is one that could, of course, be employed by a film; but movies being what they are, most screenwriters would insist on having the last program deliver additional impact—making it a funeral mass for a character who didn't make it to the end, for example. Here, the device just was what it was; although it had a very *Sopranos* feel to it, for me, it couldn't help seeming like something from a graphic novel. My next thought, bizarrely, was that in a parallel universe where Matthew Weiner was turned down by AMC and decided to do *Mad Men* as a comic book rather than a TV show, the ideal artist would be Tim Sale. The program device is not unlike some of the time-passage indicators in his collaborations with Jeph Loeb, and he's one of the few contemporary comics artists with a clean yet detailed style that lends itself equally well to expressive characters and panoramic cityscapes (for both, the best example may be *Batman: The Long Halloween*). I found myself trying to visualize Jon Hamm, Vincent Kartheiser, John Slattery and Elisabeth Moss as characters drawn by Sale; such images seemed surprisingly natural. Of course, for Sale to draw the actors would require scuttling the alternate-universe scenario and contemplating a comic book adaptation of *Mad Men*, which seems like something that could backfire with a vengeance; but if such a crazy idea is ever brought to fruition, Sale would definitely be the illustrator for the job.

Having Betty read a collection of stories by F. Scott Fitzgerald was a nice, subtle follow-up on her flirtation with the guy who name-checked "The Diamond As Big As the Ritz" last week. (The book is on the money: the Fitzgerald anthology *Babylon Revisited and Other Stories* was published in 1960, and it includes "Diamond"). Of all the strands in the episode, the Drapers cancelling their Sunday plans to spend the day with the kids, only to have the bonding count for naught when they get so drunk, they forget to make dinner, is probably the scenario that would work best as a standalone short story.

Finally, because of the abundance of "juniors" on *The Sopranos* (though there were never really any in Tony's crew, unless Uncle Jun counts), I couldn't help chuckling over the end-credits reveal that one of Peggy's nephews is named Gerry Respola Jr. I used to attribute the phenomenon to Italian-American culture (or the specific North Jersey subset thereof), until I read an interview with Terence Winter (or was it one of his *Slate* TV club entries? I forget) in which he talked about how beyond a certain point in the series, it became frustratingly difficult to keep coming up with a stream of new, real-sounding character names. If I recall correctly, Winter copped to plucking random names from the phone book and borrowing the monikers of high-school classmates out of sheer desperation. Instantly, I began to suspect that *The Sopranos'* parade of Juniors was a crutch. I could be completely wrong about that, but I nonetheless took the name of Peggy's nephew as a tip of the hat to *The Sopranos'* Juniorpalooza tendencies. If anyone on the *Mad Men* writing staff is reading this and wants to set me straight about my assumption (or—yeah, right—confirm that I'm on the money), feel free to do so.

Selected comments:

Andrew Johnston • (responses to questions/comments)
The dates on the three church programs were April 8, April 15 and April 22. I'm positive about this because the 15th is my mom's birthday and she made note of it during the episode (it also checks out by the calendar). If the chalkboard said April 9, everything would make sense instead of the way it is now, where if you literally follow the dates, Roger sleeps with the prostitute before he meets her.

Something I forgot to comment on above: Love them Sunday clothes the SC gang are sporting! Pete's tennis whites (complete with *short* shorts are a scream; ditto (to a lesser extent) Cooper's golf duds. The best joke of all, of course, is how Harry wears the same kind of clothes on Sunday that he does M-F.

Anonymous •
Mr. Johnston, wherever you are, you'll be glad to know they changed the date on the DVD to April 9th.

Andrew Johnston • (in response to comment on Brooklyn locations)
Thanks for setting me straight on my shamefully off-base assumptions about Brooklyn geography, which were the result of excessively hasty Googling and stupid leaps in logic that I made after quickly eyeballing some maps. If any of my many friends who live in Brooklyn want to use this as an excuse to laugh at me Nelson Muntz-style in person sometime, they're welcome to do so.

Andrew Johnston • (In response to a reader asking what kind of parents he had that he could sit and watched *Spaced* with them.)
I'm 40, and my mother and stepfather are 64 and 62 respectively. However, they had a kid--my brother Arthur--when my mom was 41, and raising a son at that point in her life (especially one who was as much of a music and film geek as Arthur) did a lot to keep both of them receptive to all sorts of pop culture that most people their age wouldn't touch. Watching *Spaced* (which admittedly they only discovered because I brought the DVDs on vacation; they plan to Netflix the full series) ain't the half of it: In the past three or four years, mom has seen concerts by Belle & Sebastian, Sonic Youth and Radiohead with Arthur (not because he needed a ride, but because she loves the music--and, granted, because she and Arthur are extremely close). In every case, I was as surprised as you probably are; naturally, I was more surprised still when mom and my stepfather went to see the Flaming Lips on their own initiative, without Arthur factoring into the picture at all!

Something else that plays a role in it is that my mom has loyally subscribed to every mag I've written for and has read just about every review I've published since becoming a pro movie/TV critic 11 years ago, so she's seen a lot of movies (and become obsessed with several TV series) on the basis of my recommendations. In general, though, I'd give Arthur more credit since he was living with them 24-7 for all those years before he went to college, while I was here in New York.

In the particular case of *Spaced* though, it sure doesn't hurt that my stepfather is A) English, and B) An old hippie.

That's probably more info than you (or anyone else) needed. But hey, you asked...

Mad Men Recap: Season 2, Episode 5, "The New Girl"
BY ANDREW JOHNSTON ON AUGUST 25, 2008

I was almost a little disappointed when a literal new girl showed up halfway through "The New Girl", as I was having so much fun decoding the ways the title applied to Peggy, Joan, and the visiting Bobbie Barrett (surely one of the series' most fascinating-ever characters). It's yet another entry in a very strong run of episodes and one which, in tandem with next week's installment (don't worry, you'll find no spoilers for it here) provides more in the way of semi-conventional character development than the series has in quite awhile.

The opening scene suggests another "new girl" candidate: A potential daughter from Pete and Trudy, who go to a fertility clinic in the hope of realizing the pregnancy she's long desired. The whole process turns out to be Pete's latest emasculating embarrassment, as he's peppered with awkward questions by the doc (he's of course completely sincere when he answers "no" to "Have you ever fathered a child?"). The 1962 nudist mags he's given to stimulate himself into yielding a sperm sample are good for an ironic snicker, but the best joke in that scene is the presence of a copy of *U.S. News & World Report* with a cover story that even then was completely irrelevant to the day's headlines. Industry wags have long referred to the mag as *Useless News & World Report,* and it was fascinating to see that was as true 46 years ago as it is today.

Bobbie plants herself firmly at the center of the action by coaxing Don into meeting for drinks at Sardi's, where a symbolic passing of the torch from Rachel Mencken to Bobbie occurs (Rachel has gotten married since we last saw her, and her husband has one of the greatest polyglot WASP-Jewish names I've encountered in either fiction or reality: Tilden Katz). Bobbie isn't the "new girl" just because she's the closest thing to a mistress Don has had since Rachel left, but also the first woman he's encountered since then who could qualify as his female counterpart.

In the great tradition of men who change their minds out of petulance when they see something they don't like, Don is soon en route to her beach house at Stony Brook, Long Island, a picturesque village in Suffolk County on the North Shore. On the way, Bobbie provides an abbreviated account of how she achieved success as Jimmy's manager. "This is America," she says. "Pick a a job and become the person that does it." Needless to say, that's exactly what Dick Whitman did when he became Don Draper (it's also a philosophy Bert Cooper shares, as he reveals at the climax of "Nixon versus Kennedy".) But being Don's female counterpart doesn't make Bobbie his female analogue—there are key differences in their worldview. She's got a Roger Sterling-esque love of negotiation, an activity Don says "bores" him (he clearly does everything he can to avoid negotiating on the job at SC), and her subsequent conversations with Peggy suggest she's a lot more cynical than Don.

Peggy's arrival at the courthouse is staged like a mystery with a big reveal, and indeed, as Bobbie observes, it initially does sort of seem as if she's gone a little too far above and beyond the call of duty for Don. Cue the flashbacks which shine light on what happened to her between "The Wheel" and "For Those Who Think Young" and reveal that, as Peggy sees it, she's repaying a debt. In some respects, the insertion of the flashbacks feels clunky, but as discrete scenes they play quite well, in addition to providing us with some useful info. Peggy's mom's tendency to fawn over Pegs at Anita's expense was standard procedure long before Peggy's kid came along, apparently, and Anita herself seems to be about eight months pregnant at the time of Peggy's delivery. If Peggy's kid is being passed off as Anita's, then they're presumably being presented to the world as twins (this may have been stated before; if so, I missed it).

As Peggy drives Don and Bobbie back to the city, Peggy alternates between deferring to Don and acting in a way which suggests that she now has leverage over him, and knows it. It's this side of Peggy's personality which Bobbie is intent on cultivating. During their day at Peggy's apartment, she gives Peggy advice that once again reflects her "Anything's possible when you-go after what you want" worldview. "You're never going to get that corner office until you start treating Don as an equal," she tells her. "And don't try to be a man—it won't work." And so it is that another, more abstract idea of "the new girl" enters the mix—the Helen Gurley Brown-influenced proto-feminist, an archetype that, surprisingly, Peggy may turn out to embody more completely than even Joan (who, in her conversation with Roger, displays a somewhat uncharacteristic-seeming shortage of ambition).

The flashback to Don visiting Peggy in the hospital makes it possible to argue that he, more than anyone, is responsible for Peggy's tendency to aim high. After she tells Don that she doesn't know what to do to get out of the hospital, he offers instant, decisive advise rooted in his rejection of the Dick Whitman identity, advice that's sort of the inverse of what Bobbie says about picking a job and becoming the person who does it, yet which ultimately arrives at the same place: "Move forward. This never happened. It will *shock* you how much it never happened."

That's it for the flashbacks, but it's not hard to infer what happened next. Peggy followed Don's advice, in the process taking a few months off from SC, during which he covered for her before re-hiring her as a copy writer. Somewhere along the way, she dumps the roommate and gets her own place (I'm sure I'm not the only one who initially mistook the absence of Peggy's roommate for a continuity error.)

Once again, there's plenty of ambiguity about Don's menschiness. His betrayal of Betty as a pouty response to Rachel's marriage is hardly an example of maturity, but his standing up for Peggy is admirable, and I was reasonably impressed by his resignation to facing the music when it looks like Jimmy is going to call him out over the incident with Bobbie. The most grown-up thing he does, however, is treating Peggy with respect when she follows Bobbie's advice, first asking him to repay her ASAP and then calling him "Don" instead of "Mr. Draper." (Sure, he has a surprised look on his face, but it says "I didn't know she had it in her" rather than "How dare she!"). I was fearful that Peggy's arc this season would be more about the baby than her career, but "The New Girl" (and next week's "Maidenform") prove that when she's got some fire in her belly, Peggy's journey is every bit as interesting as Don's.

Miscellaneous Notes: Many people will take Don's $150 fine for drunk driving to be another of *Mad Men*'s periodic cheap, "Ho ho ho, look how far we've come in 40-some-odd-years" jokes. The truth is more complicated: According to the Consumer Price Index Inflation Calculator, that fine comes to $1,092.54 in 2008 dollars. New York DWI law is pretty complicated—it seems that those charged with drunk driving are actually charged with two separate different offenses, "Driving While Impaired by Alcohol" (a noncriminal "traffic infraction" with a minimum fine of $300 and a max of $500 for a first offense; these charges are handled by the DMV rather than the DA, apparently), and "Driving While Intoxicated", (a criminal violation for which first-timers face a minimum fine of $500 and a max of $1000). Point being, if Don had a clean record, he could theoretically be hit for a fine that's almost $400 more (in modern dollars) than what he would face in 2008. If the accident led the cop to upgrade the offense to an "aggravated DWI" (which is done at a police officer's discretion, I think), they'd be more likely to throw the book at him.

The good ol' inflation calculator also reveals that the $110 or so that Peggy scrapes together to pay Don's fine would be $801 in 2008 money—no small sum at all, and one I dare say she shouldn't need Bobbie's encouragement to pursue its speedy return. In another Peggy note, I really liked how, as the only person on the drive home who was actually born and raised in the city, her knowledge of local freeways put Don's to shame.

During the first season, a few people complained about a product placement deal with Jack Daniels that got the whiskey shown on camera and/or mentioned verbally in three or four episodes (it was really quite subtle, especially compared to stuff like the appallingly blatant shilling for the Red Robin burger chain on *Psych* a couple of weeks ago). Well, Don and Bobbie weren't swilling a bottle of Jack Daniels as they tore it up on the road—the label is blue, not black—but the shape of the bottle sure as hell makes it look like one. Coincidence, or inside reference to last season's plugs (which I don't think are being repeated)? You be the judge.

Speaking of color changes, being the hopeless geek that I am, I couldn't suppress the urge to do a Google images search to find out if the seals of either of the Long Island counties corresponded to the patches on the cop's shoulders. The patches showed a lion against a red background, and, sure enough, the emblem of Nassau County is a lion, albeit one on a blue field. Would the producers have to get permission to use the Nassau County seal on the show? The blue-to-red switcheroo seems like the kind of thing they'd only really have a reason to do if the county had said no.

Finally, there's the actual "new girl" of the title, who didn't make much of an impression as a character (though she certainly is cute). The bit where Ken, Paul and Harry move in like sharks smelling blood was predictable, but still very funny. It also came off as fairly creepy in light of Ken's even-more-lecherous-than-before portrayal in recent episodes. I therefore enjoyed seeing him crash and burn as a result of Freddie Rumsen's impromptu performance, which was the most random, *Twin Peaks*-esque gag that the series has offered since the Chinese family left their rooster behind at the office back at the beginning of Season One. My first instinct was that some great advance in zipper technology took place circa 1962 and Freddie was trying out a brand of slacks for which Sterling Cooper was preparing a campaign, but a quick glance at the abundant online articles about the history of the zipper suggests that, from an engineering viewpoint at least, by the 1920s the zipper had been taken about as far as it could go. Rather, to paraphrase one of the most memorable descriptions in (semi)recent sports journalism, this was just Freddie being Freddie.

Mad Men Recap: Season 2, Episode 6, "Maidenform"
BY ANDREW JOHNSTON ON SEPTEMBER 2, 2008

I feel awkward whenever I cop to it, but it's true, and it probably always will be: I just don't like Peggy Olson. I like her story lines, which have offered intriguing insight into the workings of Sterling Cooper and (via this season's representation of family) the period at large. But I also find Peggy to be a dull and unaccountably naïve character whose crises at home just don't have much relevance to the larger issues on the horizon which the PR exec at the country club described in such loving detail.

I'm very much in the minority, though—after the initial airing of each episode, one of the first emails I get is always from my dad, pestering me for spoilers about Peggy's fate based on what just aired. And between the two seasons, whenever I met a fellow *Mad Men* viewer and the subject of Season Two came up, the first thing they'd want to talk about was Peggy's future at Sterling Cooper and the fate of her baby.

Peggy is a fan favorite for a number of reasons, not the least of which is that her position on the show makes speculating about her future the same thing as speculating about where the whole series is going as the timeline progresses further into the '60s. The ultimate proof of her popularity is the way even the loftiest discussion of the character (such as the commenteering here at *THND*) can quickly devolve into "'shipping" talk about Peggy and Don (or Peggy and Pete's) prospects as a couple.

The reason I'm saying all of this is that "Maidenform" is red meat for *Mad Men* 'shippers (Pete/Peggy 'shippers in particular), and I think it would be a pity if that eclipsed everything else I like about the episode—or if it eclipsed the single biggest development concerning Peggy, which is her realization that it's not enough to get Don to treat her as an equal. Getting the other guys to do so—the ones who pitch ideas over cocktails while Don is at home with Betty (or off dealing with Mistress Drama)—is every bit as important, and perhaps more difficult.

Last season, the producers apparently wanted to break period and use The Decemberist's "The Infanta" over the final scene and end credits of the early version of "Shoot" that was sent to reviewers. Presumably, they couldn't clear the song, since it wasn't used in the actual episode (I mentioned it based on the screener and came off looking like a putz). This time, it appears they did clear "The Infanta," which works even better than before now that it gives us three warrior women—Betty, Joan and Peggy—suiting up for battle in Playtex to the strains of the song, evoking an equally valid and far more energetic reading of the lyrics.

My own experience in advertising is limited, but in my years in the magazine biz, I've seen numerous examples of the phenomenon SC encounter with Playtex—a "winner" emerges in a category, yet instead of sticking with a successful recipe that the public responds to, the victor opts to emulate its less-popular competition for one reason or another (often because it's the easiest/laziest/cheapest way possible to make it seem as though you aren't resting on your laurels). Ken's wisecrack about both brands opening easily illustrates my problem with the character this year—he's been reduced to nothing more than Mr. Swinging Bachelor, with no reference made to the nascent literary career that was such a promising and unexpected plot development last season. If we don't get any forward momentum soon concerning Ken's parallel life as a writer, I'd love some retroactive coverage—say, a revelation that his creative ambitions suffered a crippling setback between seasons, causing his talent to wither and leading him to spend more and more time chasing tail as a means of validation.

From the second the character first appeared, I've been longing for an in-depth look at "Duck" Phillips, and "Maidenform" left little doubt that we're going to learn a lot more about the guy before long. Duck has thus far been played (and written) fairly straight, but here he's a terrific source of rich comic relief. I absolutely adored all of Mark Moses's interactions with Duck's dog Chauncey, and thanks to Alexander Payne's *Election*, I couldn't help hearing Ennio Morricone's "Navajo Joe" in my head during Duck's extended moment of frozen-faced panic after he learns his wife is heading back to the altar.

Although SC is packed with world class drinkers, Duck is the only one yet who's ever taken a stab at recovery, and while I'm a little disappointed that he's fallen off the wagon before we got to hear the story of the breakdown that led to him cleaning up, it's not worth complaining about under the circumstances: The scene in which his addiction trumps his feelings for Chauncey is, unquestionably, one of *Mad Men*'s funniest and most cynical scenes ever (if you've had much personal experience with alcoholics, it's also painfully realistic). I think it's not just his wife's pending remarriage that drove Duck back to the bottle—he resumed drinking after seemingly revealing much more of himself to Don than he intended to, although Don, with characteristic distraction, didn't appear to pick up on how vulnerable Duck had made himself.

After abusing Peggy too much for far too long, Joan finally cuts the poor girl loose, admitting that she can't offer Peggy any advice on how the game is played from the other side. Her final admonition, about not dressing like a girl, is something that people have seemingly been telling Peggy forever and which, by the end of the episode, finally seems to stick. Except for Pete, none of the men at S-C have ever seemed to see Peggy as a sexual being, as Ken's crass Gertrude Stein crack reminds us, and that might be for the best if she's at all serious about her career (though Don's Irene Dunne comment and its implicit defense of her sexuality may yet be seized upon by Don-Peggy 'shippers—to say nothing of the prospect of it launching, God help us, a wave of Peggy-Freddie 'shippers). Flaunting her sexuality with clients a little bit, though, may be something she has to live with to take part in after-hours pitch sessions. If she can do so while remaining in charge of the situation, she's got everything to gain—after all, what guy *doesn't* love a hard drinking babe who doesn't see anything wrong with tagging along to the strip club?

The death of Pete's father gets its first real follow-up via his brother Bud's visit to the Park Ave apartment for a cookout and discussion of their WASPy summer plans. Andrew Campbell's passing seems to have brought Pete and Bud closer together, or at least ensured that they get along better. I'd love to find out if there's more to the inside joke about their mother talking about Pete all the time, but the unfortunate reality is probably simply that she actually never talks about Pete. In any event, his claim that he's too important to SC to take a summer vacation is weak sauce, and Bud knows it. Even without taking the fertility situation into account, Pete's just too proud to summer with Trudy's parents. If he eschews a vacation and spends the whole summer working, though, at least now he's not likely to end up as a protégé of Duck's.

As always, Pete's faced with the issue of proving his manhood, and like untold millions of men before him, he turns to quick, anonymous sex to get the job done. Pete's tryst with the model is creepy and disturbing, and possessed of enough psychological realism to avoid blundering into cliché. It also adds an extra layer to his moment of eye contact with Peggy at the burlesque club—he's obviously experiencing a combination of lust and nostalgia that he doesn't quite understand, perhaps combined with a sense of "what if…?" brought on by the recent confirmation of Trudy's infertility. Because so much of the audience so eagerly want Pete to find out the truth, I'm hoping that when he does, Matthew Weiner borrows a page from the David Chase playbook and has the revelation come in a way that leaves the audience questioning their motives for so badly wanting it.

I'd be amazed if there was more to the Bobbie Barrett storyline after tonight, or at least if there was more than a cameo coda along the lines of Rachel Mencken's recent appearance. The existence of her 18-year-old son and slightly-older daughter is revealed in a way that suggests she's putting Don to a final test, and it's one he "passes" by apparently having no problem with the kids. What Bobbie *didn't* bargain on was Don's inherent conservatism, which only makes it natural that he'd wince in response to discovering he's got a rep as a cocksman instead of taking pride in word getting out. His "punishment" of her—which is thoroughly adolescent and completely unforgivable—is a total cliché, but in light of Don's characterization this season, it makes sense that he'd get so worked up. Once again, Don is furious about being taken at face value and judged on one quality alone. One might argue he's in a position to be touchier about it than usual since I get the sense he's been beating up on himself for taking the news at face value. I'm referring, of course, to the scene at the country club where he encounters the PR man who says his firm was indirectly employed by the C.I.A. during the 1961 Bay of Pigs invasion, and whose speech clearly makes Don feel kind of hollow when the veterans in the room are asked to rise during the Memorial Day celebration.

Subsequent to the fashion show, when Don blows his stack over the skimpy bathing suit, I'm convinced that his fit actually has nothing to do with jealousy and his discomfort with the prospect of Betty being leered at. The PR man's revelations rattled Don by reminding him that the world is ultimately beyond his control, which is something that spooks him deeply—and the sight of Betty acting independently just happens to provide a metaphor for the situation. Don is a jaded man who travels in jaded circles, so his encounter with the publicist probably isn't the first time he's heard Camelot compared to Versailles. The PR man's completely serious revelation that he's building a bomb shelter, however, is clearly a new one for him. "Maidenform" ends just after Memorial Day, 1962, less than five months before the event that history has come to know as the Cuban Missile Crisis.

Miscellaneous Notes: When I first heard that Matthew Weiner was going to have at least a year pass between seasons, my first reaction was a sigh of relief over realizing that 1963 would be skipped and we'd be spared from a Kennedy-assassination episode—if there's one historical incident I've well and truly OD'd on, that's it. What I didn't do was sit down to think about what history we *would* see during seasons two and three. This week's scene with the PR man would appear to constitute a very broad hint that one of this year's last episodes—perhaps the climax of the season, even—will revolve around the standoff between Khrushchev, Castro and the Kennedy brothers that brought the world to the brink of nuclear war in October, 1962. Similarly, Paul's "Jackie by day/Marilyn by night" pitch likely foreshadows the show dwelling on the August 5, 1962 death of Norma Jeane Mortenson Baker to at least some degree. At the rate time is passing on the show, I doubt that's more than three episodes away.

The firm where the PR guy at the country club says he worked and left burning behind him, Lem Jones Associates, is the company (now defunct) that was hired by the C.I.A. in real life to represent the Cuban Revolutionary Council (a sample of the propaganda distributed by Lem Jones is available online via the Google Books scan of Jon Elliston's *Psy War On Cuba*. It's kind of odd that the publicist would next land at Rogers and Cowan, a big Hollywood firm which then represented most of the Rat Pack (and which invented the Oscar campaign as we know it), but stranger things have happened.

The Man Who Shot Liberty Valance opened at the tail end of April, 1962, so it would naturally still have been in theaters a month later when Pete and Trudy get around to seeing it. Peggy must have been thinking about cheap outer borough theaters when she said Pete had saved her fifty cents, though, since according to Box Office Mojo, the average price of a ticket in 1962 was seventy cents—and Manhattan, of course, has never been known for average prices.

Attentive viewers of the opening credits may notice the surprising addition (surprising to me, at least, since I'm shamefully behind on my TV gossip) of Marti Noxon as one of *Mad Men*'s producers. Noxon earned a loyal following by writing many of *Buffy the Vampire Slayer*'s most essential episodes (including "What's My Line", Parts I & II, "Surprise", "Consequences" and "The Prom" (she also basically became Buffy's showrunner when Joss Whedon went off to do *Firefly* and *Angel*). In recent years, she's become fairly well-traveled, holding writer-producer jobs on "Brothers & Sisters", "Grey's Anatomy" and "Private Practice" that resulted in relatively few produced scripts. Hopefully she'll get more of a chance to properly strut her stuff on *Mad Men*.

The steaks that the Campbell brothers grill up with their spouses come from yet another hallowed Upper East Side institution, the Ottomanelli Brothers butcher shop at York Ave and 82nd St., which has been in business since 1900. I've never gone to check the place out, something for which, as both a devoted carnivore and a Manhattan resident for almost 20 years, I have absolutely no excuse. The Ottomanellis offer free delivery within New York City and ship nationwide by FedEx, and I wouldn't be at all surprised if they wound up getting a nice little spike in their business during the final weeks of barbecue season thanks to the long-ago patronage of the nonexistent Campbells.

Mad Men Recap: Season 2, Episode 7, "The Gold Violin"
BY ANDREW JOHNSTON ON SEPTEMBER 8, 2008

On my first viewing, I liked "The Gold Violin" pretty well but was bugged by a few things, some of which left me with an odd hunch that a number of fans would proclaim it an all-out clunker. A second viewing resolved some of my initial objections by giving me a better idea of Matthew Weiner &

Co's intent, but it didn't shake my feeling this one won't be a lot of peoples' favorite. Some of it is the unexpected return of the Barretts, which both needlessly extended a story that had come to a fairly satisfying conclusion, then pulled a 180 on the conclusion's message. Another issue might be the relatively large distance between Don's story and that of the junior executives, which allows the latter to flower but also dilutes the sense of a unified theme.

Like a number of early-mid first season episodes, "The Gold Violin" seeks to juxtapose a story about the tension between Don's past and future with one about the junior execs living lives of thwarted dreams. But here, the connection felt less organic—Ken and Salvatore's unexpected friendship felt like a self-contained short story, while Don's felt more like an excerpt from the novel (or, at the very least, like a non-entirely-hermetic story plucked from a nonsequential cycle). There have been other episodes of *Mad Men* that did this, but here the seams were just a little more visible than usual.

We begin with Don at a Cadillac dealership, where he's pondering the purchase of a 1962 El Dorado (Don isn't just looking for a toy, don't forget—he's in genuine need of a new vehicle after totaling his car in "The New Girl"). The dealer's comment that he bets Don "would be as comfortable in one of these as you are in your own skin" inaugurates a flashback to a moment ten years earlier, not more than two year's after walking away from his Dick Whitman identity, when he wasn't quite so comfortable in his own skin. At the time, ironically, he was working as a used-car dealer, and was about to sell a presumed lemon to a high school student when a Patricia Arquette-lookalike startled him by coming by in search of the real Don Draper. Spooked by the memory, Don cuts the sale short and heads back to Sterling Cooper, to meet with Roger and Duck about the Martinson's (now just "Martinson") coffee account that has gone unmentioned for several episodes.

Meanwhile, Peggy, Paul, Sal and Ken are working on the Pampers account that Sterling Cooper hopes to land, all of them vexed by the seemingly-intractible problem of the product's high price (a necessity to offset Procter & Gamble's R&D costs). Subsequent interruptions by Harry and Jane, Don's new secretary, result in Jane, Ken, Sal and Harry sneaking into Burt Cooper's office for a gander at the Mark Rothko painting on which Cooper just dropped a bundle. To Jane and Harry, it's entirely abstract—"fuzzy squares", says Jane—but a deep chord is struck within Ken by Sal's sympathetic reaction to Ken's interpretation of the painting as something that's meant to be experienced rather than merely seen.

"You're not like everyone else here," says Ken, by which he means artistically sensitive, rather than queer (Sal gets slightly defensive nonetheless). So it is that Ken seeks Sal's opinion of his latest story, which in turn leads to a Sunday night dinner invitation that gives us our first good look at Sal's (relatively) new wife, Kitty Romano.

It's the characterizations in this scene that left me thinking the episode may get branded a clunker. Ken has been portrayed as little more than Sterling Cooper's most avid pussy hound for all of the season to date, and Sal has generally come off as (almost) all bitchy snark, all the time, making his sensitivity to Ken's art somewhat unexpected (to be sure, we saw some of this when he let his guard down in "The Hobo Code," but that was much less specific). There's also the issue of his relationship with Kitty, which I appear to have completely misread when I said they seemed like genuinely loving partners earlier this season.

Ken's statement that writing is something he only does for fun, as a hobby, actually makes sense in light of what we've seen this season, and while he sniffs out Sal as more artistic than the rest of SC, Sal too sniffs him out as an idiot savant of sorts. Many people, I'm sure, will predict Sal developing a deep crush on Ken, but I think it's far more likely that he'll push Ken to actually put his gift to use, encouraging him to write, taking him to parties where he can make useful connections, that sort of thing.... as he drifts all the further away from Kitty in the process.

In Kitty's first appearances, she and Sal enjoyed a playful, easygoing chemistry that left me suspecting they might turn out to be a happy couple despite the issue of Sal's sexuality. Sal's pointed effort to keep Kitty out of the conversation pretty well torpedoes that theory. Still, Ken must have seen some of what I did, or else he wouldn't have remarked on how their relationship is the kind of thing he thinks he'd want when he tires of skirtchasing.

I was surprised by the revelations about Sal and Kitty's background. She was a neighbor from Baltimore who followed Sal's mom up to the city when he moved her there, and who kept the torch burning until he finally gave in. What surprised me the most is that Sal's mom is apparently still alive (unless that's Kitty's mom we see dozing off on the couch in the final scene at the Romano home). I guess I figured Sal wouldn't really feel the need for a full-time beard as long as his mother was alive, and she obviously wasn't around for the meal—did they park her with a neighbor for the duration, or what? (There wasn't any sign of her in the brief glimpse of Sal and Kitty getting cozy at home that we caught earlier in the season).

Like Ken and Roger, I'm increasingly intrigued by Jane Siegel, Don's new secretary (presumably one of SC's first Jewish hires since the Rachel Menken debacle). She's by far the sharpest and most professional secretary Don has had yet (I love the way she cock-blocks Duck from access to Don's liquor cabinet after he's summoned to Cooper's office), and she has a three-dimensional view of SC's workings that lets her see when it's safe to bend the rules in the interest of satisfying her curiosity (or just having a little fun). She also knows how to play the game much better than Joan does. Her exploitation of Roger's crush on her as a means of holding onto her job after Joan axes her is pitch-perfect, as is her simultaneous blowing off/stringing along of Ken. A couple of episodes ago, I took her sunburn for a throwaway sight gag, but now I see it was a pretty neat piece of groundwork being laid—thanks to the color, Jane looks like a normal human being in her confrontations with Joan, whose alabaster skin and increasingly apparent insecurity gives her the air of an elegant vampire chafing under the restrictions that limit the powers of the undead.

The return of the Barretts, via the Stork Club bash to celebrate the pickup of "Grin and Barrett" (I never got the pun in the title until now, can you believe it?) struck me as little more than a contrived way to have Betty learn of Don's affair with Bobbie. Jimmy presumably knew of the affair when he dragged his butt to SC to tell Don his alleged deepest secret, that he's really not a bad guy, and having him totally renege on that felt, to me, like a needless extension of the storyline (in addition to making Jimmy a less interesting character). And no matter how high the wall is that Bobbie has built between her personal and professional lives, I can't seeing her being at all cordial to Don after their last encounter, at least not this soon. I love how the episode ends with Betty puking inside the Cadillac, but surely the writers could have come up with a more interesting way to get us there.

At the end of the episode, the biggest thematic question remains unanswered: Who is the golden violin, apparently perfect in all ways but unable to play music? It's a metaphor for unfulfilled potential, of course, and it can't apply to Ken because he (unlike almost everyone else at SC) is doing something real with his talent, even if he doesn't take it very seriously. It could apply to a frustrated Betty, of course, but she has sufficiently few scenes in the episode to be a likely candidate. It could also apply to Don, but his lack of direct involvement in any scenes with Ken and Sal makes him an odd fit. I'm sure someone has a theory that solves everything perfectly, but for now it seems like a metaphor the writers liked too much not to use and chose to shoehorn into the episode to give it more of a theme. That the episode still plays so well under these presumed circumstances is a testament to what a talented team Matthew Weiner has assembled.

Miscellaneous Notes: Don's invitation to join the board of the Museum of Early American Folk Art (now known as the American Folk Art Museum) arrives right on time: The museum was chartered in 1961, and opened in September, 1963—making it a little hard for Bert Cooper to have already seen the first exhibit. His crack about "whirligigs" is spot on, as the museum put an early focus on weathervanes and quilts from the Northeast.

Mark Rothko, already an established painter at the time, adopted the style of the painting shown in the episode circa the late 1940s, at which point his reputation escalated significantly. This being the case, his work shouldn't have seemed "that" far out there to anyone at SC, at least anyone who knew the least bit about art (Sal's reaction struck me as just about right). I can't ID the painting shown in the episode—I even took a crack at browsing the (incomplete) Google Books scan of his catalog raisonné, but it was definitely a genuine Rothko (a reproduction of one, at least) and not a pastiche thrown together by the art department, as the end credits include a copyright notice followed by the names of the painter's children, Dr. Kate Rothko Prizel and Christopher Rothko, who control his estate.

I'm sure I'm not alone in having been convinced we'd seen the last of the young Turks that Duck brought by SC in the season premiere. After coming across as such clowns, I was surprised that they basically hit one out of the park with their extended jingle for Martinson's, which—with the right background animation—could well have gone on to attain legendary status in the world in which *Mad Men* takes place (I was more surprised still that Don, and not Duck, received credit for the "win"). Students for a Democratic Society, the group Smith's friend back in Michigan belongs to, was the most prominent leftist student group of the 1960s, and the excerpt that Smith reads to Don is a verbatim quote from the Port Huron Statement, the group's manifesto, adopted later in 1962 at its first convention. I was a little disappointed that the quote was from the version that passed at the convention, a/k/a the "compromised second draft"; I suppose it was too much to hope that Weiner had somehow gotten hold of a copy of the legendary *"original* Port Huron Statement," which one Jeffrey Lebowski claims a hand in authoring.

Mad Men Recap: Season 2, Episode 8, "A Night to Remember" & Episode 9, "Six Months' Leave"
BY ANDREW JOHNSTON ON SEPTEMBER 29, 2008

For a variety of reasons, not the least of which was my shock and grief over the suicide of David Foster Wallace, *Mad Men* Mondays just didn't happen two weeks ago. When Matt Seitz suggested recapping "A Night to Remember" and "Six Months' Leave" together in one column, I realized that the two flow together relatively seamlessly in a way very few *Mad Men* episodes do: Betty's depression in "Six Months' Leave" follows her long-simmering anger over Don's affair, which erupted earlier and further crystallized when she threw out Don after seeing one of Jimmy Barrett's Utz commercials during a rerun of *Make Room For Daddy*. On top of all this, the hour contrasts Betty, who is depressed about something immediate and personal, against the Sterling Cooper women mourning the death of Marilyn Monroe. The episodes' presentation of the challenges faced by American women in 1962 invites a tandem consideration.

Ironically, I watched "Six Months' Leave" for the second time the night before I learned of Wallace's death. The contrast between the fictional reactions to Monroe's demise and the fresh reactions to Wallace's passing was fascinating. I've always been one of those who think that people who say American pop culture is more fragmented than ever are just exaggerating—but while almost everyone in my circle of friends was affected by Wallace's death to some degree, upon hard reflection I realized that his passing really probably had an impact on only a few hundred thousand people in the U.S., while Monroe's death united millions, perhaps more, in grief. Although women were more deeply affected by it, her passing was a blow to men, too, Roger and Don's hard-shell reactions nothwithstanding. (It would have been nice to get a glimpse of Sal's response.) And it's not every day that a news story would lead to Don, Peggy and the elevator operator speaking freely with each other. If *Mad Men* sticks to schedule, the timeline will sail right by the Kennedy assassination; lacking an opportunity to present one of the few 20th century events shocking enough to unite the whole country, the creative staff may have settled on Monroe's death as the next best thing (and it also creates the intriguing historical argument that Monroe's death, even as a simple suicide, was the herald of all that would follow in the '60s, as each successive death of a politician or rock star was seen as evidence of a giant conspiracy whose motives were too complex for mere mortals to understand).

Fancy sociological BS aside, though, in many respects the divergent responses to Monroe's death are a perfect metaphor for the gulf between men and women on *Mad Men*. When Betty makes it to the riding club halfway through the episode, it starts to seem as if she's escaped her squalor (Betty doesn't need Carla or even Don to keep the house clean, but when she decides to let go, she doesn't fuck around). It's soon apparent that her true motive was to let Sarah Beth have lunch alone with Arthur. Consciously or not, Betty just closed off her safest avenue for a revenge-affair with which to torture Don. Still, as we learned in the season-opening "For Those Who Think Young," Betty has other avenues for expressing her sexuality.

"Night"'s title, of course, evokes that of Walter Lord's 1955 nonfiction book about the sinking of the R.M.S. *Titanic*, which leads one to expect a much bigger crisis than Betty's embarrassment at the dinner party (I'm inclined to think that, per Don, it's the drunken antics of Mrs. Colson that the guests are more likely to remember than anything). The title might have been a better fit for "Leave," where it could have applied to either the death of Marilyn Monroe or Don and Roger's night out with Freddie, which ends disastrously for two of the three of them.

We never got to see how Don and Betty patched things up after "The Wheel" (or how long it took them to do so), but the opening scene of "Night", in which Betty exerts herself riding like never before, makes it clear that she's building up a strong head of steam and is ready to blow. She returns from the ride before Don has even woken, and we're soon treated to another example of the domestic laziness that always drives Betty bananas. (Don doesn't seem to mind breaking out the tools on Sally's behalf, as in "Marriage of Figaro", but whenever Betty asks him to do something, his first response is always, "Why can't we call a repairman?") This time, however, Betty's frustrated response is further evidence that her knowledge of Don's affair has turned her into a ticking bomb.

Betty's passive-aggressive insistence on perfection—we get a doozy of an example when she destroys that chair—comes to an end after she searches Don's desk for evidence to prove Jimmy's allegations of the Don-Bobbie affair (at first, I thought she'd find something Dick Whitman-related instead) and then completely falls apart after she gets her annoyance about the Heineken gambit off her chest and throws Don out, creating the circumstances necessary for the house to slide into chaos. Neatness, as we've always seen, is a point of pride for Betty, but all of us, at some point, arrive at a place where we just don't have the strength.

If I had written this recap on schedule, I wouldn't have had the opportunity to look at Paramount's amazing new Blu-ray discs of the *Godfather* films (using the same restoration being shown at Film Forum as its source material), and thereby wouldn't be in a position to compare Don and Betty's final conversations to some of the great (if somewhat overly hysterical, thanks to Diane Keaton's acting) shouting matches between Michael Corleone and Kay Adams. Because we know Don and Betty will presumably get back together (it's too early for a permanent split if the series is aiming for a long run), nothing in the scene at the end of "Night" has the chilling force of the door being shut in Kay's face after she sees a parade of soldiers kissing his hand, proving the falsehood of his answer a moment earlier when he let her ask one question—only one—about the family business, which he pledges to answer honestly.

Using similar terms and language, Don baits Betty into asking him about the affair with Bobbie, which he promptly denies. He's as convincing a liar as ever, but Betty doesn't buy it for a second. After this, the terms of the confrontation change—now, Betty is Kay at the end of *Godfather II,* telling Michael that if he doesn't really put his money where mouth as far as Corleone legitimacy goes, he'll be looking at a lonely life indeed. Despite having strayed, the Don Draper of Season Two really does seem intent on being a better man, but he's still screwed up enough to think he can achieve this by hiding information from Betty. As rough a spot as their relationship is in at the end of "Leave", you can't deny that his relationships with Sally and Bobby have strengthened significantly this season—a fact that should have some interesting effects on the separation-in-progress.

Once Don's Betty-targeting marketing technique was in play, he was thereafter a victim of bad luck: The dinner party seems coincidental—I don't think Don needed Duck as a witness to prove the trick worked, and he never seemed completely comfortable having Duck there. Duck's presence was pretty clearly requested by Roger, who, within the context of the business world, is star-struck by Crab's gig with Rogers & Cowan and eager to form an alliance between SC and the public relations giant. The gambit may have succeeded because of how well Don knows Betty; the flipside of that—even though she's forever complaining about his inscrutability and refusal to discuss his past—is that she knows Don pretty darn well, too. Under the circumstances, the poor guy didn't stand a chance

Peggy's continued rise at Sterling Cooper may seem like no more than fallout from the heart-rending story of Freddie Rumsen's departure from the agency that drives "Six Months' Leave," but in fact it's the reverse of Joan's plot line in "A Night to Remember." Peggy ascends into Freddie Rumsen's job because, despite his drinking, he was a clear-eyed judge of talent who saw the wisdom of giving her a break long ago. In "Night," Joan proves ideally suited to the requirements of Harry's new TV department via her skill as a pitchwoman and her knack for insight into soap opera-caliber TV; third on the list of assets are her looks, to which clients are as vulnerable as anyone else. Yet it's important to note that the clients, having no prior impression of Joan, soak in her skills alongside the va-va-voom factor; for the lads at SC who are used to seeing Joan flaunt her body daily, her looks would seem to cancel out any possibility of talent.

Because Peggy has always had a touch of the librarian to her, clients have generally been inclined to look at her work first and pay attention to her sex appeal second. In the case of Father Gill, even if he was attracted to Peggy (an issue that's open for debate), he couldn't do anything about it (at least not with having to, oh, throw his entire life down the toilet for a woman who clearly has no interest in him). Because of this, Peggy is pretty offended—and rightly so—when the little old ladies running the CYO dance don't realize that they're in the clients' role here, and fail to show due respect for her job. Peggy takes a shot at reminding Father Gill of her authority by bringing the padre to the office so he can see her in action. Unbeknownst to her, Gill has a second agenda—getting Peggy to come clean about secretly being a single mother. He brings with him enough bait to catch half the fish in the North Atlantic, but she doesn't take any of it.

Peggy's rise from the steno pool to senior writer in just over two years is the kind of feat that would earn a male ad man the label "prodigy." But as far as the men of SC are concerned, poor Peggy's accomplishments will (for the time being, anyway) come with an asterisk attached. To Pete, she only made it so far because of the patronage of Freddie. To Don, her success is entirely his responsibility, a means of saying "Fuck you!" to Pete and Duck after they "ambushed" Don in Roger's office, making it impossible for him to mount a coordinated defense of Freddie.

Freddie Rumsen's story line is, to my mind, one of the most tragic and heart-rending the series has given us. Part of is is because I really love Freddie as a character—until Duck came along, he was the only guy at SC who really seemed like an "old advertising hand." Roger has never looked at the industry from anything but an ivy-tower perspective, and most of his gnomic insights into the field sound like they were cribbed from a book, and while Bert Cooper's knowledge of the field is deep and nuanced, he plays the game at an Olympian level nobody else at SC can access. Freddie is the only one who seemed like an industry lifer—a trench veteran who entered the field with natural instincts that sharpened over the years; a man inclined to party with junior execs half his age not because everyone in his cohort has cleaned up or died, but because he has a true zeal for the business that other old-timers lost long ago.

Freddie's story is long overdue vis-à-vis the depiction of alcoholism on *Mad Men*: It's the first time the show has argued that there are alcoholics and there are *alcoholics*. There are those who can keep a bottle in their office and celebrate a win the way, say, Don or Ken might, and there are those incapable of getting out of bed without taking a drink, and who use alcohol as a means of pushing the rest of the world away from them. If you're unfortunate enough to have had much experience with that kind of alcoholic, Freddie's last night on the town is truly painful to watch: At one level, like Peggy, you might think that in light of all the forgiveness that gets thrown around SC, Freddie deserves another chance. On the other hand, though, it's fairly indisputable that it's just a matter of time until the Freddie-style alcoholic pisses himself again (or does something worse) as part of a long, slow slide into self-destruction.

Clearly, Freddie's final scene with Don and Roger faintly hints that, lacking any direction in life without his job, he might take his own life. I'd much rather see him dry out and land at another agency, but one of the problems when one develops an affection for this kind of alcoholic is that one tends to root for unlikely or improbable outcomes when the dry facts make the likeliest outcome all too evident. I'm told that there's an AA saying to the effect of "the definition of insanity is doing the same thing over and over while expecting different results." The statement is equally relevant to alcoholics and to people who care for them.

It's fascinating how easily the drinkers jumped to the conclusion that it only made sense for Duck, as a (supposed) teetotaler, to bear a serious animus toward Freddie. People today don't often jump to the automatic conclusion that everybody who doesn't smoke weed has an *ipso facto* hatred of stoners or that all vegans have it in for carnivores. *Mad Men* takes place just three decades after the end of prohibition, meaning Roger, Duck and Freddie were all adults (perhaps albeit just barely) when the 21st amendment was ratified, making it possible for them to drink (legally) for the first time in their lives). Is it possible that kneejerk anti-alcoholism, or anti-teetotalerism among social drinkers as well as addicts, were more common when America's greatest failed social experiment was still part of living memory?

Equally interesting (in a way much more specific to how the season is playing out) was the revelation of Pete's particular contempt for alcoholics like Freddie, who he sneeringly refers to as "those people." We haven't gotten many details about the late Andrew Campbell's drinking habits (other than the mere fact that he was a WASP, which brings with it baggage and preconceptions galore), but it's obvious that at some point Pete was severely traumatized by a full-on, binge-drinking, pants-pissing, can't-stand-up-for-falling-down alcoholic, and that had a huge negative influence on the development of his personality and worldview. We've only seen Duck slide off the wagon once thus far, but if he continues to drink, and if his drinking gains momentum, whatever respect and regard Pete might have for him would turn to ash the moment Pete caught wind of it.

After Don and Roger bid Freddie adieu, they go out for a nightcap, and Don gives Roger a pep talk which doubles as an explanation of his desire to improve himself. Roger, unfortunately, misunderstands Don, and, in a bombshell move, he tells his wife Mona that he wants a divorce. Roger suggested the possibility of running off together to Joan more than once in Season One, but he never seemed too serious about it. His general attitude—extending to his wife and daughter as well as his mistresses—is that if you pay another man to handle your women problems, everything will take care of itself. After slowly backsliding toward his S1 level of decadence, Roger has reached escape velocity from his own life and is making a mistake he's sure to regret (and for which Bert Cooper is sure to crucify him) given the importance his profession places on appearances.

The episode ends on a note of slight unclarity: Whom, exactly, is Roger dumping Mona for? If it's Jane, then things between them must have gotten much more serious off-camera than we realized; having the relationship reach that level without much to tip the audience off feels like a bit of a cheat, given the way *Mad Men* has tended to dole out info to the audience. If it's Joan for whom he's getting a divorce, the move is clearly intended to take her by surprise as much as Mona or anyone else. If Joan won't accept his flirtatious entreaties to get back together, Roger thinks, I may as well break out my nuclear option while I still have the time. The facts will be revealed (or cleared up) soon enough; in the meantime, I expect a lot of interesting discussion from fans arguing both sides.

Miscellaneous Notes: TV shows set in New York have a long history of giving out bogus addresses for the buildings characters live in, but that's been happening less and less of late, probably because HDTV makes it a lot easier to toss in "easter eggs" that viewers can actually pick up on (and because obsessive TV nerds just love looking that stuff up on the Internet). *30 Rock* in particular has been jammed full of actual NYC addresses used in contexts where writers would once break out the geographical equivalent of a "555" phone number. The point? Any serious *30 Rock* fan knows that Liz Lemon's address is 160 Riverside Dr., a very nice-looking building which has its entrance on W. 88th St. Freddie Rumsen, we learn tonight, lives at 152 Riverside, which is just around the corner, between 87th and 88th. Freddie's building doesn't look quite as nice as Liz's—at least not today—but being on the avenue itself gives him a better shot at a nice view. I bet Liz's building is already part of one Upper West Side walking tour or another; the inclusion (or not) of Freddie's will make for a pretty interesting index to the "market penetration" (as it were) of *Mad Men*.

Since my footnotes have come to seem a little repetitive of late when discussing historical facts ("Weiner and the researchers got this right...", "Weiner & Co. got that right..."), I'm going to take a different tack and remind them that historical accuracy shouldn't come at the expense of continuity, as "Six Months' Leave" takes what seemed like a timeline that was pretty meticulously developed over the course of S1 and then smashes it it pieces.

I'm referring, of course, to the reference to Freddie having known Roger's father. It was fairly definitively established in the first season that Sterling Sr. perished in World War I, after he'd co-founded the agency and sired Roger but before the agency had become much of a success. For Freddie to have realistically worked at SC while Sterling Sr. was there, he'd need to have been born circa 1897 (making him a 20-year-old newbie in 1917, just before Sterling's enlistment) and 65 years old in "Six Months' Leave". Joel Murray is 45 in real life, and I doubt I could accept Freddie as being any older than 52 or so without major cosmetic makeup being brought into play. The Signal Corps position that Roger says Freddie held would be believable for someone in their mid-late 30s, the age Freddie would have been during WWII if born in 1897, but it leaves unanswered the question of why Freddie wouldn't have enlisted (or been drafted) for WWI at an age when he was a much more appropriate candidate for military service. The issue of how Roger, who was in the Navy in the Pacific, would have known Freddie in the war if the latter was in the Army and in Europe may seem like another bumble, but it can be easily fanwanked by Freddie being a prewar employee of SC. Some people may not have a problem with any of this, but having Freddie be 60+ is something I can't easily swallow.

On a lighter note, via a *New York Times* blog which in turn linked to a blog run by one of my best friend's closest college pals which in turn linked to a Flickr collection, I found this incredible collection of *Mad Men*-themed illustrations on Flickr by a woman who uses the alias "Dyna

Moe". Apparently Rich Somer came across Dyna's unrelated art last year and commissioned her to do the Christmas card he planned to give other cast members. The experience turned her into a *Mad Man* fanatic, and she now illustrates each episode with an image conveniently sized to serve as computer desktop wallpaper (some have also been resized for use as iPhone wallpapers). The illustrations (another of which opens this week's notes section, above) are just cooler than hell, and I can't urge you strongly enough to check them out.

Finally, allow me to extend my congratulations to Matthew Weiner and his crackerjack cast and crew for their stunning success at the Emmys last week. Sure, it sucks that none of the acting nominees won, but as John Slattery's knowing and gracious nod to richly deserving winner Željko Ivanek—both of whom have spent years in the trenches—reminds us, individual recognition often tastes sweeter the longer one has been working for it. The basic cable drama explosion has been a godsend for actors like Slattery and Ivanek, brilliant guys who work mostly on the stage or on East Coast-based TV shows and have been semi-anonymously racking up Tony nominations, Ben Brantley raves and Drama Desk awards over the years. This year, it was just Ivanek's turn (his terrific work in *John Adams* and *In Bruges* didn't hurt things either). Slattery and Hamm are sure to be recognized by the academy in the future; this year, the awards *Mad Men* received—Outstanding Writing for a Drama Series and the big magilla itself, Outstanding Drama Series, are the ones the show needed to win to establish itself. As one of the few first-year shows in history to successfully grab the brass ring, it seems almost certain now that Matthew Weiner will have the freedom to do what he wants with the show and its overall direction. Based on Aaron Staton's beard at the ceremony, I assume S2 has officially wrapped; when production begins on the third season, I'm hopeful that it'll do so with a new sense of confidence that takes this brilliant series even further into the stratosphere than ever.

Mad Men Recap: Season 2, Episode 10, "The Inheritance"
BY ANDREW JOHNSTON ON OCTOBER 6, 2008

After hitting fans with bombshells a-plenty in "Six Months' Leave," it's only to be expected from *Mad Men* that the follow-up would go in an entirely different direction. Well, that's partly true—certainly, Betty's angst and its effects on her marriage to Don are among the prime orders of business here. The heavy focus on Betty and Pete Campbell and their respective problems with aging parents gives the episode a very melancholy feeling as, despite being surrounded by family, circumstances leave them feeling very much alone.

When we last saw Betty's father Gene, it was just a few months after her mother's death, and he'd just started carrying on with his new girlfriend Gloria, which created a rift between Betty and Don. With the passage of almost two years, their bond is that much tighter, and Betty's less comfortable about it than ever. Her physical distance from her dad (unlike her brother William, who stayed nearby) made it all too easy for William and Gloria to join forces (or so Betty believes) in taking everything they please from the house, disinheriting Betty in practice if not on paper. I'm inclined to think Betty is overreacting, but William's failure to tell Betty about the stroke for three days—or to even mention earlier strokes—certainly doesn't speak well of him.

As for Pete, Trudy's inability to conceive is causing him ever more headaches as he labors under the implicit promise he made to give her parents a grandchild in exchange for "help" buying their apartment. Presumably because of their lack of a connection to the "old money" mindframe, Trudy's parents apparently don't have a problem with adoption. Pete does, however, and one gets the sense that it was drilled into him by his family and isn't really a personal thing. When Pete's mother catches wind of the possibility of an adoption and tells Pete he can kiss the family goodbye if he goes down that road with Trudy, he twists the knife in his mother by revealing just how puny a sum she'll have to live on for the rest of her days thanks to his father's devotion to keeping up appearances.

Especially after the scene between Pete and Peggy at SC, I suspect a lot of fans will be spinning theories about scenarios in which Pete and Peggy's baby could be adopted by Trudy. I don't see that happening—it seems way too soap-opera and there are a ton of hoops that would have to be jumped through. However, I'd buy a situation in which Peggy somehow let the truth slip to Pete, who would later drunkenly confess the truth to Trudy, thereby casting a long, dark shadow over the relationship that keeps the two from ever really trusting each other again.

It seems likely that Don is using the visit to Betty's father as an opportunity to get cracking on mending the relationship, and Don keeps a respectful distance while also making it clear that he's ready to help Betty in any way he can. The only fresh intimacy between them comes when Betty, who's been sleeping on the bed in the spare room, rouses Don, who's been sleeping on the floor, and mounts him. It's a fascinating sex scene—on the one hand, it only makes sense for Betty to turn to good old-fashioned carnal energy in response to all the stress the visit has put her under, notwithstanding her feud with Don. On the other, the texture of the scene almost makes it feel like it's actually a dream that Don is having. Subsequent events, however, make it pretty clear that the tryst was for real.

Somewhat unusually, the episode basically dispenses with plot business when there are still several minutes to go, using the remaining time for a series of brief character studies in loneliness which were key to why I found the episode so deeply affecting. When Don and Betty return to Ossining, he's operating under the assumption (or "desperate hope," take your pick) that the experience of visiting her father together brought them close enough to cancel out their recent differences. Before the stroke, Don and Gene had a fairly cordial relationship, but now he's ranting that Don is not to be trusted because he has no "people" in the world—a slur that surely slices deep for Don, as practically everything he's done since ditching the "Dick Whitman" identity has been in the interest of acquiring people and setting down roots.

More than anything else, Don wants to move back in as if nothing had ever happened, but he encounters no such luck: Betty soon makes it quite clear that she doesn't think Don should stick around, and Don is quickly on the brink of tears. We've seldom seen him in such a vulnerable state, and while Jon Hamm plays the moment to perfection, what follows—which I'll discuss momentarily—makes his performance all the more impressive.

The next morning, the Draper dog leads Betty to the treehouse Don built in "Marriage of Figaro," which is being used as a hide-out by none other than her old partner in existential despair, Glen Bishop. Glen ran away from home a few days earlier, seeking to avoid being sent off to live with his father and "mean" stepmother. Life with his mother doesn't seem like the world's greatest alternative—ignoring her kids, she prefers to devote her time to political activism and going on dates (though I'm sure Glen is exaggerating her activity in the latter department.

In many ways, it's a replay of the season one scene in which Betty squeezed Glen for dirt on Helen, but with a key difference: That time, Betty was seeking info to help her feel superior to Helen; this time, she's driven by an apparent instinct that Helen's post-divorce life, for better or worse, may turn out to be a preview of her own.

Betty is so starved for true empathy that she loses sight of reality for a second and lets Glen cross a line when he takes her hand and announces his intent to "rescue" her. This quickly leads to a phone call to Helen, who thanks Betty for taking care of Glen while sternly admonishing her that the weird connection between Betty and Glen must end immediately. In response, Betty does the closest thing she can do to playing a trump card and telling Helen that Don has left. Helen—instantly stigmatized no longer—reaches out to Betty, offering the kind of support and grown-up advice she needs if she's going to take baby steps toward her own life. "The hardest part," says Helen, "is realizing you're in charge." And, as Bert Cooper said, loyalty's been made from stranger stuff.

Don, of course, is a perpetual outsider who always carries a little cloud of loneliness with him, and he probably feels a little more like an outsider than ever when he makes an early return to the SC office—it's largely empty, and he hasn't a clue why. Turns out a party celebrating Harry Crane's impending fatherhood is in progress, and the celebration—or is it his frustration with SC in general?—makes Don snap. Don's decision to bigfoot Paul off the trip and go to California for the engineering conference with Pete is the decision of a lonely man, one who's confident and aggressive but lonely nonetheless. Sitting next to Pete on the plane and sucking down one cigarette after another, Don has the look of a rapacious predator contemplating its next move, ensuring that the prospect of Don at liberty in L.A. is as frightening as it is intriguing.

Miscellaneous Notes:

Since there wasn't a convenient place to address the situation in the body of the recap itself, I've held my comments on the Paul and Sheila situation for down here. I like Sheila a lot, and while Paul is one of my favorite *Mad Men* characters, I would never deny that he's an unbelievable blowhard. Sheila clearly seems smart enough to see through that, so there must be another side to him that we haven't seen yet but which does the trick for her. She certainly deserves much better treatment than what Paul gives her in this episode, however—his "you can work at a supermarket anywhere" line was particularly crass. After Don boots him off the trip, his decision not to tell her and to act like he canceled because he had a change of heart is perhaps even worse, but it falls under the umbrella of classic cad behavior without really having a racial tinge to it. His speech on the bus could well be the most inane that he's ever had on the show, and more than ever it makes me want an episode that gives us a little more of a glance at what makes this guy tick.

As to their trip to register voters in Mississippi ... my immediate suspicion was that 1962 was a little early for that sort of thing, which some quick research seems to bear out (for lack of time, I used the Wikipedia articles "African-American_Civil_Rights_Movement_(1955–1968)" and "Timeline_of_the_African-American_Civil_Rights_Movement" as my sources) Certainly, the first freedom rides took place in the summer of 1961, but 1962 seems to have been a fairly quiet year in the Civil Rights struggle, with far more activism and protest from locals on the ground than by liberals from up North. 1963 and 1964 were the true watershed years of the struggle (it's *amazing* how many famous events from the crusade took place in 1963). Still, cheesy though Paul may be, he deserves credit for volunteering on behalf of the call, especially for doing so ahead of the curve.

Andrew passed away on October 26, 2008. The next recap was written by his close friend Matt Zoller Seitz. It's title and dedication are given here.

Mad Men Recap: Season 2, Episode 11, "The Jet Set"; Episode 12, "The Mountain King"; Episode 13, "Meditations in an Emergency"
BY MATT ZOLLER SEITZ ON OCTOBER 27, 2008

Editor's note: This column is dedicated to the memory of House contributor, Time Out New York *editor and regular* Mad Men *recapper Andrew Johnston, who passed away Sunday, Oct. 26 at age 40, following a long battle with cancer. There will also be a memorial Wednesday, October 29 at 5:30 p.m.; if you were a friend of Andrew's and would like to attend, email Matt at reeling@aol.com for details.]*

Title Index

X

Y

CPSIA information can be obtained
at www.ICGtesting.com
Printed in the USA
BVHW070058110222
628632BV00001B/43